D0920470

n

Genesis

with an
Introduction to
Narrative Literature

GEORGE W. COATS

The Forms of the Old Testament Literature
VOLUME I
Rolf Knierim and Gene M. Tucker, editors

WILLIAM B. EERDMANS PUBLISHING COMPANY
GRAND RAPIDS, MICHIGAN

Copyright © 1983 by William B. Eerdmans Publishing Company
255 Jefferson Ave. S.E., Grand Rapids, MI 49503

Reprinted, December 1987

Library of Congress Cataloging in Publication Data

Coats, George W.
  Genesis, with an introduction to narrative.

  (The Forms of the Old Testament literature; v. 1)
  Bibliography: passim.
  1. Bible. O.T. Genesis—Criticism, interpretation,
etc. 2. Narration in the Bible. I. Title. II. Series.
BS1235.2.C62   1983   222'.110663   83-16457
ISBN 0-8028-1954-0

CONTENTS

ABBREVIATIONS AND SYMBOLS

I. Miscellaneous abbreviations and symbols

D	Deuteronomic source
Diss.	Dissertation
Dtr	Deuteronomistic source
E	Elohistic source
Fest.	*Festschrift*
J	Yahwistic source
LXX	Septuagint
MT	Masoretic Text
OL	Old Latin
P	Priestly source
PN	personal name
R	redactor
Rp, etc.	redactor of Priestly source, etc.
Sam Pent	Samaritan Pentateuch
Tiq soph	Tiqqun sopherim
*	When placed before a word or text citation, the asterisk indicates a hypothetical form presumed to underlie the present form of the word or text.
→	The arrow indicates a cross reference to another section of the commentary.
<	(is) derived from
√	the root or stem of a word

II. Publications

AfO	*Archiv für Orientforschung*
AJSL	*American Journal of Semitic Languages and Literatures*
AnBib	Analecta biblica
ANET	J. B. Pritchard, ed., *Ancient Near Eastern Texts Relating to the Old Testament* (3rd ed.; Princeton: Princeton University Press, 1969)
AOAT	Alter Orient und Altes Testament

vi

ASTI	*Annual of the Swedish Theological Institute in Jerusalem*
ATANT	Abhandlungen zur Theologie des Alten und Neuen Testaments
AusBR	*Australian Biblical Review*
AzT	Arbeiten zur Theologie
BASOR	*Bulletin of the American Schools of Oriental Research*
BBB	Bonner biblische Beiträge
BHT	Beiträge zur historischen Theologie
Bib	*Biblica*
BibLeb	*Bibel und Leben*
BibS(N)	Biblische Studien (Neukirchen, 1951-)
BK	*Bibel und Kirche*
BKAT	Biblischer Kommentar: Altes Testament
BLit	*Bibel und Liturgie*
BR	*Biblical Research*
BTS	*Bible et terre sainte*
BWANT	Beiträge zur Wissenschaft von Alten und Neuen Testament
BZ	*Biblische Zeitschrift*
BZAW	Beihefte zur Zeitschrift für die Alttestamentliche Wissenschaft
CBQ	*Catholic Biblical Quarterly*
CBQMS	Catholic Biblical Quarterly—Monograph Series
EvT	*Evangelische Theologie*
ExpTim	*Expository Times*
FRLANT	Forschungen zur Religion und Literatur des Alten und Neuen Testaments
HKAT	Handkommentar zum Alten Testament
HTR	*Harvard Theological Review*
HUCA	*Hebrew Union College Annual*
Int	*Interpretation*
JAAR	*Journal of the American Academy of Religion*
JAOS	*Journal of the American Oriental Society*
JBL	*Journal of Biblical Literature*
JBR	*Journal of Bible and Religion*
JCS	*Journal of Cuneiform Studies*
JEOL	*Jaarbericht van het Voorazietisch Egyptisch Genotschap ex oriente lux*
JNES	*Journal of Near Eastern Studies*
JQR	*Jewish Quarterly Review*
JSOT	*Journal for the Study of the Old Testament*

JSOTSup	Journal for the Study of the Old Testament, Supplements
JSS	*Journal of Semitic Studies*
JTS	*Journal of Theological Studies*
KD	*Kerygma und Dogma*
OLZ	*Orientalische Literaturzeitung*
OTL	Old Testament Library
OTS	*Oudtestamentische Studiën*
OTWSA	Ou-Testamentiese Werkgemeenskap in Suid-Afrika
PJ	*Palästinajahrbuch*
PTMS	Pittsburgh Theological Monograph Series
RB	*Revue biblique*
RHR	*Revue de l'histoire des religions*
RSV	*Revised Standard Version*
RTR	*Reformed Theological Review*
SBLASP	Society of Biblical Literature Abstracts and Seminar Papers
SBLMS	SBL Monograph Series
SBS	Stuttgarter Bibelstudien
SBT	Studies in Biblical Theology
Scr	*Scripture*
Sem	*Semitica*
SJT	*Scottish Journal of Theology*
SNTSMS	Society for New Testament Studies Monograph Series
ST	*Studia theologica*
TLZ	*Theologische Literaturzeitung*
TTZ	*Trierer theologische Zeitschrift*
TZ	*Theologische Zeitschrift*
VT	*Vetus Testamentum*
VTSup	Vetus Testamentum, Supplements
WMANT	Wissenschaftliche Monographien zum Alten und Neuen Testament
WO	*Die Welt des Orients*
WZGreifswald	*Wissenschaftliche Zeitschrift der Universität Greifswald*
WZHalle	*Wissenschaftliche Zeitschrift der Martin-Luther-Universität*
WZLeipzig	*Wissenschaftliche Zeitschrift der Karl-Marx-Universität*
ZA	*Zeitschrift für Assyriologie*
ZAW	*Zeitschrift für die alttestamentliche Wissenschaft*
ZDMG	*Zeitschrift der deutschen morgenländischen Gesellschaft*
ZTK	*Zeitschrift für Theologie und Kirche*

EDITORS' FOREWORD

THIS BOOK is the second in a series of twenty-four volumes planned for publication throughout the nineteen-eighties. The series eventually will present a form-critical analysis of every book and each unit of the Old Testament (Hebrew Bible) according to a standard outline and methodology. The aims of the work are fundamentally exegetical, attempting to understand the biblical literature from the viewpoint of a particular set of questions. Each volume in the series will also give an account of the history of the form-critical discussion of the material in question, attempt to bring consistency to the terminology for the genres and formulas of the biblical literature, and expose the exegetical procedure in such a way as to enable students and pastors to engage in their own analysis and interpretation. It is hoped, therefore, that the audience will be a broad one, including not only biblical scholars but also students, pastors, priests, and rabbis who are engaged in biblical interpretation.

There is a difference between the planned order of appearance of the individual volumes and their position in the series. While the series follows basically the sequence of the books of the Hebrew Bible, the individual volumes will appear in accordance with the projected working schedules of the individual contributors. The number of twenty-four volumes has been chosen for merely practical reasons which make it necessary to combine several biblical books in one volume at times, and at times to have two authors contribute to the same volume. Volume XIII is an exception to the arrangement according to the sequence of the Hebrew canon in that it omits Lamentations. The commentary on Lamentations will be published with that on the book of Psalms.

The initiation of this series is the result of deliberations and plans which began some fifteen years ago. At that time the current editors perceived the need for a comprehensive reference work which would enable scholars and students of the Hebrew scriptures to gain from the insights that form-critical work had accumulated throughout seven decades, and at the same time to participate more effectively in such work themselves. An international and interconfessional team of scholars was assembled, and has been expanded in recent years.

Several possible approaches and formats for publication presented themselves. The work could not be a handbook of the form-critical method with some examples of its application. Nor would it be satisfactory to present an encyclopedia of the genres identified in the Old Testament literature. The reference work would have to demonstrate the method on all of the texts, and identify genres only through the actual interpretation of the texts themselves. Hence, the work had to be a commentary following the sequence of the books in the Hebrew Bible (the

Kittel edition of the *Biblia Hebraica* then and the *Biblia Hebraica Stuttgartensia* now).

The main purpose of this project is to lead the student to the Old Testament texts themselves, and not just to form-critical studies of the texts. It should be stressed that the commentary is confined to the form-critical interpretation of the texts. Consequently, the reader should not expect here a full-fledged exegetical commentary which deals with the broad range of issues concerning the meaning of the text. In order to keep the focus as clearly as possible on a particular set of questions, matters of text, translation, philology, verse-by-verse explanation, etc. are raised only when they appear directly relevant to the form-critical analysis and interpretation.

The adoption of a commentary format and specific methodological deliberations imply a conclusion which has become crucial for all the work of form criticism. If the results of form criticism are to be verifiable and generally intelligible, then the determination of typical forms and genres, their settings and functions, has to take place through the analysis of the forms in and of the texts themselves. This leads to two consequences for the volumes in this series. First, each interpretation of a text begins with the presentation of the *structure* of that text in outline form. The ensuing discussion of this structure attempts to distinguish the typical from the individual or unique elements, and to proceed on this basis to the determination of the *genre,* its *setting,* and its *intention.* Traditio-historical factors are discussed throughout this process where relevant; e.g., is there evidence of a written or oral stage of the material earlier than the actual text before the reader?

Second, the interpretation of the texts accepts the fundamental premise that we possess all texts basically at their latest written stages, technically speaking, at the levels of the final redactions. Any access to the texts, therefore, must confront and analyze that latest edition first, i.e., a specific version of that edition as represented in a particular text tradition. Consequently, the commentary proceeds from the analysis of the larger literary corpora created by the redactions back to any prior discernible stages in their literary history. Larger units are examined first, and then their subsections. Therefore, in most instances the first unit examined in terms of structure, genre, setting, and intention is the entire biblical book in question; next the commentary treats the individual larger and then smaller units.

The original plan of the project was to record critically all the relevant results of previous form-critical studies concerning the texts in question. While this remains one of the goals of the series, it had to be expanded to allow for more of the research of the individual contributors. This approach has proved to be important not only with regard to the ongoing insights of the contributors, but also in view of the significant developments which have taken place in the field in recent years. The team of scholars responsible for the series is committed to following a basic design throughout the commentary, but differences of emphasis and even to some extent of approach will be recognized as more volumes appear. Each author will ultimately be responsible for his own contribution.

The use of the commentary is by and large self-explanatory, but a few comments may prove helpful to the reader. This work is designed to be used alongside a Hebrew text or a translation of the Bible. The format of the interpretation of the texts, large or small, is the same throughout, except in cases—as partly in this volume—where the biblical material itself suggests a different form of presentation. Individual books and major literary corpora are introduced by a general bibliography referring to wider information on the subjects discussed, and to works relevant for the subunits of that literary body. Whenever available, a special form-critical bibliography for a specific unit under discussion will conclude the discussion of that unit. In the outline of the structure of units, the system of sigla attempts to indicate the relationship and interdependence of the parts within that structure. The traditional chapter and verse divisions of the Hebrew text are supplied in the right-hand margin of the outlines. Where there is a difference between the Hebrew and English versification the latter is also supplied in parentheses according to the *Revised Standard Version*.

In addition to the commentary on the biblical books, this volume includes an introduction to the major genres found in the Old Testament narrative literature and a glossary of the genres discussed in the commentary. Most of the definitions in the glossary were prepared by Professor Coats, but some have arisen from the work of other members of the project on other parts of the Old Testament. Each subsequent volume will include such a glossary. Eventually, upon the completion of the commentary series, all of the glossaries will be revised in the light of the analysis of each book of the Old Testament and published as Volume XXIV of the series. The individual volumes will not contain special indices but the indices for the entire series will be published as Volume XXIII.

The editors wish to acknowledge with appreciation the contribution of numerous persons and institutions to the work of the project. All of the contributors have received significant financial, secretarial, and student assistance from their respective institutions. In particular, the editors have received extensive support from their Universities. Without such concrete expressions of encouragement the work scarcely could have gone on. At Claremont, the Institute for Antiquity and Christianity has from its own inception provided office facilities, a supportive staff, and the atmosphere which stimulates not only individual but also team research. Emory University and the Candler School of Theology have likewise provided tangible support and encouragement.

The editors are indebted to Christine Bucher, Old Testament graduate student at Claremont Graduate School and research associate to the FOTL project at the Institute for Antiquity and Christianity, for her significant contribution to the editorial process.

ROLF KNIERIM
GENE M. TUCKER

Preface

A PREFACE SHOULD document contributions from friends and colleagues to the production of a book. For the insight and patience of my colleagues in the form-critical project I am most grateful. For the stimulation of countless students in my seminars on exegesis of Genesis or preaching from the Pentateuch, especially for the good humor of students who confess a seminary major in Genesis, and the several students whose work as assistants facilitated the production of the manuscript, I am most grateful. I am grateful also for my faculty colleagues at Lexington Theological Seminary who must have thought that I know nothing in the Old Testament except Genesis, yet were willing to approve two sabbatical proposals related to this Genesis project. Finally, the financial support at various intervals over the ten years of this project from Lexington Theological Seminary, Humboldt Stiftung, Fulbright Commission, the American Philosophical Society, and the National Endowment for the Humanities made free time available for concentrated work on the text.

The traditions in Genesis depict the pain and turmoil, hatred and strife, separation and death for generations of a family. But the traditions also speak of hope for reconciliation. These friends of mine from the ancient world have offered me a hope that I could not find in myself. I can only wish for the same experience for all who struggle with their story.

GEORGE W. COATS
Lexington Theological Seminary

INTRODUCTION TO NARRATIVE LITERATURE

BIBLIOGRAPHY

Th.M. Andersson, *The Icelandic Family Saga* (Cambridge: Harvard, 1967); K. Baltzer, *Die Biographie der Propheten* (Neukirchen-Vluyn: Neukirchener Verlag, 1975); W. Bascom, "The Forms of Folklore: Prose Narratives," *Journal of American Folklore* 78 (1965) 3-20; B.S. Childs, "The Etiological Tale Re-examined," *VT* 24 (1974) 387-97; idem, *Myth and Reality in the Old Testament* (SBT 1/27; London: SCM, 1960); R.C. Culley, *Studies in the Structure of Hebrew Narrative* (Philadelphia: Fortress, 1976); D.M. Gunn, "The 'Battle Report': Oral or Scribal Convention?" *JBL* 93 (1974) 513-18; R.M. Hals, "Legend: A Case Study in Old Testament Form-Critical Terminology," *CBQ* 34 (1972) 166-76; A. Jolles, *Einfache Formen* (Tübingen: Niemeyer, 1958); B. O. Long, *The Problem of Etiological Narrative in the Old Testament* (BZAW 108; Berlin: Töpelmann, 1968); idem, "Recent Field Studies in Oral Literature and Their Bearing on OT Criticism," *VT* 26 (1976) 187-98; A. Olrik, "Epic Laws of Folk Narrative" (tr. J.P. Steager and A. Dundes), in *The Study of Folklore* (ed. A. Dundes; Englewood Cliffs: Prentice-Hall, 1965) 129-41; A. Rofé, "The Classification of the Prophetical Stories," *JBL* 89 (1970) 427-40; R. Wellek and A. Warren, *Theory of Literature* (3rd ed.; New York: Harcourt, Brace, and World, 1956); C. Westermann, *The Promises to the Fathers: Studies on the Patriarchal Narratives* (tr. D.E. Green; Philadelphia: Fortress, 1980); R.J. Williams, "The Fable in the Ancient Near East," in *A Stubborn Faith* (*Fest.* W.A. Irwin; ed. E.C. Hobbs; Dallas: Southern Methodist University Press, 1956) 3-26.

I. PROLEGOMENA

Narratives in the OT deserve serious attention as examples of ancient literary art. This assertion may appear to be obvious. Yet, its importance as an assumption for form-critical analysis and the difficulties experienced by contemporary cultures in taking it seriously require its consideration at the beginning of this introduction. The difficulties arise from a penchant among members of western audiences, particularly American audiences, for destroying the narrative in an effort to discover the "real" history experienced by its heroes and hidden behind its forms. There is perhaps a popular view that narrative can be appreciated only as "a document or case history, as—what for its own purposes of illusion it sometimes professes to be—a confession, a true story, a history of a life and its times" (Wellek and Warren, 212). An implicit—or even at times explicit—consequence is the belief that narrative appreciated for its own merits as imaginative art is "harmful or at best self-indulgent" (Wellek and Warren, 212). The same problem might be expressed as follows: "There are today two absolutely contrary approaches or methodologies, between which there can be hardly any agreement granted the present state of scholarship. . . . The one side tends to accept the Genesis narratives as directly as possible as accounts of events that took place just as described, preserved by an uninterrupted tradition. The other side tends to emphasize the work of writers and narrators throughout the historical period of Israel in shaping stories that were much earlier, asking about the course of tradition taken by these narratives *within Israel*. To them, the question of what the narratives can tell us about the patriarchal period itself appears very difficult or even impossible to answer" (Westermann, *Promises*, 1-2). One might add, however, that the narratives themselves can still merit our serious consideration as works of ancient literary art.

The goal for this form-critical analysis of OT narrative is not to reconstruct the history of the patriarchs or Moses. It is rather to show that the value of the literary form resides in the form itself rather than in its contribution to a reconstruction of historical process. For the historian it is relevant to ask whether a report about a battle between X and Y is historically accurate. In that case, however, the narrative artifact is but a shard, a piece of the ancient world valuable for reconstructing a larger and quite different original. The goal of this form-critical analysis of OT narrative calls instead for evaluation of the narrative for itself, even if the history it projects proves to be less than the accurate witness sought by the historian.

OT narrative shares characteristics with narrative art, both ancient and modern, for depicting its environment in symbolic, verbal form. Specifically, it embraces events that happened to principals within a specified period of time. Moreover, the narrative depicts the principal people embroiled in those time periods by *description* of the details that constitute the events, and by *dialogue* among the principals who participate in the process of events. Indeed, in OT narratives, dialogue carries as much of the weight in the depiction of the period as does the description. In the following examples of form-critical exposition, the term "narrative" is held as a broad and neutral term, inclusive of various "narrative" genres that develop particular structures and serve varied intentions within the general concern to depict a sequence of events from a specified period of time. The narrative is the art form, symbolic and imaginative in its representation, that combines description and dialogue in order to depict principals in a particular span of time. The terms "narrate" and "narration" also belong in this fund of general, neutral categories. The verb "narrate" denotes the act of describing the events, while the noun "narration" refers to the process of narrating.

The task of this introduction is, then, to clarify the most distinctive "narrative" genres that emerge from the following discussion. The goal is in part to control the technical terminology used to expose the various form-critical units. This terminology has, unfortunately, provoked a series of problems that must be addressed, however briefly, by anyone who would undertake a form-critical survey of OT narratives. The terms for the genres have been drawn by and large from fields of literature outside the OT, indeed, from outside the period of time that produced the principal narratives. They apply, therefore, to the OT literature only with a limited degree of accuracy. Objections invariably arise. Yet, the technical vocabulary has some currency and tradition in the discipline of OT studies. The goal of this introduction is not to play a name game. It is to identify specific kinds of narrative literature. Giving a name to the genre is necessary but only as a convenience for the discipline. It would thus be of some merit to avoid the name game by using esoteric, descriptive terms for the classes drawn from distinctive elements of content (see Westermann, *Promises*). The advantage of such a procedure would be to avoid the technical vocabulary with its inherent set of problems altogether. Yet, if the technical vocabulary has currency relevant to the characteristics of the narrative genres identified from particular texts, not in abstraction from the texts, then it seems appropriate to define the vocabulary so that it can be used with precision and then to apply that vocabulary to the narrative units of the OT. The goal of the following discussion is therefore to identify the major narrative genres, to suggest terminology for them, and then to provide sufficient definition to facilitate precision in their use. The goal does not call for a resolution of all the problems in the history of the terms. It calls only for identification of legitimate characteristics signaled by the terms so that the reader can know what they stand for in the following analyses.

The criteria for establishing these categories are: (1) a distinctive structure, (2) distinctive vocabulary patterns, perhaps appearing as indicators of the structure, (3) a typical setting, and (4) a qualifying function of the literary piece within its setting, thus a distinctive intention. If a piece of narrative meets one or more of these criteria, particularly if the characteristics recur in several pieces of narrative, then there is fundamental reason for identifying the piece as a representative of a narrative genre. The viability of the genre is the key concern.

4

II. THE PRINCIPAL NARRATIVE GENRES IN THE OLD TESTAMENT

A. SAGA

A SAGA is a long, prose, traditional narrative. It has typically an *episodic* structure developed around stereotyped themes or topics. These episodic units might be pieces of narrative tradition that were in themselves originally independent of the saga. Indeed, they may include narratives that represent quite distinctive genres in themselves. Thus, a saga will comprise a series of TALES, REPORTS, LEGENDS, ANECDOTES, HYMNS, and various other smaller pieces. These episodes narrate deeds or virtues from the past to the extent that they contribute to the composition of the present narrator's world. That world is the real world, not a world of fantasy or mythology. It would be possible, however, for the saga to embrace FABLE or MYTH in its compass and thus to transform such genres dealing with a world of fantasy into pictures of the real world.

It should be noted here that the term "saga cycle" probably falls under serious attack from this definition of saga. The implication of the definition is that those larger units previously labeled "saga cycle" have far more cohesion than suggested by the term "cycle." That cohesive narrative carries an intrinsic function for the society that produced it and ought not to be represented simply as a redactional collection of totally distinct and independent sagas. In most cases, however, it is probably true that those units described here as "saga" were in previous form-critical works called "saga cycle."

The saga falls into three subcategories: (1) the primeval saga, or a narrative account of the beginning time, the time that produced the world as it is from an original ideal world; (2) the family saga, or a narrative account of the events that compose the past of the family unit; and (3) the heroic saga, or a narrative account of the events that compose the past of a people's leader who, by virtue of his identification with his people, made it possible for the people to endure (see Westermann, *Promises*, 31-35).

(1) The primeval saga shares structural characteristics with the other two classes of saga by virtue of its episodic series. It has no single plot that runs throughout the whole series, but rather recounts those events of the distant past, before this age, that produced this age from the ideal original. Two principal subjects characteristic of the primeval saga appear prominently in the OT, although certainly other subjects contributed to the traditional structure: (a) a creation narrative or some other account of the beginning of human culture, and (b) a flood narrative or some other account of a cosmic destruction of the world. Generally, the second topic will lead to a renewal of the first, with some indication of the process that brought the world in its renewed form to its present stage. For both, the perspective of the narration is worldwide, although some concern to identify a particular group in the worldwide scene may also appear. Thus, the Gilgamesh Epic is not a part of a primeval saga, although it looks back on primeval tradition. In the primeval tradition some point of identification with historical culture can be seen. Utnapishtim, for example, was a relative of Gilgamesh, and thus he provides a point of contact between the primeval past and the historical peoples associated with the city of Gilgamesh. In the OT primeval saga, Noah was the righteous father of all the world's population, but from him comes the line of

Shem and, eventually, of Terah and Abraham. As an example of primeval saga, see the Yahwist's version in Genesis 1–11.

(2) Family saga shares the structural characteristics of primeval saga: it is a long, traditional, prose narrative with episodic units. In content the family saga is distinctive. Its perspective is still this world. Indeed, its narration depicts events of this period in world history. It focuses its concerns, however, not on the affairs of all the peoples of the world, as would primeval saga, but rather on the activities of a family, exemplified primarily by the affairs of the patriarchal head of the family. Nevertheless, the family saga is not simply about the life of the familial patriarch. It centers on those events that compose the internal affairs of the family headed by the patriarch. Thus, typical episodic units represent the travel of the family, relationships within the family commonly depicted as strife and separation of family members from the unit (see the Icelandic sagas), birth, marriage, death of family members, and some indication about the primary family structure (who the head of the family is and how he will be succeeded). Family saga, moreover, typically comprises some account of the conception and birth of male heirs (see Westermann, *Promises,* 12-30). As an example of family saga in the OT, see the Yahwist's version of the Abraham saga, Genesis 12–25.

(3) The heroic saga again employs episodic units in order to build its structure for a long, traditional account of events in the past. In this case, however, the events do not embrace the affairs of a family or tribe, but rather the events in the life of a central figure significant for the life of the people who remember him. Thus, typically, the saga includes some account of the hero's birth, marriage, vocational commitment, and death. In addition, some display of the hero's virtues as complements to his deeds rounds off the narrative account of the saga.

It seems inappropriate to define this genre of narrative as (→) biography (contrast Baltzer), since the concern is not simply to describe the hero as he really was or as he really acted, an intention the storyteller might readily have embraced, but rather to interpret the hero according to stereotyped, but imaginative, categories. Again, it seems appropriate to classify this prose narrative as saga rather than *Vita,* even though the definitions of *Vita* seem to have the same genre in view (see Rofé), primarily because the narrative shares with the family saga and the primeval saga the typical episodic structure. Its perspective is consistently limited to this world, a real world defined by real people struggling with real limitations. Its interests are larger than family interests, perhaps already moving into a nationalistic stance. The genre is nonetheless the same. As an example of heroic saga, see the Yahwist's story of Moses, Exodus 1–Deuteronomy 34.

The saga reflects, in all probability, the productivity of the storyteller within the structures of ancient society. The family sagas, for example, come to us through the hands of literary figures, the authors or redactors of the Yahwist or the priestly writers, but behind the written form of the saga lies the work of the oral storyteller. Details about this stage in the creative formation of the sagas are not available. Much rests on hypothetical reconstruction. Yet, it seems to be a fair reconstruction of a sociological institution to suggest that the saga represents the construction of a lengthy story from shorter, moveable, traditional episodes (see Long, "Recent Field Studies"; Culley). Such a context for construction would account for recurring episodic types, such as the threat to the ancestress (Genesis

12; 20; 26) and, in many cases, the variations in stories commonly attributed to distinct literary sources.

This observation would qualify the setting of the saga. The ancient society might have supported a segment responsible for public entertainment as well as public moral indoctrination. This institutional concern would have functioned as a part of the family structure. Thus, family members would have been responsible for telling the stories of the family's past, even when the society moves beyond family or tribal structures to national orientation. The storytelling function in the ancient society cannot be limited to the affairs of the family, however. Stories could be told in the cult or in the royal court or in the town gate at the public meeting of the elders. Storytelling itself is an institution with a specific function for the ancient society.

The intention of the saga must be related in some manner to entertainment. Yet, it would be too simplistic to define saga only in terms of entertainment. Storytelling preserves the traditions of a family or a people so that in the story the moral fiber of the group can be constituted. This intention may be expressed in terms of legitimation for the group by showing the genealogical, geographical, or historical origin of the group. It may accomplish that goal by setting out models for the group's behavior. But in whatever the particular manner, the saga establishes the heritage for the group's moral development.

B. TALE

A TALE is a short narrative, characterized by a minimum number of characters (two or, on occasion, three), a single scene, and a simple plot (see Olrik). Typically, the tale will establish the circumstances for its plot (exposition), then develop a point of tension as the subject of the plot. The plot unfolds as an arc running from the tension to a resolution of the tension (see Westermann, *Promises*, 27-30). The brevity of the narration is a relative factor, but the complexity of the plot remains rather limited.

The tale may have been originally an independent element of folk tradition. It might also have functioned as a dependent part of the saga. It is not possible to determine the history of the genre clearly enough to know whether the tale was originally an independent narrative, subsequently embraced by the saga-teller as a part of the longer story, or whether it was from the beginning a part of the larger whole. The crucial point is that the tale features a distinctive, if limited, structure. The term (→) "story" might be legitimately used for this genre. Yet, "story" has a broader field of meaning. It can refer to narratives of this genre, the saga, or the novella. A common use of the term qualifies the narrative in Genesis 37–47 as "the Joseph story." It seems advisable, therefore, to reserve the term "story" for more general use and to employ "tale" for the genre described here. An example of the genre "tale" is the narrative about a threat to the ancestress (Gen. 12:9–13:1).

The tale derives from the same setting as the saga. Thus, it appears in written form as a part of the saga or even as an independent narrative. It doubtlessly belonged to the repertoire of the oral storyteller. Consequently, the tale would have been available for use in the saga or for brief narration in its own right. Like the saga, the tale might have been told in a number of different societal institutions. The family, the cult, the court, or any other institution might have supported storytelling as entertainment and as edification for the audiences attracted by the program.

C. NOVELLA

The NOVELLA shares characteristics of structure with the tale. Thus, it can develop a point of tension over an arc of narration to a final resolution. Its perspective is this world, not a world of fantasy. Its narration recounts events as they might have happened. The pattern of narration is not controlled by a cause-effect sequence of events but by the concern for the integrity of the plot. Moreover, like the tale, it too might have been included as an episode in a larger saga, or it might have been broken at key spots in order to include within its structure some element of narration originally independent of its plot (Genesis 37–47 as a frame for Genesis 38). Yet, its structural character is quite different from that of the tale or saga: It is not singular but complex; it can employ a series of subplots in careful support of the principal theme; it involves more than the typical two figures for a scene; and its presentation of principals tends to be much more subtle and psychologically sophisticated.

The novella does not derive from the world of the storyteller. It is not a genre set within the processes of oral tradition. According to Olrik's laws, the novella must be understood from the beginning as a kind of literature produced by an author as an original piece of art. It may employ (oral) tradition, and the tradition may reveal a history even in the realm of oral storytelling. As a distinct genre, however, the novella transforms whatever tradition it employs into a new work of art, marked by its own internal unity.

The genre serves the purposes of entertainment. Its function is distinct from saga, however, in that it does not preserve the stories simply for entertainment, but rather develops the particular intentions of the author. The author may seek to entertain his audience by presenting humorous (→ Abraham-Lot Novella) or theological (→ Servant of Abraham Novella) situations. He may speak to a problem within the structures of his society (→ Joseph Novella). The intention can thus be shaped by the particular goals of the artist who composes the narration.

D. LEGEND

The LEGEND is a genre of narrative fundamentally distinct from the saga and its field of related forms. Its structure does not represent a plot based on narration of tension, increasing to a point of resolution (→ tale). To the contrary, it employs a relatively static narration. The structure of the legend features recurring emphasis on some particular characteristic of the narrative's hero. Typically that characteristic is a virtue of high value. Thus, by emphasizing the commandment of God to sacrifice Isaac, Genesis 22 represents Abraham as a man of virtuous faith. His obedience exemplifies the obedience that all faithful persons should experience. The structure does not develop an arc of tension that moves from point of complication to point of resolution. It spotlights the virtue and addresses the same virtue from various points of view. The narrative thus does not appear to move at all, at least not as a part of its principal structural pattern. To the contrary, it is static.

The legend should be defined not by its content, but rather by its characteristic structure. A legend may be about a holy person, and the virtue it highlights may be a religious one, such as the religious obedience and faith of Abraham. But the legend may also be about a political person, and the virtue it highlights may be a political one (→ Genesis 39–41). Moreover, the legend should not be defined by any particular subject. The legend will typically depict a person as a hero whose virtues can be identified in narrative form. It may, however, depict a place as one whose attributes, such as a special event characteristic for the place, can compose the structural pattern of a narrative. Thus, the HIEROS LOGOS, or the sacred words used for showing the origin of a holy place, would share certain characteristics with etiology, but it would also reveal its nature as a cultic legend intended as an account of the foundation of a sanctuary by a depiction of the event or the construction that marked the place as holy.

The legend belongs to the repertoire of the storyteller. Thus, legends might be told in cultic shrines, at the royal court, among family members. It is important to avoid the temptation to locate the setting of a legend, for example, in the holy shrine associated with the legend simply because the content of the legend happens to mention, or even to devote its entire narration to, a ceremony there. The legend might belong to the ceremony, but it cannot be limited to that setting.

The goal of the legend is edification of its audience. Thus, the hero may serve as a model whose virtue can be duplicated by subsequent generations. Indeed, the model can serve as a standard of judgment by which political or religious criticism can be effected. If the society knows that a politician should act in a particular way, it can call particular politicians to account for behavior that violates the norm.

E. HISTORY

HISTORY as a genre of literature represents that kind of writing designed to record the events of the past as they actually occurred. Its structure is controlled, then, not by the concerns of aesthetics, nor by the symbolic nature of a plot, but by the chronological stages or cause-effect sequences of events as the author(s) understood them. It is not structured to maintain interest or to provoke anticipation for a resolution of tension. It is designed simply to record. The validity of any example from the genre is not determined by the accuracy of its record as controlled by the standards of modern history, but rather by the success or failure on the part of any given example for publishing its record. As an example of history, see the Deuteronomistic History or the Chronicles.

A BIOGRAPHY is a particular kind of history writing. Its concern is to document the events of a particular life throughout its duration. The structure is controlled by the record of events in the chronology of the life rather than by stereotyped or symbolic themes (contrast the [→] heroic saga).

The setting for history and biography differs markedly from the setting for saga and legend. History writing marks a movement away from the contexts of the family or tribe, with their storytelling concerns, to the record-keeping responsibilities of the nation. History writing would thus be identified in some

9

manner with the affairs of the royal court, with its archives. It derives from the concern to document the past of the people in order to validate the present administration.

F. REPORT

This genre shares with history the intention to record without developing the points of tension characteristic for a plot. It is basically brief, with a single event the subject of its record. Again, the accuracy of its reporting does not alter the character of the genre. As an example of the genre, see Gen 35:8.

Reports might be made by anyone. It is thus difficult to limit a report to one institutional setting. The court would certainly cultivate report making. AN-NALS would provide a clear representation of a series of reports. Other institutions, however, might also provide reports of key events in the past.

A particular kind of report records an event as an experience in the life of a person. For this report, the technical term ANECDOTE would be appropriate. The anecdote maintains the same relationship to report that biography maintains to history.

G. FABLE

This genre depicts a world of fantasy (see Williams), with the principal figures drawn typically, but not necessarily, from human and subhuman creatures. The subhuman creatures may be either animal or plant. The narrative itself does not develop a plot with tension increased to the point of denouement. Rather, it describes a static situation. Typically, a presumptuous character has an overblown ego pricked by a pointed moral (→ Num 22:22-35).

H. ETIOLOGY

This genre must not be confused with a (→) tale expanded with an etiological suffix. The ETIOLOGY must be defined as a narrative designed in its basic structure to support some kind of explanation for a situation or name that exists at the time of the storyteller. Thus, a typical etiology will build a connection between a saying in the body of the genre and a conclusion that provides the explanation. The connection might be a simple wordplay (→ Exod 15:23). If the connection is fundamental to the narrative, the unit qualifies as an example of etiology (see Long, *Etiological Narrative*).

I. MYTH

This term can be limited to a narrative genre, although it has wide currency beyond its strict form-critical application. The genre it might most appropriately represent is a narrative form, set in a fantasy world, designed to account for the real world by reference to the activities of the gods in the divine world (see Childs, *Myth*). The OT has relatively few myths in its collection of narrative forms (→ Gen 6:1-4).

GENESIS

CHAPTER 1
The Pentateuch / Hexateuch: The Framework

BIBLIOGRAPHY

A. Alt, "The God of the Fathers," in *Essays on Old Testament History and Religion* (tr. R.A. Wilson; Garden City, N.Y.: Doubleday, 1968) 1-100; Chr. Barth, "Zur Bedeutung der Wüstentradition," in *Volume du Congrès Genève* (VTSup 15; Leiden: Brill, 1966) 14-23; J. Blenkinsopp, "Theme and Motif in the Succession History (2 Sam 11:2ff.) and the Yahwist Corpus," in *Volume du Congrès Genève* (VTSup 15; Leiden: Brill, 1966) 44-57; idem, "The Structure of P," *CBQ* 38 (1976) 275-92; R. Borchert, "Stil und Aufbau der priesterschriftlichen Erzählung" (Diss., Heidelberg, 1957); C.H.W. Brekelmans, "Het 'historische Credo' van Israël," *Tijdschrift voor Theologie* 3 (1963) 1-10; W. Brueggemann, "David and His Theologian," *CBQ* 30 (1968) 156-81; idem, "The Kerygma of the Priestly Writers," *ZAW* 84 (1972) 397-413; C. Carmichael, "A New View of the Origin of the Deuteronomic Credo," *VT* 19 (1969) 273-89; B.S. Childs, *Introduction to the Old Testament as Scripture* (Philadelphia: Fortress, 1979); D.J.A. Clines, *The Theme of the Pentateuch* (JSOTSup 10; Sheffield: University Press, 1978); G.W. Coats, "An Exposition for the Wilderness Traditions," *VT* 22 (1972) 288-95; idem, *From Canaan to Egypt: Structural and Theological Context for the Joseph Study* (CBQMS 4; Washington: Catholic Biblical Association, 1976); idem, "A Structural Transition in Exodus," *VT* 22 (1972) 129-42; idem, "The Wilderness Itinerary," *CBQ* 34 (1972) 135-52; F.M. Cross, "The Priestly Work," in *Canaanite Myth and Hebrew Epic: Essays in the History of the Religion of Israel* (Cambridge: Harvard University Press, 1973) 293-325; idem, "Yahweh and the God of the Patriarchs," *HTR* 55 (1962) 225-59; O. Eissfeldt, "Jahwe, der Gott der Väter," *TLZ* 88 (1963) 481-90; K. Elliger, "Sinn und Ursprung der priesterlichen Geschichtserzählung," *ZTK* 49 (1952) 121-42; P. Ellis, *The Yahwist: The Bible's First Theologian* (Notre Dame: Fides, 1968); J.M. Grintz, "Do Not Eat on the Blood! Reconsiderations in Setting and Dating of the Priestly Code," *ASTI* 8 (1970/71) 78-105; H. Gunkel, *Genesis* (3rd ed.; HKAT 1/1; Göttingen: Vandenhoeck und Ruprecht, 1964); M. Haran, "Shiloh and Jerusalem. The Origin of the Priestly Tradition in the Pentateuch," *JBL* 81 (1962) 14-24; M.-L. Henry, *Jahwist und Priesterschrift: Glaubenszeugnisse des Alten Testaments* (AzT 3; Stuttgart: Calwer, 1960); G. Hölscher, *Geschichtsschreibung in Israel. Untersuchungen zum Jahwisten und Elohisten* (Lund: Gleerup, 1952); H.B. Huffmon, "The Exodus, Sinai, and the Credo," *CBQ* 27 (1965) 101-13; J.P. Hyatt, "Jahweh as 'the God of My Father'," *VT* 5 (1955) 130-36; idem, "Were There an Ancient Historical Credo in Israel and an Independent Sinai Tradition?" in *Translating and Understanding the Old Testament* (*Fest.* H.G. May; ed. H.T. Frank and W.L. Reed; Nashville: Abingdon, 1970)

152-70; A.W. Jenks, *The Elohist and North Israelite Traditions* (SBLMS 22; Missoula: Scholars Press, 1977); R. Kessler, "Die Querverweise im Pentateuch. Überlieferungs-geschichtliche Untersuchung der expliziten Querverbindungen innerhalb des vorpriesterlichen Pentateuchs" (Diss., Heidelberg, 1972); N. Lohfink, "Die Priesterschrift und die Grenzen des Wachstums," *Stimmen der Zeit* 99/7 (1974) 435-50; D.J. McCarthy, "What was Israel's Historical Creed?" *Lexington Theological Quarterly* 4 (1969) 46-53; S. McEvenue, *The Narrative Style of the Priestly Writer* (AnBib 50; Rome: Biblical Institute Press, 1971); idem, "Word and Fulfillment. A Stylistic Feature of the Priestly Writer," *Semitics* 1 (1970) 104-10; S. Mowinckel, *Tetrateuch-Pentateuch-Hexateuch* (BZAW 90; Berlin: Töpelmann, 1964); M. Noth, *A History of Pentateuchal Traditions* (tr. B.W. Anderson; Englewood Cliffs: Prentice-Hall, 1972); G. von Rad, "The Form-Critical Problem of the Hexateuch," in *The Problem of the Hexateuch and Other Essays* (tr. E.W. Trueman Dicken; Edinburgh: Oliver and Boyd, 1966) 1-78; idem, *Genesis, a Commentary* (tr. J.H. Marks; rev. ed.; OTL; Philadelphia: Westminster, 1972); idem, *Die Priesterschrift im Hexateuch, literarisch untersucht und theologisch gewertet* (BWANT 13; Stuttgart: Kohlhammer, 1934); R. Rendtorff, "The 'Yahwist' as Theologian? The Dilemma of Pentateuchal Criticism" (tr. J.B. Geyer), *JSOT* 3 (1977) 2-10; idem, *Das überlieferungsgeschichtliche Problem des Pentateuch* (BZAW 147; Berlin: Walter deGruyter, 1976); J.A. Sanders, *Torah and Canon* (Philadelphia: Fortress, 1972); J. Scharbert, "Der Sinn der Toledot-Formel in der Pries-terschrift," in *Wort—Gebot—Glaube* (*Fest.* W. Eichrodt; ed. H.J. Stoebe; ATANT 59; Zürich: Zwingli, 1970) 45-56; H.H. Schmid, *Der sogenannte Jahwist. Beobachtungen und Fragen zur Pentateuchforschung* (Zürich: Theologischer Verlag, 1976); H. Seebass, *Der Erzvater Israel und die Einführung der Jahweverehrung in Kanaan* (BZAW 98; Berlin: Töpelmann, 1966); J.A. Thompson, "The Cultic Credo and the Sinai Tradition," *RTR* 27 (1968) 53-64; J.G. Vink, *The Date and Origin of the Priestly Code in the Old Testament* (Leiden: Brill, 1969); Th. C. Vriezen, "The Credo in the Old Testament," in *Studies on the Psalms* (OTWSA; Potchefstroom: Beperk, 1963) 5-17; P. Weimar, "Die Toledoth-Formel in der priesterschriftlichen Geschichtsdarstellung," *BZ* 18 (1974) 65-93; H.W. Wolff, "The Elohistic Fragments in the Pentateuch" (tr. K.R. Crim), *Int* 26 (1972) 158-73; idem, "The Kerygma of the Yahwist" (tr. W.A. Benware), *Int* 20 (1966) 131-58; W. Zimmerli, "Sinaibund und Abrahamsbund. Ein Beitrag zum Verständnis der Priester-schrift," *TZ* 16 (1960) 268-80; idem, "Promise and Fulfillment" (tr. J. Wharton), in *Essays on Old Testament Hermeneutics* (ed. C. Westermann; tr. ed. J.L. Mays; Richmond: John Knox, 1960) 89-122.

THE PENTATEUCH, Gen 1:1 – Deut 34:12

Structure

I. The patriarchal sagas	Gen 1:1–50:26
A. The primeval saga	1:1–11:32
B. The Abraham saga	12:1–25:18
C. The Isaac saga	25:19–36:43
D. The Jacob saga	37:1–50:26
II. The Moses saga	Exod 1:1–Deut 34:12
A. Birth	Exod 1:1–2:10
B. Marriage	2:11-22
C. Call	2:23–4:31
D. Execution of the call commission	5:1–6:1

E. Call	6:2–7:7
F. Execution of the call commission	Exod 7:8–Num 36:13
1. Exodus	Exod 7:8–12:36
2. Wilderness	Exod 12:37–Num 36:13
G. Death of Moses	Deut 1:1–34:12
1. Moses' farewell speech	1:1–30:20
2. Moses death report	31:1-30
3. Poems	32:1–33:29
4. Moses' death report	34:1-12

According to the traditional division, three large units constitute the scope of the MT: the Torah, the Prophets, and the Writings. The first major unit to consider under form-critical categories would therefore be the Torah. Immediately, however, the Torah presents a major problem. Is there any sense in which the Torah as a unit has form-critical integrity? Or is it a segment of the Bible far too diverse to merit an evaluation as a form-critical unit? The term "Torah" is in itself one that derives from the history of the canon established within a specific religious community (→ 2 Chr 23:18). It connotes something about function within a specific community of faith. That point alone would suggest that "Torah" is properly a unit of literature with some degree of form-critical integrity. The problem that calls for evaluation, however, concerns the structural unity that might characterize the Torah. It is just at this point that the structural term for the unit ought to appear. The Torah comprises five distinct elements, the first five books of the MT. Its structure suggests, therefore, the traditional synonym for Torah, the Pentateuch, if not for a discussion of the history of the text, then at least for a discussion of the form-critical integrity of the text.

Yet, the problem for analyzing structure in the unit remains. Is the Pentateuch simply a random collection of writings? Or is there some principle of unity that holds the structure of the Pentateuch together? Although the question must be asked for each book, it should be posed first to the unit as a whole.

Structural analysis of the Pentateuch reveals two basic units of narrative: the patriarchal sagas and the Moses saga. Yet, in this statement of structure, the form-critical problem of the Pentateuch comes most sharply into view, for there is a fundamental disunity between the patriarchal sagas and the Moses saga. The patriarchal sagas narrate stories about the fathers and their families in their life settings in Canaan. In this literature the culture appears to be semi-nomadic, the religion a mobile one tied not to a particular place, but rather to a particular tribal patriarch. Whenever the patriarch moves, the God of the patriarch moves with him. Even at the end of the series, the subject of the tradition is, at most, *the sons of Jacob* at home in Canaan. The Moses saga, to the contrary, recounts the events of Moses in Egypt, the process that brought him to his people, *the sons of Israel*, the formation of the group into a working unit, and the events of trial and victory that brought them to the land of Canaan. It may be that the religion of this group was nonetheless similar to the religion of the God of the fathers (see Hyatt, "Jahweh"). In any case, the religion of Yahweh, perhaps closely tied to Mt. Sinai, would appear to be quite distinct from the religion of the God of the fathers. In the history of the text and traditions, as well as in the history of the people, these two segments demonstrate their original disunity.

Moreover, the tradition reveals various points that suggest evidence for the process of union between these originally distinct segments. The Joseph novella, Genesis 37–47, appears as a major literary work designed to bridge the gap between the sons of Jacob in Canaan and the sons of Israel in Egypt (Coats, *From Canaan*). Also, the definition of Yahweh, the God who revealed himself to Moses, as the God of the fathers (→ Exod 3:6-15) derives from a stage in the history of the tradition that sought to identify the God of the fathers with the God of Moses (see Alt). The form-critical integrity of the Pentateuch depends on the success of these bonds.

Given the union of the traditions about the fathers with the traditions about Moses, a union that has its literary expression in the Joseph story, one can then describe the unity of the Pentateuch in terms of patriarchal sagas joined with the Moses saga. The Pentateuch begins with the primeval saga as a preface to the patriarchs, and it concludes with the death of Moses and its corresponding affirmation of Moses' career.

However, the problem of unity in the structure of the Pentateuch is not resolved completely by these observations. To the contrary, the text reveals a second pattern of structure, not tied to the limits and functions of saga, but moving beyond those configurations to a more theologically oriented structure. Since this structure includes the tradition of the conquest in the book of Joshua, it suggests a form-critical integrity for the Hexateuch.

THE HEXATEUCH, Gen 1:1– Josh 24:33

Structure

I. The patriarchal theme	
A. The primeval saga (exposition)	Gen 1:1–11:32
1. Creation	1:1–2:4a
2. Creation and fall of human beings	2:4b–4:26
a. Paradise	2:4b–3:24
b. Tale of two brothers	4:1-26
3. Flood	5:1–9:29
4. Dispersal of human beings	10:1–11:32
a. Table of nations	10:1-32
b. Tower	11:1-32
B. The Abraham saga	12:1–25:18
1. Narrative	12:1–22:24
2. Death reports	23:1–25:18
C. The Isaac saga	25:19–36:43
1. Narrative	25:19–35:15
2. Death reports	35:16–36:43
D. The Jacob saga	37:1–50:26
1. Joseph novella	37:1–47:27
2. Death reports	47:28–50:26
II. The exodus theme	Exod 1:1–12:36

16

A. Exposition	1:1-14
B. Birth	1:15–2:10
C. Marriage	2:11-22
D. Call	2:23–4:31
E. Execution of the call commission	5:1–6:1
F. Call	6:2–7:7
G. Execution of the call commission	7:8–12:36
III. The wilderness theme	Exod 12:37–Deut 34:12
A. Exposition	Exod 12:37–13:22
B. God's aid in the wilderness	14:1–17:16
C. Judicial order	18:1-27
D. Sinai	Exod 19:1–Num 10:36
E. God's aid in the wilderness	Num 11:1–36:13
F. Moses' last speech	Deut 1.1–34.12
IV. The conquest theme	Josh 1:1–24:33
A. Exposition	1:1–5:12
B. Call	5:13-15
C. Conquest tales	6:1–11:23
D. Division of the land	12:1–22:34
E. Joshua's last speech	23:1–24:33

The structure of the Hexateuch both complements the structure of the Pentateuch and at times contradicts it. Its theological patterns suggest that the unity of narration does not cease with the death of Moses but moves into the traditions of conquest in Joshua. Yet, the unity in structure remains a problem. Not only does the primary problem evident from the Pentateuch appear also for the structure of the Hexateuch, but a second problem arises as well: What is the relationship between the Moses saga and the narrative construction of the Joshua traditions?

The key for analyzing the structure of the Hexateuch lies in a series of texts that provide exposition for narration of the saga tradition under the stamp of God's mighty acts. For the first of these themes of theological tradition, Genesis 1–11 and 12:1-9 serve as exposition. This exposition announces God's act that resolves a crisis posed by broken intimacy within the community of his creatures. God's act will meet the crisis by offering blessing to the world through the patriarchal figures, a blessing that assumes the form of reconciliation and union among members of key human groups. In addition, the blessing offers to the patriarchs a series of promises: land, posterity, son, blessing, and guidance. The promise motif is a structural arc for describing the unity between Genesis and Joshua: the conquest fulfills the promise for land given to the patriarchs (Zimmerli, "Promise").

The second theme, the exodus from Egypt, begins with an exposition in Exod 1:1-14 (Coats, "Transition"). These verses mark a crisis for the sons of Jacob created by the pharaoh, king of Egypt, when he imposed oppressive labor on his slave gangs. Resolution of the crisis will therefore involve redemption from that oppression.

The third theme marked by an explicit structural element is the wilderness wanderings. Exod 12:37–13:22 sets the pattern for this theme as God's leadership in the journey from Egypt to Canaan (Coats, "Exposition"). Indeed, the symbols of the motif appear here as prime forms of God's presence for his people: the pillar of cloud and the pillar of fire. Moreover, the exposition introduces an itinerary chain that provides structure for the unity of the theme (so, Coats, "Itinerary"). From the city of Ramses to the plains of the Jordan Valley where the land awaits their entry, the people follow the leadership of Moses and, through him, Yahweh. The wilderness theme includes the traditions about the event at Sinai as one of the various stations in the wilderness itinerary. In the final form of the text, Sinai is not a distinct theme, even though the content of the Sinai tradition may be quite different from its wilderness context. Here God shows Israel how to respond to the fruits of his presence.

Finally, Josh 1:1–5:12 introduces the conquest, that mighty act of God that secured the land for the Israelites. Characteristic for this theme is the leitmotif of fear among the Canaanites. Their hearts melted, and thus they could offer no resistance to the invading Israelites. With this theme the point of tension introduced by the promise for land to the patriarchs comes to its conclusion (→ Josh 1–11).

The term "theme" offers some problem at this point in definition of structure. "Theme" doubtlessly refers to a dominant element of content such as oppression, leadership, or fear. Yet, this element establishes the key for structural unity in the larger narration. Thus, by "theme" the critic also means the formative unifying principle for constructing a lengthy narrative. It is properly a structure term, characterized by an exposition introducing the key leitmotif and a composition that moves from the introduction to some recognizable conclusion. The composition may include diverse materials such as distinct sagas, tales, and novellas. It may include simply a saga. But the point is that the leitmotif combines the diverse units into a larger body of narration.

It is instructive to ask what kind of structure might be characteristic for the sources that make up the Pentateuch/Hexateuch. The structure of the priestly source is as follows:

I. The patriarchal theme	Gen 1:1–50:26
A. Primeval event	1:1–2:4a
1. Creation	1:1–2:3
2. *Toledoth* formula	2:4a
B. *Toledoth* series	
1. Flood	
a. Genealogy of Adam (5:1 formula)	5:1-32
b. Flood (6:9 formula)	6:1–9:29
c. Genealogy for sons of Noah (10:1 formula)	10:1-32
2. Patriarchs	
a. First patriarch	
1) Shem formula	11:10
2) Terah formula	11:27
3) Abraham tradition	12:1–25:11
b. Second patriarch	
1) Ishmael formula	25:12

The priestly source preserves the problem of the Pentateuch/Hexateuch within its limits. It is characteristically statistical in form, formulaic in style. Its narration appears to lose vitality in its concern to construct the tradition in symmetrical patterns with emphasis on key periods. Indeed, it is possible to argue that the source is no longer narrative at all (so, Cross, "Priestly Work") but only a schematized report of events which constitute the narrative tradition for the older sources. The creation tradition provides ample evidence for such a tendency. Yet, in the midst of such clearly marked stylistic elements that unify the whole source, the division between patriarchal theme and Moses saga noted above remains obvious. The patriarchal theme reveals a structure organized by a series of *toledoth* formulas: "These are the generations of PN." The first entry in the series, 2:4a, functions as a prolepsis for the entire theme, suggesting that the series covers the history of the entire creation. The preceding report of creation sets the stage for this prolepsis by enumerating the stages of creation itself in a six-day scheme, with the seventh day marked for special observance by the completion of all divine creation acts. Then the series begins in 5:1 with a headline as the title of the series. Following the headline is a genealogy that runs from Adam to Noah in ten generations. The genealogy provides structural context for the flood story, the events of the tenth generation. This series begins with a *toledoth* formula for Shem, the son of Noah (11:10), and it ends with a *toledoth* formula for Terah, the father of Abraham (11:27). Moreover, the *toledoth* formula for Terah marks the beginning of P's narration of the Abraham tradition. At the end of the Abraham tradition, two *toledoth* formulas appear, one for Ishmael (25:12) and one for Isaac (25:19). The Isaac formula then introduces the tradition about Jacob and Esau. At the end of the Jacob-Esau tradition, three *toledoth* formulas appear, two for Esau (36:1, 9) and one for Jacob (37:2). The Jacob formula then introduces the account of the descent into Egypt under the authority of Joseph. The similar formula in Num 3:1 does not belong to the series but is simply a divergent use of the same formulaic construction. It would appear, then, that the patriarchal theme involves a stereotyped structure that binds the primeval event(s) to the patriarchs but separates the theme sharply from the narration in the remaining parts of the unit. The structure is not broken by the absence of a *toledoth* formula for Abraham since the formula for Terah plays the same role in the construction of the theme.

The content for these periods in the patriarchal theme highlights two major covenants: the covenant that establishes intimacy between Abraham and God (El Shaddai), and the prior covenant with Noah that guarantees the stability of the earth. These two periods emerge from a narrative pattern that emphasizes God's command and the obedient execution of the command by his creation (so, Blenkinsopp, "Structure of P"). But more content than the covenant tradition appears. In addition to the creation and flood, P narrates the purchase of a burial plot for the patriarchal family, the division of the family because of Esau's treachery, and a subsequent renaming of Jacob. Moreover, various pieces of priestly tradition suggest a broader range of narrative material. It may be that these pieces must be identified simply as expansion of received tradition (Cross, "Priestly Work"). Yet, the structure of P in the patriarchal theme is not simply an expansion but quite distinctive. It suggests strongly that P has independent form-critical integrity and cannot be treated simply as a dependent expansion of JE. Furthermore, it seems to be clear that narrative tradition does appear in P and will not support the judgment that P is not a narrative.

This clear-cut structure for P shifts, however, when the narrative moves from patriarchs to exodus. P accomplishes the shift by a statistical report, a name list of persons who joined Joseph in Egypt (→ Gen 46:8-27; Exod 1:1-7). In the exodus theme, P develops a different pattern of structure. An exposition marks the issue for narration as the contrast between fertility among the Israelites and the resulting oppression from the Egyptians. The substance of the narration employs a description of God's call to Moses (→ Exodus 6) and the obedient execution of that call (→ Exodus 7–12). Indeed, the period is marked for P by a notation that divine instructions for ritual celebration were properly executed (12:43-51). With the proper ritual act, the exodus occurs (see Blenkinsopp, "Structure of P"). P's material is nonetheless narrative. It runs from introduction of a crisis, the Egyptian oppression, to resolution of the crisis in the celebration of the exodus-Passover ritual.

P's narration of the wilderness theme returns to the characteristic statistical series. A wilderness itinerary provides structure for various elements of narrative tradition. This device is doubtlessly the work of the final redactor, at least as the narrative now stands, although in its final form it gives credence to the hypothesis that P is an expansion of JE. The itinerary, however, reveals evidence of rootage in a priestly scheme for organizing the wilderness tradition. For example, the itinerary builds on the priestly notation of station in Exod 14:1-4. The narrative tradition thus provides essential material for the completion of the itinerary chain.

Since the itinerary moves from Ramses to the Jordan Valley, its pattern suggests that the priestly source may involve text material in the book of Joshua. The exposition for the conquest theme in Joshua 1–5 is now more completely controlled by the redaction of Dtr (→ Joshua: the Framework), but priestly tradition may lie behind it (Blenkinsopp, "Structure of P"; Mowinckel).

In contrast to P, J preserves the structure of successive sagas:

I. The patriarchal theme	Gen 1:1–50:26
A. Primeval saga	1:1–11:32
1. Paradise	
2. Flood	
3. Tower	
B. The Abraham saga	12:1–25:34
C. The Jacob-Esau saga	26:1–36:43
D. The Joseph novella	37:1–50:26
II. The exodus theme	Exod 1:1–12:51
A. Exposition	1:8-12
B. Moses	
1. Birth	(1:15-21) 2:1-10
2. Marriage	2:11-22
3. Vocation	3:1–12:39*
a. Call	3:1–4:31*
b. Negotiations	5:1–12:36*
c. Exodus	12:37-39
III. Wilderness	Exod 13:1–Deut 34:12
A. Moses' leadership, God's leadership	
1. Sea	13:17–15:21*
2. Springs	15:22–17:7*
3. Mosaic virtue	17:8-16
4. Legal system	18
5. Sinai	19–34*
6. Quail	Num 11*
7. Mosaic virtue	12
8. Spy report	13–14*
9. Dathan-Abiram rebellion	16
10. Conquest	20–21*
B. Balaam	22–24
C. Baal-peor	25*
D. Preparation for conquest	32
E. Death of Moses	Deut 34*

In contrast to the statistically oriented style of P, the Yahwist preserves the flavor of folk tradition. That flavor occurs, however, at the expense of strict unity in structure. The form-critical problem of the Pentateuch/Hexateuch emerges clearly from the Yahwist's narration. The patriarchal sagas stand juxtaposed with the Moses saga. Even though the Joseph story provides the bridge between the two, it does not close the gap (von Rad, *Genesis,* 20-23). Moreover, the primeval saga sets the stage for the patriarchal sagas and only through them does it relate to the remaining traditions of the unit. The patriarchal sagas themselves feature tradition about strife within the family, with the typical tradition describing broken intimacy with little or no hope for reconciliation. The individual sagas have nevertheless been unified under the theme of divine promise, and the promise reaches some fulfillment in the exodus theme. The patriarchal family has now multiplied so extensively that they can be described as a numerous people, large enough to threaten the stability of the Egyptians. Yet, they possess no land. Thus, the promise establishes a point of tension that leads the Yahwist through narration of oppression and slavery in Egypt, the context for the exodus as the event of Yahweh's greatest act of redemption, to the wilderness, with Yahweh's leadership and aid in the face of crisis and the gift of the law at Sinai.

It is, unfortunately, not altogether clear where the Yahwist's narration comes to an end. It may be that some traditions about the conquest of Transjordan mark the end of the series. This material would have included the Balaam legend and the material about Baal-peor. But some additional possibilities might also be considered. In contrast to the structure of the narrative as a succession of theologically oriented themes of tradition, the Yahwist unifies the narrative under the stamp of a Moses heroic saga. This structure suggests that the source may have included some account of the death of Moses (Deuteronomy 34?). The promise motif in the patriarchal theme might also suggest a theme for the conquest as an essential part of the Yahwist tradition, thus calling for some continuation of the source into Joshua (→ Joshua 1–5). Does the promise element in Genesis not require completion at some point that marks the fulfillment of the promise (see Zimmerli, "Promise")? Unfortunately, the presence of J in Joshua cannot be clearly documented.

The Elohist appears now only in a series of fragments (see Wolff, "Fragments"). It is not yet clear whether these fragments represent an originally independent and complete source parallel to J (so, Jenks; Wolff, "Fragments"), or whether the fragments were from the beginning nothing more than expansions of J (so, Coats, *From Canaan*). It does appear to be clear, however, that the E fragments do not offer any kind of form-critical integrity as they now stand (see Kessler). At every point Elohistic fragments now function as expansions of J, dependent on the Yahwistic structure, rather than as independent elements, distinct from the structure of J. Moreover, the Elohistic expansions do not appear to alter the original structure of the Yahwistic source. They are, rather, theological or traditio-historical commentaries on the J source which supports them. Therefore, the Elohist does not merit a distinct section in this evaluation of the Pentateuch/Hexateuch.

It is quite clear that the Yahwist did not create the tradition represented by the Yahwistic narrative of the Pentateuch. To the contrary, the tradition in J derives from folk institutions preserved over a long period of time, perhaps in written form (so, Noth's G [*Grundschrift*]), more probably in oral form (see Gunkel). It is significant, for example, that several small units of tradition, such as Deut 26:5-11 or Josh 24:1-15, preserve the tradition in a context of cultic recital. They appear to be cultic confessions of faith or credos (so, von Rad, "Problem") with articles of confession that follow basically the outline of the Hexateuch.

The credo suggests a new dimension of the form-critical problem in the Hexateuch, however. Here, the patriarchal theme and the exodus theme have already grown together, and, at least in part, the sequence of the patriarchs—Abraham, Isaac, Jacob—already appears as the established order of the tradition (→ The Patriarchal Theme). Indeed, the goal of the credo is clearly an affirmation that God gave the people of the patriarchal clans the land he had promised. Thus, the arc of tension between promise and fulfillment seems already to be the functional control for the structure of the tradition. The new dimension of the problem in the outline of the tradition can be expressed under two rubrics: (1) There is no reference in the credos to the primeval tradition. Does this fact suggest that primeval history was not a part of the folk, cultic outline of tradition? Perhaps the outstanding achievement of the Yahwist in his theological redaction of the tradition was to prefix the primeval saga to the patriarchal theme (so, von Rad, "Problem"). But the conclusion remains hypothetical. Since the primeval saga attaches directly to the patriarchal traditions rather than functioning as a distinct theme, or even as a preface to all the themes, perhaps the credo outline assumes the primeval element in its oblique allusion to the patriarchs. Thus, in Deut 26:5, the patriarchal theme begins with a reference to "a wandering Aramean." Not all the patriarchal traditions come to expression in the allusion—the wandering Aramean is only Jacob. But Abraham and Isaac appear alongside Jacob in Josh 24:3-4. It would not be adequate to assert that the credo tradition represented by Deuteronomy 26 knows nothing of Abraham or Isaac.

(2) There is no reference to Sinai in the outline of the credo, at least not until the very latest ones. Indeed, it has long been recognized that the Sinai traditions appear to be literarily secondary in their present position in the Pentateuch/Hexateuch narrative (see von Rad, "Problem"). Does the absence of Sinai not suggest that originally the Sinai traditions were quite distinct from the credo traditions? Were they not preserved by an originally separate group of people? In that case, they would have grown together with the credo traditions in the process of unification that welded diverse groups into the people of God (see von Rad, "Problem"). Yet, the same kind of observation noted above about the primeval tradition merits attention here. The structure of the Sinai traditions as they now stand does not support a notion that they constitute a distinct theme in the structure of the whole. To the contrary, they appear as tradition attached to a particular station in the wilderness intinerary. They are but part of the diverse traditions now constituting the wilderness theme. The point does not prove that Sinai was not originally distinct and independent from the credo traditions, but it does argue for caution (see Huffmon; Hyatt, "Credo").

The same kind of question about original unity in the credo traditions can be raised about each distinctive theme of the tradition. Perhaps the exodus theme was originally distinct and independent from the theme about the conquest, and perhaps the two distinct themes grew together with diverse traditions from the wilderness serving as the bridge between them (so, Noth). In this case, one would be forced to conclude that the apparent unity given these themes by the Moses saga is a secondary stage in the process. The location of the Moses traditions themselves would then appear unsettled. Moses could have been originally at home in the exodus or the wilderness or even the Sinai traditions, but he would not have been an original part of all three (so, Noth). The character of the pentateuchal themes, however, does not support this conclusion. The themes of tradition were originally quite distinct but not independent. Thus, it appears to be clear at this stage of research in the Pentateuch that the form-critical problem of the Pentateuch/Hexateuch is the relationship between the patriarchal sagas and the Moses saga, a problem addressed specifically by the Joseph story.

One further problem requires consideration. In the history of the credo tradition, what happened in the relationship between the Moses saga and the Joshua traditions? Exodus, wilderness, and Sinai appear to be united under the stamp of the Moses saga. But what relationship does the Moses saga have to the conquest traditions? What role does Moses play for a conquest theme? Conquest traditions appear in Numbers, structured into the scheme of the wilderness theme, and Moses has some role to play in them. Thus, he assumes responsibility for dispensation of the land (→ Numbers 31–32). Yet, there is a pronounced tendency in the tradition to hold Moses away from the traditions about conquest. The root for the tendency doubtlessly lies buried deep in the tradition that Moses died before he entered the land. The Moses saga does not infringe on the traditions of Joshua. To the contrary, in both tradition and text structure, a great gap between Moses and Joshua insures that the Moses saga not be simply identified with the traditions of the conquest. Even though in the theology represented by the credo the conquest theme and thus the book of Joshua play a major role for the structure of the two bodies of tradition, the units do not merge. Thus, the proper form-critical unit would appear to be the Pentateuch.

It is not yet clear whether the texts representing the credo tradition are older or younger than the Yahwist (see Huffmon). The pattern of tradition noted above would suggest that even the earliest credos preserved in the MT represent a relatively late period in the history of the traditions. Even if they should prove younger than the Yahwist, they nonetheless preserve the outline of the Hexateuch in a cultic context as tradition recited by the people in various acts of worship. It would be plausible to hypothesize that the tradition lived in that setting over an extended period of time, even before the period of the Yahwist. Thus, while the form-critical unit would appear to be the Pentateuch, the tradition history suggests proper attention to the Hexateuch as a unified scope of tradition.

Genre

The Pentateuch as it now stands can be understood as TORAH, a unique combination of story and commandment that makes a fundamental statement about what God expects by saying as forcefully as possible what the people of God is (Sanders). If "Pentateuch" is a term for this unit of Bible that reflects its structure, then "Torah" is a term for the same unit that denotes its genre and intention. The priestly source follows the same pattern. It cannot be defined as (→) saga or as a series of sagas. Its character as strict narrative recedes behind its concern to provide instructions in the will of God (cf. Cross, "Priestly Work"). In contrast, the Yahwist preserves the character of the tradition as narrative SAGA. This point can be seen in the juxtaposition of the patriarchal sagas with the Moses saga. Indeed, it is precisely in this character of saga cycle that the disunity of the

24

Yahwist as theologian can be most adequately understood (see Rendtorff, "Yahwist"). Yet, in the middle of the complex combination of stories characteristic for the Yahwist emerges the character of the story to address its audience with moral instruction. Thus, it would appear that as early as the Yahwist, the proper designation for the display of these traditions is Torah. Moreover, there is some connection between the traditions of the Torah and the traditions of the credo. The function of the traditions in the credo suggests that Torah is essentially existential. It is a genre with traditional content that announces not only who the ancestors were and what God expected of them, but also who each subsequent generation was and what God expected of them.

Setting

The Pentateuch as it now stands is the product of a literary setting, the work of redaction and composition that produced the traditions of the past in a complete structure. It would be a simple procedure to conclude that behind the Yahwistic or priestly literary settings such Torah tradition derived from the cult. Indeed, would it not follow that the home for literary redactional activity was the cult? Certainly, the credos suggest that the Torah tradition was recited within the cult as an expression of loyalty and obedience by the people to the God who acted on their behalf (→ Deut 26:5-11). The Sinai traditions may derive from a similar setting. Yet, some caution seems necessary just at this point, for such an existential story cannot be strictly limited to a cultic observance. The Torah story belongs also to the realm of the storyteller, perhaps as a part of the cult, but also as a part of the people (→ Exod 13:14-16). Thus, it seems appropriate to suggest that the setting for the final form of the Pentateuch as well as for P may well be cultic recitation (→ Neh 8:1-8), but cult in a wider sense than that suggested simply by celebration and rituals. It would live in the cultic vitality of the family group. The Yahwist, on the other hand, shows the influence not only of the family as a locus of folk culture, but also of the royal court (Brueggemann, "David and His Theologian"). Yet, here too setting cannot be limited to a single institutional event. The Yahwistic narrative functions not only as a critical hedge around the power of the court but also as a source of instruction for the people. Its setting is thus in the folk, a literary context that gives expression to the diverse existential traditions that live among the people. At its earliest level this setting probably can most clearly be seen as the family, although certainly the family group should be understood in its larger, tribal pattern.

Intention

The Torah performs in the medium of writing those traditions that constitute the people in their characteristic dress. It says in the form of story what the essential character and moral obligations for any current audience might be by depicting the character and moral obligation of the normative past. The priestly narrative accomplishes this goal in terms of cultic ritual. Thus, the exodus occurs when the Passover ritual is properly celebrated, or the creation reaches completion in proper observation of the Sabbath. The Yahwist, on the other hand, preserves Torah by preserving the saga. In the saga there is a clear announcement of obligation presented by God to the people. However, the tradition functions not only as an address to the people with the power of divine obligation. It is also an address by the people to God and to themselves in an effort to say that in these events and obligations the people define themselves. They are who they are because they and their fathers were who they were. If for P the ritual accomplishes this existential reality, for J the story does it.

CHAPTER 2
THE PATRIARCHAL THEME
(THE BOOK OF GENESIS):
THE FRAMEWORK

BIBLIOGRAPHY

A. Alt, "The God of the Fathers," in *Essays on Old Testament History and Religion* (tr. R.A. Wilson; Garden City, N.Y.: Doubleday, 1968) 1-100; idem, "Zum 'Gott der Väter'," *PJ* 36 (1940) 100-3; K.T. Anderson, "Der Gott meines Vaters," *ST* 16 (1963) 170-88; I. Blythin, "The Patriarchs and the Promise," *SJT* 21 (1968) 56-73; W. Brueggemann, *Genesis, A Bible Commentary for Teaching and Preachng (Interpretation*; Atlanta: John Knox, 1982); H. Cazelles, "Der Gott der Patriarchen," *BLit* 2 (1961) 39-49; B.S. Childs, *Introduction to the Old Testament as Scripture* (Philadelphia: Fortress, 1979); W.M. Clark, "The Origin and Development of the Land Promise Theme in the Old Testament" (Diss , Yale, 1964); F.M. Cross, "Yahweh and the God of the Patriarchs," *HTR* 55 (1962) 225-59; O. Eissfeldt, "Jahwe, der Gott der Väter," *TLZ* 88 (1963) 418-90; idem, "Der kanaanäische El als Geber der den israelitischen Erzvätern geltenden Nachkommenschaft und Landbesitzverheissung," *WZHalle* 12 (1968) 45-53; J.P. Fokkelman, *Narrative Art in Genesis: Specimens of Stylistic and Structural Analysis* (Amsterdam: Van Gorcum, 1975); H. Gunkel, *Genesis* (3rd ed.; HKAT 1/1; Göttingen: Vandenhoeck und Ruprecht, 1964); M. Haran, "The Religion of the Patriarchs: An Attempt at a Synthesis," *ASTI* 4 (1965) 30-55; H. Hirsch, "Gott der Väter," *AfO* 21 (1966) 56-58; J. Hoftijzer, *Die Verheissungen an die drei Erzväter* (Leiden: Brill, 1956); H. Junker, "Aufbau und theologischer Hauptinhalt des Buches Genesis," *BK* 17 (1962) 70-78; K. Koch, "Die Sohnverheissung an den ugaritischen Daniel," *ZA* 24 (1967) 211-21; S.E. Lowenstamm, "Divine Grants of Land to the Patriarchs," *JAOS* 91 (1971) 494-503; H.G. May, "The God of My Father: A Study of Patriarchal Religion," *JBR* 9 (1941) 155-58; M. Noth, *A History of Pentateuchal Traditions* (tr. B.W. Anderson; Englewood Cliffs: Prentice-Hall, 1972); G. von Rad, *Genesis, a Commentary* (tr. J.H. Marks; rev. ed.; OTL; Philadelphia: Westminster, 1972); C. Sant, "Links between the Three Main Divisions of the Book of Genesis," *Melita Theologica* 15 (1963) 41-49; 16 (1964) 56-64; idem, "The Non-Promise Narratives in Genesis," *Melita Theologica* 14 (1962) 62-74; idem, "The Promise Narratives in Genesis," *Melita Theologica* 12 (1960) 14-27; J. Scharbert, "Der Sinn der Toledot-Formel in der Priesterschrift," in *Wort—Gebot—Glaube* (*Fest.* W. Eichrodt; ed. H.J. Stoebe; ATANT 59; Zürich: Zwingli, 1970) 45-56; J. Schreiner, "Segen für die Völker in der Verheissung an die Väter," *BZ* 6 (1962) 1-31; H. Seebass, *Der Erzvater Israel und die Einführung der Jahweverehrung in Kanaan* (BZAW 98; Berlin: Töpelmann, 1966); G. Wallis, "Die Tradition von den drei Ahnvätern," *ZAW* 81 (1968) 18-40; P. Weimar, "Die Toledot-Formel in der priesterschriftlichen Geschichtsdarstellung," *BZ* 18 (1974) 65-93; C. Westermann, *Genesis* (BKAT 1/1; Neukirchen-Vluyn: Neukirchener Verlag, 1974-); idem, *The Promises to the Fathers: Studies on the Patriarchal Narratives* (tr. D.E. Green; Philadelphia: Fortress, 1980).

THE PATRIARCHAL THEME, 1:1–50:26

Structure

I. The primeval saga	1:1–11:9
A. Creation	1:1–4:26
1. Enumeration report	1:1–2:4a
2. Paradise tale	2:4b–3:24
3. Genealogy	4:1-26
B. Flood	5:1–9:29
1. Genealogy	5:1-32
2. Tale	6:1–9:17
3. Curse	9:18-29
C. Tower	10:1–11:9
1. Genealogy	10:1-32
2. Tale	11:1-9
II. The Abraham saga	11:10–25:26
A. Genealogy	11:10-32
B. Narrative	12:1–22:19
1. Exposition (A)	12:1-9
2. Threat to the ancestress (B)	12:10-20
3. Abraham-Lot (C)	13:1–14:24
4. Covenant (D)	15:1-21
5. Family strife (1)	16:1-15
6. Covenant (D')	17:1-27
7. Family strife (2)	18:1-15
8. Abraham-Lot (C')	18:16–19:38
9. Threat to the ancestress (B'α)	20:1-18
10. Family strife (3)	21:1-21
11. Beer-sheba etiology (B'β)	21:22-34
12. Legend (A')	22:1-19
C. Death reports	22:20–25:26
1. Nahor genealogy	22:20-24
2. Death of Sarah	23:1-20
3. Wife for Isaac	24:1-67
4. Marriage report	25:1-6
5. Death of Abraham	25:7-11
6. Succession	25:12-26
a. Ishmael	25:12-18
b. Isaac	25:19-26
III. The Isaac saga	25:19–37:2
A. Narrative	25:19–35:15
1. Exposition	25:19-34
2. Threat to the ancestress	26:1-33

The first major unit of narrative in the OT, the patriarchal theme, corresponds to the division in the Pentateuch classically named the book of Genesis. Analysis of the unit with a form-critical methodology is justified, however, not because of the historical accident that made the unit the first book of the OT. The second major unit of the Hexateuch, the exodus theme, does not correspond to the second book of the OT, but rather only to a part of it (→ Exod 1:1–12:36). A form-critical analysis of the unit is justified by virtue of the structural unity developed in the narrative, the structure marking a beginning and an ending at joints that happen to correspond to the limits of the book. Thus, although the subject of this section happens to be the patriarchal theme, a narrative that reveals various structural devices as unifying tools, it is synonymous with the book of Genesis.

The first point to emphasize in the analysis of this unit is that the primeval saga does not function simply as an introduction to the entire Pentateuch/Hexateuch, but rather as a fundamental element within the patriarchal theme. To be sure, as the introduction to the patriarchal theme, it is also the introduction to the Pentateuch/Hexateuch. Indeed, the theological questions posed by the primeval saga reach across the scope of the Pentateuch/Hexateuch. Yet, it seems to be necessary to conclude that such overarching relevance of the primeval saga comes through the patriarchal sagas rather than as an immediate point of contact with exodus, wilderness, Sinai, or conquest.

The structural cohesion of this unit derives first from the genealogical framework of the final redaction. Creation itself ties into the history of God's world through a *toledoth* formula (→ 2:4a). Then each major stage in the entire unit begins or ends under the structural control of a new formula (5:1; 10:1; 11:10; 25:12, 19; 36:1; 37:2). It is significant that in this tradition creation is not immediately celebrated by any given generation but always inherited by each new generation through the series of genealogical stages that compose world history. It is significant, moreover, that the patriarchal material belongs to those generations. The patriarchs emerge in the middle of history documented by the *toledoth* formulas, not at the beginning of history, not even at the beginning of Israel's history.

Beyond the genealogical framework, structural cohesion of the unit appears more clearly in terms of the individual sources that compose its content.

The priestly framework for the patriarchal theme is as follows:

I. The primeval period	1:1–10:32*
A. Creation	1:1–2:4a
B. Flood	5:1–10:32*
1. Genealogy	5:1-32*
2. Tale	6:1–9:29*
3. Genealogy	10:1-32*
II. Abraham	11:1–25:34*
A. Narrative	
1. Genealogy	11:1–12:20*
2. Abraham-Lot	13:1-18*
3. Crisis	16:1-16*
4. Covenant	17:1-27
5. Fulfillment	21:1b-5
B. Death reports	
1. Sarah	23:1-20
2. Abraham	25:7-11a

The priestly narrative is relatively short and demonstrates structural cohesion organized around the genealogical succession from creation to the death and burial of Jacob. The genealogy develops not only through the primeval history that ties creation to several lists, but also in the patriarchal stories that recount narrative components in relationship to death reports, a genealogical element. Thus, the Abraham story includes accounts of the deaths of Sarah and Abraham (23:1-20; 25:7-11a), the Isaac story an account of the death of Isaac (35:27-29), and the Jacob story an account of the death of Jacob (49:29–50:13). Moreover, the genealogical structure provides connection between the stories, suggesting that the story content in each section is the substance of a genealogical stage. Its unity derives also from the focal importance of the covenant, first to Noah (→ 9:1-17), then to Abraham (→ 17:1-27). In both cases, covenant means God's unconditional promise to his creation. In the first case, the promise guarantees the stability of creation. The second one ties the covenant to the patriarch's fertility and possession of a land that can give support to such divine fertility. The priestly narrative thus develops a span of unity around the theme of God's promises to the patriarchs.

Moreover, this theme demonstrates an exclusive character in the promise. Thus, in the Abraham saga, the promise to the patriarch passes to Isaac, not to Ishmael. It is somewhat surprising that Ishmael receives circumcision, the sign of the covenant, and is heir to a similar promise. The promise of the covenant nonetheless passes over Ishmael, the firstborn, and resides in Isaac. The same pattern then emerges in the Isaac story, where the promise passes over Esau, the firstborn, who marries outside the proper channels, to Jacob, who marries within the family. Here, as in the Abraham story, the promise is confirmed in an occasion of revelation to the patriarch that repeats the content of the covenantal promise first given to Abraham (35:9-15). The patriarch who receives the promise, however, is Jacob, not Isaac. Although the account refers to the promise in connection with both Abraham and Isaac, no P narrative recounts explicitly that Isaac received the promise. That movement in P's tradition is built into the initial statement establishing the promise for both Abraham and Isaac. The Jacob element in the series is quite brief, composed not of narrative elements, but only of a name list (→ 46:6-27) and the corresponding account of the patriarch's death. The element nonetheless prepares the stage for P's account of the exodus by placing the patriarchal family in Egypt with Joseph and enumerating the size of the family itself. Thus, the promise theme, oriented in P around posterity and land, concludes with a sizable family ready to return to Canaan and possess the land.

Behind the promise theme lurks evidence of a narrative constructed out of a strife theme. Thus, Isaac and Ishmael oppose each other as narrative principals in development of the covenant theme. Jacob and Esau also stand as opposites in the cohesion of the family, with Esau excluded because of his marriage. Yet, the strife theme remains quite muted for P. The focal emphasis on the promise renders the strife element only as background, an assumption about the context for fulfillment of the promise (see Westermann, *Promises*; Brueggemann).

Structure in the JE form of the patriarchal theme is as follows:

I. Primeval saga			2:1–11:9
A. Paradise tale			2:1–3:24
B. Two brothers			4:1-26
1. Tale			1-16
2. Genealogy			17-26
C. Flood			6:1–10:32*
1. Tale			6:1–8:22*
2. Genealogy			10:1-32*
D. Tower			11:1-9
II. Abraham saga			11:10–26:6
A. Narrative			11:10–22:19
1. Exposition	(A)		11:10–12:9*
2. Threat to the ancestress	(B)		12:10-20
3. Abraham-Lot	(C)		13:1–14:24*
4. Covenant	(D)		15:1-21
5. Family strife		(1)	16:1–18:15*
a. Ishmael			16:1-15
b. Isaac			18:1-15
6. Abraham-Lot	(C')		18:16–19:38*
7. Threat to the ancestress	(B'α)		20:1-18
8. Family strife		(2)	21:1-21*
9. Beer-sheba etiology	(B'β)		21:22-34
10. Legend	(A')		22:1-19
B. Death reports			
1. Nahor genealogy			22:20-24
2. Wife for Isaac			24:1-67
3. Marriage			25:1-6*
III. Jacob-Esau saga			25:21–35:22a

A. Narrative		25:21–35:7
1. Exposition		
a. Birth report		25:21-26a
b. Principals		25:27-28
c. Tale		25:29-34
2. Threat to the ancestress		26:1-33
3. Family strife		27:1–33:17
a. Tale of strife		27:1-40
b. Jacob-Esau		27:41–33:17
1) Complication		27:41-45
2) Bethel *hieros logos*		28:10-22
3) Jacob-Laban		29:1–32:1 (*RSV* 31:55)
4) Mahanaim		32:2-3 (*RSV* 32:1-2)
5) Resolution		32:4–33:17 (*RSV* 32:3–33:17)
4. Shechem *hieros logos*		33:18-20
5. Threat to the daughter		34:1-31
6. Pilgrimage		35:1-7
B. Death reports		
1. Deborah		35:8
2. Rachel		35:16-20
3. Rebellion of Reuben		35:21-22a
IV. Joseph story		37–50
A. Novella		37:1–47:27
B. Death reports		
1. Instructions for burial		47:29-31
2. Blessing		48:1–49:27*
3. Death and burial		50:1-14
4. Joseph recapitulation		50:15-21
5. Death of Joseph		50:22-26

The J narratives can be understood more adequately under the theme of strife in the family than under the theme of the divine promise for a son, posterity, or land. The divine promise is present in these older narratives, but it does not represent the organizing principle for construction of a theme. Moreover, the promise-fulfillment span of tension that can be seen in P is not yet a structural principle in J. The Yahwistic narrative appears much more comparable to the family saga of Iceland, with its accounts of strife within the family. The concern is not simply to recount how a strife-torn family experiences reconciliation but also to narrate the strife that continues to tear human community apart.

The primeval saga is not simply an extension of the patriarchal theme, as it is in P, but a unique narrative unit in its own right. This point stands out even more sharply by virtue of 12:1-4a, an exposition for the following patriarchal traditions that creates a clear demarcation between primeval saga and patriarchal theme. It functions to highlight *blessing* as the basic leitmotif for the unit. Yet, it raises the questions of human-divine community and thus prepares the way for the strife stories in the patriarchal theme. It suggests also an overarching pattern that ties to the exodus-wilderness-conquest. In what manner is the people of

Abraham or Jacob blessed? In what manner do the families of the world derive blessing from them? The Joseph story responds explicitly to the question. In anticipation of a common future, the brothers lay aside suspicion occasioned by strife and speak with one another. A family torn by strife will again recognize each other as brothers.

In J, the saga structure of the tradition differs from the P framework. The Abraham saga orients around the leitmotif of blessing, confirmed by Abraham's act of faith (→ Genesis 22). Moreover, the deathbed scene concerns not so much the death and burial of the patriarch and his associates as the necessary patriarchal act of securing a proper bride for the heir (→ Genesis 24). For J there is no Isaac saga. Even the necessary deathbed scene concerned with securing a bride for Jacob loses contact with Isaac tradition and appears now more directly as Jacob-Esau tradition. P's distinct Jacob saga stands in J as a novella about the affairs of Joseph and the other sons of Jacob. It may be that behind the J tradition lay a stage in the tradition's oral history that offered more narration about Isaac. Indeed, it may be that the Isaac tradition was the original form of the patriarchal theme, the locus for both the strife motif and the promise (see Noth, 103). Such a hypothesis would imply that the patriarchal figures have been aligned in the traditional genealogical series as an artificial means of structuring the tradition into a unified theme, the product of a unification among originally diverse people who had preserved traditions about their own patriarchal figures (see Noth, 56-58). But that possibility must remain hypothetical.

Genre

A cycle of SAGAS—a primeval saga and two family sagas—constitutes the span of traditions in the patriarchal theme. This designation is perhaps obscure for the final Rjep and P. Yet, the lines of the family sagas still appear in the middle of the genealogical narrative, and the primeval saga stands out despite the extension of the genealogical frame into the following narratives. In J, the genre is clear: Family strife sagas joined into a cycle unified under the theme of blessing (or curse) constitute the compass of narrative in the patriarchal theme.

Setting

P and J employ the sagas in a literary construct that lends itself to the theological interests of each source. Behind the sources, the institutional context for the narrative remains apparent. Family sagas derive from the concern of the family to report the problems that give history to the community.

Intention

The patriarchal theme in P and J recounts the concern of the source to show the presence of blessing and its consequence despite strife in the family. Earlier forms of the family saga develop family history in terms of strife without reconciliation as a natural counterpart of the blessing.

CHAPTER 3

THE PRIMEVAL SAGA

BIBLIOGRAPHY

B.S. Childs, *Introduction to the Old Testament as Scripture* (Philadelphia: Fortress, 1979); H. Gunkel, *Genesis* (HKAT 1/1; 3rd ed.; Göttingen: Vandenhoeck und Ruprecht, 1964); M. Noth, *A History of Pentateuchal Traditions* (tr. B.W. Anderson; Englewood Cliffs: Prentice-Hall, 1972); G. von Rad, *Genesis, a Commentary* (tr. J.H. Marks; rev. ed.; OTL; Philadelphia: Westminster, 1972); C. Westermann, *Genesis* (BKAT 1/1; Neukirchen-Vluyn: Neukirchener Verlag, 1974); idem, *The Promises to the Fathers: Studies on the Patriarchal Narratives* (tr. D.E. Green; Philadelphia: Fortress, 1980) 1-94.

THE PRIMEVAL SAGA AS A WHOLE, 1:1– 11:9

Structure

I. Creation	1:1–4:26
A. Enumeration report	1:1–2:4a
B. Paradise and fall	2:4b–3:24
C. Genealogy	4:1-26
II. Flood	5:1–9:29
III. Tower	10:1–11:9
A. Genealogy	10:1-32
B. Tale	11:1-9

The first major unit of the OT contains a narrative description of events from long ago and far away. The principals in the narrative thus have no immediate contact with the culture or times of historical Israel. They are subjects of world history in a primeval period. Nonetheless, it is clear that this first major unit of the Pentateuch sets the context for Israel's own heritage. The following narrative about the patriarchs does not begin in midstream but rather assumes a context that pushes back to the beginning of the entire creation. Israel's own personal traditions thus appear as a reflex to a universal context. In relationship to the patriarchs, the primeval saga represents an etiology for Israel itself (see von Rad, *Genesis*, 24).

In this larger unit, three major elements of genealogy serve as a framework for three major elements of narrative. The unit thus comprises two characteristic types of material: tale set in close conjunction with more statistically oriented tradition (see Westermann, *Genesis*, 783-84). The framework elements embrace not only larger narrative units, but also some very short, perhaps very ancient,

35

reports (→ 6:1-4). The framework quality, however, appears most clearly in a series of formulas introduced by 5:1: "This is the book of the generations of Adam." The series, commonly called the *Toledoth* Book (see von Rad, *Genesis*, 33-34; Noth, *History*, 10-12), is not an independent unit imposed secondarily on the narrative, but a basic structural pattern which gives cohesion to the range of material in the unit (Westermann, *Genesis*, 481-82). The *toledoth* series, as well as the older genealogical material, should not therefore be consigned to an insignificant collection of bits and pieces. Its importance derives rather from the structure of the whole, a structure that, for example, places Abraham in the theologically significant tenth generation (11:1-32), just as it does Noah (5:1-32).

The unit begins with creation, not with the beginning of any particular culture. But where does it end? In what manner does the narration develop a climax? The *toledoth* series moves into the patriarchal sagas and suggests a structure for the entire book of Genesis. In contrast, the tale about the tower in 11:1-9 binds off the series of narratives about the people of the world. This element would thus mark the end of the primeval saga. Moreover, the genealogy in 11:10-32 provides a transition to the Abraham saga. The transition, however, is not a climax for the primeval saga, nor is it accurate to describe the narration simply as an increasing cacophony of sin, with the final crescendo set in the tower narrative of 11:1-9 (so, Clark, 206). Rather, the climax comes in the middle of the unit with the flood narrative. In this case the creation-fall narratives would be set opposite the tower narrative as support for the denouement. The structure of this narrative triangle would be ABA'. This analysis suggests that the order of units established by the saga is not strictly chronological but complementary (see Westermann, *Genesis*, 771). It suggests, moreover, that the weight of structure for the whole rests on key passages in the flood story, particularly on 8:20-22 and 9:1-17, a point supported in general by Mesopotamian parallels (see Clark).

The priestly version of the primeval saga reveals a distinctive structure:

I. Creation report	1:1–2:4a; 5:1-32
A. Report	1:1–2:4a
B. Genealogy	5:1-32
II. Flood	6:1–9:29*; 10:1–11:32*
A. Tale	6:1–9:29*
B. Genealogy	10:1–11:32*

The *toledoth* formulas constitute the skeleton from which the priestly narrative derives its unity. The series thus establishes an atmosphere of the universal for P's primeval saga. (See Westermann, *Genesis*, 8-24, for comments on the dominance of the genealogies.) But at the same time, the series marks unity in P between the primeval saga and the patriarchal sagas.

The primeval narrative in P does not reflect the same pattern of structure as the one preserved in the received text. Rather than building a center around two supports, here two narrative units are placed in opposition. A creation report establishes the beginning without reference to human failure. Moreover, its enumeration of the acts of God in creation stands outside the structure of the *toledoth* formulas and suggests an introduction not to the primeval saga alone, but to all the priestly story. The flood narrative contrasts with the beginning by depicting sin and destruction. The beginning describes creation as order called out of chaos. The ending describes destruction as chaos called into the order. The unit nonetheless lends its weight to the thesis that the denouement of the primeval saga must be sought in the flood tale. For P this high point must be the covenant (9:1-17). Moreover, the priestly covenant tradition, with its world focus signed by the rainbow as a symbol for the security of the new world order, stands in close relationship to the Abraham covenant (Genesis 17), with its focus on Israel signed by the circumcision of the flesh. The inner action of the two is basic for P's contribution to the entire Pentateuch/Hexateuch narration (→ *Toledoth* Book, 5:1). It suggests that the covenant between God and the entire world, unsecured by any ritual, is mediated to the world through the ritual obedience of Israel to God's intimate call for covenant.

The Yahwist's version of the primeval saga develops with more color and diversity than does its counterpart:

I. Paradise and fall	
A. Tale of Paradise and fall	2:4b–3:24
B. Genealogy	4:1-26
II. Flood	
A. Sons of God	6:1-4
B. Flood	6:1–8:22*
C. Curse on Canaan	9:1-29
III. Dispersal	
A. Genealogy	10:1-32*
B. Tower	11:1-9

The genealogies here do not carry the weight they do for P. They appear rather as transition pieces or frames for narrative elements. It is precisely in their function as carriers, however, that their theological significance appears (so, 4:46; 5:29). This material thus depends far more heavily on the narrative. Moreover, the structure in J is the ABA' pattern noted above. The crux for this pattern would be 8:20-22, with its complement in 6:7, if not in 3:17 or 4:12. The crux in J, like the covenant in P, promises stability. But the connection of the crux with 4:12 calls for a wandering father, and its relationship with 11:1-9 promises a fate characterized by separation, remarkably similar to the separation Cain takes as condemnation. Moreover, the impact of the structure is not so much a highlight of ever increasing sin. The hubris of the tower people is not as blatant as the hubris of Cain, although it shares essentially the same rootage. Rather, the structure in its complementary elements suggests a permanent problem: God's creatures separate themselves into isolated groups, and those groups constitute the context for J's Abraham narrative. The crux in 8:20-22 does not remove the isolation; it only promises stability and harvest in the middle of the isolation. God will not again curse the ground. (Notice the connection established by 'ădāmâ, the word for "ground," in 8:21 and 4:11.)

What were the antecedents for the traditions in this primeval saga like? It may be the case that distinct and independent tales circulated among the folk in the beginning. Indeed, the goal of form criticism was initially described as an adequate definition of the smallest, originally distinct and independent unit of narrative, doubtlessly a unit that lived in the oral tradition of the people (see Gunkel, 3-4). Yet, it is necessary to recognize that those small tales lie deeply buried in larger narrative and often can be recovered only with an alarming degree of hypothetical reconstruction. Indeed, parallels to the primeval saga now suggest that the small tale may not have had an independent role to play apart from its position in the larger saga.

The traditio-historical antecedents of the primeval saga are numerous, and Babylonian and Egyptian parallels demand special attention. *Enuma Elish* and the Gilgamesh Epic, both from Mesopotamia, and the Memphis creation documents from Egypt are most widely known. But of perhaps more importance are the Sumerian king list and the Atrahasis Epic, since here various narrative elements are set together in something of the same series as the OT primeval saga (see Clark). It is significant, however, that not many of these points of contact for developing a tradition history appear in the OT. Deutero-Isaiah employs creation motifs for specific theological goals. Job leans heavily on creation themes. Ezekiel alludes to the first king in the Garden. But these points are late in the history of OT literature, and at no point in these parallels can the entire range of the primeval saga be seen. It is not difficult to conclude, then, that for the OT the Yahwist was first to introduce the primeval saga with its creation motifs (see von Rad, *Genesis*, 23-24).

Genre

As a narrative about the distant past and a distant land, this unit qualifies as a primeval SAGA (→ narrative genres). As primeval saga the unit moves away from its mythological antecedents, although fragments of MYTH still appear (→ 6:1-4). The broken quality of the mythological tradition (→ 1:1–2:4a), with the events of the primeval world set as immediate context for the patriarchs, confirms the designation of the unit as SAGA. These observations obtain also for J's primeval saga. For P, however, the independence of the unit fades into the structure for the patriarchal narrative, and its generic characteristics also shift (→ Genesis). The primeval narrative for P would thus be an element in the larger priestly chronology, while the J material would stand much closer to the traditional genre of primeval saga (see Westermann, *Genesis*, 784).

Setting

For the received text, the setting of the unit is the redaction of literary sources, a function of Israelite society interested in preserving tradition as a key for maintaining identity. P and J also reflect a literary setting, the function of the individual sources oriented toward a particular theological goal. In each case, the primeval saga or the primeval period in a larger chronology is related to the patriarchal theme. The family setting for those narratives must have exerted an influence on this unit. Yet, behind the literary connection with family tradition, the primeval saga shows a connection with a more sophisticated world. The structural pattern of sin-judgment may suggest influence from the legal court. Mythological antecedents doubtlessly lived in the ritual of the cult. Neither of these points, however, adequately defines the setting for the primeval tradition. The Garden, the first human creature as a primeval king, even the concern to establish stability by ritual, all share elements from the royal court (see Clark). It seems probable, therefore, that the earliest stages of the primeval saga reflect the concerns of royal theology, either as support for the power of the king or as a hedge to control the power of the king.

Intention

For the final form of the text, as well as for J and P, the primeval saga establishes a context for the patriarchs. Its intention, however, is not simply to place the patriarchs in a world scene, but more precisely to depict a typical state of affairs for people and to suggest that the patriarchs are a part of that state. The narrative does not elevate the ancestors of Israel beyond the affairs of the human world but rather places them in that world. It suggests that whatever identity the narrative offers to Israel must be won by struggle with a very real world. How can people like Adam and Cain or even the righteous but drunk Noah provide a context for Abraham, Isaac, and Jacob?

Moreover, whatever stability might have been offered by the perpetual repetition of creation in a cultic act, controlled by the king or the priest or even the prophet, is here denied. Stability (and thus the power of royal man) comes only through the events God established with his people once, long ago and far away. The narrative draws a hedge around efforts (by the royal man?) to establish power by establishing world stability in the cult.

For P, these intentions can be accomplished only through the covenantal relationships established in the flood as a prefiguration for relationships established with Abraham. The concern for proper order, both in the royal man and for all creatures, thus appears in a ritual dress. But it hangs on obedience as a sign of righteousness. J, on the other hand, addresses a human problem with the vitality of a theologian. His understanding of Israel, worked out in some greater detail in the patriarchal theme, gains its first, perhaps its sharpest, hearing here. Human beings lose the blessing of God; the family of Abraham offers restoration.

Bibliography

W. Brueggemann, "David and His Theologian," *CBQ* 30 (1968) 156-81; idem, "From Dust to Kingship," *ZAW* 84 (1972) 1-18; idem, "Kingship and Chaos (A Study in Tenth Century Theology)," *CBQ* 33 (1971) 317-32; idem, "Life and Death in Tenth Century Israel," *JAAR* 40 (1972) 96-109; idem, "Weariness, Exile, and Chaos (A Motif in Royal Theology)," *CBQ* 34 (1972) 19-38; W.M. Clark, "The Flood and the Structure of the Pre-patriarchal History," *ZAW* 83 (1971) 184-211; D.J.A. Clines, "Theme in Genesis 1–11," *CBQ* 38 (1976) 483-507; G.W. Coats, "The God of Death: Power and Obedience in the Primeval History," *Int* 29 (1975) 227-39; E. Combs, "The Political Teaching of Genesis I–XI," in *Studia Biblica 1978* (JSOTSup 11; Sheffield: University Press, 1979) 105-110; T.E. Fretheim, *Creation, Fall, and Flood: Studies in Genesis 1–11* (Minneapolis: Augsburg, 1969); S. Mowinckel and W.F. Albright, "The Babylonian Matter in the Predeuteronomic Primeval History (JE) in Gen 1–11," *JBL* 58 (1939) 87-103; W. Richter, "Urgeschichte und Hoftheologie," *BZ* 10 (1966) 96-105; J.F.A. Sawyer, "The Meaning of *běṣelem 'ĕlōhîm* ('In the Image of God') in Genesis I–XI," *JTS* 25 (1974) 418-26; W. von Soden, "Verschlüsselte Kritik an Salomo in der Urgeschichte des Jahwisten?" *WO* 7/2 (1974) 228-40.

CHAPTER 4
THE INDIVIDUAL UNITS

CREATION REPORT, 1:1 – 2:4a

Structure

The creation report in 1:1–2:4a establishes the context for all subsequent units in the book of Genesis, including the tale in 2:4b–3:24. It is possible to explore whether the beginning reported here is absolute. Can one not conclude, particularly on the basis of v. 2, that God simply establishes order in the midst of a chaos already in existence? (On the relationship between v. 2 and ancient Near Eastern parallels, see Schmidt, 78-86.) Yet, as far as this unit is concerned, the question of preexistent material does not play a large role. The unit develops its structure toward a different end: All that exists derives from God, not only the substance of creation, but also the sequence of days and nights that gives those structures a history (see Anderson, *Creation,* 40-41 and passim).

The pattern of structure developed by this unit comprises a systematic display of eight stages in creation, cast into a six-day enumeration scheme, framed by an introduction in vv. 1-2 and its parallel conclusion in 2:1-4a. The introduction, 1:1-2, can be understood linguistically as a dependent clause for the principal clause in v. 3. On the basis of an analysis of form, however, this possible reading cannot be adopted (see von Rad, *Genesis*, 48).

Support for this conclusion derives not only from the regular pattern of structure in each section of the six-day scheme, a pattern that begins in v. 3 and thus excludes vv. 1-2 from dependent relationship (see Anderson, "Stylistic Study," 154-56), but also from the intimate parallel formation between vv. 1-2 and the conclusion in 2:1-4a. First, the opening reference to "the heavens and the earth" *('ēt haššāmayim wĕ'ēt hā'āreṣ)*, as well as the verb "create" *(bārā')* constructed as an active perfect (Qal) and controlled by the adverbial "in the beginning" *(bĕrē'šît)*, stands parallel to the closing phrase in 2:4a, with its reference to "the heavens and the earth" *(haššāmayim wĕhā'āreṣ)*, as well as its verb "create" *(bārā')*, constructed as a passive infinitive construct (Niphal) and controlled by a preposition, "when they were created" *(bĕhibbārĕ'ām)*. The formula in v. 4a, "These are the generations" *('ēlleh tôlĕdôt)*, does not, however, look back on previously narrated events, but rather introduces new elements of narration (Childs, *Introduction*, 149). It thus cannot be understood simply as a subscription to the stages of creation in 1:1–2:3. But it does not look forward simply to 2:4b–3:24. It does not build its immediate sequence with the so-called *Toledoth* Book (→ 5:1), but rather places the generations described in the stages of creation as the beginning context for everything, including even the *Toledoth* Book. Second, the introduction in 1:1-2, with its reference to the heavens and the earth and its explication of the earth as "formless and void" *(tōhû wābōhû)*, also parallels 2:1 (Anderson, "Stylistic Study," 159-62), with its reference to "the heavens and the earth" *(haššāmayim wĕhā'āreṣ)* and its explication of both in relationship to "all their hosts" *(wĕkol ṣĕbā'ām)*.

Moreover, the parallel frame established by 1:1-2 with both 2:1 and 2:4a also suggests that 2:2-3 stands outside the scheme of days enumerated in 1:3-31. The seventh day appears in this context. It is quite clear that such a disjunction is not absolute. The day featured in 2:2-3 must be understood in relationship to the scheme of days in 1:3-31. This point is established not only by the enumeration scheme that comes to its end in 2:2-3, but also by the blessing on the day (2:3), a motif that echoes the blessing of 1:22 and 28. The disjunction serves thus to highlight 2:2-3 as a conclusion of the scheme, not as another in the successive stages within the scheme. Hence the seventh day is categorically (formally) different from the other six days. And significantly, the blessing for the seventh day is categorically different from the blessing for the animals or the human beings. There is no admonition to produce. Rather, the blessing of the seventh day centers in the completion of work and the corresponding rest (Schmidt, 154-59). In that center, vv. 2-3 function fittingly as a conclusion of the unit.

The principal body of the report, 1:3-31, encapsulates eight stages of creation into six enumerated periods. The six periods are marked regularly by a conclusion formula. The first of these formulas (v. 5b) employs a cardinal numeral, the remaining five (vv. 8b, 13, 19, 23, 31b) ordinal numerals: "It was evening, and it was morning, day one." "It was evening, and it was morning, the

43

second day." No structural significance accrues to this shift. The sequence simply provides the outer framework of the element and anticipates the conclusion in 2:2-3. The structural significance in the series of enumerations, however, marks a contrasting system of structure. The dominant form of the received text emphasizes the order of days, with focus on the seventh day. The tradition embraced by this series emphasizes a set of eight events, with the focus on the creation of the human beings.

The pattern of each stage follows a sequence that suggests a regular, even ideal, structure. The ideal form might have involved the following elements: command in jussive or, once, cohortative, execution of the command, an act of creation, valuation (see Schmidt, 52). This ideal pattern is present in 1:11-12, 14-18, 24-25. Variations in the pattern can be summarized as follows: In the first stage, the execution formula, "and it was so" *(wayĕhî-kēn),* does not appear. Rather, the execution of the opening jussive is attached directly to the content of the verse: "And there was light." Moreover, the formula for valuation follows the execution of the command rather than the description of God's act, and a naming element appears following the act. In the second stage, the notice of execution follows the act rather than the command. There is, moreover, no valuation note following the act. There is only a naming element. The third stage comprises two commands, thus two different moments of creation. The first, vv. 9-10, has no notice of God involved in a creative act (but see LXX). Otherwise, all the elements of the ideal pattern appear, including the naming. It is perhaps significant to note that the naming element appears here for the last time in the unit and thus highlights the first three moments of creation as a distinct section vis-à-vis all that follows. These three moments depend on an act of separation (the light from the dark, the waters above from the waters below, and the waters from the dry land). The following moments outfit the created order with its essential life. Here the verbs reflect a divine extension of the initial series of separations (on the verbs, see Westermann, *Genesis,* 119). Yet, if this transition was at one time significant in the structure of the unit, it is no longer so. Its significance has now been lost in the compression of the report into its present six-day scheme. The second moment, vv. 11-12, shows no variation from the ideal pattern. One should note, nonetheless, that the act described in v. 12 is not *directly* God's act, but rather the act of the earth. The point may cast v. 12 more nearly as a continuation of the execution formula in v. 11b (see the comments below). Whether significant weight can be hung on the earth as a partner in creation is not likely (see Schmidt, 108-9; in contrast, cf. the comments by Westermann, *Genesis,* 122). The fourth stage shows no variation from the ideal pattern.

In the fifth stage there is no formula to show that the command was executed. Rather, the report moves immediately to a description of God's act (so, 1:6-7). As an addition to the act, v. 22 reports God's blessing on the creation produced by the act. The sixth stage again compresses two moments into one frame. The first moment shows no variation from the ideal pattern. The second opens with a command that has no immediate notice of execution (but see v. 30b). Rather, as in vv. 6 and 20, so here the frame moves immediately to a description of God's act. Moreover, the command is formulated here as a cohortative plural: "Let us make man. . . ." Also, the sequence of this stage is expanded. Rather than including an execution formula (v. 30b), the structure jumps readily to a report of divine act (v. 27). This element, with its regular valuation in v. 31, now frames a blessing (v. 28; cf. v. 22), a designation of food available for man and animals (vv. 29-30b) and the notice of execution (v. 30b). The designation of food for the creatures may be secondary, an addition that points forward to the flood. The reference forward, however, would not in itself reduce the element to a secondary status (see Steck, 139). In any case, the disruption of the normal pattern here is a peculiarity that characterizes this crucial stage. The blessing is also a peculiarity, although v. 22 paves the way for it and establishes some basis for a continuing tension between man and beast. The peculiarity resides, of course, in the admonition not only to be fruitful, but also to rule. Moreover, the blessing here contrasts with the judgment in the flood, reducing all life to death, with minimum exceptions, and parallels the blessing following the flood. It is thus of central importance for the theological structure of the unit (see Brueggemann, "Kerygma"). Finally, one can note that the valuation formula in v. 31 also highlights this stage as a pinnacle, a major goal toward which the entire sequence of days moves.

These eight moments compressed into six stages or panels can be structured into two series of parallel units. Thus, panel one parallels four, two parallels five, and three, six (see Anderson, "Stylistic Study"). The structure would again point to the cohesion of the center element that excludes the seventh day as a part of the conclusion, and it places emphasis on the third- and sixth-day events as climactic. The creation event in the one panel provides the context for the creatures whose creation appears in the other.

The unit as it stands is a part of P; indeed, it establishes a context which is brought sharply to focus in the priestly account of the flood. Its emphasis on the blessing (1:28) as well as on the Sabbath (2:2-3) highlights characteristic concerns for P (see Brueggemann, "Kerygma"). Although the present form of the text employs a command-execution pattern, this pattern is perhaps a reinterpretation of an older version of the unit centered on a description of God's act, without reference to a command (so, Schmidt, 163-78; von Rad, *Genesis*, 64-65). Units like 1:11-12, 14-18, 24-25, and even 3-5 would tend to support this view. Yet, there is a problem in the structure that demands careful evaluation. Is the description of Yahweh's act an independent element in each stage? Or is it a dependent element, an elaboration of the formula used to assert the execution of God's command? A simple structure, such as 1:11-12, juxtaposes the two elements and suggests that v. 12a may be understood as an elaboration of the formula in v. 11b. A unit that displaces the execution formula (1:6-8, 26-31) or uses no execution formula at all (1:20-23) may more easily be described in terms of unity (see Steck). The formula would in that case be a link between the command and the longer description of the act (so, Steck, 35-39). Moreover, it is clear that such a narrative pattern is typical for P and does not in any respect suggest disunity. But the point applies also to arguments that would dissect the unit into parallel sources. A form-critical analysis will not support such a division.

On the other hand, the first panel separates the execution formula from the description of the act with a formula of valuation, and the valuation assumes that something has been completed. In their present form vv. 3-5 support the notion that two distinct levels of the tradition can be seen. It is not clear, however, whether those levels suggest an ancient text that has not been reinterpreted or simply a displacement of a text element (v. 4a). It seems appropriate not to press the analysis to a reconstruction of a hypothetical antecedent text (contrary to Schmidt). That an early tradition may have been recast under the stamp of the divine command is, however, plausible. The point would be supported, if not by a disjunction in the P text itself, then by a comparison between the P text and the J parallel. J does not, of course, make use of the word-execution pattern. Moreover, the affinity of the conclusion with the same perspective suggests that the description of creation by act at least lies in the background of P's work.

It is clear that the imagery of the unit derives from a common tradition in a large cultural context. Particularly v. 2 projects images that were at home in the mythological heritage of Babylon and Canaan. This point can be seen first in the description of God's movement over the seas. The hovering connotation of the wind suggests not so much the spirit of God but rather a part of the chaos that God responds to (see Schmidt, 81-84). The darkness, if not also the void and formlessness, may derive from a similar context. Does the Hebrew term "deep" *(tĕhôm)* not capture the imagery of Tiamat and her struggle with Marduk, the creator? These images lie beneath the surface of this unit; yet, at some stage in the process of formulation the unit has recast those images. There is no longer a struggle between God and some opposing force. Now the description of creation centers on proper order at the behest of God's word. Even the reformulation of tradition in terms of creation by the word has roots in the cultural context. Egyptian tradition (the Memphis creation tradition) suggests a cultural context for the patterns now dominant in the unit. Indeed, even the conclusion with its goal in the rest of God may pick up significant cultural parallels (so, Schmidt, 154-59).

In the stereotyped structure of this unit, formulas play a large role. It is not possible to penetrate the peculiarity of this structure without attention to them. (1) Speech formula: "And God said. . . ." The formula introduces speeches by designating who the speaker is and, commonly, to whom he speaks. It plays a large role in all OT narrative and demonstrates, on balance, that the dominant movement of narrative derives not so much from the description of event as from the construction of speeches. (2) Execution formula: "And it was so." The formula does not stand necessarily at the end of a narrative unit, but more commonly as a link between two dependent parts (see Steck). Its peculiar structural intention is to show the interaction between command and fulfillment. (3) Naming formula: "God named the light day." The formula can commonly be combined with an inflected form of the verb "name" *(qārā' 1 . . .)* to reveal a wordplay with a preceding or following element. It is thus closely tied to an etiological formula (→ 4:25). (4) *Toledoth* formula: "These are the generations of. . . ." A demonstrative pronoun, *'ēlleh,* introduces the technical term *tôlĕdôt,* and the context of the generation is named. It functions to head a story or a larger unit of stories about the subject of the formula. For details, see 5:1. (5) Two other formulas of the unit are not so commonly employed by OT narrative and can simply be listed: valuation formula and conclusion to enumeration panels. (6) The blessing in 1:28 carries a major part of P's theology and represents a stereotyped formulation, especially characteristic for P (Brueggemann, "Kerygma"). Introduced with the verb "bless" *(wayĕbārek)* and constructed with imperatives, the blessing establishes the right of its subject to fertility. Cf. also 9:1-2.

Genre

If ancient Near Eastern myths lie behind this unit, it is nonetheless clear that the unit is no longer (→) myth. The generic character of parallel mythology is not reproduced in the narrative itself. Nor can the unit properly stand as a (→) tale: It develops no plot; there is no arc of tension, no resolution of crisis. The dominant structural characteristic, an enumeration of days with a specific sequence of events in each day, destroys any story quality by its regular progression and suggests the unit has more in common with (→) genealogy, even with (→) hymns or wisdom tradition, than with tale. Moreover, it is clear that while a common tradition may tie the unit with hymns in the Psalter that list the acts of creation (Pss. 135:6-7; 136:5-9), the unit is not itself a hymn. It sets out doctrine (so, von Rad, *Genesis,* 63) and teaches a particular world view. But it does not approach that task philosophically, as if the doctrine could be established by logical argument. It sets out its teaching in the form of history. Again, such an observation does not mean that the unit is (→) history writing. Rather, the unit employs event as a costume to identify its teaching. It thus seems most appropriate to label the unit a REPORT, a genre that communicates events for the sake of the communication, not for the sake of building interest or developing plot. As a report, the unit can communicate its teaching (about the Sabbath) in terms of event (the first Sabbath) and relate all subsequent events to the power of its position. All orders of creation derive from God. All events of creation derive from this primary event.

One should note that to label a unit a report is not to say anything about the accuracy of the report as a historical document. It casts the events it reports as history; it does not guarantee the validity of its reporting. There is thus no basis in the identification of genre for an argument with science, unless science casts itself as a new mythology. In the identification of genre there is basis only for an argument with mythology. This tradition is not yet tale and no longer myth. Thus, it is not to be celebrated like myth. It is now simply report, to be communicated like any report.

Setting

Two institutions make immediate claims as candidates for a definition of setting. (1) The cult comes to the fore because of the emphasis on the Sabbath in 2:2-3. Moreover, if the genre is bound up with teaching and doctrine, the cult would offer an attractive context for understanding its characteristics. Would the source identification not point to the cult as well? Yet, there are problems. The mythological antecedents were preserved and celebrated in the cult, but this text shows some interest in breaking those images. Would the change in genre not mean a change in setting as well? (2) The royal court also demands some consideration. The man here as in the counterpart in 2:4b–3:24 is in some manner royal man (Schmidt, 140-42). This point can be represented most sharply in the description of the man as "image of God" *(bĕṣelem 'ĕlōhîm)* and in his commission to exercise dominion over creation (v. 28; Schmidt, 132-42). Yet, the king depends in some manner on the repetition patterns of creation tradition as a key to his power. Indeed, creation tradition may stem from the concern to preserve recognizable orders of the world, a concern open to the control of the king in annual repetition patterns of the cult (see Westermann, *Genesis,* 128). The movement away from annual repetition to report of an event that happened once would tend, however, to weaken an appeal to royal court. The tradition that lies behind the priestly unit may derive from court theology, or better, from the cult controlled by the court. In its present form, however, it is no longer that. It can only derive from the setting that produced the entire priestly form of the Pentateuch (see Westermann, *Genesis,* 126-30).

This designation means, however, that setting here as an analytical category is different from analysis of setting in, for example, the Psalms. It is possible to see settings in institutions which flourished in Israel's life. It is possible that traditions such as this one functioned as oral narrative resources for those institutions. But when the tradition enters a literary framework, as this one has, setting means something new. The question no longer concerns a setting in the social institutions, but rather a setting in the literature of Israel. Thus, conclusions about setting must be advanced with caution. The warning applies, moreover, to all of the narrative tradition in the Pentateuch/Hexateuch. It may be that a narrative piece will still show setting in the life of the people very clearly, but this question can be answered only in terms of the tradition history (see Westermann, *Genesis,* 127).

Intention

As a part of a larger priestly narration, this unit claims the origin of all things, as well as the origin of all events, to be in God. Moreover, the claim is that the origin was at the beginning, once and for all, rather than repeated as a part of an annual celebration. That origin sets the context for all subsequent things and events. In effect, it demythologizes both the world and its history. But it also suggests that the beginning is important to each successive generation of people only through the history it establishes, not as a primeval and absolute source. It is thus subordinated to God's history of the people. That subordination is a part of the demythologizing reflected in the tradition's formulation or reformulation. Indeed, the subordination functions to protect the mystery of creation from the abuse that civilization might foist upon it (Coats, "God of Death"; see also Westermann, *Genesis,* 238). In the protection, the unit facilitates human praise of God as the Lord of creation.

Bibliography

B. W. Anderson, "A Stylistic Study of the Priestly Creation Story," in *Canon and Authority: Essays on the Theology and Religion of the Old Testament* (ed. G. W. Coats and B. O. Long; Philadelphia: Fortress, 1977) 148-62; idem, *Creation versus Chaos: The Reinterpretation of Mythical Symbolism in the Bible* (New York: Association, 1967); P. Beauchamp, *Création et séparation: étude exégétique du chapitre premier de la Genèse* (Paris: Aubier-Montaigue, 1964); W. Brueggemann, "David and His Theologian," *CBQ* 30 (1968) 156-81; idem, "The Kerygma of the Priestly Writers," *ZAW* 84 (1972) 397-413; G. W. Coats, "The God of Death: Power and Obedience in the Primeval History," *Int* 29 (1974) 227-40; L. R. Fisher, "An Ugaritic Ritual and Genesis 1:1-5," *Ugaritica* 6 (1969) 197-205; H. Gunkel, *Schöpfung und Chaos in Urzeit und Endzeit. Eine religionsgeschichtliche Untersuchung über Gen 1 und Ap Joh 12* (Göttingen: Vandenhoeck und Ruprecht, 1895); G. Hasel, "The Significance of the Cosmology in Genesis 1 in Relation to Ancient Near Eastern Parallels," *Andrews University Seminary Studies* 10 (1972) 1-20; F. Hvidberg, "The Canaanite Background of Gen I-III," *VT* 10 (1960) 285-94; A. Kapelrud, "The Mythological Features in Genesis Chapter I and the Author's Intentions," *VT* 24 (1974) 178-86; K. Koch, "Wort und Einheit des Schöpfergottes in Memphis und Jerusalem," *ZTK* 62 (1965) 251-93; H. J. Kraus, "Die Entstehungsgeschichte der priesterlichen Schöpfungslehre Gen 1," *Fuldaer Hefte* 13 (1960) 76-94; W. R. Lane, "The Initiation of Creation," *VT* 13 (1963) 63-73; H. Lubsczyk, "Wortschöpfung und Tatschöpfung. Zur Entwicklung der priesterlichen Schöpfungslehre in Gen 1:1–2:4a," *BibLeb* 6 (1965) 191-208; T. Mettinger, "Abbild oder Urbild? 'Imago Dei' in traditionsgeschichtlicher Sicht," *ZAW* 86 (1974) 403-24; G. von Rad, "The Theological Problem of the Old Testament Doctrine of Creation," in *The Problem of the Hexateuch and Other Essays* (tr. E. W. Trueman Dicken; London: Oliver and Boyd, 1966) 131-43; W. H. Schmidt, *Die Schöpfungsgeschichte der Priesterschrift. Zur Überlieferungsgeschichte von Genesis 1:1-2, 4a und 2:4b–3:24* (3rd ed.; WMANT 17; Neukirchen-Vluyn: Neukirchener Verlag, 1973); O. H. Steck, *Der Schöpfungsbericht der Priesterschrift. Studien zur literarkritischen und überlieferungsgeschichtlichen Problematik von Genesis 1:1–2:4a* (FRLANT 115; Göttingen: Vandenhoeck und Ruprecht, 1975); W. Wegner, "Creation and Salvation: A Study of Genesis 1 and 2," *CTM* 37 (1966) 520-42; C. Westermann, "God and His Creation," *Union Seminary Quarterly Review* 18 (1963) 197-209; idem, *The Genesis Accounts of Creation* (tr. N. E. Wagner; Philadelphia: Fortress, 1964).

PARADISE TALE, 2:4b – 3:24

Structure

I. Introduction — 2:4b-7
  A. Description of precreation — 4b-6
  B. Creation of man — 7
II. Creation of paradise — 8-17
  A. General introduction — 8
  B. Creation of the Garden — 9-14
    1. Trees — 9
      a. For food — 9a
      b. Particular trees — 9b
    2. Rivers — 10-14
      a. For water — 10
      b. Naming — 11-14
  C. Responsibility — 15-17
    1. Positive — 15
    2. Negative — 16-17
III. Creation of helper — 18-25
  A. God's plan — 18-23
    1. General introduction — 18
    2. Animals — 19-20
      a. Act — 19aα
      b. Naming — 19aβb-20a
      c. Valuation — 20b
    3. Woman — 21-24

The report of creation events in 1:1–2:4a sets the context for this tale. As far as the final form of the text is concerned, the events narrated by this tale are postcreation. If, then, any mythological flavor should be left in, for example, vv. 4b-6, it would be seasoned by the priestly report of beginnings. For this tale at least, if not for all the following units in the primeval saga, the opening creation report is a pace-setting preface (→ 1:1–2:4a). The unit presents its tradition, nonetheless, as primeval. Creation of the world, even creation of human beings, appears in the introduction, not in the body of the pericope and thus not as the core of the narrative. The narrative, however, concerns human beings generally, a picture of events that demonstrates that human beings in the world are limited, less than divine.

The structure of the unit leans on two pillars: an account of paradise gained (2:8-17) and an account of paradise lost (3:1-24). This pattern suggests a similarity with other stories of fall and judgment (see Westermann, *Promises,* 44-56). These two pillars enframe a digression (3:20-21) and an account of God's plan to create a helper for the man (2:18-25). Finally, the pattern created by the two major pillars in the narration assumes an introduction to the context (2:4b-7).

The introduction develops first by means of a dependent clause, a typical mark for introducing narrative units (see 4:1; 16:1) or major breaks within a unit (3:1). Moreover, the syntax recalls the dependent phrase governed by a preposition in the beginning lines of creation accounts outside the OT (see *Enuma Elish*) and suggests that the introduction here follows a convention rather widespread in ancient narrative art. The dependent clauses in v. 4b, a general summary statement of creation that, incidentally, reverses the order of the phrase from 1:1 and 2:1, 4a to "the earth and the heavens," and vv. 5-6, a description of precreation that reverses the imagery of 1:1 2, lead to the major independent clause in v. 7, a crisp statement of the creation of man. The entire sentence thus functions as introduction, including the report of the creation of the man (contrast Westermann, *Genesis,* 261). All are in some manner summary statements, establishing context. All give witness to the perspective of the story: The events narrated here are primeval, but they are postcreation. Therefore, the goal of the narration cannot be to recount the creation of the world or even the creation of man (contrast Schmidt, 196-205).

The structure of the unit does not support arguments that the paradise-gained story is independent of the paradise-lost story. Rather, the two elements stand together as one unit, the one a reflex to the other. This point is clear not only from recurring motifs at key points, such as the tree of life or the tree of the knowledge of good and evil, but also by the dialectic expressed in the parallel, paradise gained-paradise lost. Moreover, the two pillars show a strong bond with the introduction, especially in the explicit allusion to the introduction in v. 23b (cf. v. 7a). In the introduction man is created as a living being. In the judgment he is denied access to the tree of life. Thus, the judgment that removes the man from the tree of life to till the ground from which he was taken tolls with dire tones the parallel statement in 2:7: This man is dust, and dust without life is like the Garden without water. Moreover, the judgment against the man contrasts sharply with the positive responsibility he carries to till the ground (2:15). The principal point here is that while vv. 23 and 24 share a certain redundancy, they function as complements in the parallelism of the element. It is therefore difficult to shunt v. 23 off from vv. 22 and 24, either literarily or as a sign of growth in the tradition's history (contrast Schmidt, 220). The weight for this point rests not so much on the designation of the human creature as dust (v. 19b), but on the contrast between the sentence to till the ground (3:23) and the responsibility to till the Garden (2:15).

The judgment element, however, has a double function. It not only parallels the introduction and its intimate connection with the description of paradise gained, but it also offers a dramatic climax to the plot that unfolds in the body of the unit. The story thus has no gradual relaxation of tension, as OT stories commonly do. It ends sharply with a final judgment that is as harsh as the judgment of the Flood Tale. In order to demonstrate this point, it is necessary to describe the plot. The first element in the body of the narration depicts the creation of the Garden. The depiction assumes the creation of the world. It is thus not properly a creation report, a parallel in tradition or form to 1:1–2:4a. It does not describe the creation of the cosmos, or even the earth. It is, rather, simply an account of paradise gained. V. 8 is a general statement of this event, vv. 9-17 a detailed narrative of the same event.

(1) Thus, vv. 9-14 specify what v. 8a reports generally. To plant a garden means to produce trees that are good for fruit. No syntactical or traditio-historical reasons deny v. 9b to the detailed account in v. 9a. The noun *'ēṣ* ("tree") appears three times in the verse. In the first instance, it is controlled by the particle *kol* and qualified twice, once by a Niphal participle that functions as an adjective and once by an adjective. "And out of the ground the Lord God made to grow every tree that is pleasant to the sight and good for food." These are all the trees in general, desirable to see and good to eat. The other two occurrences refer to two particular trees: "the tree of life in the midst of the garden" and "the tree of the knowledge of good and evil." The particularity does not, however, mark the trees as secondary in the narrative; rather, it marks them as foreshadowing motifs. It leaves them unintegrated, but nonetheless tantalizing. Vv. 10-14 then provide data necessary for the Garden. These data need not be secondary in the narrative. That they shift the style from narrative to list, like the genealogies, is clear (Westermann, *Genesis,* 265). The earth had no water, according to the introduction, or at least only primordial water (so, vv. 5-6); the Garden has water. Indeed, from the Garden's water spring four world rivers. And from the water the Garden and the world receive fertility. The world geography in vv. 11-14 is thus not intended so much as an incidental collection of facts, but rather as an affirmation that fertility in all the world derives not from foreign gods or cultic rituals, but from the Garden God created for man.

(2) Moreover, vv. 15-17 specify in detail what v. 8b reports generally. V. 8b notes that God put Adam in the Garden. Vv. 15-17 repeat that move, but not as a formal doublet. Rather, these verses make quite detailed what v. 8b reports only generally. First, Adam has positive responsibility for the Garden. That responsibility is signaled by two imperfect verbs in construct: "God *took* Adam and *put* him in the Garden of Eden." The extension contrasts with the briefer notice in v. 8b. But also, two infinitives construct define his responsibility: "to till it *[lĕ'obdāh]* and to keep it *[ûlĕšomrāh]*." The Garden requires that his work be responsibly defended so that the order it represents may be preserved. The positive character of this responsibility contrasts sharply with the negative character of v. 23. In the contrast, they function as foreshadowing, but the foreshadowing is formally positive.

This positive character shifts in vv. 16-17, where God addresses the man directly: "You may freely eat of every tree of the garden. But of the tree of the knowledge of good and evil you shall not eat, for in the day that you eat of it you shall die." It may be that the "knowledge of good and evil" means assumption of political power not properly man's (see Clark, "Legal Background"; Coats, "God of Death"). But in the context of the story this tree bodes its own contrast to the tree of life: "In the day that you eat of it you shall die." On the surface, the prohibition is straightforward, a negative pole in contrast to the positive in v. 15, formulated in apodictic style and specifying the consequences of violation. Its prohibition assumes, moreover, that the human creature may eat from the tree of life. If that assumption is correct, the image would be that regular eating from the tree insures life against death, not that having once eaten, death would never come. But the verse does more—it foreshadows the development of the plot and thus represents the principal point of tension which moves the story. It stands as if its dire threat were an inevitable fate (Westermann, *Genesis*, 260-62). But it should be clear that the point of tension that feeds the story here is not the creation of man. It is not a tradition like 1:1–2:4a. The point of tension lies in man's relationship with God as it works itself out in the Garden (contrast Westermann, *Genesis*, 262).

The next element of narration, 2:18-25, appears virtually as a digression between the two major pillars of the unit (see Westermann, *Genesis*, 260). Yet, it prepares the way for the fourth element by introducing the animals (cf. 3:1) and the woman (cf. 3:1-13). It can thus be understood as a delay in the plot's development. Again, the element moves from a general statement to a particular statement. V. 18 is the general statement, a divine speech announcing God's plan for creating a helper for Adam. Vv. 19-20 spell out details with the creation of animals and Adam's reaction to them. The designation of names by Adam symbolizes his authority over them (thus, 1:28; see Schmidt, 200). V. 20b, a valuation of this step in God's plan, sets the stage for the next element by reporting failure. No helper fit for intimacy with man appeared among the animals.

The next element, vv. 21-23, opens with a detailed description of God's work in building the woman. V. 23, in all probability originally independent from the story context (see Schmidt, 203), represents a valuation and naming of the woman. Whereas the animals were rejected as candidates for a proper helper for man, woman is accepted precisely because of the intimate relationship in her creation from man's bone. The intimacy of kinship marks her as the proper helper (→ 29:14). The etiological formula in v. 24 is rooted in this intimate relationship and suggests moreover that the goal of the entire unit moves toward the etiology (see Schmidt, 203-4; Westermann, *Genesis*, 260-61). It moves from the beginning to explain the union of flesh in the relationship. Over against the virtual independence of this digression, v. 25 functions as a transition. In vv. 18-24 there is no reference to the Garden, the prohibited tree, the dawning tension. In v. 25 the man and his wife, introduced by the ideal relationship described in vv. 18-24, are depicted as naked and unashamed. Their situation is still ideal, but both terms anticipate the crisis of the next unit (cf. 3:7, 10).

The fourth major element of narration begins in 3:1a with a sentence cast in nominal sequence. The sentence order does not, however, signal a new unit. To the contrary, it marks the exposition for a new element in the continuing unit.

As expositions commonly do, this verse exposes a new principal actor for the narrative and new circumstances. But it also demonstrates, in comparison to 2:4b-7, that a story unit may have more than one exposition element and that expositions may appear not only at the beginning of a story, but also at the beginning of any major element involving new principals or circumstances. This exposition introduces the snake. But at the same time, it ties the snake into the preceding element in two ways: (1) It names the snake as one of the creatures of the field which the Lord God made (→ 2:19). It is thus not a primordial Satan. (2) It relates the snake to the man and woman by suggesting that it was more naked—or wiser—than any other creature (Heb. *'ārûm*; cf. 2:25: "The two human beings were naked *['ārûmmîm]*"; the wordplay depends on paronomasia). The snake was also capable of intimacy. Despite the role of this exposition for introduction, it serves a relatively small element, vv. 1-5. In effect, it sets the necessary stage for the temptation dialogue in vv. 1b-5.

The temptation dialogue is simple in its structure, particularly in view of the heavy weight it carries as preparation for the key element in vv. 6-7. It does not involve the whole slate of characters; only two appear. The dialogue unfolds completely between the woman and the snake. It opens with a simple question about God's instructions, assuming the instructions had been addressed to both the man and the woman: "Did God say: 'You [plur.] shall not eat of any tree in the Garden!'?" The question, formulated in the extreme, immediately draws the woman into debate. Her response has two parts: (1) She corrects the snake by making clear what the range of behavior permitted by God's instructions was. (2) She cites God's prohibition, with its sanction. The debate can now move to its center. The snake first denies the truth of God's sanction: "You will not die." There is no argument against the sanction. Rather, the snake leaves the denial to stand alone and moves to God's motivations: God told the human couple this lie in order to prevent them from becoming like him, "knowing good and evil." The snake argues, in effect, that eating from the tree of knowledge will not bring death from God, but the life of God, the power of divine discrimination (see Clark, "Legal Background"). The temptation thus places before the human couple an invitation to become like God, to live not under the command to be responsible, but under the power to decide what responsible is. And that is all the snake does. He played his role with the woman and now he disappears from the story.

The fall itself is distinguished from the temptation element by the lapse of dialogue. These two verses, again involving only two actors, appear entirely as narrative (cf. also 4:8). The woman discovers that the tree is good and delightful; indeed, it is desirable for making one wise. The focus of her discovery is not on the invitation to wisdom, however; it is on pleasure. So she ate, and she gave some to Adam, who also ate. The tempted woman becomes the tempter for the man. And the awful event is done, captured in v. 7 by simple clauses: "Then the eyes of both were opened, and they knew that they were naked." The verse stands in contrast to v. 25, not so much by suggesting that before the fall the couple did not know that they were naked, but rather by suggesting that before the fall their nakedness did not bother them. They were not ashamed; they were intimate. Now they discover that they are naked, and they become ashamed. Their intimacy is broken, so they make aprons for themselves. These verses constitute the peripeteia for the entire unit. The story had warned the audience that dire events lay on the horizon, but the tension unfolded out of the possibility that the human couple might be obedient. Now the die is cast. They were not obedient, and the fate foreshadowed in 2:17 must now claim its own victims.

The next unit, 3:8-13, functions ambiguously for the whole. The exposition in v. 8 sets the stage for the dialogue in vv. 9-13. The couple, now guilty, must hide from the presence of the Lord. Structurally, the exposition and the dialogue it introduces function as a delay. To hide from the presence of the Lord is to delay the fate that must come. Theologically, the exposition carries as much weight as vv. 6-7. The presence of the Lord identifies the people of the Lord (see Exod 33:16). Without the presence of the Lord there is no people. Ironically, then, the act of Adam immediately following the fall sets in motion the fate he won with his disobedience. But the exposition accomplishes more: The natural intimacy between creature and creator captured by the imagery of the Garden now appears to be broken. The human couple has proven untrustworthy, and their effort to hide emphasizes their untrustworthy character. Intimacy between God and human beings dissolves.

The dialogue in vv. 9-13 carries this motif even further. God summons the man (without the woman) to a hearing: "Where are you?" The question appears on the surface to be simple, an inquiry for information. But in terms of the dialogue, it carries the force of a summons—it does not leave Adam with the choice to remain hidden. Is there nonetheless some ray of divine grace in the summons? The man cannot remain hidden from the source of his life. To the contrary, God seeks him out, and the confrontation does not spell his immediate death (on the element of grace in this unit, see Westermann, *Promises*, 55-56). Yet, if there is grace in the move, the grace is subordinated in the narrative to the renewed tension produced by the ensuing dialogue. Adam explains why he hid: He was naked and afraid. God responds with a challenge, in effect an accusation: "Who told you that you were naked?" But the following question gets to the point: "Have you eaten. . . ?" The question, like the one in v. 9, does not call for information. It is, though perhaps not formally, at least in content an accusation: "You have eaten. . . ." And Adam responds to the accusation with a confession.

The confession in v. 12 and the renewed dialogue in v. 13 reintroduce the woman into the proceedings. Adam's confession is clear in the last word of v. 12: "I ate." The first part of the confession, however, lays the blame on the woman (cf. vv. 1-7). Then v. 13 addresses a formal accusation to the woman. It is not possible, on the basis of the loose relationship of the woman to the proceedings, to say that v. 13 is secondary, although the problem may suggest something about the tradition's history. But neither is it possible to say that the unit lays structural focus on the bond between the man and the woman. The etiology in 1:18-24 has an intrinsic role, although it may have been originally an independent tradition, but the role is a digression in the narrative plot. The story itself depends not so much on the bond that makes man and woman one, but on the fall that leaves them separated: "Don't blame me, Lord. That woman you gave me did it." And even the woman looks for another party to blame. The fall brings an inevitable fate on the couple. They do not die immediately, but suffer a fate worse than death—they do not stand together any longer. They do not stand together with nature, and they do not stand together with God. The contrast with 2:24 depicts a painful change in status.

The response of God is cast first as three distinct speeches, addressed to the three distinct actors in the drama. Each has an etiological element, but each carries out the force of the judgment. The sentence against the serpent is structured now in the pattern of an oracle of judgment. A dependent clause, "because you have done this" *(kî 'āśîtā zō't)*, functions as an indictment and provides a foundation for the following judgment. The judgment opens with a curse formula: "Cursed are you. . ." *('ārûr 'attâ)*. The specification following is to be interpreted in the context of the curse. The first part of the specification depicts an element of the natural world and thus has an etiological ring. Anyone who asks why the serpent must crawl on its belly can find an answer narrated here. V. 15 carries the fate of the serpent to a new form of world reality: "I will put enmity between you and the woman. . . ." The judgment against the woman, v. 16, is not constructed with indictment or curse; otherwise it follows the same pattern as the first. An etiological note, "I will greatly multiply your pain in childbearing. . . ," precedes a description of the new relationship the man and woman share: "Your desire shall be for your husband, and he shall rule over you." This is not the mutuality captured by the bond of 2:24 or the intimacy of 2:23. This is a different relationship, a relationship of opposition that is not creative. Finally, vv. 17-19 present the judgment against the man. Again cast in an indictment-sentence structure, the element follows a pattern like vv. 14-15. A dependent clause begins with "because" *(kî)* and sets the indictment. The following is a curse, but not a curse against man, at least not directly: "Cursed is the ground because of you . . ." *('ărûrâ hā'ădāmâ ba'ăbûrekā)*. The sentence following the curse carries an etiological ring: "In toil you shall eat of it [the ground] all the days of your life." Vv. 18-19 depict the new world order for man, an order that threatens him in two ways: (1) The opposition between man and ground produced thorns and thistles, along with plants to eat. That means sweat instead of ease. (2) The end of man's toil is his own return to the ground *(hā'ădāmâ)*, the center of the curse. V. 19b captures the same threat with the noun "dust" *('āpār)*, an allusion that recalls 2:7.

The three oracles do not represent the primary conclusion of the unit, however (see Westermann, *Genesis*, 266-67; Schmidt, 214-17). One cannot object at this point, then, that the conclusion does not correspond with the development of tension since the tension builds on an immediate fate: "In the day that you eat of it you shall die." Rather, the question about resolution of tension must be addressed to the following verses. The element in vv. 20-21 obviously does not fulfill the role of conclusion; it is a delay. Indeed, it appears in every way as literarily secondary in the story. It is an interruption that duplicates information already established by the story. (1) Adam gives his wife a name, but she already has a name (2:23b). The naming etiology that follows develops from assonance: "The mother of all living" *('ēm kol-ḥāy)* sounds somewhat like Eve *(ḥawwâ)*. But the etiology is secondary, virtually an epilogue hung onto the end of the story. (2) God gives the man and woman garments of skin, but Adam and his wife already had garments of fig leaves (cf. 3:7). There is no etiological mark here. Neither is there structural or content evidence of interest in labeling this gift a sign of God's grace. It is only information to show the progress of civilization (see Westermann, *Genesis*). The quest for a narrative climax thus moves to the next element, vv. 22-24.

These verses also function as judgment on the human pair for their disobedience. But contrary to the poetic oracles, here the primary narrative develops its conclusion. Structure in these verses appears essentially on the pattern of indictment-judgment. The scheme is marred, however, by a shift from first-person-plural speech in v. 22 to third-person narration in vv. 23-24. The indictment does not employ a *kî*-clause or a curse. It opens with a simple statement of fact: "Behold, the man has become like one of us, knowing good and evil." The allusion refers to the man's act of eating from the forbidden tree. But remarkably, it now has only the man in view, just as the initial prohibition is addressed only to the man (see the comments below on the tradition history).

The second part of the indictment is introduced with the particle *pen* ("lest") and refers to the second tree. If the man now eats the fruit of the second tree, which was not denied him initially, he will be like God. Man's sin is disobedience, but the threat he poses is hubris, desire to become like God. The weight of the structure lies on disobedience; the *pen*-clause and its threat raise the specter of apotheosis. The judgment element, vv. 23-24, builds on a synonymous parallel pattern, ABAC. The first section in the parallel describes the judgment, with an accompanying final infinitive: "The Lord God sent him forth from the Garden of Eden to till the ground from which he was taken." The final clause contrasts with man's original purpose (2:15); indeed, his original creation represents an explicit source for the allusion (2:7). Now, tilling the ground has a negative ring. The ground is away from the Garden; its productivity, despite man's tilling, cannot be like that of the Garden. The opposition thus recalls the curse in vv. 16-17. This negative quality is expanded by the parallel with v. 24. V. 24a parallels v. 23a exactly (on the verb "drive out" *[gāraš]*, cf. 4:14). V. 24b then advances the point of v. 23b with new information. Two guards, the cherubim and a flaming, turning sword, block the way back to the Tree of Life. The allusion to the Tree of Life cannot be secondary. It stands at the center of the climax, for to be driven out of Eden, to have one's way to the Tree of Life blocked by such creatures, must mean death (cf. Ezek 28:17-19). God's judgment of death for disobedience is thus not ignored but tragically fulfilled.

It would seem clear, then, that despite complexities in structure that point to a tradition history, the story ends where the plot intends it to end. The man violated the law of obedience placed on him by God. His punishment is death on that very day. And that happens, despite delays, despite signs of God's grace (if any should be there). The basic structure thus unfolds on two pillars: the creation of paradise and the loss of paradise. The second pillar can be understood under the structural pattern of sin and judgment (see Westermann, *Promises*, 49-56). The judgment, despite man's continued life, is death. Alienation from the source of his life, opposition from that which gives him life, is the order he has to live in or die in.

The unit belongs to the Yahwist. It marks the beginning of the J narrative, significantly not so much with an affirmation that all that is and happens derives from God (so, P), but rather with a description of human plight, the violation of created orders that permeates all of creation. Certain secondary elements in the narrative, such as 3:20-21, characterize the latest stage. Use of the sentences in vv. 14-19 is central to the Yahwist's narration and may reflect the hand of the Yahwist. The pre-Yahwistic narrative derives from the combination of a paradise story, perhaps reporting the disobedience and fall of only one person, with tradition about man and woman in an intimate marriage bond. If the paradise story originally involved only one person (see Westermann, *Genesis,* 266; Ezekiel 28), then the role of the woman in the temptation element would be the result of the combination. Would the pattern for the combination derive from a paradise tradition that casts the tempter not as a naked (wise) snake, but as a naked (and wise) woman (cf. the Gilgamesh Epic)?

Formulas and stereotyped expressions in this pericope include: (1) An apodictically formulated prohibition in 2:17 that denies the privilege of action without designation of exceptions and seals the power of the assertion with a statement of judgment. The judgment typically concludes with the formulation *môt tāmût* ("you shall surely die"). (2) A naming formula for etiologies that employs the verb "name" *(qārā')* and builds on some kind of wordplay in a preceding or following part of the verse. In 2:23 the name for the woman is *'iššâ* ("woman"), and the following *kî*-clause reports that she was taken "from the man" *(mē'îš)*. (3) A speech formula that appears widely in narrative as an introduction to a speech. It notes who makes the speech and, in most occasions, to whom the speech is addressed, as, for example, in 3:2. (4) A formal accusation, drawn from the pre-official legal process as a kind of summons to legal action, that typically begins with the interrogative particle *lāmmâ* (*"Why* have you done this thing?"). Or, in 3:13, a more stylized formula functions in the same way: "What have you done?" *(mah-zō't 'āśît)*. In both cases, the formula is constructed in the second person as a direct challenge to some previous act. The position of such an accusation calls for some kind of response from the addressee (so, Boecker). (5) An oracle of judgment from God to the addressee that typically employs some statement of indictment as the foundation for a sentence as divine judgment, as in 3:14-15. The form appears widely in the prophets (so, von Waldow), but it cannot be limited to a prophetic setting. It doubtlessly derived primarily from a legal context but was used widely as a literary form, quite apart from either a prophetic or a legal setting. (6) A curse formula that employs the passive participle *'ārûr* ("cursed"), with a definition of the one to be cursed and the content of the curse. The formula in 3:14 establishes the pattern.

Genre

As a part of the final form of the Pentateuch, and as a part of the Yahwist's narrative, the paradise story stands as an element in the primeval SAGA. As an element in the saga, and perhaps as a narrative that was once not associated with a saga, the unit would nevertheless demonstrate its own internal identity. It has a plot that comes to a conclusion. It follows a general narrative pattern of employing only three actors (God, man, snake) or at most four (the woman) but only two at a time: God-man; man-woman; woman-snake. Indeed, where it might focus on three or even four actors, the third and fourth fall into the background. It is thus not surprising that the prohibition, as well as the expulsion on the basis of the prohibition, involves only the man and God. The temptation involves only the woman and the snake, with the snake disappearing when the temptation is complete. Or, later, the temptation involves the woman and the man. The structure is complex rather than simple, but that feature reflects the tradition's history. Its place of action is the Garden of Eden, the beginning time before human beings gained their later state. But the story moves from the world of a god and his garden to the present. Its concern is to show the origin of the present situation. The story thus loses its affinity for mythological forms, both in tradition and in genre. As it stands in J, and thus for the final form of the text, the narrative is a TALE, an account of this world and these people.

Earlier stages in the tradition may have been mythology. The parallel in Ezekiel 28 ties the tradition to this world by making the Paradise Man the king of Tyre (see also the Gilgamesh Epic). There is, however, something remote and primordial in the king of Tyre, as there is in Enkidu, and these qualities point to MYTH as the background for the paradise tale.

Setting

The primary form, J, and its incorporation into the final form of the Pentateuch/Hexateuch reflect a setting in a literary mold. Some artisan employed this unit as the beginning of a longer narrative, and that artisan we may call the Yahwist (see von Rad, *Genesis*).

As a tale the unit derives in some manner from the royal court (see Richter). The Paradise Man is the royal man; his garden, his animals, his wife constitute his court. He exercises dominion over them as he names them (cf. 1:28). The Paradise Man thus wields power in his garden, power to know good and evil, to discriminate between alternatives for the future of his subjects. Yet, the tale is not simply a propaganda piece for the royal man. His knowledge of good and evil was originally denied him. His grasp of it was an act of disobedience, an affront to God. His expulsion from the Garden is a denial of his power. The story thus derives from circles (wisdom?) who stand over against the king to admonish, instruct, and correct him, or finally to impeach him.

Intention

Just as the final form of the text begins with a statement of creation that must be mediated to historical creatures through God's saving events, so with this story the final form of the text affirms the initial act of human disobedience and resulting expulsion from the Garden of God as the model of human resistance to dependency on God. J begins his entire narration by depicting the plight human creatures share. They stand in opposition to each other, to the created world, and to God. And the opposition, the loss of intimacy with all parts of life, creates their death. The story casts its presentation of the condemnation of the human pair to death under the stamp of the creatures' rise to power. As they grasp what was rightfully God's, they discover that they have created for themselves only death. J deals with this facet of human experience throughout his story. Indeed, the primary intention of J is to explore the limitations in human experience not only in terms of the order humans must live in as creatures, but in all the relationships of their experience. The story for J, then, leads necessarily to the next unit (see Westermann, *Genesis*, 374-80), but it casts the next unit and all following units against this one primeval event. The mythological background for the tradition is broken, and human (royal) power is limited.

At earlier stages, the tradition may have served as a critical judgment on the power of the king. It reflects the efforts to limit and thus to instruct the king in his administration of state affairs. It calls on mythological tradition which, by annual repetition in the ritual of the royal cult, secured the stability of the king's world. It suggests, however, by breaking the myth, that the power of the creation belongs only to God.

Bibliography

L. Alonso-Schökel, "Sapiential and Covenant Themes in Genesis 2–3," *Theology Digest* 13 (1965) 3-10; J. A. Bailey, "Initiation and the Primal Woman in Gilgamesh and Genesis 2–3," *JBL* 89 (1970) 137-50; J. Begrich, "Die Paradieserzählung. Eine literargeschicht-liche Studie," *ZAW* 50 (1932) 93-116; H. J. Boecker, *Redeformen des Rechtslebens im Alten Testament* (WMANT 14; Neukirchen-Vluyn: Neukirchener Verlag, 1964); W. Brueggemann, "Of the Same Flesh and Bone (Gen 2:23a)," *CBQ* 32 (1970) 532-42; idem, "From Dust to Kingship," *ZAW* 84 (1972) 1-18; idem, "Kingship and Chaos (A Study in Tenth Century Israel)," *JAAR* 40 (1972) 96-109; K. Budde, *Die biblische Para-diesgeschichte* (BZAW 60; Giessen: Töpelmann, 1932); W. M. Clark, "A Legal Back-ground to the Yahwist's Use of 'Good and Evil' in Genesis 2–3," *JBL* 88 (1969) 266-78; D.J.A. Clines, "The Tree of Knowledge and the Law of Yahweh," *VT* 24 (1974) 8-14; G. W. Coats, "The God of Death: Power and Obedience in the Primeval History," *Int* 29 (1975) 227-39; I. Engnell, " 'Knowledge' and 'Life' in the Creation Story," in *Wisdom in Israel and in the Ancient Near East* (*Fest.* H. H. Rowley; ed. M. Noth and D. Winton Thomas; VTSup 4; Leiden: Brill, 1960) 103-19; W. Fuss, *Die sogenannte Paradieserzähl-ung. Aufbau, Herkunft und Theologische Bedeutung* (Gerd Mohn: Gütersloher, 1968); E. Haag, *Der Mensch am Anfang: Die alttestamentliche Paradiesvorstellung nach Genesis 2–3* (Trierer Theologische Studien 24; Trier: Paulinus Verlag, 1970); H. Haag, "Die Kom-position der Sündenfallerzählung," *Tübinger Theologische Quartalschrift* 146 (1966) 1-7; idem, "Die Themata der Sündenfall-Geschichte," in *Lex tua veritas* (*Fest.* H. Junker; ed. H. Gross and P. Mussner; Trier: Paulinus Verlag, 1961) 101-11; N. Habel, "Ezekiel 28 and the Fall of the First Man," *CTM* 38 (1967) 516-24; K. R. Joines, "The Serpent in Gen 3," *ZAW* 87 (1975) 1-11; N. Lohfink, "Die Erzählung vom Sündenfall," in *Das Siegeslied am Schilfmeer* (Frankfurt: Knecht, 1965) 81-101; idem, "Gen 2–3 as 'Historical Etiology'," *Theology Digest* 13 (1965) 11-17; H. P. Müller, "Mythische Elemente in der jahwistischen Schöpfungserzählung," *ZTK* 69 (1972) 259-89; E. Nielsen, "Creation and the Fall of Man. A Cross-Disciplinary Investigation," *HUCA* 43 (1972) 1-22; W. Reiser, "Die Verwandtschaftsformel in Gen 2:23," *TZ* 16 (1960) 1-4; W. Richter, "Urgeschichte und Hoftheologie," *BZ* 10 (1966) 96-105; L. Ruppert, "Die Sündenfallerzählung (Gen 3) in vorjahwistischer Tradition und Interpretation," *BZ* 15 (1971) 185-202; J. Scharbert, "Quellen und Redaktion in Gen 2:4b–4:16," *BZ* 18 (1974) 45-64; W. H. Schmidt, *Die Schöpfungsgeschichte der Priesterschrift. Zur Überlieferungsgeschichte von Genesis 1:1– 2:4a und 2:4b–3:24* (WMANT 17; 3rd ed.; Neukirchen-Vluyn: Neukirchener Verlag, 1970); O. H. Steck, *Die Paradieserzählung: Eine Auslegung von Genesis 2:46–3:24* (BibS[N] 60; Neukirchen-Vluyn: Neukirchener Verlag, 1970); P.E.S. Thompson, "The Yahwist Cre-ation Story," *VT* 21 (1971) 197-208; W. Trilling, *Denn Staub bist du. . . . Eine Einführung in den Bericht von Paradies und Sündenfall* (Freiburg: Herder, 1965); E. von Waldow, *Der traditionsgeschichtliche Hintergrund der prophetischen Gerichtsreden* (BZAW 85; Berlin: Töpelmann, 1963); J. Walsh, "Genesis 2:4b–3:24: A Synchronic Approach," *JBL* 96 (1977) 161-77; C. Westermann, "Der Mensch im Urgeschehen," *KD* 13 (1967) 232-46.

ADAM GENEALOGY (J), 4:1-26

Structure

I. First generation: Adam   1-16

The immediate context for this J unit is the paradise tale in 2:4b–3:24. The genealogy thus binds the beginning narrative (J) with the following material, particularly with the narrative of the flood in order to show continuity of event between the two.

The genealogy begins with vv. 1-2. These verses have now been incorporated into the narrative structure of the tale of the two brothers (→ 4:1-16). This point is particularly clear in the style of the opening, a nominal construction (v. 1), in comparison with the beginning of other genealogical units (cf. 4:17, 25). Yet, in content as well as in intention, v. 1 duplicates individual entries of the genealogy (cf. v. 17). V. 2a is shorter, with no notation of conception or explanation of the name for Abel, who is known only in reference to his brother. This element seems thus more oriented to the tale than to the genealogy. If one considers, however, v. 2b to be a part of the genealogy, then the pattern more closely approximates the entries of the genealogy, at least the entries in vv. 20-21 (see Westermann, *Genesis,* 439-40).

If the first two verses of the chapter constitute the beginning of the Adam genealogy, continued by vv. 17-24, then the basic structural characteristics emerge. (1) The genealogy comprises seven generations, a whole unit, particularly for J (see Westermann, *Genesis,* 439). (2) The genealogy embraces the tale of the two brothers, suggesting a framing function (→ Numbers 33). (3) Two distinct styles break the body of the genealogy. (a) The opening elements concentrate on successive generations, a father-son chain. Combined with the generation entry are, on occasion, various items of information about the progress of culture achieved by the generations. Cain and Abel introduce farming and herding, Enoch a city. (b) V. 19 builds not so much on successive stages of generations as on the internal relationships, the structure of Lamech's family (see Wilson, 138-58; Westermann, *Genesis,* 446-47). Again, items of information about developing human culture appear. Lamech's sons are the first to dwell in tents (v. 20), the first to play the lyre (v. 21), and the first to forge bronze and iron (v. 22a). Moreover, the entry embraces a longer saying about Lamech (→ 4:23-24). The saying is doubtlessly secondary in the genealogy, but it nonetheless contributes to the expansive style of the entry. The alternate style recalls the expansive quality of the first entry, but it also suggests that the genealogy places importance on the Lamech segment (see Westermann, *Genesis,* 447). Its structure elevates the special group.

The genealogy belongs to the Yahwist. Genealogies with traditional elements already incorporated are attested outside the OT (see Westermann, *Genesis,* 441; Reiser). The genealogy reflected in this list has a tradition history (see the P parallel in ch. 5), but earlier forms of the genealogy cannot be reconstructed beyond the suggestion that vv. 1-2 have been altered to fit the tale or that vv. 19-24 show evidence of expansion.

Genre

The GENEALOGY builds on a system of enumeration rather than a style of narration. It is more nearly akin to (→) list than to (→) story genres, although it can encompass story in its scope. Moreover, genealogy can designate a broader group of lists, with various genres emerging from the general combination. This list belongs to a genre that traces generations over a long period of time. It is thus *linear* in form and function. The last verse, however, seeks to expand a generation into its various segments. It is thus *segmented* in form and function (see Wilson, 158).

Setting

The genealogy has a firm setting in J as a part of a larger piece of literature (→ The Book of Genesis). Genealogy derives ultimately from tribal circles as a means for the history and validation of tribal units (see Wilson).

Intention

For J, the genealogy provides a bridge between the paradise tale and the flood tale. It also provides a literary vehicle for framing smaller pieces of tradition, such as the tale of the two brothers. Moreover, it incorporates references to the development of culture as parts of the productivity from the people of the list. It thus shows culture as the work of human beings, not the sacral product of ancient mythology. This work is nevertheless a goal for which God created human beings (see Westermann, *Genesis,* 405-6). The Cain-Abel tale and the Lamech song show that the cultural progress is unfortunately burdened by a disjunction, a break between brothers that can lead to uncontrolled vengeance. One might note here the relationship between the genealogy of J and the J note in 5:29. Is the Lamech entry only preparation for the next stage of tradition represented by Noah? (Cf. P in ch. 5.)

Prior stages of the genealogy must have involved accounts of the growth of culture and human relations from the primeval period. It is not appropriate to argue that the genealogy presupposes no flood story since it places the beginning of various elements of later culture before the flood. Rather, the genealogy presupposes that cultural elements were carried over to the postflood period (see Westermann, *Genesis,* 441-42).

Bibliography

J. Gabriel, "Die Kainitengenealogie: Gen 4:17-24," *Bib* 40 (1959) 409-27; M. D. Johnson, *The Purpose of the Biblical Genealogies with Special Reference to the Setting of the Genealogies of Jesus* (SNTSMS 8; Cambridge: Cambridge University Press, 1969); A. Malamat, "King Lists of the Old Babylonian Period and Biblical Genealogies," *JAOS* 88 (1968) 163-73; R. R. Wilson, *Genealogy and History in the Biblical World* (New Haven: Yale University Press, 1977).

TALE OF TWO BROTHERS, 4:1-16

Structure

I. Exposition	1-2
A. Birth reports	1-2a
1. Cain	1
2. Abel	2a
B. Profession	2b
II. Rejection	3-15
A. Temptation	3-7
1. Offering	3-5
2. Accusation	6-7
B. Fall	8
C. Judgment dialogue	9-15a
1. Opening question	9a
2. Cain's explanation	9b
3. Judgment	10-12
a. Accusation	10
b. Judgment	11-12
4. Cain's lament	13-14
5. Oath	15a
III. Conclusion	15b-16
A. Protection oath fulfilled	15b
B. Sentence executed	16

The context for the tale of the two brothers derives from the creation/paradise narratives immediately preceding. Indeed, the bond between the paradise tale (J) and this pericope involves not only narrative continuity, but also structuring patterns. The genealogy that binds the paradise tale to the flood tale frames the tale of the two brothers. The events of this tale are thus a part of the primeval history, a narrative about individual persons in the process of becoming historical generations.

The structure of the unit involves an exposition, vv. 1-2, and a conclusion, v. 16, framing the major body of narrative in vv. 3-15. (1) The exposition encompasses all of vv. 1-2, even though v. 1 must also be considered a logical, if not a structural, part of the genealogy that continues in v. 17. It is normally the case in the primeval history that narrative units are connected by genealogies. It is not surprising, then, to find genealogy tradition in v. 1; the surprise lies rather in the style of the notice. One might expect a consecutive imperfect verb as the opening (cf. 4:17, 25), but the sentence employs nominal structure typical for a narrative exposition (cf. 3:1). If v. 1 belonged originally to the genealogy (so, Westermann, *Genesis,* 388-89), then it has been recast as the opening lines of the tale. Moreover, v. 2a builds on v. 1 (thus the formulation: "And again she bore . . ."). It does not resemble the genealogies; there is no notation of conception or designation of a saying to explain the name. The verse does, however, introduce a principal in the tale, just as v. 1 does. It is clear, then, that vv. 1-2a function together as an introduction of the two actors at the center of the tale. V. 2b then defines the way of life for each, a datum necessary for the plot that follows.

The conclusion, v. 16, parallels the introduction not only by its description of Cain's departure, but specifically in the relationship between Cain and the Lord. The mother's birth saying in v. 1b, a play on the name and the verb *qānîtî 'îš* ("I have gotten a man . . ."), also notes the presence of the Lord. The conclusion, however, emphasizes Cain's loss of the presence: "Cain went away from the presence of the Lord." The land of Nod, Cain's destination (and a play on Cain's state after God's punishment in vv. 12, 14; *nōd* means "to wander, lament"), is thus a place without the Lord.

The tale itself employs two elements of structure that depend on speeches (vv. 3-7, 9-16), connected by a simple verse of narrative (v. 8). The first involves no exchange between the two brothers. It reports the sacrificial ritual of, and the formal response to, each (vv. 3-5a). V. 5b sets the stage for the story by depicting Cain's emotion: "Cain was very angry, and his countenance fell." Yahweh's speech follows, an accusation against Cain along with some paternal advice. One can almost hear Jacob addressing Reuben or Judah. Indeed, the point of tension that sets the plot for the story is the same as that in the Joseph novella (→ Genesis 37–50). The trouble is not between Cain and the Lord; it is between Cain and Abel.

V. 8 accomplishes quickly what the point of tension anticipates (contrast Westermann, *Genesis*). Some early versions of the Cain-Abel exchange (LXX, Sam Pent) carry a Cain speech to Abel (see also *RSV*), but the story in the MT has no speech. It may be translated simply: "So, Cain spoke to Abel his brother. And when they were in the field. . . ." Without a speech, then, the structural element notes that Cain leads Abel into a field and kills him (compare the style of 3:6-7). Thus, the relationship between brothers raises the specter of opposition noted in the Garden between the man and the woman. The act may be quantitatively different, but its quality is the same.

The second structural element, vv. 9-16, can be defined in terms of a gradual reduction in tension. What will the Lord do with the guilty one? Again, the element is patterned like its paradise counterpart (cf. 3:8-12). An opening question confronts Cain with the necessary procedure (cf. 3:9). Cain's explanation is as weak as Adam's (cf. 3:10), indeed, almost insolent in its refusal to address the challenge (so, Rieman). Vv. 10-12 must then be understood as a formal accusation (cf. 3:11), which, by virtue of its legal quality, calls for some kind of response (see Boecker). The story, however, does not allow the Lord to wait for Cain's self-defense; it moves immediately from accusation to judgment (vv. 11-12). The judgment employs the same curse pattern as 3:14-17: "You are cursed" (*'ārûr 'āttâ*).

And the key term in the content of the curse is, again, "the ground" *(hā'ădāmâ)*. Indeed, one wonders whether the pattern intends a conscious reversal from 3:17: "Cursed is the ground because of you." "Cursed are you because of the ground" (note the causative connotation of the preposition *min* in 4:11). The sentence in v. 12 then spells out the details of the judgment. When Cain "tills" *(ta'ăbōd)* the ground, it will not give him its fare (cf. 3:18-19a). The meaning is plain, but it is also interpreted by v. 12b. Cain is alienated from the ground, and as a consequence he must be a fugitive and a wanderer, unable to establish relationships anywhere.

Cain responds in vv. 13-14 with a lamentation (cf. Westermann, *Genesis,* 421). The structure of the lamentation follows the pattern of the personal lament in the Psalter (see Westermann, *Genesis,* 421-23). The lamentation does not suggest that the judgment has been softened (contrast Westermann, *Genesis,* 389). To the contrary, it suggests that such life is worse than death: "My punishment is greater than I can bear." V. 14a describes the nature of that alienation: To be driven away "from the ground" *(mē'al pěnê hā'ădāmâ)* is to have all relationships, particularly with the family, broken (cf. 3:24 with the same verb). Moreover, it is to have one's relationship with the Lord broken (cf. 3:10). Life must be lived with various oppositions, but these oppositions spell death.

Vv. 14b-15 pick up the same theme. As a wanderer, Cain faces potential death at every hand. The mark of v. 15, a protection from such death, must then serve as a constant reminder of the opposition. As a protective device against potential enemies, it may stay death; in that sense, the anticipated punishment is softened. But at the same time it serves as a constant reminder of Cain's banishment, his isolation from other people. The story concludes with Cain's moving to the land of Nod, an ironic wordplay on his isolation.

The story belongs to J and represents a natural parallel to J's paradise tale (see Westermann, *Promises,* on the structure of sin and punishment stories). A varied history of the two-brothers tradition lies behind the tale (see Westermann, *Genesis,* 390). One might note especially the Egyptian story of Seth and Osiris as an element in the background of this tale.

Formulas and stereotyped expressions include a speech formula in vv. 6, 8, 9, 10, 13, 15 (→ 1:1–2:4a); an accusation in vv. 6, 10 (→ 2:4b–3:24); and a curse in v. 11 (→ 2:4b–3:24).

Genre

Various characteristics of TALE dominate the development of plot in this narrative. (1) There are only three acting principals, with only two involved in any given event. This point is clear in all three elements of the middle section in the unit. The sacrifices engage Yahweh with Abel or Yahweh with Cain but not Yahweh with both Cain and Abel. Yahweh's accusation in vv. 6-7 confronts Cain without reference to Abel. Indeed, the weight of the accusation in the whole element reduces Abel to a supporting role—he is not a principal in the scene at all. In the middle element, the narrative involves a Cain-Abel opposition, even though Abel remains passive. The final element sets Cain in opposition to Yahweh. (2) The plot is simple. No digressions disturb the structure to suggest a complex tradition history or a shift in genre.

The tale is, moreover, a part of the primeval SAGA (see Westermann, *Gen-*

esis, 432). It does not suffice, then, to designate the genre as an ethnological tale, an account of the beginning of particular tribes or basic professions. There is, of course, reference to the origin of professions—the one brother is a farmer, the other a shepherd—but the reference is incidental. The perspective of the tale is universal. The story describes a primal event, like the one in 2:4b–3:24. And the primal event depicts the fate of all subsequent creation, not in terms of tribes or unions, but in terms of individuals. Each faces a threat of becoming a wanderer and a fugitive.

Setting

The tale of the two brothers belongs to the larger complex of J's narrative and, as a part of the primeval saga J prefixed to the patriarchs, demands consideration as an element of literature from the ancient world. That the tale derives from oral tradition is doubtlessly true, but where the oral stage of the tradition might have been preserved can be fixed only by assumptions. It is reasonable to assume that this tale, like the one reporting the struggle of Jacob and Esau, circulated primarily in the "family" as family tradition. If this guess has any weight, it would be necessary immediately to say that the "family" here refers to a larger societal complex than father-mother-children. And it is in such large complexes that struggles for power appear (→ 2:4b–3:24). One must consider seriously the importance of the family, in both its narrower definition and its broader contexts, for the preservation and, indeed, the formation of narrative tradition. This comment applies not only for the family saga (→ Genesis 12–25; 26–50), but also for items in the primeval saga, or, indeed, for the entire primeval saga (→ The Primeval Saga).

Intention

The tale narrates an event of the primeval period, as a parallel to the paradise tale but not as a simple extension of it, in order to show that the break in human society from primeval times forward involves not only husband-wife but also brother-brother relationships. Moreover, it establishes a parallel contact with the tower tale. The break thus involves not only brother-brother, but peoples as well. Human creatures live in strife and instability, a style of life that brings about violence and dissolution of relationships.

Bibliography

H. J. Boecker, *Redeformen des Rechtslebens im Alten Testament* (WMANT 14; Neukirchen-Vluyn: Neukirchener Verlag, 1964); H. Heyde, *Kain, der erste Jahwe-Verehrer. Die ursprüngliche Bedeutung der Saga von Kain und ihre Auswirkungen in Israel* (AzT 1/23; Stuttgart: Calwer, 1965); S. Levin, "The More Savory Offering: A Key to the Problem of Gen 4:3-5," *JBL* 98 (1979) 85; J. M. Miller, "The Descendants of Cain: Notes on Genesis 4," *ZAW* 86 (1974) 164-74; A. Olrik, "Epic Laws of Folk Narrative" (tr. J. P. Steager and A. Dundes), in *The Study of Folklore* (ed. A. Dundes; Englewood Cliffs: Prentice Hall, 1965) 129-41; P. Rieman, "Am I My Brother's Keeper?" *Int* 24 (1970) 482-91; W. Zimmerli, "Zur Exegese von Genesis 4:1-16," *Der evangelische Erzieher* 20 (1968) 200-3.

SONG OF LAMECH, 4:23-24

Structure

I. Speech formula	23aα
II. Song	23aβb-24
A. Call to attention	23aβ
B. Boast	23b
C. Vengeance formula	24

This very early poem derives its context from the genealogy that precedes it (→ 4:1-26). Indeed, it has now been incorporated as a part of the final entry in the genealogy, not only by the common subject, Lamech, but also by the address to the two wives (cf. v. 19). Nevertheless, the context is rough and shows clearly that the poem has been introduced secondarily into the final stage of the genealogy: (1) The poem is introduced by a speech formula in contrast to the style of enumeration that dominates the genealogy. (2) The poetic structure of the poem stands out against the enumeration of the genealogy (see Gevirtz).

The poem itself comprises three lines, each developed with a marked parallelism. The first line is a call to attention (→ Isa 32:9), with strictly synonymous parallelism. Constructed on the basis of a 2:2:2:2 meter, the line names the wives, then calls them to hear the words of the singer. The second line is a boast of strength used against an enemy in greater degree than the enemy's provocation, the parallelism again strictly synonymous, although not in the same meter. The third line is more difficult to analyze, although it is marked by paronomasia. Like line two, this element begins with *kî*, but the *kî* is redundant in the third line and suggests that the line may be a secondary expansion. To support this suggestion one might note that the line breaks the pattern established in v. 23 by using a synthetic parallel (see Westermann, *Genesis,* 454-55, who observes that without the context, the third line could be read as prose). If the third line should be taken as an expansion of the basic poem, its function would be to tie the poem to its context in the genealogy already equipped with the tale of the two brothers, for the entire line is an allusion to 4:15.

In its genealogical context, the poem belongs to the Yahwist. The poem is nonetheless earlier than J and reflects life among the folk as a piece of popular poetry. Indeed, it seems inappropriate to tie this poem directly to any one of the several pentateuchal sources. It is more likely that this early piece represents one of the sources for J, and that in its structure it preserves a kernel of folk tradition. Moreover, the parallel with Isa 32:9 suggests that a typical formulation for a call to attention serves the structure of this poem, a line not dependent on a common tradition history but formulated, nevertheless, out of a common function.

Genre

In J, the poem is a part of the GENEALOGY for Lamech. It thus functions as genealogical information, just as 4:17b or, for that matter, the tale of the two brothers. Apart from J, the poem may be categorized as a boasting SONG (not a [→] taunt).

Setting

J uses the song as the conclusion of the genealogy. Its setting in the literature cannot be overemphasized (→ 4:1-26). As a boasting song, the poem belongs to the social transactions of the people. It is the work a victor might display to his brace of women (see Westermann, *Genesis,* 454-57). The contact of such a poem with the family would be obvious, but the contact might also assume a situation of threat to which the head of the family must respond.

Intention

For J, the poem closes the genealogy, including the tale of the two brothers. Its reference to the vengeance associated with Cain shows a reason for its inclusion in this context, but it also shows mounting violence as a characteristic of human culture. This negative pole outweighs the positive signs of culture's progress, such as the origin of music on the lyre and pipe or the origin of economic systems such as farming and herding. The double stamp on human society demonstrates a field of tension as the native habitat for human beings. For the poem taken by itself, boasting rises to center stage. It is a boast that already contains the violence depicted in J. But the function of the boast ties to the call to attention; it is a demonstration of strength for the benefit of the women.

Bibliography

S. Gevirtz, *Patterns in the Early Poetry of Israel* (Studies in Ancient Oriental Civilizations 32; Chicago: University of Chicago Press, 1963) 25-34.

TRANSITION, 4:25-26

Structure

I. First generation: Adam   25
   A. Birth report: Seth
   B. Saying
II. Second generation: Seth   26
   A. Birth report: Enosh
   B. Event in world history

This small unit features a genealogy constructed from only two generations. In its present form, this unit assumes a relationship with the genealogy in 4:1-24, as the particle "again" (*'ôd*) makes quite clear. Moreover, the explanation for the name in v. 25b alludes to the tale of the two brothers and again demonstrates the relationship. This genealogy is not, however, a continuation or even a parallel to the preceding genealogy, nor a part of the following one, although it does parallel the latter. It is an independent unit. If it was originally a part of a longer genealogy that extended to Noah (cf. 5:1-29), the list can no longer be reconstructed as it was. It must now be evaluated for itself. As an originally independent piece, it has been adapted for its position here as a bridge to the priestly genealogy in ch. 5. It shows how one can explain the contradiction between the Adam genealogy that makes no reference to Cain and the J context that includes Cain. The unit must, then, be defined as Rjp.

The structure in the unit unfolds in terms of the two successive generations.

The first stage, v. 25, reports the birth of a son, followed by a naming etiology (see Long). The etiology reports first the act of naming, with a typical verb, "call" *(qārā': wattiqrā')*, followed by a designation of the name. In contrast to v. 26, the naming formula here employs a feminine verb. The second part of the entry (v. 25b) begins with a *kî* and offers a foundation for the name in the development of the sentence. The foundation derives from paronomasia (the name, *šēt*, plays on the verb in v. 25b, *šāt*). In its present form, the foundation is clearly secondary to the tale of the two brothers. An earlier form might have developed an explanation of the name from an independent sentence (see Westermann, *Genesis*, 459). The second entry (v. 2b) has a naming formula but no etiology. Rather, v. 26a provides the genealogical context for v. 26b, information about the advance of culture (→ 4:1-24). There is no structural explanation for the introduction of the name Yahweh here, perhaps in contradiction to Exodus 3 (see Westermann, *Genesis*, 460-63).

Genre

The unit is a linear GENEALOGY, the type associated typically with primeval history. Moreover, it includes a naming ETIOLOGY. It is typical for the genre to include items of information such as v. 26b.

Setting

In its present form, the unit has a setting in the redaction process that joined J and P. Such genealogies in the folk tradition derive from the interests of the family to preserve the heritage, both in terms of family or tribal origins and by reference to particular items of information associated with the generations.

Intention

The unit bridges the genealogy in 4:1-24, including the tale of the two brothers and its corresponding Cain entry in the genealogy, with the genealogy in 5:1-32, a genealogy that follows a Seth line.

Bibliography

B. O. Long, *The Problem of Etiological Narrative in the Old Testament* (BZAW 108; Berlin: Töpelmann, 1968); R. R. Wilson, *Genealogy and History in the Biblical World* (New Haven: Yale University Press, 1977).

ADAM GENEALOGY (P), 5:1– 9:29

Structure

I. Introduction	5:1-2
A. Formula	1a
B. Creation report	1b-2
II. Generations	5:3–9:29
A. First generation: Adam	5:3-5
1. Birth report: Seth	3
2. Length of life after birth	4
3. Death report	5
B. Second generation: Seth	6-8

1. Birth report: Enosh	6
2. Length of life after birth	7
3. Death report	8
C. Third generation: Enosh	9-11
1. Birth report: Kenan	9
2. Length of life after birth	10
3. Death report	11
D. Fourth generation: Kenan	12-14
1. Birth report: Mahalalel	12
2. Length of life after birth	13
3. Death report	14
E. Fifth generation: Mahalalel	15-17
1. Birth report: Jared	15
2. Length of life after birth	16
3. Death report	17
F. Sixth generation: Jared	18-20
1. Birth report: Enoch	18
2. Length of life after birth	19
3. Death report	20
G. Seventh generation: Enoch	21-24
1. Birth report: Methuselah	21
2. Length of life after birth	22
3. Death report	23-24
H. Eighth generation: Methuselah	25-27
1. Birth report: Lamech	25
2. Length of life after birth	26
3. Death report	27
I. Ninth generation: Lamech	28-31
1. Birth report: Noah	28-29
a. Birth	28
b. Prophecy	29
2. Length of life after birth	30
3. Death report	31
J. Tenth generation: Noah	5:32–9:29
1. Birth report: Shem, Ham, Japheth	5:32
2. Noah tradition	6:1–9:27
3. Length of life after flood	9:28
4. Death report	9:29

The context for this genealogy (P) parallels the context for the Yahwistic genealogy in 4:1-24. 4:25-26 is a secondary link between the two genealogies designed to smooth contradictions. Further significance of the final form of the text, however, cannot be determined from the structure. For both genealogies, then, the context is the creation report of 1:1–2:4a.

The genealogy opens with an introduction (vv. 1-2) composed of a *toledoth* formula ("This is the book of the generations of Adam") and an allusion to 1:26-27. The formula connects with similar constructions in 6:9; 10:1; 11:10, 27; 25:12, 19; 36:1, 9; 37:2 (see also Num 3:1; Ruth 4:18). The other formulas follow

70

a stereotyped pattern, connecting the noun "generations" *(tôlĕdōt)* to a demonstrative pronoun, "these" *('ēlleh)*, and defining it more precisely by a construct bond with a proper noun: "These are the generations of Noah." In this case the stereotype is broken by the addition of the noun "book" *(sēper)* constructed with a singular demonstrative: "This is the book of the generations of Adam." This distinct form suggests that this verse functions as the head of a series of formulas and that the series functions together as a key for organizing the material in the book of Genesis. It gives a sense of progression in the order of events as well as continuity for the total period. The function of continuity is also highlighted by 2:4a, a preface to the series that connects immediately with 5:1.

It is, however, too much to take 5:1 as a superscription to a book containing the *toledoth* material. The series functions to give structure for narrative through its enumeration. The "book" of the generations of Adam would be the narrative embraced by the formula (see also the itinerary chain in the wilderness theme; → Numbers 33). Vv. 1b-2 begin like the traditional opening of a creation narrative (→ 2:4b-7), and the selection of vocabulary recalls Genesis 1. If the pattern were followed, the main clause in v. 2b would suggest that the point of this allusion is to emphasize the blessing on Adam (along with the naming). What could be a better introduction for a genealogy from P than a blessing, recalling the commission in 1:28 to fill the earth?

The entries in the genealogy follow a regular pattern over the course of ten generations. The pattern comprises three parts: (1) a birth report, accompanied by the age of the father, (2) a notice of the years of life for the father following the report, and (3) a death report. The death report regularly notes the total number of years in the entry's life and the fact of his death. The variations from this regular structure are: (a) In the first panel, Seth's relationship with Adam is described in the same terms as those used for Adam's relationship with God in 1:26 (see also 5:1). The father-son relationship here clearly intends setting the life (and the narratives) of the human creature in relationship to God. (b) In the seventh panel, the middle element changes its verb from "lived" *(wayĕḥî)* to "walked with God" *(wayyithallēk . . . 'et-hā'ĕlōhîm)*. And the final element reports the total years of the entry's life, plus a unique note: "Enoch walked with God, and he was not *[wĕ'ênennû],* for God took him." Although this peculiarity may belong to a distinct Enoch tradition, no further details can be reconstructed. (c) The next break in the pattern comes in the ninth panel. V. 29 is constructed as a naming etiology, with v. 29a the naming formula, v. 29b the play on the name in a saying. The verse, however, alludes to 3:17-18 and shows the development of the panel as a part of the larger picture of the Pentateuch (see Westermann, *Genesis,* 487-88). (d) The final break in the regular construction of the genealogical entries comes in the tenth panel, the generation of Noah. V. 32 contains a report of the birth of Noah's sons. That the entry reports three sons rather than one already differs from the other nine panels and suggests that some unusual focus resides here. Indeed, the break in the ninth panel places similar focus on Noah. Yet, v. 32 contains only a birth report. It thus appears to be, in itself, incomplete. The open character of the entry suggests, however, not that some portion of the text has been lost or restructured in a different place, but that the entry intentionally builds a bridge around the following narratives in order to include them within the scope of the genealogy. The tenth generation, then, extends from 5:32 through 9:29. This extension is accomplished first by 9:18-19, a genealogical expansion of 5:32. Indeed, 9:19 contains information typical for the structure of a genealogy. Moreover, the impact of the extension is to include the entire flood story, 6:1–9:17, as a part of the genealogical information. In keeping with this function, 5:32 and 9:18-19 emphasize the three sons of Noah, and 9:19 picks up the motif of repopulation for the world (→ 10:32). The verses thus clearly frame the flood story and provide a connecting frame for 9:20-27 as well (for a somewhat different view, see Westermann, *Genesis*, 645-46).

But the tenth generation does not end with 9:18-19. These verses only expand what already was reported by 5:32. The end of the tenth generation comes in 9:28-29 with a notation of the life of Noah after the flood. This note provides a key to the peculiar function of the unit. Then a death report, including a summary statement of Noah's total life span, rounds off the panel. This conclusion to the tenth generation functions not as an epilogue to the flood story, but as the conclusion for the genealogy. One may conclude, then, that P employs genealogical tradition as a framework for narrative, just as in the tale of the two brothers J used genealogical tradition as a context for narrative.

Antecedents in a tradition history for this unit are difficult to establish. The J genealogy in ch. 4 seems to be parallel (see Westermann, *Genesis*, 472-73). Whether the structure in a ten-generation scheme in the Babylonian king list, with very long reigns for the kings before the flood, represents an antecedent for this text is at the moment uncertain (see Malamat).

Formulas and stereotyped expressions appear as basic building components for genealogies. Of particular importance are the formulaic structures of all three principal elements: birth report, statement of age, and death report.

Genre

This list is a linear GENEALOGY for the primeval period (→ 4:1-26). Whether the unit can be associated generically with the Babylonian king list remains uncertain.

Setting

In its present form, the genealogy has a setting in the literary and theological structure of P. There is no evidence of a political setting (contrast the Babylonian king list). Earlier levels are difficult to determine, particularly in the form of a primeval genealogy. Genealogy in its linear construct derives from tribal or family groups.

Intention

P connects the genealogy with the creation report, setting all that the genealogy embraces under the stamp of God's act in creation. The connection also suggests that the flood and all subsequent events in human history stand under the creation opening, indeed, under the blessing to fill the earth. As a literary device, the genealogy serves as a redactional framework for narrative tradition and even for larger sections of narrative material such as the flood tale.

Bibliography

M. Barnouin, "Recherches numériques sur la généalogie de Gen V," *RB* 77 (1970) 347-65; R. Borchert, "Stil und Aufbau der priesterlichen Erzählung" (Diss., Heidelberg, 1957);

W. W. Hallo, "Beginning and End of the Sumerian King List in the Nippur Recension," *JCS* 17 (1963) 52-57; T. C. Hartman, "Some Thoughts on the Sumerian King List and Genesis 5 and 11b," *JBL* 91 (1972) 25-32; M. D. Johnson, *The Purpose of the Biblical Genealogies with Special Reference to the Setting of the Genealogies of Jesus* (SNTSMS 8; Cambridge: Cambridge University Press, 1969); A. Malamat, "King Lists of the Old Babylonian Period and Biblical Genealogies," *JAOS* 83 (1968) 163-73; R. R. Wilson, *Genealogy and History in the Biblical World* (New Haven: Yale University Press, 1977).

FLOOD TALE, 6:1 – 9:19

Structure

I. Exposition (myth of the giants)	6:1-4
II. Judgment	6:5-8
A. Divine perception	5-6
1. God's act	5
2. Valuation	6
B. Sentence speech	7
C. Noah's favor	8
III. Exposition	6:9-11
A. *Toledoth* formula	9aα
B. Noah's favor	9aβb-10
1. Righteousness	9aβb
2. Son list	10
C. Condition of the earth	11
IV. Judgment	6:12–7:24
A. Divine perception	6:12
B. Sentence speech	6:13-21
1. Sentence	13
2. Instructions for building the ark	14-16
3. Sentence	17
4. Noah's favor	18-21
a. Covenant	18a
b. Instructions for survival	18b-21
C. Execution of instructions	6:22
D. Sentence speech	7:1-4
1. Instructions for survival	1-3
a. Family	1
b. Living creatures	2-3
2. Sentence	4
E. Execution of instructions	5-24
1. General introduction	5
2. Survival	6-16
a. First panel	6-10
1) Age of Noah	6
2) Survival	7-9
a) Family	7
b) Living creatures	8-9
3) Flood report	10

The context for the flood story is established explicitly by the genealogy in ch. 5. The tenth generation in the structure of that genealogy is open and embraces the Noah tradition (→ 5:1–9:29). The flood event thus counts as one of several in a series of events embraced by the genealogy.

The flood narrative itself unfolds as a circle. It opens with an announcement of God's decision to destroy life on the earth and ends with a commitment to maintain the stability of the earth for the sake of life. Moreover, the narrative pattern is tied closely to the traditions of creation. Here the point of tension arises from the nature of God's central act. He created the world, but what happens when the human creature falls and thus breaks the intimacy of the created order? If God punishes, can humanity survive?

In its present form, the flood story does not appear to be very well unified (contrast Anderson). This point emerges most clearly in the beginning of the story by comparison of doublets in the functional structure of the pericope. An exposition in 6:9-11—with an introduction of Noah as a righteous man (note the nominal sentence order) and the father of three sons, and a description of conditions on the earth—parallels an exposition in 6:1-4, which describes the conditions on the earth. In both cases, the exposition is set off from two elements of a second movement, each introduced in the same manner: In 6:5, "the Lord saw . . ." *(wayyar' yahweh kî . . .)*, and in 6:12, "God saw . . ." *(wayyar' 'ĕlōhîm 'et . . .)*. The substance of the second movement is identical in both 6:5-6 and 6:12–7:24: (1) a description of the state of the earth as God saw it, and (2) a speech with God's judgment against the earth because of its corruption. This movement is distinct from the exposition by virtue of its function in setting out the crisis of the plot: God intends to destroy the world; how can humanity survive (cf. the Babylonian flood traditions, the struggle between Ea and Enlil)? It is interesting that one parallel introduces the righteous Noah as a part of the exposition, the other as a postlude to the crisis (cf. 6:8). The redundancy continues in the remaining elements of the unit, although the functional parts are not set out so clearly in parallel to each other. Rather, they tend to intertwine. The speech in 6:13-21 and the execution of instructions in 6:22 stand parallel to the speech in 7:1-4. But the execution of instructions in 7:5-24 clearly combines the parallel elements (see 7:6-10 and 11-16). The flood itself (7:17-23) reveals doublets (see vv. 17 and 18). The re-creation of the earth, certainly the goal of the narrative, doubles back on itself (8:1-7 par. 8:8-12). Perhaps most important, the conclusion in 8:21-22 is paralleled in the key section, 9:1-17. The most obvious purpose in the redundant structure is the preservation of the parallel lines (see von Rad, *Genesis,* 119; contrast Anderson). It is thus necessary to establish basic observations about structure and genre on the parallels rather than on the combined text.

The structure of P's flood tale is as follows:

I. Exposition	6:9-11
A. *Toledoth* formula	9aα
B. Righteous Noah	9aβb-10
C. Corrupt and violent earth	11
II. Judgment	6:12-21
A. Divine perception	12

The context for P's version of the flood derives from the genealogy in ch. 5, and particularly from the tenth entry in the genealogy which embraces the flood tradition. If 9:18-19 belongs to J, then the natural frame for P's flood story would be 5:32 with 9:28-29, the elements of the genealogy panel. A problem appears, however, in P's exposition, 6:9. (1) The opening formula from the *toledoth* series, "these are the generations of Noah," can be used for the beginning of a genealogy (→ 5:1–9:29). The formula appears again with a genealogy in 10:1 and 11:10. Yet, the formula should not simply be taken as the opening clause for a genealogy, as a standard genre element (contrast McEvenue, 37-41). This point is clear from the use of the formula in 37:1 with a major narrative following. Indeed, that the formula appears with different kinds of genealogies (cf. 5:1; 10:1) would suggest already that its function cannot tie the formula to one particular genre (see McEvenue, 38 n. 28). It functions rather as a floating rubric available for various positions (cf. 2:4a). (2) V. 10 could be taken as a continuation of the genealogical frame (see McEvenue), thus doubling 5:32. The parallel function of the note, however, does not appear in 9:28-29 with the completion of the genealogical frame, but rather in 9:18-19 (see the comments below on 9:18-19).

The narrative itself unfolds in four principal parts. The exposition (6:9-11) and the conclusion (9:18-19) frame an element of judgment and destruction contrasted with an element of re-creation and renewal of commitment.

The exposition not only introduces the principal characters in this drama, Noah and God (v. 9b), but with v. 11 sets out a basic structural opposition that characterizes the entire story: righteous Noah:corrupt and violent earth. The redundancy between v. 11 and 12 must then be interpreted in terms of structural function, not simply in terms of content correspondence (contrast McEvenue, 28-29, who picks up a functional element on p. 32). The same opposition appears, with its elements reversed, in the body of the unit: destruction of the corrupt and violent earth through the judgment of God: re-creation of the earth with the righteous Noah. Moreover, in such an exposition v. 10 has a crucial role to play. The three sons, though crucial for the structure of the subsequent unit in P (→ 10:1-32), play at best a subordinate role in the flood story (7:13) and appear generally as an extension of the principal character. "Noah and his sons" is by far the most common designation (so, 6:18). For the exposition, however, v. 10 stands alone, not subordinated to any other part of the opening. The sons are the fruit of the righteous man's seed.

The significance of the exposition comes to light in the conclusion, 9:18-19. In both exposition and conclusion, but at no point in the body of the story, references to the sons come sharply to the fore in a stereotyped combination of names: "Shem, Ham, and Japheth" (cf. 7:13). Two conclusions about structure derive from this observation: (1) The exposition, 6:10, and the conclusion, 9:18-19, constitute an inclusion for P's account of the flood, similar to the inclusion in P's account of the creation. This point seems valid even if 9:18-19 should be considered finally a part of an older story (see von Rad, *Genesis*), for the verses clearly anticipate the story in 9:20-27. As an anticipation, they have a redactional function, presupposing not simply the J story in 9:20-27 but the organization of the Noah traditions generally, including 9:20-27. Moreover, as a key to the organization of the Noah traditions, these verses would relate not only to the P exposition in 9:10, but also to the genealogy in 5:32. (2) As the conclusion for the P flood story, these verses participate in the opposition structure characteristic for 6:9, 11: righteous man with three sons: three sons from the ark. For P, the plan of the story, foreshadowed by 6:10 and even more directly by 6:18, comes to fruition in the repopulation of the world through Shem, Ham, and Japheth.

The first major narrative unit opens with a statement of God's perception that the earth was corrupt. This assertion is more than a general introduction to the element, however. It functions as the basis for the judgment oracle in the following speech. This function is also established by the speech in v. 13. The first part of the speech announces the divine judgment twice (vv. 13aα, 13b), with a causal *(kî)* clause between them stating the reason for the judgment (v. 13aβ). The speech loses its character as judgment, however, when it continues with instructions for building the ark, vv. 14-16. The same pattern appears again, with v. 17 an announcement of judgment against all life and vv. 18-21 instructions for survival. The instructions for survival begin, significantly, with an allusion to the covenant, a device that ties this positive statement in the first narrative element with the survival of Noah and his descendants in the second (cf. 9:8-9). Moreover, it continues with a stereotyped list of survivors (6:18b-19). And the list recurs at key points in the developing narrative (on the list, see McEvenue, 47-50). Thus, the same opposition noted in the exposition appears here: corrupt earth: Noah and his family in the ark. Indeed, the opposition here already foreshadows the conclusion in P by reference to the covenant (v. 18). The opposite side of divine destruction is divine commitment (9:1-17).

The structural exchange between command and execution, so typical for OT narrative (see Genesis 1), surfaces in the completion of this element. The formulaic reference to execution in 7:5, 9 must be so common in Hebrew narrative that observations about peculiarity in P's style of narration cannot rest adequately on it (but see McEvenue, 33). 6:22 and 7:11-21 execute the judgment and instructions in 6:13-21. 6:22 is a general statement of completion, although it is attached directly to the Noah-God relationship. 7:11-21 follows the structure of the judgment speech in 6:13-21 with a report in narration about the flood (7:11), survival of the flood (7:12-16), and the death that came from it (7:18-21). The parallel could be described as ABAC:ACA. But the judgment execution is set off from the speech by the date in v. 11, and the date in itself highlights vv. 11-21 as a high point in the unit, parallel with the date in 8:13 where the second high point appears. (On the dates in P, see McEvenue, 54-59.)

The second major body of the narrative describes God's response to the tragedy. The opening of this element (8:1a) grounds God's re-creation in his act of remembering Noah (no reference to the sons or the women). The allusion to the covenant in 6:18, contrary to the detailed description of the event in 9:8-17, also addresses Noah. Remembering is not covenantal in this instance, however, since the covenant is established at the conclusion of the pericope. It is only personal, sparked by God's relationship to the righteous man. Following the motivation, the narrative describes God's act of (re-)creation. Without use of speeches, the description builds on a division between the waters and the emerging and drying ground. Vv. 1b-3a establish the initial separation, vv. 3b-5 the date of the separation, vv. 6-14* confirmation of the new creation as life supporting. The style of narration changes in vv. 15-19—speech is again a key structural element. With the change, the narrative comes to its focus: the emergence of the living creatures, both human and subhuman, from the ark. In comparison with Genesis 1, only the last stage of re-creation involves a command-execution pattern. The detailed description of the execution in 8:18-19 is clearly a part of the execution of the command (but cf. Genesis 1).

9:1-17 completes the re-creation section. As in the initial act of creation (1:28), so here God blesses the new human community. The blessing appears in vv. 1 and 7 as a frame for the element. The basic content is like 1:28: "Be fruitful and multiply and fill the earth." The reference to subduing the earth and having dominion over the subhuman creatures is not paralleled here in the same words, but 9:2 must represent an extension of that clause. Indeed, the presentation of the animals as food here in explicit contrast to the food stipulation in 1:29 suggests that the parallel is an interpretative basis at least at the hands of P if not earlier in the tradition (cf. also 9:6). Moreover, the blessing is completed by the prohibitions against eating meat with blood. Vv. 5b-6 extend the prohibition against blood in meat to a prohibition of blood vengeance. V. 5b is a statement of capital punishment for murder. The executor is God, however, not the man's brother. V. 6 then builds on a parallel couplet to establish an irony. Literally, the couplet reads: "The shedder *[šōpēk]* of the blood of man *[dam hā'ādām]*, by man *[bā'ādām]* his blood will be shed *[dāmô yiššāpēk]*." The one who sheds the blood of a man will have his blood shed by a man; that is blood vengence. But the man who executes the killer becomes himself a shedder of blood, thus creating a tragic chain. The answer to the chain is to leave the life and death of each man to God (v. 5b). The motivation for this irony lies in the affirmation that God made the man in his own image (cf. 1:27), and as a consequence of the image his life belongs to God.

The final section of the narrative, 9:8-17, is perhaps the most important, for here the text describes God's covenant with his creatures, a natural continuation of the blessing. Like the blessing, the element develops within an inclusion (see vv. 9, 17). It features a series of speeches, each with its own distinctive weight. The first speech, vv. 9-11, announces the covenant in two parallel lines: the first names the recipients, the second the content of the covenant. One must note here the structural parallel with the first movements of P's text, not only in terms of establishing the covenant (see 6:18), but also in contrast to the plan to destroy all flesh (see 6:13, particularly "all flesh" *[kol-bāśār]*, in contrast to 9:11, particularly "all flesh" *[kol-bāśār]*; on the inclusion, see McEvenue, 46). The second speech, vv. 12-16, names the sign of the covenant, the rainbow, and defines its function as a guarantee that God would remember (contrast 8:1) the commitment of the covenant (v. 11). The final speech, v. 17, summarizes the sign announcement.

One may ask here concerning the nature of the covenant: Does God not commit himself unconditionally to the terms of the covenant? Is this commitment not at the basis of the term "everlasting covenant" *(běrît 'ôlām)*? The divine commitment is not that punishment for capital crimes would be dropped, but that total destruction, a return of chaos, would never again occur. Yet, the connection with the blessing, vv. 1-7, must be considered. At least a part of the commitment central to this final element in the flood story is the prohibition concerning blood, both in animals and in the brother. Is that prohibition not explicitly the content of the covenant established between God and "every living creature of all flesh that is upon the earth"? The prohibition is rooted in the blessing, however, not in the covenant. Although the two are connected, the covenant itself maintains its character as God's act, sealed by God's sign. In that case, it parallels the covenant as oath in Genesis 17.

It is clear, moreover, that this presentation of covenant serves P as a central crux for the primeval history. The structure does not develop its point of tension into a story or plot; there is no developed arc of tension here. Rather, in systematic display of corrupt earth : righteous Noah; re-created earth : covenant, the unit moves through any possible story to its emphasis on the final measure. That emphasis carries not only the flood unit, but also the entire priestly primeval saga (→ Genesis 1–11).

In comparison, the structure of J's flood tale is as follows:

I. Exposition	6:1-4
II. Judgment	6:5-8; 7:1-4
A. Judgment	6:5-7
1. Divine perception: "The Lord saw . . ."	5-6
2. Sentence speech	7
B. Instructions for survival	6:8; 7:1-4
1. Noah's favor	6:8
2. Oracle	7:1-4
a. Instructions for survival	1-3
b. Judgment	4
C. Execution	7:5-24*
1. Noah	5
2. Survival	6-10*, 16b
3. Report of the flood	17b, 22-24
III. Renewal	8:1-22*

A. End of the flood   2b
B. Dry earth test   6, 8-12, 13b
C. Commitments   20-22

The context for J's account of the flood is established by the genealogy of 4:1-24 and its completion in the P genealogy of Genesis 5. The significance of the larger context, Genesis 4 and 5, appears not only in the form of the received text, but also in the J fragment of 5:29. The genealogical framework is thus not the result of simple historical interest in the line of generations from Adam, but rather a structure designed explicitly for display of context in the narrative units. The genealogy of ch. 4 places special emphasis on the generation of Lamech (→ 4:1-26). With the unit in ch. 4, however, the relevance of such emphasis is not apparent. With 5:29, that relevance becomes clear. The son of Lamech is Noah, and Lamech's birth saying, an etiology built on assonance with the verb in the following saying, sets the context for the flood. Moreover, the etiology foreshadows 8:21-22.

For J, the structure of the unit comprises two principal elements, introduced by an exposition. The exposition has no parallel here in a framing conclusion. Indeed, the exposition may be understood as an originally distinct story in itself (→ 6:1-4). The element preserves vestiges of a plot line built, like 4:1-16 or 11:1-9, on the scheme of a violation-punishment arc. But the plot has now been broken by the disjunction between vv. 3 and 4 (see Westermann, *Genesis*). Indeed, the punishment announced in v. 3 has relatively little to do with the violation in vv. 1-2. It appears more as a description of normal experience for human beings than as punishment for either the "sons of God" or the "daughters of men." Moreover, the description leaves v. 4 hanging. The last part of v. 4a makes an explicit effort to tie the information given in v. 4 to the event in vv. 1-2 and gives witness thereby to the disjunction. In its present form (J), then, 6:1-4 is no longer a story but only a description, and as description, it doubles as exposition for the J flood narrative (see v. 11 in P).

The conclusion builds a framing parallel more directly with 6:5-7, the first part of the first major narrative element (on the parallel, see the comments below). Vv. 5-6 relate to v. 7 as an indictment relates to a sentence (cf. also P, 6:12-13). The first part of the divine indictment, v. 5, is external, objective. "The Lord saw . . ." (cf. also P). Moreover, what God saw is total disruption in the human community: "The wickedness of man was great. . . . Every imagination of the thoughts of his heart was only evil continually *[kol-yēṣer maḥšĕbōt libbô raq ra' kol-hayyôm]*." The disruption, certainly prefigured in the judgment against Adam and Cain, leads in v. 6 to an internal, subjective response. But the response reflects a central pillar for J: "The Lord was sorry that he had made man . . . and it grieved him to his heart." The judgment is then in v. 7, a speech: All must die (cf. 6:13, P). The sentence formulates its dire judgment in reference to the ground: "I will blot out man whom I have created from the face of the ground *[pĕnê-hā'ǎdāmâ]*." The formulation thus echoes 3:23 and 4:11-12.

In contrast to the wickedness of human society, 6:8 sounds a note of hope: Noah found favor. It is striking that Noah appears for the first time at a relatively late point in the development of J's story. The nature of his favor before God is not spelled out in detail. Indeed, there is no moral quality noted to set Noah on such a plane. He simply found favor, and the favor sets Noah over against the people who grieved God to his heart. It may be that between 6:8 and 7:1-5 some description of instructions to build an ark appeared, along with some notation that Noah did it. The speech in 7:1-4 would assume some awareness of an ark present for Noah's use (perhaps assumed simply by the traditional association between the hero of the story and a boat). But it also shifts the designation of relationship between Noah and God. In 7:1, Noah has more than favor before God—he is now righteous *(ṣaddîq)*. (Cf. 6:9, P.) Since "righteous" describes a state derived from a relationship, not a standing quality, one might think that Noah had shown himself to be righteous by obeying instructions to build the ark. In any case, for J the subtle introduction of Noah moves to an explicit speech of God with instructions for survival (cf. 6:19-21, P). Vv. 6-10, 16b then report in detail what v. 5 reports in general. The instructions were carried out as Yahweh gave them, and Yahweh himself brings them to a conclusion (v. 16b). Vv. 17b, 22-23 draw the tragic conclusion for the element.

The second major element stands in opposition to the first: God destroyed all life except Noah: God re-creates life from Noah. The first part of this element describes the end of the flood, the drying of the earth. The details of this element reside basically in the exchange between Noah and the dove, a threefold probe to determine if the ground could support life. On three occasions Noah set a dove free. On the first, the dove returned. The conclusion: "The waters were still on the face of the whole earth *['al-pĕnê kol-hā'āreṣ]*." After seven days, the second occasion resulted in the return of the dove with a fresh olive leaf. The conclusion: "Noah knew that the waters had subsided from the earth *[mē'al hā'āreṣ]*." On the third occasion, he set the dove free, and it did not return. The conclusion here is confirmed by Noah's own probe: "Noah removed the covering of the ark and looked. And behold, the face of the ground *[pĕnê hā'ădāmâ]* was dry." The shift in terminology emphasizes the ground in the final phase. Thus, Noah establishes a relationship with the ground after the flood.

It is significant to note that the second major element in the story occurs without speech. This point also applies, in effect, to the conclusion, 8:20-22. Noah's first act is to build an altar and offer sacrifice (see the Gilgamesh Epic). These events are related to a description of Yahweh's response as a series of consecutive sentences: "Noah built an altar to Yahweh, and he took. . . , and he offered a sacrifice on the altar. And Yahweh smelled the pleasing smell and Yahweh said. . . ." The relationship is thus not explicitly causative, but it is clear that Noah's sacrifice is bound at least temporally to Yahweh's acts, and the acts constitute a response. Moreover, the response includes not only a description of Yahweh smelling, but also a divine soliloquy: "Yahweh said in his heart. . . ." The parallel with 6:6-7 is thus established.

The soliloquy, however, carries the parallel further. In v. 21, two promises to refrain from total destruction of the creation frame an allusion to 6:5. The promises focus on (1) the curse on the ground because of man *(lĕqallēl 'ôd 'et-hā'ădāmâ)* and (2) the destruction of all life *(kol-ḥay ka'ăšer 'āśîtî)*. The first alludes to the sentence in 6:6, if not also to 3:17-19 and 4:11. Its impact is to resolve the standing curse in terms of two promises: the human creatures will not be destroyed (6:6), and the ground will support them (3:17-19; 4:11; cf. also 5:29). The second confirms the first with a promise that God will never again destroy all of creation. These two promises are complemented by v. 22, for here the stability of human and subhuman life is tied to the stability of the seasons and times. Human creatures do not need further ritualistic guarantees for the stability of the world. The peculiar item in the structure of the unit, however, is the piece framed by the promises in v. 21: "For the imagination of man's heart is evil from his youth" *(kî yēṣer lēb hā'ādām ra' minnĕ'urāyw)*. The description obtains at the moment of the promise; the promise is given in spite of it. Moreover, its parallel 6:5 is clear. Even though God will not again do what he did, his human creatures are the same as they were before the flood. One should note that the story does not describe an increasing cacophony of sin, with the flood at its zenith. Rather, it describes a state of human life.

It is important to understand the structure of the J unit in terms of the two major elements that constitute its center. They do not develop as crisis–resolution of crisis (→ Genesis 37–50). Rather, they follow a different pattern, a contrasting complement (→ 2:4b–3:24). In this case, then, it is not quite adequate to inquire about the resolution of tension, or even the arc of tension that holds the plot of the narrative together. To be sure, one can find tensions: How will creation survive the flood? Will the creature be any different? But the answers to these questions do not move the story. They are clear virtually from the beginning (6:5-8). Rather, the structure is somewhat static, and as a consequence, its vitality appears elusive (see Petersen). The reason for this elusive character in the narrative lies at least in part in the structural center it carries for the whole J primeval saga (see Clark, "Flood"; Steck; Rendtorff), for here appears a resolution of a curse established in 3:17-19 (cf. also 5:29). Indeed, here is a foreshadowing of the consequences imposed on the human creatures in 11:1-9. The curse is removed, but for J the blessing is not yet established. What P affirms as central to human creation J holds in abeyance.

Antecedents to the J version are plentiful (see Westermann, *Genesis*); at least the Gilgamesh Epic and the Atrahasis Epic might be named. The J version differs from its counterparts in describing the flood and its consequences entirely in terms of the actions of Yahweh internalized, his reflection on the violence of man, and not in terms of struggles among the gods. Moreover, the event is set within the context of a genealogical scheme that embraces all of the primeval saga, as if to say these primeval events belong to the same history as the events of the patriarchal traditions.

In addition to several examples of narrative formulas common to the primeval saga (discussed above, → 1:1–2:4a; 2:4b–3:24), two new items deserve attention here. (1) A dating formula (7:11; 8:4, 5, 13, 14) attests an event by fixing the year, the month, and the day the event occurred: "In the six hundred and first year, in the first month, the first day of the month. . . ." If a renewed formula occurs in close proximity to the full designation of date, it might drop selected parts: "In the second month, on the twenty-seventh day of the month. . . ." (2) An age formula (7:6) establishes the statistic in relationship to a particular event of seminal importance for the subject's life. This element is related to the age formula in the genealogy, although in the narrative it plays a quite distinct role. In addition to these two formulaic items, one should note the importance of the stereotyped blessing, 9:1-2. Governed by the key verb *wayĕbārek* ("he blessed"), the blessing speech uses imperatives to establish the fertility of the recipient (→ 1:28).

Genre

Questions about genre must be answered on several different planes. (1) In the final form of the text, no conclusions need to be drawn. The level represents an artificial combination of two originally distinct accounts, the one perhaps aware of the other but not simply a revision of it.

(2) The priestly account of the flood is hardly a story. It is more nearly parallel to the priestly creation report (→ 1:1–2:4a), a vehicle for the presentation of priestly theology. Its systematic order, its failure to develop a point of tension that might serve as the basis of a plot, its structural focus on re-creation with blessing and covenant, place it as a part of a larger whole. Like its counterpart in 1:1–2:4a, this unit is a REPORT of the event for the sake of communicating theology.

(3) The Yahwist's version of the flood is less systematic than its counterpart in P. It stands more nearly in relationship to the paradise tale as a continuation of the larger story line rather than as an independent unit incorporated into a larger story. Even in its dependent role, however, some generic features suggest possibilities for definition. (a) Noah is first a man of favor before God, then righteous. (b) The other creatures are corrupt. Indeed, man remains rather static throughout the scope of the narration, as if the narration focused its structure on that negative virtue. Would these structural characteristics not suggest that the unit should properly be understood as (→) legend? Moreover, as legend, its loss of vitality in narrative style would be more understandable (cf. Petersen). Yet, the structure of the story does not carry the weight for an argument that the unit is legend. The story is not so much about righteous Noah or even about the evil people as it is about Noah's relationship (as the new man) with nature and, through that event, with God. Nature erupts; it cannot really be trusted. Will it not do that again? The conclusion in 8:21-22 bears this point out: God guarantees the order of nature. If humanity does not survive, it will not again be due to the orders of the created world. The two structural poles then suggest a parallel with 2:4b–3:24. Defining the genre as TALE does not necessitate a decision that the unit must have been originally independent. This tale and the tale of paradise function together.

(4) Even at earlier levels the flood tradition circulated in relationship to other tradition units (see the Atrahasis Epic). It might be appropriate to imagine that this example of the flood tradition is also rooted in a poetic epic. Moreover, it is also possible that the flood tradition derives from an originally independent poetic epic, but these possibilities remain hypothetical.

Setting

(1) For the final form of the text, as well as for P and J, the setting for the flood narrative is the literary or redactional work of the larger context (→ The Pentateuch/Hexateuch).

(2) The flood tradition, like the larger body of the primeval saga, belongs to that place in Israel's life that sought to communicate some sense of stability and rootage for the everyday, recurring world of Israel's experience. The close junction of interests between the cult and the royal court would come into consideration here. The peculiar form of Israel's primeval saga, however, suggests that the traditions have been taken out of the hands of the court-cult in a process of historicizing. Stability is not to be maintained by the recurring activities of

ritual or royal decree. It is to be remembered as an event at the beginning of this history.

Intention

(1) The flood narrative is the crux of the primeval saga. It accounts for the conditions that make life in subsequent periods possible, but also for the conditions that make life pleasant or tragic. Moreover, it separates subsequent periods of life from that distant, different period before the flood. This point applies for the final text as well as for P and J.

(2) In P, the focal intention is to show the introduction of God's covenant with human creatures, the reformation of his blessing despite the tragedy of the flood. The new period is laden with a portent of mixed quality. Human creatures may now kill, to be sure only for food and only if the blood is properly avoided, but the stipulations lead to efforts to control killing of fellow human beings as well.

(3) In J, the flood establishes a new relationship among humans, nature, and God, uncontaminated by the curse on the ground (see 3:17, 23; 4:14). It should be clear, however, that the crux does not remove the judgment of death in 3:23-24 or the judgment of dislocation in 4:14; it removes the ground's resistance to human life. The crux counteracts the curse, but it is not yet a blessing.

Bibliography

B. W. Anderson, "From Analysis to Synthesis: The Interpretation of Genesis 1–11," *JBL* 97 (1978) 5-22; W. Brueggemann, "David and His Theologian," *CBQ* 30 (1968) 156-81; W. M. Clark, "The Flood and the Structure of the Pre-patriarchal History," *ZAW* 83 (1971) 184-211; idem, "The righteousness of Noah," *VT* 21 (1971) 261-80; E. Fisher, "*Gilgamesh* and Genesis: The Flood Story in Context," *CBQ* 32 (1970) 392-403; A. R. Hulst, "*Kol baśar* in der priesterlichen Fluterzählung," *OTS* 12 (1958) 28-68; K. H. Kaspar, "Der priesterschriftliche Bericht vom 'Noahbund'. Eine exegetisch-theologische Untersuchung zu Gen 9:1-17" (Diss., Münster, 1969); M. Kessler, "Rhetorical Criticism of Genesis 7," in *Rhetorical Criticism* (*Fest.* J. Muilenburg; ed. J. J. Jackson and M. Kessler; PTMS 1; Pittsburgh: Pickwick Press, 1974) 1-17; S. McEvenue, *The Narrative Style of the Priestly Writer* (AnBib 50; Rome: Biblical Institute Press, 1971); R. A. F. MacKenzie, "The Divine Soliloquies in Genesis," *CBQ* 17 (1955) 277-86; G. Morawe, "Erwägungen zu Gen 7:11 und 8:2. Ein Beitrag zur Überlieferungsgeschichte des priesterschriftlichen Flutberichtes," *Theologische Versuche* 3 (1971) 357-66; D. L. Petersen, "The Yahwist on the Flood," *VT* 26 (1976) 438-46; B. Porten and U. Rappaport, "Poetic Structure in Genesis 9:7," *VT* 21 (1971) 363-69; R. Rendtorff, "Genesis 8:21 und die Urgeschichte des Jahwisten," *KD* 7 (1961) 69-78; O. H. Steck, "Genesis 12:1-3 und die Urgeschichte des Jahwisten," in *Probleme biblischer Theologie* (*Fest.* G. von Rad; ed. H. W. Wolff; Munich: Kaiser, 1971) 525-54; G. J. Wenham, "The Coherence of the Flood Narrative," *VT* 28 (1978) 336-48.

MYTH OF THE GIANTS, 6:1-4

Structure

I. Exposition	1
II. Crisis	2

III. Judgment 3
IV. Conclusion 4
    A. Nephilim 4a
    B. Heroes 4b

This small unit now stands as the exposition for J's account of the flood. As exposition, it depicts an example of the "wickedness of humanity," but its structure suggests that it may be considered a narrative unit in itself. It features a point of tension and offers a resolution to the tension, characteristics that at least enable reconstruction of a plot.

The structural elements are now brief. (1) An exposition (v. 1) introduces not so much the principal figures in the narrative as simply the circumstances that provide the context for the key event. Human creatures were multiplying "on the face of the ground" *('al-pĕnê-hā'ădāmâ)*, almost in contradiction to the curse in 3:17 or 4:11, or the rejection in 3:23, and the product of the multiplication included daughters. The exposition is neutral; it does not show implicit judgment, but simply states the circumstances. (2) The complication appears in v. 2. The sons of God take the daughters of men as they want. Again, the verse fails to make explicit the direction of its implicit complication. As it now stands, it is only a report of an event. It suggests crisis (→ Genesis 34), but the crisis is not spelled out in detail. As a consequence one may conclude that the element anticipates something more. (3) The next element, however, breaks the story development with a divine oracle of judgment: "My spirit shall not abide in man forever, for he is flesh, but his days shall be a hundred and twenty years." On the surface there is no connection with the preceding elements. If one interprets the role of this verse from the total structure of the unit, however, some conclusions are possible: (a) References to "sons of God" and "daughters of men" assume classes, those derived from God and thus divine and those derived from humanity and thus mortal (see Childs, *Myth,* 49-57). (b) The complication is not so much the physical assault by the gods on the "daughters of men," unable to resist the divine wiles, but rather the loss of limitations on the definition of human beings. A combination of divine and human would not produce a divine man but a violation of created order. (c) The oracle thus moves the story away from its apparent plot to a theological issue: Humans cannot live as God (→ 3:22-24). Rather than developing the story as its opening calls for, the unit imposes a new structure of fall and punishment (see Westermann, *Promises*).

This structural analysis suggests, moreover, that v. 3 must be seen as a limitation, not as a description of the current standard. Its assumption is that as a mixture with the gods, human creatures could live forever (→ 3:22). The judgment oracle makes such a prospect impossible. (4) The final element hangs rather loosely on the unit. Neither of its two points develops the limitation theme of v. 3 or the plot of vv. 1-2. Rather, they suggest a cultural identity for the offspring from the union. V. 4a connects the offspring with the Nephilim, the giants of tradition (→ Num 13:33), v. 4b with "the heroes" *(haggibbōrîm)*. These connections, not necessarily independent, point to an original etiological structure for the unit (see Childs, *Myth*). Moreover, the etiological goal may have been the conclusion of the plot introduced in vv. 1-2, but it does not follow directly from

v. 2 (see the suggestions of Westermann, *Genesis,* 495). If an original story concluded with the information in v. 4, its internal connections have now been lost.

For J, the unit is hardly independent. Rather, it reflects the careful incorporation of ancient material into a larger unit, the flood tale. Behind J, one may reconstruct a story of divine-human cohabitation, pointed by a plot similar to Genesis 34 toward an eventual etiological goal.

Genre

As a part of J, the unit would have no independent generic definition. Rather, it appears as a genre element, an exposition for the flood tale (→ 6:1–9:19). It is relatively clear, however, that J adapts a MYTH set in the primeval period for his purposes (see Childs, *Myth*). Although these verses are no longer myth, they reflect an earlier stage as myth.

Setting

The setting in the literature of J is clear. The setting for the stage that broke an earlier myth and raised the issue of faith for Israel cannot be tied to an institution (see Westermann, *Genesis*). The myth reconstructed from the present form of the text does not suggest bonds with some cultic ritual. Rather, it is broader, a part of popular culture.

Intention

J uses the story to depict the wide range of violation against divinely ordered limitations in human culture. The unit thus immediately precedes J's general statement in v. 5. The broken myth suggests that life cannot be passed along without end by physical procreation—or by cultic ritual that facilitates procreation. Rather, human culture depends on God's order, i.e., God's act in limiting the world. Its intention would have been to place the origin of those limitations, i.e., the death of human creatures, in the primeval period. The myth would have had an etiological goal: the origin of the Nephilim or the heroes. Whether it had some further intention is no longer clear. Perhaps its goal was a dramatic presentation (fertility?) of the relations between the "sons of God" and the "daughters of men" (see Westermann, *Genesis,* 499-500).

Bibliography

B. S. Childs, *Myth and Reality in the Old Testament* (SBT 1/27; London: SCM, 1960); J. Scharbert, "Traditions- und Redaktionsgeschichte von Gen 6:1-4," *BZ* 11 (1967) 66-78; W. H. Schmidt, "Mythos im Alten Testament," *EvT* 27 (1967) 237-54.

NOACHIAN APOPHTHEGM, 9:18-29

Structure

I. Exposition	18-20
A. Introduction of principals	18-19
1. Three sons from the ark	18
2. Dispersal over the world	19
B. Noah as vineyard keeper	20

This unit is set in a context by an exposition, vv. 18-20 (J), and a genealogical conclusion, vv. 28-29 (P). The conclusion completes the genealogical entry
for Noah from 5:32 (→ 5:1-32). Its construction refers to the flood, not the subject
of this unit. The reference serves as a point of crucial importance for the entry,
normally filled by a notation of the birth of the first son. The element then notes
the number of years in the life of the entry from the reference and the total number
of years to his death. The conclusion does not relate in substance to the unit, but
only establishes the Noachian context for the unit.

The introduction comprises two points. The first, vv. 18-19, introduces the
three sons of Noah who are the subjects of the unit. These sons have not appeared
previously in the scope of J's narrative. Moreover, two items of information about
the sons complete the element. (1) The middle son is identified as the father of
Canaan, suggesting unusual significance for the name. The unit will be, in some
manner, about Ham or Canaan. Indeed, the original structure of the tradition may
have involved Shem, Japheth, and Canaan (see von Rad, *Genesis,* 135-36). (2) The
three sons are identified as the fathers of the earth's people (→ 10:1-32). The
second element, v. 20, identifies Noah in terms of his contribution to a new,
emerging culture. Noah was the first man to work the ground *(hā'ǎdāmâ),* and
that means the first who planted the vineyard. This kind of information properly
belongs in a genealogy (see Westermann, *Genesis,* 648). Indeed, the reference to
the three sons resembles genealogical formations (cf. 5:28-30). But it now introduces the principal figures of a narrative and alludes, by reference to the vineyard,
to the coming problem.

Two elements compose the remaining part of the narrative (J). The first is
entirely narration. In crisp, consecutive sentences, the text reports Noah's drunkenness, Ham's violation, and the response of Shem and Japheth. The second is
introduced by a note concerning Noah's discovery of the violation, then a display
of two patriarchal speeches. The first speech is a curse against Canaan (not Ham).
In content, it subjects Canaan to his brothers as a slave or servant. The curse does
not specify the crime; the context notes only that Ham saw his father naked (some
taboo in the area of incest?). The violation scene, then, only provides context; it
is not substantially a part of the curse. The second speech contains a blessing for
Shem (Israel) and, by extension, for Japheth. The blessing formula in v. 26 identifies Yahweh as the God of Shem and the source of the blessing. The next

movement repeats the subordination of Canaan as his slave or servant. The blessing in the name of Yahweh means the curse on Canaan. The blessing does not open a period of fortune for Shem; it only repeats the misfortune for Canaan (for a different formulation, see Koch, 72-73).

Moreover, the entry for Japheth is positive in the sense that Canaan is to be his slave as well. But it also subordinates Japheth to Shem: "Let him dwell in the tents of Shem." Again, the contact between the narrative element and the speech seems minimal. There is no justification in the narrative for the elevation of Shem over Japheth. The good act by the two brothers (v. 23) thus provides only a context for the blessing—it does not provide the motivation.

Thus, the central part of the unit is not a story, but a speech, a curse on Canaan. The blessing on Shem and, by extension, on Japheth exhibits by contrast an emphasis on the curse (thus, the repeated reference to Canaan as slave in both vv. 26 and 27). It may be that a story, perhaps involving an incestuous taboo (→ 19:30-38), perhaps involving an account of the first cultivation of the grape (see von Rad, *Genesis,* 136), lies behind the present form of the narrative.

The structures of a curse and a blessing appear here as part of the stereotyped language of the pericope. Each is controlled by a passive participle from the appropriate verb. Each is followed by the subject of the formula and a dependent clause with the details of the act. The break in the pattern is in the blessing. Rather than a blessing on Shem, the statement pronounces the blessing on Yahweh. But the definition of Yahweh as the God of Shem and the following statement of Canaan's slavery elevate Shem as the opposite of Canaan. The structure of the element thus builds clearly on opposition, a characteristic pattern in J's primeval saga.

Genre

In its present form, the unit is an APOPHTHEGM, a narrative designed as support for a saying. If a story can be reconstructed behind this form, it would be a (→) tale about taboo-incest (→ 19:30-38), and its generic character would be explicitly ethnological tale.

Setting

The imagery of family life is strong (→ Genesis 27). Indeed, the patriarchal curse-blessing as well as the genealogical structure would place some weight on family structures (see Westermann, *Genesis,* 649). In its content, the curse itself presupposes contact with Israel's Canaanite neighbors, with the genre suggesting again a family or tribal setting.

Intention

The unit sets Canaan under the thumb of Shem. Its intention is not so much to develop the blessing of Shem as it is to emphasize the curse against Canaan by Yahweh, the God of Shem. To some extent, that curse echoes the curse against Cain. The echo appears both in the verb as a passive participle, "cursed be Canaan" (*'ārûr kĕnā'an*) and in his designation as "slave" (*'ebed*). The Cain counterpart, 4:11-12, is "cursed are you from the ground. . . . For you shall serve the ground [*kî ta'ābōd 'et-hā'ădāmâ*]. . . ." The imagery must arise, then, from the struggles of Israel against its Canaanite neighbors; it is thus explicitly ethnological. The genealogical frame sets that struggle into the context of primeval history, the immediate reflex of new life under Noah's contribution to culture.

Bibliography

F. W. Bassett, "Noah's Nakedness and the Curse of Canaan. A Case of Incest?" *VT* 21 (1971) 232-37; J. Hoftijzer, "Some Remarks to the Tale of Noah's Drunkenness," *OTS* 12 (1958) 22-27; K. Koch, "Die Hebräer vom Auszug aus Ägypten bis zum Grossreich Davids," *VT* 19 (1969) 37-81; D. Neiman, "The Date and Circumstances of the Cursing of Canaan," *Lown Institute Studies and Texts* 3 (1966) 113-34; L. Rost, "Noah der Weinbauer: Bemerkungen zu Gen 9:18ff.," in *Geschichte und Altes Testament (Fest.* A. Alt; BHT 16; Tübingen: Siebeck, 1953) 169-78; W. Schottroff, *Der altisraelitische Fluchspruch* (WMANT 30; Neukirchen-Vluyn: Neukirchener Verlag, 1969); A. van Selms, "The Canaanites in the Book of Genesis," *OTS* 12 (1958) 182-213.

NOAH GENEALOGY, 10:1-32

Structure

Since the genealogy in Genesis 5 leaves the tenth generation open in order to include the Noah material as a part of its compass, it connects immediately to the genealogy in Genesis 10. The *toledoth* formula in 10:1a therefore establishes the larger context by its cohesion with the formula in 5:1. Indeed, the series now underway functions in the context provided by 2:4a. The enumeration begins with the stages of creation and continues through the genealogy of Adam (Adam to Noah) to the genealogy of Noah's sons.

This genealogy is not constructed like the Adam genealogy, however. In the present form of the text, the series does not develop the consecutive stages to an ordered and emphasized conclusion. Rather, it presents three tables of genealogy, each more or less synchronic with the other. Moreover, the entries for each generation in the table do not follow the regular pattern of ch. 5, but rather develop distinct groups or segments. The first group, the sons of Japheth, appears in units characterized by a brief introduction, "the sons of Japheth," and a name list. There is no note about a father "begetting" a son, no statement of total years, no death report. If one understands v. 5 as a conclusion to the entire table of Japheth (see below), then the entry also contains no note of progress in the culture, no event that expands the entry with distinct data. There is only a series of name lists. Perhaps the most distinctive character of the Japheth table, then, is that instead of moving to the third generation, the second generation branches to synchronic lists and thus parallels the conception of the unit. The table ends in v. 5 with a note that from these people the coastland nations "spread" (*niprĕdû*, Niphal < √ *prd*), and the movement produced "land," "language," and "family" for each nation. (Note that MT does not have the formula "These are the sons of Japheth." Rather, the three following nouns refer to the coastland nations spread from Japheth. But compare the conclusion for the sons of Ham, v. 20, and the sons of Shem, v. 31.)

The second table, the sons of Ham, begins in the same style. The initial distinction is that rather than branching to synchronic lists, v. 7b moves the series to the third generation. The style breaks, however, in v. 8 and moves back to the second generation. In this stage of the table, three synchronic entries appear (the introduction in v. 6 lists four sons of Ham), and the entries are totally different from the preceding lists. (1) Cush reports only one son, Nimrod, but the entry moves immediately to notations about advancements in culture. Nimrod was a "mighty man," a "hero" (*gibbōr*). Moreover, he was a "mighty hunter" (*gibbōr ṣayid*) before Yahweh (on the earth). Indeed, he was a king (v. 10), and he built cities (vv. 11-12; cf. 4:17). (2) The second entry, Egypt, has only a name list, although the list is introduced like v. 8, not like vv. 2, 3, 4. (3) The third entry, Canaan, introduced like the second, is initially a name list, although in v. 16 the list shifts from personal names to gentilic names. No longer like the personal names Sidon or Heth, the names are formed with an ending, such as "Jebusites," "Amorites." V. 18b follows the pattern of v. 5b, although the vocabulary is markedly different: "Afterward the families of the Canaanites spread abroad" (*nāpōṣû*; Niphal $<$ √ *pwṣ*). V. 19 rounds off the entry with a designation of land occupied by the Canaanites. This element stands virtually outside the entry but compares to the list of cities built by Nimrod (vv. 11-12). The table concludes in v. 20 with a stereotyped formula, "These are the sons of Ham" (*'ēlleh běnê-ḥām*), and a recognition that the sons possessed families, languages, lands, and nations.

The third table, the sons of Shem, begins with a genealogical note that Shem "begat" children. The name lists of the first and second generations (vv. 22-23) appear simply as lists, like the sons of Japheth. V. 24 returns, however, to the "begat" style. In the fourth generation, two sons appear, but the list follows only one, who then "begets" thirteen sons. V. 30, like v. 19, defines the territory. V. 31 then brings the table to its stereotyped conclusion (cf. v. 20).

V. 32 is the conclusion to the whole unit, parallel to v. 1. (Note the repetition of the key term "generations" *[tôlědōtām].*) The conclusion states that the table presents "nations" (*běgôyēhem*), although it makes no reference to languages. The final element, however, is more important: "From these the nations were spread [*niprědû*, Niphal $<$ √ *prd*] in the earth after the flood." With this comment the series of tables reaches its goal.

The structure of the unit can be clarified by separating P from its Yahwistic counterpart. In P, the structure of the unit appears in regular patterns:

I. Introduction	1a
II. Tables	2-31*
A. Sons of Japheth	2-5
1. First generation	2
2. Second generation	3-5
a. Sons of Gomer	3
b. Sons of Javan	4
3. Conclusion	5
B. Sons of Ham	6-20*
1. First generation: sons of Ham	6
2. Second generation: sons of Cush	7a
3. Third generation: sons of Raamah	7b
4. Conclusion	20
C. Sons of Shem	22-31*
1. First generation: sons of Shem	22
2. Second generation: sons of Aram	23
3. Conclusion	31
III. Conclusion	32

The P introduction, the *toledoth* formula, links the table of nations to the unity established in 2:4a. Its perspective derives more immediately from the flood tradition, both in terms of connection with the genealogy that embraces the flood and in terms of the subject, the sons of Noah. The *toledoth* formula series thus presupposes the narrative material that the individual formulas embrace. Moreover, the parallel between the opening *toledoth* formula and the conclusion in v. 32 points again to the embracing function of the series. Indeed, the formula in v. 32 as conclusion would point to the position of 2:4a as concluding element in the opening unit of P (see also 11:10-32). The unit then comprises three sections composed entirely from name lists. The first table has only two generations, although the second has two synchronic parts. The second table has three generations, the third only two. For details, see the comments above.

In J, the structure is as follows:

I. Sons of Ham	8-14
A. Nimrod, son of Cush	8-12
1. Birth report	8a
2. Profession	8b-9
3. Kingdoms and cities	10-12
B. Sons of Egypt	13-14
C. Sons of Canaan	15-19
1. Name list	15-18a
2. Territorial limits	18b-19
II. Sons of Shem	21-30*
A. First generation: sons of Shem	21
B. Second generation: son of Arpachshad	24a
C. Third generation: son of Shelah	24b
D. Fourth generation: sons of Eber	25
E. Fifth generation: sons of Joktan	26-30
1. Name list	26-29
2. Territorial limits	30

The J counterpart has only two tables, each constructed in its own peculiar way. In the first table, structure is developed by means of three synchronic branches. The contribution of Nimrod to the culture of the world sets the Cush branch apart from all other entries in the unit. Following a simple enumeration of names for Egypt, the sons of Canaan segment displays a distinct development. A list of names leads to some specification of geographic locale (vv. 18b-19). This element ties to the second table. Though developing diachronically, the fifth entry also specifies territorial claims (v. 30). The one break in the structure of this table expands the fourth generation, the sons of Eber (v. 25), with a notation that two sons were born, Peleg and Joktan. There is an item of information with Peleg: "For in his days the earth was divided." The comment, however, is not so much a part of the tradition about spreading out in the world as it is a simple wordplay on the name *(peleg-niplĕgâ)*. For further details, see the comments above.

The genealogy employs stereotyped expressions and formulas as basic building blocks. (1) Introductions involve simply a designation of subject: "The sons of Japheth." (2) Conclusions join the designation with a demonstrative pronoun: "These *[ʾēlleh]* are the sons of Ham." These two variations belong to a single formula, available for either introduction or conclusion. It should be noted that

v. 5 does not have the conclusion formula in Hebrew, even though the form of the pericope suggests that it should be there. The conclusion is marked rather by a note that the people spread. Other stereotyped expressions include a birth report and designations of genealogical information.

Genre

The unit is a segmented GENEALOGY, structured with synchronic branches. In addition, it contains two different types of genealogical material: (1) An explicit witness to the linear succession of generations through the reproduction of the stages in the generations. This stage does not yet lend itself to the concerns of a "table" (note the verbal construction of the series). (2) A simple name LIST, with an introduction that designates the generation to which the name list belongs (note the nominal construction of the series). The successive structure is implied by the whole unit, not explicit in this stage. Indeed, in this stage, the genre has deteriorated. It should perhaps no longer be designated (→) genealogy, but rather simply an organizational LIST (→ Exod 1:1-5; see Westermann, *Genesis*, 671-72).

The priestly form of the genealogy reflects the organization of the tradition into tables for the nations. In each table, the genealogy is linear; yet, the tables provide the appearance of the segmentation into branches. The J genealogy also suggests segmentation by virtue of the grouping into the sons of Ham and the sons of Shem. But again, the content of each group is linear.

Setting

The tradition preserved in this unit ranges from the literary construct of P or Rp to the early, tribal self-definition of a people in a struggle with other people. The earliest forms may still reflect the concern of a family or larger family unit to achieve self-identity in the context of the world's families and geographical organizations. As a part of J, the tradition no longer reflects the history of a particular family, but rather the more systematic concerns of organization. This level is more national or prenational tribal than family (thus, the inclusion of territorial domain). Also, at this level the organization scheme does not derive from the reflective display of the whole world. At its earliest level (including J), the tradition is not a table of nations but a definition of people in Palestine (Canaanites and the children of Eber). In P, the distinctions break down; the concern is defined completely by P's own organization (see Westermann, *Genesis*, 671-73).

Intention

In its latest stages (in P, but perhaps already suggested in J), the table intends to display the organization of the world in terms of the three sons of Noah. Thus, the simple lists tend to depict a status in world reality, and significantly, the notices that people spread to various parts of the world as well as the geographical definitions follow simple lists. An earlier form of genealogy (J) focuses on the primeval history as a series of successive generations (→ 4:1-26) and embraces information that characterizes differences in particular stages of the genealogy. Both forms, however, affirm that all the peoples of the earth derive from God's creation. Even the enemy or the pagan was at one time a brother (see Westermann, *Genesis*, 704-6).

Bibliography

F. C. Burkitt, "Note on the Table of Nations (Genesis X)," *JTS* 21 (1920) 233-38; J. M. Fenasse, "La table des peuples," *BTS* 52 (1963) 2; A. H. Sayce, "The Tenth Chapter of Genesis," *JBL* 44 (1925) 193-202; J. Simons, "The 'Table of Nations' (Gen. 10): Its General Structure and Meaning," *OTS* 10 (1954) 155-84; R. R. Wilson, *Genealogy and History in the Biblical World* (New Haven: Yale University Press, 1977); M. H. Woudstra, "The *Toledot* of the Book of Genesis and Their Redemptive-Historical Significance," *Calvin Theological Journal* 5 (1970) 184-89.

TALE OF THE TOWER, 11:1-9

Structure

I. Exposition	1
II. Complication: the act of men	2-4
A. Initial act	2
B. Proposals	3-4
1. Construction of bricks	3
a. Speech	3a
b. Act	3b
2. Construction of city and tower (speech)	4
III. Resolution: God's response	5-8
A. Initial act	5
B. Proposal speech	6-7
1. Indictment	6
2. Judgment	7
C. Execution of judgment	8
IV. Conclusion	9

The tale of the tower contradicts the context that surrounds it in the present form of the text. In ch. 10, the concluding v. 32 and its counterparts in vv. 5 and 20 accomplish distribution of people to their respective lands and their respective languages. 11:1 appears as a sharp contradiction: "The whole earth had one language and few words." The problem is not solved by noting that the genealogy in ch. 10 is complemented by narrative in ch. 11 without necessitating a chronological sequence. The final text might be explained in that manner. The context is clarified, however, if the tower tale is set in its proper context as a part of J. The J genealogy in ch. 10 did not develop a table of nations as a world pattern, but rather as Canaanites vis-à-vis the children of Eber. Moreover, the children of Eber live in the hill country of the east, and 11:2 describes the migration of people from the east as the point of departure for the story.

The story features a structure already familiar in J (→ Paradise, Flood, Cain). An exposition and conclusion frame two major elements of narrative that complement each other as opposites. The exposition introduces the subject: "The whole earth had one language" (on the opening convention, → 2:4b–3:24). The conclusion brackets the subject with its counterpart: "The Lord confused the language of all the earth." This bracket stands now as the foundation side of an etymological etiology built on a wordplay between the name "Babel" *(bābel)* and the verb in the saying, "confuse" *(bālal)*. The etiology is clearly secondary in the unit, not the goal of the whole. But the secondary character of the etiology here does not mean that the confusion motif in the story is secondary. The final line of the conclusion picks up a motif from the story (vv. 4, 8) and sets it as a consequence of God's action: "From there [place or confusion of language?] the Lord scattered [hĕpîṣām] them abroad over the face of all the earth." One should note that this conclusion is broader than the comment in 10:18b and does not contradict the J context.

The two components of the story form a complementary opposition. The first, vv. 2-4, focuses on the decision of men to build a city and a tower with its top in the heavens. V. 2 is a general statement of human preparation: They found a place. Vv. 3-4 comprise two speeches, each constructed as cohortative with introductory petition "come" (hābâ), each reporting the plans of the human community: "Come, let us make bricks. . . . Come, let us build ourselves a city, . . ." The sequence in the scene grounds the decision to build a city in the fear that if a city or a tower and a name are not established, the community will be scattered: "Lest we be scattered over the face of all the earth" (pen-nāpûṣ 'al-pĕnê kol-hā'āreṣ). The second part of the story describes the action of God. Like v. 2, v. 5 is a general statement of God's act: God found the same place the people had discovered (on the irony of this statement, see von Rad, Genesis, 149). Vv. 6-7 then present the divine oracle, a decision about God's plans for the human community. V. 6 is cast as the foundation for the decision. Like Gen 3:22-24, the decision calls for preventative action against further abuse. The decision is expressly to confuse the language, not to scatter the people over the face of the earth, although the people cited the fear of scattering as the basis for their action. Moreover, the consequence of the confusion as far as the divine oracle is concerned is not a scattering, but the loss of ability to hear (and understand) the neighbor's speech. V. 8 then reports that the divine decision was carried out. That meant (1) the people were scattered, and (2) they left off building the city. Thus, the two parts tie closely together. Being unable to build the city means being scattered over the face of all the earth, and the confusion of language is the cause for leaving the construction of the city.

In its present form, then, the story is of one piece, a consistent part of the J context. It may be that the motifs of scattering and the confusion of language were originally distinct. It may be that a tradition about building a city has grown together with a distinct tradition about building a tower (see Westermann, Genesis, 711-21). These items form the tradition history behind the text. For the text, however, building the city leads to confusion of language, and confusion of language leads to scattering over the face of the earth.

Genre

Like the counterparts in J, the paradise story, the Cain narrative, and the flood story, this narrative is a TALE. Indeed, its structure follows the model of its counterparts.

Setting

The unit is a part of J and belongs in its latest stage to the J complex as given context in the redaction of the Pentateuch (→ Pentateuch/Hexateuch). As a part of J, it has a literary (and theological) setting. In a pre-Yahwistic level, the question of setting is more difficult. It is clear that the setting cannot be defined simply as Babylon or a tower in Babylon, or even as a historical Israelite counterpart. Since the story reveals a somewhat negative attitude toward Babylon, tower temples, or big cities, one might conclude that the tale circulated among the circles of folk singers who recited the traditions of the past in order to account for the character of the present. A more precise definition of setting is not possible.

Intention

The story accomplishes for J what the table of nations accomplishes for P. The successors to Noah spread throughout the world and have their own language. Thus, a basic element of common experience in the world of human beings has its beginning in the primeval world (→ Genesis 10). For J, however, the element has a negative cast. The dispersal and the multiplication of languages comes as a result of divine reaction against human action. The pattern, already apparent from the first of J's primeval tales (husband against wife; man and woman against god), present in successive tales (brother against brother; humans against god), now adds a new step. The people cannot understand each other, and so they must live apart, separated into their own lands and languages.

Bibliography

B. S. Childs, "The Etiological Tale Re-examined," *VT* 24 (1974) 387-97; J. P. Fokkelman, *Narrative Art in Genesis: Specimens of Stylistic and Structural Analysis* (Amsterdam: Van Gorcum, 1975); A. Frenz, "Der Turmbau," *VT* 19 (1969) 183-95; H. Junker, "Die Zerstreuung der Völker nach der biblischen Urgeschichte," *TTZ* 70 (1961) 182-85; I. Kikawada, "The Shape of Genesis 11:1-9," in *Rhetorical Criticism (Fest.* J. Muilenburg; ed. J. J. Jackson and M. Kessler; PTMS 1; Pittsburgh: Pickwick, 1974) 18-32; K. Seybold, "Der Turmbau zu Babel. Zur Entstehung von Genesis 11:1-9," *VT* 26 (1976) 453-79.

CHAPTER 5
The ABRAHAM SAGA

BIBLIOGRAPHY

O. Eissfeldt, *Stammessage und Menschheitserzählung in der Genesis* (Berlin: Akademie, 1965); A. Jepsen, "Zur Überlieferungsgeschichte der Vätergestalten," *WZLeipzig* 3 (1953/54) 139-55; H. Junker, "Die Patriarchengeschichte. Ihre literarische Art und ihr geschichtlicher Charakter," *TTZ* 57 (1948) 38-45; C. A. Keller, "Grundsätzliches zur Auslegung der Abraham-Überlieferung," *TZ* 12 (1956) 425-45; R. Kilian, *Die vorpriesterlichen Abrahamüberlieferungen, literarkritisch und traditionsgeschichtlich untersucht* (BBB 24; Bonn: Hanstein, 1966); J. Muilenburg, "Abraham and the Nations: Blessing and World History," *Int* 19 (1965) 387-98; G. von Rad, *Genesis, a Commentary* (tr. J. H. Marks; rev. ed.; OTL; Philadelphia: Westminster, 1972); J. van Seters, *Abraham in History and Tradition* (New Haven: Yale University Press, 1975); C. Westermann, *Genesis* (BKAT 1/1; Neukirchen-Vluyn: Neukirchener Verlag, 1974-); idem, *The Promises to the Fathers: Studies on the Patriarchal Narratives* (tr. D. E. Green; Philadelphia: Fortress, 1980).

THE ABRAHAM SAGA AS A WHOLE, 11:10-25:26

Structure

I. Narrative inclusion			11:10-22:19
A. Exposition	(A)		11:10-12:9
B. Threat to the ancestress	(B)		12:10-20
C. Family novella: Abram-Lot	(C)		13:1-14:24
D. Covenant	(D)		15:1-21
E. Tale of family strife		(1)	16:1-16
(Annunciation and birth of Ishmael)			
F. Covenant			17:1-27
G. Tale of family strife		(2)	18:1-15
(Annunciation of Isaac)			
H. Family novella: Abraham-Lot	(C')		18:16-19:38
1. Intercession			18:16-33
2. Lot's salvation			19:1-29
3. Incest			19:30-38
I. Threat to the ancestress	(B'α)		20:1-18
J. Tale of family strife		(3)	21:1-21
K. Beer-sheba etiology	(B'β)		21:22-34
L. Abraham legend	(A')		22:1-19
II. Death reports			22:20-25:26
A. Nahor genealogy			22:20-24

B. Sarah's burial	23:1-20
C. Abraham's deathbed	24:1-67
D. Abraham's second marriage	25:1-6
E. Abraham's death	25:7-11
F. Following generations	25:12-26
1. Ishmael	12-18
2. Isaac	19-26

An analysis of form in the Abraham narrative must consider the saga first as a whole and only thereafter as individual units. This point obtains not only because in the whole a narrative continuation of the primeval saga appears, but also because a marked element of structural and narrative unity sets this whole apart from its surroundings. The whole has two major structural patterns, each with its own integrity. (1) A narrative inclusion begins with an exposition, moves to a center focused on the covenant between Abraham and God, then returns to a theological conclusion designed to confirm the character of Abraham as it was set forth in the exposition. Moreover, the content of the covenant focuses on a promise from God to the patriarch, a promise foreshadowed by the exposition and confirmed by the test of Abraham's faith. This pattern of structure can be diagramed in reference to the outline above as ABCDD'C'B'α-B'βA'. This palistrophe is then combined with elements of an extensive narration about the familial relationships of members in Abraham's house: Sarah-Hagar: Isaac-Ishmael. The pattern of this narrative element can be diagramed by the serial elements 1,2,3. Moreover, element 2 intervenes between D and D', the center of the palistrophe, and element 3 interrupts a traditional unity between B'α and B'β. (2) A collection of units in 22:20–25:26 involves accounts of death and burial for the patriarch or members of his family, along with some indication of the familial succession from his house or from the house of his relatives. These units recount the last acts of the patriarch as a traditional theme distinct from the plot of the narrative inclusion.

This larger narrative whole represents a combination of at least two narrative sources. There is no evidence from form-critical analysis of structure that would support a clear separation between the Yahwist and the Elohist. At most, the Elohistic elements seem to be an expansion of the Yahwist's narrative, not a distinct narrative unit that has an independent form-critical integrity (→ Genesis 15). The two sources that present a self-contained unity subject to structure and genre analysis are thus P and JE.

The priestly structure for the Abraham saga is as follows:

I. Exposition	11:10–12:9*
II. Narrative inclusion	
A. Birth of Ishmael	16:15-16
B. Covenant	17:1-27
C. Birth of Isaac	21:1b-5
III. Death reports	
A. Death of Sarah	23:1-20
B. Death of Abraham	25:7-11
C. Successive generations	

1. Ishmael	25:12-18
2. Isaac	25:19-20, 26b

The two items of structure noted in the final form of the text emerge as characteristic structure in P, a narrative inclusion and a collection of units concerned with the death and burial of the patriarchal figure or members of his family and with the designation of familial succession. But P is distinct from the final text in the details, particularly those in the first major element. (1) The exposition for P does not tie directly with the narrative inclusion but anticipates rather the entire range of the Abraham narrative. Indeed, the structure of the exposition, a genealogy that merges with an itinerary, sets the Abraham narrative into direct relationship with the enumeration structure of the primeval history. It recognizes that a new narration begins. But it assumes an immediate continuity with the preceding narration in much the same way that Genesis 5 assumes for P that the flood story is a continuation of the story that began with Adam. (2) The narrative inclusion is considerably shorter; yet, it is significant that its center is still the Abrahamic covenant. The two sons of Abraham's house provide substance for the framing narration. Thus, the possibilities for narrative conflict are also here. This point is the subject of P's development in Genesis 17, the establishment of the covenant. For here, with sharp focus on the promise for subsequent posterity, Abraham receives God's announcement that Ishmael cannot be the son of the promise. Rather, Sarah, the mother of the promise, will give birth to a son whose name shall be Isaac. This contrast is the subject for a narrative tension. The tension, however, does not develop, at least not in the priestly narrative elements now preserved. Rather, P features simply birth reports as if the narrative theme now serves only the demonstration of the promise fulfilled and, of more significance, the covenantal ritual of circumcision (cf. 21:1b-5). The most important element for the structure of P would thus be covenant, a parallel with the P primeval saga with its center on the covenant with Noah (→ 9:1-17). Moreover, the Lot tradition does not appear in P as a fully developed narrative. At most, only allusions to the contrast between Abraham and Lot can be found (see 13:6, 11b, 12abα; 19:29), and these allusions hardly constitute a major narrative theme, if indeed they can be adequately separated from their JE context at all. Rather, they underwrite P's emphasis on the Abraham covenantal relationships (so, 19:29).

The second element of structure contains the same death-and-burial motif. First, a rather detailed account of Abraham's negotiations for purchase of a burial plot provides substance for the death report for Sarah. But this unit also paves the way for the death-and-burial report for other patriarchal figures (→ 25:7-11; 50:1-15). The account of Abraham's burial fits into this pattern, however, not only by virtue of place but also by reference to both Isaac and Ishmael as sons responsible for the burial. The traditional conflict from the narrative inclusion is not apparent here (see von Rad, *Genesis*). Yet, these final elements hark back to Genesis 17 in order to make the direction of the familial succession clear. The two sons are represented with two units of tradition. Ishmael's entry features a genealogy that recognizes fulfillment of the promise to Abraham in Genesis 17. Ishmael became a nation, with a twelve-tribe construction. But the entry also features a death report, in which Ishmael's standing conflict with his brother, if not his subordination to his brother (note v. 11), disappears. In contrast to this line of report for Ishmael, the Isaac entry breaks off after only two verses. The assumption here is that the entire Isaac narrative constitutes the subject for the entry. And in this narrative, Isaac's ascendancy is clear.

The problem in structure for P, then, is that there is no real distinction between primeval saga and Abraham saga and no distinction between Abraham saga and the Isaac-Jacob saga. For P, the entire line of narration in Genesis merges into a single unit, with structural centers in the Noah-Abraham covenant traditions.

The Abraham saga in JE reveals the following structure:

I. Narrative inclusion
   A. Exposition   (A)   11:10–12:9*
   B. Threat to the ancestress   (B)   12:10-20
   C. Abraham-Lot   (C)   13:1–14:24
   D. Covenant   (D)   15:1-21
   E. Family strife
      1. Ishmael annunciation   (1)   16:1-14
      2. Isaac annunciation   (2)   18:1-15
   F. Abraham-Lot   (C')
      1. Intercession   18:16-33
      2. Lot's salvation   19:1-28 (29?)
      3. Incest   19:30-38
   G. Threat to the ancestress   (B'α)   20:1-18
   H. Family strife   (3)   21:1-21
   I. Beer-sheba etiology   (B'β)   21:22-34
   J. Abraham legend   (A')   22:1-19
II. Death reports
   A. Nahor genealogy   22:20-24
   B. Abraham's deathbed   24
   C. Abraham's second marriage   25:1-6
   D. Isaac's succession   25:21-26

Thus, the narrative in JE accounts for the primary structural characteristics in the final form of the text. The two major elements, a narrative inclusion and a group of traditions about Abraham's last days, build the scope of the unit. The first element reveals the structural patterns of the palistrophe noted for the final text. Indeed, in this case the inclusion structure is clearer. The exposition, a theologically pregnant unit designed to show Abraham as a man of faith whose obedience leads to a divine promise for posterity and blessing (→ 11:10–12:9), stands against the legend in Genesis 22, again a theologically pregnant unit designed to emphasize Abraham's obedience as a virtue of edifying proportions. The faith of the patriarch, first perceived in 12:1-4, gains final confirmation in 22:1-19. Moreover, the threat to the ancestress in 12:10-20, a unit that apparently interrupts the context created by the itinerary, balances the threat to the ancestress in ch. 20. Following the one and preceding the other are items of the Lot tradition. Finally, at the center of the pattern is the covenant text, ch. 15, which places emphasis on the promise of Yahweh to Abraham. Yet, just here a problem in the history of the Abraham tradition emerges, for none of the narrative elements in the palistrophe features the promise to Abraham as an original goal of the plot. The narrative inclusion does not build on the promise to a point of fulfillment.

This structural inclusion then merges with the narrative elements associated with the Sarah-Hagar: Isaac-Ishmael opposition. Elements 1 and 2 stand together, intervening between the center D and the Abraham-Lot tradition, C'. Element 3 breaks the traditional relationship between Genesis 20, B'α, and 21:22-34, B'β. The impact of this structure is to emphasize two different lines of narrative development, each equally important for the goals of the whole. The first represents Abraham as the patriarch of faith. Exposition and legend combine to support the covenant text at the center. The Lot tradition sets out a comic contrast with the man of faith, not as a competitor, not as an example of the man of unfaith, but as a comic-tragic buffoon (→ Genesis 19). But the narrative can also characterize Abraham himself as the opposition (→ 12:10-20; 20:1-18). The relationship of intimacy with God and family, apparent in 12:1-4, evaporates in 12:10-20. The covenant reconfirms that intimacy for Abraham's future, including the promises. But again the intimacy evaporates, 20:1-18, and as a necessary consequence, a probe of Abraham himself leads to reconfirmation of his obedience. The complementary narrative model in elements 1, 2, and 3 reduces Abraham to a relatively passive figure in the affairs of his household, with Sarah-Hagar or Isaac-Ishmael at center stage. The narrative line here is rooted in the covenant center, the outgrowth of God's promise to Abraham for a son. But with the promise comes the familial strife (→ Genesis 16; 18; 21). In these relationships, the character of Abraham's blessed family emerges in all its human resistance and struggle. The impact of the two structural models is that if blessing for the nations of the world is to come from this family, it must do so not because the family is itself a model, nor because Abraham is himself free of involvement in family strife, but rather because in Abraham's obedience (ch. 22) a stance toward the future as the arena of God's promise can emerge.

With these structural observations in hand, one may ask where the traditio-historical kernel of the Abraham tradition lies. Is it not in the promise of God to the patriarch? If so, the next question must be: Which promise? The promises for a land, for great posterity, for a son, for room to live, for becoming a nation, for redemption from slavery, all compete for attention. Many of these promises are clearly secondary in the narrative tradition (see Westermann, *Promises*). Can any one qualify as primary, as the content of the traditio-historical kernel of the tradition? This kernel lies, in all probability, in the promise for a son, from which the other promises developed as secondary expansions.

In this saga, at least two more extensive narrative units can be identified. The one deals with Abraham-Lot, the other with Sarah-Hagar. In these elements lies evidence for the tendency of the larger unit to incorporate smaller, distinct narrative units. Moreover, a novella in Genesis 24, relatively unrelated to the larger structure, rounds out the evidence for this tendency. In each case, older oral tradition may lie behind the unit. As far as the unit is concerned, however, the narration cannot be analyzed satisfactorily as a cycle of stories, originally small and independent. Rather, each reveals a structural interdependency, suggesting that the primary limits of the narrative involve the larger whole. The remaining narratives are the threat to the ancestress and the local traditions in 21:22-34; neither of these units treats the theme of promise as a major narrative goal. Indeed,

101

in the Sarah-Hagar narrative, the dominant theme is familial strife rather than promise. The promise comes to the fore in Genesis 15, but whether this chapter represents the oldest Abraham narrative—and thus a source for defending a thesis that promise is the primary theme in the Abraham narrative—is not at all certain.

The oldest Abraham tradition is doubtlessly centered in a combination of promise and strife motifs. The promise kernel would be the blessing-son tradition, but the substance of the tradition does not appear simply in terms of promise-fulfillment. Although the oldest traditions may have included the promise theme, the substance of the narrative seems more directly to be strife as the characteristic of the Abrahamic family. Indeed, the promise for a son rather than land or great posterity seems subordinated to the theme of strife over possession of inheritance. It would seem, then, that the traditio-historical root for the Abraham tradition featured an opposition between a promise for blessing and a tendency for strife, themes already apparent in the primeval saga.

Genre

The total unit of narrative can be understood together as a family SAGA. Saga presents the history of a family in such a manner that the qualifying principles of the family appear most sharply in the foreground. Here are the traditions that tell the family what it means to be the family of Abraham. Such tradition is distinguished from (→) history writing by virtue of its concern to narrate not simply the course of events dictated by the cause-effect sequence of the past, but rather the central kernel of the past that encapsulates each successive generation. It is much more symbolic than objective representation; it is an art form, not an objective scientific datum. And though the symbol emerges as an art form, the power of the art form belongs to the quality of the family life itself.

Setting

Family saga is bound in essence to the interests and life of the family. This saga was doubtlessly preserved in the framework of the family. In addition, however, one should say that the setting lies in the art and skill of the story-teller, who shapes the roots that define for each generation what it means to be family.

Intention

This larger unity of narrative presents the Abraham tradition as the story of a family in order to show in the narration what the character of the family is. A central focus of this concern is the promise to Abraham, the oath which at the same time contains the content of God's covenant. The oath is originally given to the childless family as a promise for the birth of a son, then subsequently expanded to include the birth of a great nation, the gift of a land, and a blessing. At the same time, however, the narrative depicts the struggles of the family to secure relationships of intimacy. The struggles break the family in open strife. With these traditions, the character of blessing is set into question. How can God's blessing for the nations derive from a family that cannot yet live with itself? Genesis 22 is thus a theological and traditional key for the intention of the saga. The man of faith proves himself prepared for his future despite the pressures of the present (→ Genesis 22).

CHAPTER 6
The Individual Units

BIBLIOGRAPHY

M. Noth, *A History of Pentateuchal Traditions* (tr. B. W. Anderson; Englewood Cliffs: Prentice-Hall, 1972); G. von Rad, *Genesis, a Commentary* (tr. J. H. Marks; rev. ed.; OTL; Philadelphia: Westminster, 1972); J. van Seters, *Abraham in History and Tradition* (New Haven: Yale University Press, 1975); C. Westermann, *Genesis* (BKAT 1/1; Neukirchen-Vluyn: Neukirchener Verlag, 1974-); idem, *The Promises to the Fathers: Studies on the Patriarchal Narratives* (tr. D. E. Green; Philadelphia: Fortress, 1980).

SHEM GENEALOGY, 11:10 – 25:11

Structure

I. Introduction	11:10aα
II. Generations	11:10aβb–25:11
A. First generation: Shem	11:10aβb-11
1. Birth report: Arpachshad	10aβb
2. Length of life after birth	11
B. Second generation: Arpachshad	12-13
1. Birth report: Shelah	12
2. Length of life after birth	13
C. Third generation: Shelah	14-15
1. Birth report: Eber	14
2. Length of life after birth	15
D. Fourth generation: Eber	16-17
1. Birth report: Peleg	16
2. Length of life after birth	17
E. Fifth generation: Peleg	18-19
1. Birth report: Reu	18
2. Length of life after birth	19
F. Sixth generation: Reu	20-21
1. Birth report: Serug	20
2. Length of life after birth	21
G. Seventh generation: Serug	22-23
1. Birth report: Nahor	22
2. Length of life after birth	23
H. Eighth generation: Nahor	24-25

As it now stands, this pericope is structured as a linear genealogy, embracing itinerary traditions and extensive narrative. The genealogy begins with a *toledoth* formula, placing the scope of the unit into the larger context established by the formula in 5:1. Moreover, it embraces the entire scope of the Abraham saga as a part of the larger context, the so-called *Toledoth* Book. The patriarchal narratives represent the substance of a tenth generation, just as the Noah narratives represent the substance of a tenth generation.

The character of this bond with the larger context (→ The Patriarchal Theme) depends, however, on examination of the component sources. It seems appropriate, therefore, to display the structure of P without further comment on the final form of the genealogy. The structure in P is regular:

II. Generations   11:10aβb–25:11
    A. First generation: Shem   11:10aβb-11
    B. Second generation: Arpachshad   12-13
    C. Third generation: Shelah   14-15
    D. Fourth generation: Eber   16-17
    E. Fifth generation: Peleg   18-19
    F. Sixth generation: Reu   20-21
    G. Seventh generation: Serug   22-23
    H. Eighth generation: Nahor   24-25
    I. Ninth Generation: Terah   26-32*
    J. Tenth generation: Abram   12:4b–25:11
       1. Age   12:4b
       2. Itinerary   12:5
       3. Narratives   16:1–23:20*
       4. Death reports   25:7-11*

The genealogy in this unit cannot be separated from the genealogies of the so-called *Toledoth* Book (→ Genesis 5; 10). This point is confirmed by the *toledoth* formula in v. 10aα, a structural link that ties the unit to other units introduced by the *toledoth* formula (see 2:4a; 5:1; 10:1). As a part of the *toledoth* series, this formula suggests that 11:10–25:11* is a proper continuation of the priestly primeval saga, a presentation of the sons of Shem as the successors to the sons of Adam (cf. also the pattern of construction in each generation, both here and in Genesis 5). On the other hand, the genealogy here cannot be separated from the patriarchal traditions in P. This point is confirmed by the structure of the genealogy in ten steps, with the tenth step a frame for the priestly Abraham saga (→ Genesis 5). One may properly suggest, therefore, that this unit is a part of a larger context established by the primeval history. The first segment of the larger unit has a universal perspective, this one the particular perspective of the patriarchal narratives. Noah was the father of all the earth's people. One of Noah's sons was the father of a particular group of people. It is interesting to note that the priestly table of nations (Genesis 10) does not fit as readily into the pattern of the *toledoth* chain, but simply describes the growth of population in the world from the seed of Noah (see Westermann, *Genesis*, 743-46).

The nature of the unity established by the *toledoth* series must be carefully evaluated, however. The genealogy with ten generations accomplishes its structural function here in precisely the same way that the ten-generations structure functioned in the primeval saga. Does the structure therefore not point to a closer bond between primeval sagas and the sagas about the patriarchs for P than is to be seen in the transition from patriarchs to the exodus or from the wilderness to the conquest? Moreover, the theme of intimacy in human relationships for both the primeval saga and the patriarchal sagas suggests that the primeval history stands in unique relationship to the patriarchs. It is an introduction to the entire Pentateuch/Hexateuch only insofar as the theme of the patriarchs mediates its function as the introduction to the remaining themes of tradition. This context confirms that for the OT, the primeval history is not to be considered for itself but only in relationship to the patriarchs.

The succession of generations appears in a regular pattern from the first through the eighth generation. The exception to this structure occurs in the first generation with a note that Arpachshad was born two years after the flood (cf. 5:3). Otherwise, each panel notes the age of a father at the birth of a son and the length of life and productivity that the father enjoyed after the son's birth. The genealogy in Genesis 5 employs exactly the same pattern, with the addition of a death report composed of the total numbers of years in the entry's life and the notice of his death. The ninth generation breaks the pattern. The birth report is marked with three sons rather than one. (Cf. 5:32.) The ninth generation in 5:25-31 is expanded with v. 29, a part of J. But the redactional pattern is the same. The report is followed by a *toledoth* formula, a structural feature that shows the formula as a piece that functions more widely than as an introduction to a genealogy. Here it can only place emphasis on the generation of Terah, in anticipation of the following panel. V. 31 is an item of information incorporated into this generation in the form of an itinerary entry. Terah left Ur and came to Haran, even though his destination was Canaan. The motif clearly anticipates the following patriarchal stories and thus emphasizes the structural function of this unit as a redactional frame. V. 32 concludes the entry with a death-report formula like the genealogy in ch. 5 but as a unique item here.

The tenth generation also breaks the pattern (cf. 5:32). As in the regular entries, so here the age of the generation father is noted. But the point of the age is not the birth of a son but rather a continuation of the itinerary opened in the ninth generation. After the death of Terah in Haran, Abram left Haran and came to Canaan (cf. 11:31). Thus, in a subtle structure P joins genealogy with itinerary as a means for joining primeval history with patriarchs: From Shem to Abram also means from Ur to Canaan. Moreover, the genealogical entry, anticipating some notice of the birth of a son, is left provocatively open in 11:32. The structure cannot be complete without the body of the patriarchal traditions.

The structure of J, however, is quite different.

I. Exposition	11:27aβb-30
A. Birth report: Terah	27aβb
1. Sons	27aβ
2. Grandson	27b
B. Death report	20
C. Marriage report	29-30
1. Names of wives	29a
2. Identity	29b-30
a. Genealogy of Milcah	29b
b. Crisis for Sarai	30
II. Oracle of promise	12:1-3
A. Instructions	1
B. Promises	2-3
III. Execution	4a, 6-9
A. Itinerary	4a, 6
B. Theophany	7
C. Itinerary	8-9

1. First station   8
2. Second station   9

The most obvious difference between the J form of this unit and its priestly counterpart is, of course, that J does not present the structure of the entire Abraham saga in the framework of a genealogy. The first element in J's unit may presuppose a genealogy, constructed in a linear pattern for two generations, and that genealogy may appear in fragmentary form in 10:24-26, but there is no explicit contact for the central figures that come to the fore here. Rather, the opening is loose, almost abrupt. Following P's *toledoth* formula in 11:27, J defines the subjects of his presentation with a birth report. But the birth report here is not like the birth report in each generation of P's genealogy, not even like the birth report in J's genealogies (cf. Genesis 4). In inverted sentence order, the text notes that Terah fathered three sons (on inverted sentence structure with the same verb, cf. J in 10:8, 13, 15, 24, 25, 26), and he also became a grandfather. (The allusions to Lot here and in 12:4aβ anticipate the tradition in Genesis 13.) This information derives from a genealogy, but here it lies at hand simply as an introduction to following items. Moreover, v. 28 reports the death of the father of the generation, a feature common in P's genealogy but irregular in J. Further, the report does not mark the transfer to a new generation—Haran is a brother to Abram and Nahor. It signals, rather, a series of acts by Abram and Nahor as representatives of the family. Both marry. Nahor's wife is identified by her family, and the rudiments of genealogy return. Abram's wife, however, is identified by a crisis—she was barren. This theme does not reflect simply the interests of a genealogy; it is the subject for narrative development.

The oracle in 12:1-3 cannot be understood apart from the context in 11:30. It is composed of two principal elements: (1) a set of instructions to Abram, built on the patterns of an itinerary: "Go from . . . to . . ."; and (2) a set of promises constructed as purpose or goal for the instructions: "so that I may make you a great nation, so that I may bless you. . . ." The promises depend on the instructions, but under the assumption of obedience to the instructions, the promises counteract the crisis of 11:30: Abram's wife is barren: God promises Abram that he will become a great nation. Thus, the structural pattern of opposite complements characterizes this J piece (see also 2:4b–3:24; 6:1–8:22; 11:1-9).

Moreover, the promise that Abram will become a great nation is coupled with promises for blessing and a great name. The blessing resides in the multiplication of seed to the stature of a great nation, to be sure. But the reference to a blessing for Abram is tied more directly to the promise for a great name. For Yahweh to bless Abram is for him to make the name great, a prospect that is tied to Abram's fruitfulness.

The verb in v. 2b is a problem. As a 2nd m.s. imperative, it disrupts the series of verbs constructed as imperfect with simple *waw*. If one should reconstruct a similar verb by adding a *yod* to the preserved form of the text, then the series would be intact: ". . . so that I may make your name great, so that it may be a blessing." In that case, one could conclude that the blessing refers explicitly to the name—to have a great name is to have a blessing. In any case, the close connection between blessing and name here stands as an opposition to the rejection of the tower people: "Let us build a city . . . that we may make a name for ourselves." If, on the other hand, the verb in v. 2b should be translated as a 2nd m.s. imperative, it would move the speech forward to the next line: "Be a blessing, so that I may bless those who bless you, and those who curse you I shall curse." The people of the tower had no name; thus they could not understand one another, and they were scattered. Abram will have a name, however, and anyone who curses him will be cursed (cf. 4:11: Cursed "from the ground" [min-hā'ădāmâ]). That means a loss of intimacy in the human community, a loss of intimacy with nature (→ Genesis 16). And anyone who blesses him will be blessed. V. 3b continues: "In you all the families of the ground [mišpĕḥōt hā'ădāmâ] will be blessed." That means intimacy in the human community and intimacy with nature. To live in intimacy is a blessing denied to Cain and to the people of the tower, but it is an intimacy now open to all the nations through their relationship with Abram and his descendants.

The parallel breaks at one further point. The first line of the couplet uses the same verb in both halves: "I shall bless those who bless you." Cf. Num 24:9. But the second line breaks the parallel by using two different verbs in the parallel halves: "The one who holds you in contempt I shall curse." (Contrast Num 24:9.) For the significance of this change, cf. Genesis 16.

This oracle is then followed by a note that Abram executed the instructions as received and took Lot along. The pattern of the following verses is set by itinerary elements, each potentially a frame for distinct material. V. 4a should be defined structurally as the opening half of an itinerary frame: "Abram departed. . . ." The second half of the frame is in v. 5: "Abram passed through the land to the oak of Moreh." The practical impact of the frame is to include the P material in vv. 4b-5. The itinerary is continued in v. 8abα and again in v. 9. Between vv. 6 and 8 is a theophany report, v. 7a, simply a note that Yahweh appeared and spoke to Abram (see Westermann, *Promises,* 22-23, who suggests that this verse summarizes an old narrative, now no longer preserved). His speech, v. 7b, is a promise to give the land to Abram's descendants. V. 7b reports that in response Abram built an altar to Yahweh. Moreover, between vv. 8abα and 9 is a similar notice that Abram built an altar to the Lord and called on the name of the Lord. As a structural framework, the itinerary thus embraces various kinds of tradition (→ Wilderness Theme: The Framework).

The formula in v. 9 does not represent a conclusion to the series. Indeed, it is not complete. The first half of the formula notes departure from the previous site, but there is no notice of arrival. The frame is left open in much the same way that P leaves a genealogy entry open in order to include narrative tradition. This open structure anticipates the following Abraham narrative. Thus, for J the unit is not genealogy, but itinerary, and into the itinerary J inserts his own interpretation of the coming narration (see Wolff). The blessing parallel, particularly the saying "I will bless those who bless you, and him who curses you I will curse," may belong to ancient tradition (see Gen 27:29; Num 22:6; 24:9). The itinerary may also belong to ancient tradition, the pattern of an ancient pilgrimage route. The formative stage for this unit, however, belongs directly to the Yahwist. Moreover, the saying establishes the structural opposition for the relationship. In the primeval saga, the key leitmotif is "curse" ('ārar and qālal); in the patriarchs, it is "blessing" (bārak).

Genre

For the final form of the text, the unit is a GENEALOGY that embraces the whole of the Abraham story in its linear presentation of ten generations. This genre belongs to P. Indeed, the redactor incorporates priestly tradition into his scheme of the *Toledoth* Book, a structural framework that combines both the primeval saga and the patriarchal sagas. For J, the unit is an exposition for the Abraham saga. As transition, it harks back to past narratives and looks forward to the coming ones. In the process, it establishes the dominant leitmotif for its story (→ Exod 1:1-14; 13:17-22) in the structure of an itinerary.

Stereotyped forms and formulas follow a pattern dictated by the genealogy. They feature a regular succession of panels, but with no death REPORTS for any except the tenth generation (→ Genesis 5). The ITINERARY follows a pattern of movement, with notations of departure and arrival (→ Numbers 33). The blessing (→) speeches are not yet formulas but promises for blessing that depend on obedience to instructions or relationships to Abram.

Setting

The unit is redactional. It presupposes the organizational activity of P and J. Rpj is hardly more than a combination of the two sources. (On genealogy generally, → Genesis 5. On itinerary, → Numbers 33.)

Intention

The unit functions as a bond for coupling patriarchal traditions with the primeval saga. In the final form of the text, as well as in P, this intention is accomplished by means of the genealogy that puts both primeval saga and Abraham saga together in the *toledoth* series. For J, the intention focuses on introduction of the Abraham saga with the basic leitmotif for the story, but it does so in the context of transition from the primeval saga. In the primeval saga, the prospects for intimacy in all aspects of life lie under a curse. In the patriarchs, that curse may be transformed into blessing. For both J and P, the unit suggests that primeval saga and Abraham saga constitute a unity of essential importance.

Bibliography

G. W. Coats, "The Curse in God's Blessing: Gen 12:1-4a in the Structure and Theology of the Yahwist," in *Die Botschaft und die Boten* (*Fest.* H. W. Wolff; ed. Jörg Jeremias and L. Perlitt; Neukirchen-Vluyn: Neukirchener Verlag, 1981) 31-41; T. C. Hartman, "Some Thoughts on the Sumerian King List and Genesis 5 and 11B," *JBL* 91 (1972) 25-32; E. Ruprecht, "Vorgegebene Tradition und theologische Gestaltung in Genesis 12:1-3," *VT* 29 (1979) 171-88; J. Scharbert, " 'Fluchen' und 'Segnen' im AT," *Bib* 39 (1958) 1-26; idem, "Die Geschichte der bārûk-Formel," *BZ* 17 (1973) 1-28; H. W. Wolff, "The Kerygma of the Yahwist" (tr. W. A. Benware), *Int* 20 (1966) 131-58.

TALE OF A THREAT TO THE ANCESTRESS, 12:9 – 13:1

Structure

I. Introduction	12:9-10
A. Itinerary	9
B. Exposition	10
II. Complication	12:11-16

The story in this unit (J) has been given a context in the Abraham saga by the itinerary that frames it. 12:9 notes that "Abram journeyed on, still going toward the Negeb." In correspondence, 13:1 completes the frame: "Abram went up. . . , he and his wife, and all that he had, and Lot with him, into the Negeb" (→ 12:1-9). The itinerary in 13:1 has closer contact with the story, however. Its reference to movement, "he went up from Egypt" (*wayya'al . . . mimmiṣrayim*), corresponds with the opening phrase of movement, "he went down to Egypt" (*wayyēred . . . miṣraymâ*). Moreover, its allusion to Egypt as the point of departure functions as a continuation of the note in 12:20, the execution of the pharaoh's orders. But this contact is artificial and reflects adaptation of the itinerary frame for the sake of the narrative. It is as if the itinerary builds a bridge around the story, and the bridge highlights the story as somewhat isolated from its larger narrative context (see Koch, 116-17; van Seters, 170). Yet, the story develops a plot that calls on a particular context for its central affirmation. In 12:3 (J), Yahweh announces to Abram, "I will bless those who bless you, and him who curses you I will curse. . . ." The story involves the pharaoh in relationship to Abram and his blessing (see Polzin).

The story itself displays a structure with four parts: an exposition, v. 10; a complication, vv. 11-16; a resolution, vv. 17-19; and a conclusion, v. 20. (1) The exposition opens in a fashion typical for tales, with an imperfect consecutive from the verb "be" (*wayĕhî*): "(Once) there was a famine. . . ." The purpose of the exposition is to define external circumstances for the story's narration and the principal figure who responds: "(Once) there was a famine. . . . So Abram went to Egypt . . . because the famine was severe. . . ." These items of information give the audience what they need to know in order to participate in the story. Moreover, the exposition corresponds with the conclusion in v. 20: "Abram went down to Egypt"/"They sent him on his way."

(2) The complication in vv. 11-16 sets Abram into a particular relationship with the pharaoh. Sarai remains passive in the story, addressed but silent. The

110

first part of the complication, an address to Sarai, lays out a prediction about the pharaoh's response to Abram's beautiful wife. Moreover, he proposes a plan to forestall the dire consequences he anticipates: "When the Egyptians see you . . . they will kill me, but they will let you live. Say you are my sister, that it may go well with me." The implications of the plan are clear: (a) She is not his sister (contrast the explanation in Genesis 20). (b) To say that she is his sister is to invite overtures or more from those who hear. The second part of the complication notes the fulfillment of Abram's predictions, with the appropriate consequences. The Egyptians did see her, and as a result, the pharaoh took her into the royal harem and paid Abram for the privilege. The list of payment in v. 16 is in itself a stereotype, designed to depict the very wealthy. The complication thus presents a positive note. Abram, a stranger (cf. v. 10, *lāgûr* ["to sojourn"]), becomes a wealthy man by the generosity of his host. The primary character of the element as complication, however, lies in the loss Abram sustains—Sarai is no longer in his house. For the sake of his life (as well as the wealth, as Polzin suggests), he submits her to intentional adultery in the pharaoh's house. Thus, the intimacy represented by Abram and Sarai is broken without a notation of Sarai's response (→ Genesis 2–3).

(3) The resolution, vv. 17-20, opens with a notation of divine plagues against the whole house of the pharaoh because of Sarai. The plagues are not explained further. They may be punishment for the sin of adultery, although nothing explicit enters the story that would relate the plagues to a theological construct of sin and punishment. The context might suggest, rather, that the plagues derive from the pharaoh's unwitting violation of Abram and his family structure, even though Abram seems to have facilitated the violation with his plan. In any case, because of the plagues, the pharaoh confronts Abram. His speech is first an accusation, constructed with legal, preofficial formulaic language (see Boecker). V. 19b, then, marks the peripeteia of the story. On the basis of his accusations, the pharaoh announces his judgment: Sarai will be restored to her husband. After the restoration, Abram leaves Egypt with his wealth and his wife. But the judgment has a negative cast about it as well: Abram must leave Egypt; he is formally deported.

(4) The conclusion completes the narrative of the confrontation between the pharaoh and Abram, the execution of the pharaoh's sentence on his guest. Officials of the court escort Abram out of the country: "They sent him on the way, with his wife and all that he had." The theme of division that characterizes the relationship between Abram and his wife in the complication thus reaches fulfillment in the relationship between Abram and the pharaoh. Abram may be wealthy, and the pharaoh's house may be free of plagues, but the pharaoh and Abram stand opposed to each other. The issue here does not appear, at least explicitly, as Sarai's childlessness, a challenge to the promise of God. To be sure, one may ask how Sarai can bear Abram's promised seed if she is endangered in the harem of the pharaoh. The promised seed remains at best in the background, however, overshadowed here by the relationship between Abram and the pharaoh. A foreigner who has called down the plagues of Yahweh by his relationship with the wife of this blessed man must separate himself from the source of divine blessing.

The story follows the patterns of folk narrative. A limited number of principals engage in dramatic contact. The plot line is simple, employing speech as well as narration at key points in its display. The peripeteia has some unexpected qualities that alter the course of the story, breaking the tension not by an act of the human principals but by divine intervention. The conclusion eases the audience out of the experience. Moreover, the narrative employs formulas from preofficial legal circles. The story in J may thus stand very close to oral tradition (see van Seters, 170). For subsequent stages in the tradition's history, → Genesis 20; 26. Even behind Gen 12:10-20 an oral tradition probably developed a basic narrative pattern: (1) The patriarch traveled to a foreign land (Gerar rather than Egypt?). (2) The king (or pharaoh) took the beautiful wife into the royal harem, and adultery followed. (3) The crime comes to the attention of the king (by a foreign god or soothsayer?). (4) The king responds with a formal challenge to the patriarch (and deportation? → 26:1-18). (5) The patriarch becomes wealthy (see Koch, 125-26).

Stereotyped expressions and formulas in the pericope include the structure of the exposition in v. 10 and preofficial legal accusations of v. 18: "What is this you have done to me? Why did you not tell me that she was your wife?" Two structural aspects of this accusation call for comment. (1) "What have you done to me?" In itself a stereotyped formula of preofficial legal dispute, this question addresses Abram directly with a second-person verbal form (→ 3:13). (2) The following questions, introduced by *lāmmâ* ("why") and constructed again with second-person verbs, spell out the context of the accusation (→ Exod 17:3).

Genre

As a relatively independent, distinct narrative in the Abraham saga of J, as well as in whatever oral levels one might reconstruct for the story, this unit can be defined as a TALE.

Setting

The setting for this story within the framework of J is, of course, the literary, theological construct of the Yahwist. Even in this setting in the literature, however, one cannot fail to preceive the popular cast of the unit (see van Seters). It derives from whatever circumstance the people might have constructed for telling stories. Since the story involves a husband and wife, it might have been preserved in family circles (see Westermann, *Genesis*). If that was the case, the fundamental reason lies not in the content of the story, but rather in the occasion family life offers for telling stories. In that case, the setting might properly be defined as family, or larger family, tribal gatherings.

Intention

The tale is told to entertain. But in the process questions of family existence are raised sharply. How did this family become rich? Or more to the point, why is the relationship with Egypt as it is? Or even more, why is the relationship between husband and wife, Abram and Sarai, as it is (→ Genesis 2–3)? The narrative thus intends to portray a new stage in the struggle for intimacy. Abram, the man of proverbial faith, loses intimacy with his wife, and only by the intervention of God is the intimacy restored. The tale does not concern the promise for numerous descendants or even for a son (→ 26:1-17), except insofar as the larger context of J imposes it on the narrative plan.

Bibliography

H. J. Boecker, *Redeformen des Rechtslebens im Alten Testament* (WMANT 14; Neukirchen-Vluyn: Neukirchener Verlag, 1964); C. A. Keller, "Die Gefährdung der Ahnfrau," *ZAW* 66 (1954) 181-91; K. Koch, *The Growth of the Biblical Tradition: The Form-Critical Method* (tr. S. M. Cupitt; New York: Scribners, 1969): D. L. Petersen, "A Thrice-Told Tale: Genre, Theme, and Motif," *BR* 18 (1973) 30-43; R. Polzin, " 'The Ancestress of Israel in Danger' in Danger," in *Semeia 3: Classical Hebrew Narrative* (ed. R. C. Culley; Missoula, Montana: Scholars Press, 1975) 81-98.

ABRAHAM-LOT NOVELLA, 11:10 – 12:9; 13:1 – 14:24; 18:16 – 19:38

Structure

I. Introduction	11:10–12:9*
II. Separation	13:1-18
III. Rescue	14:1-24
IV. Intercession	18:16-33
V. Destruction of Sodom	19:1-38
A. Rescue	
B. Incest	

The Abraham-Lot tradition forms a remarkably well-unified narration within the scope of the Abraham saga (see von Rad, *Genesis,* 225). The tradition opens with genealogical information intertwined with the general introduction to the Abraham saga. Thus, in J, 11:27b reports the birth of Lot to Haran, while 12:4a notes that Lot accompanied Abram in the journey from Haran in obedient response to God's call. Moreover, the transitional itinerary in 13:1 suggests that Lot was involved in the Egyptian journey represented by 12:10-20. The point in these brief allusions is simply to incorporate Lot as an intrinsic figure in the Abraham narration.

Ch. 13 constitutes the first major unit of Lot tradition, a unit marked by the separation between Abram and Lot. The narrative here represents Lot as rather clever, manipulating a conflict with Abram over space for maintaining his wealth into possession of choice territory. Thus, it is quite appropriate to describe the Abraham-Lot narration in terms of a narrative contrast (so, Jepsen). Moreover, the contrast foreshadows subsequent elements by placing Lot in jeopardy (13:13). Yet, to describe the contrast in terms of competition, on the analogy of Ishmael-Isaac or Jacob-Esau/Jacob-Laban, fails to penetrate the character of the tradition. Lot does not represent a competitor for Abram, even in ch. 13. Abram remains somewhat aloof from the accidental fumbling of Lot (see his apparently wise choice of the best land that leads him into contact with the wicked city of Sodom, 13:13).

There is some difficulty in the transition between chs. 13 and 14. In ch. 13, Lot is a wealthy nomad, possessor of so many cattle that his servants necessarily come into conflict with the servants of Abram. As a resolution of the conflict, he separates from Abram in order to establish possession of the good land in the Jordan Valley. But in ch. 14, he is an inhabitant of the city, a subject of the king of Sodom. There is, of course, some preparation for that conflict in 13:12, a depiction of the basic contrast in terms of dwelling: "Abram dwelt in the land of Canaan, while Lot dwelt among the cities of the valley and moved his *tent* as far

113

as Sodom." Lot dwells in a tent, but the tent now resides in relationship to a city. Thus, already in ch. 13 some ambiguous quality in Lot's circumstances emerges.

Ch. 14 functions in its present form not simply as a chronicle of battles waged by the king of Elam and his allies, but as an Abraham-Lot narrative. When the king of Elam defeats the king of Sodom, he takes spoil, which includes Lot and his family (14:12). Lot is not the political figure involved in the war, neither the overlord nor the aggressor. He is merely one among the citizens of Sodom taken as spoil by the victor. He is totally passive, a point emphasized by the opening of the unit in vv. 1-11 without a word about Lot. Moreover, Abram hears of Lot's capture, moves to the rescue with relatively few men, and emerges as the family hero. Lot, however, remains passive. He is rescued, but he makes no contribution to the rescue (see 14:16). The unit comes to its end with an account of Abram's relationship with the king of Sodom, qualified with an account of his relationship with the king of Salem. Indeed, it is somewhat surprising that the relationship with the king of Sodom, whom Abram also rescued, is somewhat negative (→ 14:17-24). It anticipates some continuation of the struggle. But there is no word about Lot. It is as if Lot's role in the account has receded behind the king of Sodom to a new subordination. As a subject of the king, Lot shares the anticipated struggle with the king, but competitor with Abram or narrative opposition in contrast to Abram he is not.

In 18:16-33, Abraham comes again to the defense of Sodom, but the defense only assumes the Abraham-Lot tradition—it does not develop that tradition explicitly (on the unity of these verses with the Abraham-Lot complex, see von Rad, *Genesis*, 225). Nevertheless, the assumption is a necessary one. The subject of Abraham's defense is Sodom. Abraham ironically defends the city and its inhabitants whose king had accused him of misappropriation of spoil. Moreover, the defense also assumes an intervention on Lot's behalf, like the intervention in ch. 14. Lot, the one who chose the best land, must again be rescued from conflict associated with that land. Indeed, the best land is now the evil land (13:13); the entire dialogue in 18:23-33 emphasizes the evil quality of the inhabitants in the land's city (→ 18:16-33). The implication of the unit is that Lot, an inhabitant of the city, might escape the divine, cosmic destruction by virtue of his righteousness. But Lot has not been depicted as righteous. The question posed by the unit, then, focuses on Lot's fate. Can he escape the destruction intended for the land of his own choice?

Ch. 19 divides into two parts, an account of the destruction of Sodom in vv. 1-29 and an account of incest in vv. 30-38. The first account proves the character of the men of the city, a theme established first in 13:13. It also depicts Lot as a host who takes his responsibility seriously. The serious defense of the guests who come to him compares favorably to the hospitality offered the same guests by Abraham in 18:1-15. Lot thus secures salvation from the destruction for himself and his family. Despite this positive note, the narrative reduces Lot to a figure of comic tragedy. Abraham has no active role to play in this chapter. The comparison now derives only from context. This point alone would suggest that the narrative does not play on an opposition between Abraham and Lot. The comparison is rather that of hero and fool. As soon as the fool attempts to defend his guests in an active manner, he loses his position of strength and must be rescued by the guests he sought to protect. He becomes passive, and in his passive position his initial offer of his daughters for the gratification of his evil neighbors appears the more tragic. It is a fruitless effort of a figure who cannot affect the course of events that involves his own family and, of course, himself. In this context, the second account, 19:30-38, rounds out the tragic comedy. The survivor of the destruction becomes the father of two groups of people, but he does not choose to do so. Rather, his daughters, once offered without their consent to the pleasure of the evil neighbors, now take their pleasure with their father. This they do by first reducing the father to drunken insensibility. The father of the two peoples becomes their tribal patriarch in an incestuous relationship—that is tragic enough. But he does so in a completely passive way, unaware of the event that embroils him. Beyond this occasion the tradition has nothing more to say about Lot.

The Lot tradition is rooted most firmly in 19:30-38 (see Lods, Noth, Kilian). But that the tradition was originally attached to a place or told to glorify the wild freedom of the mothers seems doubtful. At least as far as the tradition now preserved is concerned, its ethnological tendencies are Israelite, presenting Lot as a buffoon, and the daughters as supporting figures.

Genre
In the present form of the text, the Abraham-Lot narrative is a subplot in the Abraham saga. Yet, its remarkable unity (see von Rad, *Genesis,* 225), its subtle development of character, and its position of an initial crisis resolved only by the final scene suggest creative composition. It seems possible that the genre of the whole as it was before incorporation into J's Abraham SAGA should be understood as NOVELLA, a genre that by virtue of its complex structure can commonly be split apart in order to include new elements of narrative (→ Genesis 37–50).

Setting
The text as it now stands derives from the literary, redactional setting of J. A novella presupposes literary activity, the act of the redactor if not directly the act of the storyteller. For this novella, the interests of a popular audience, perhaps within the context of the family, come first to mind. Older forms of the tradition may suggest a Moabite or pre-Moabite populace rather than the Israelite characteristics of the final form in the text.

Intention
The novella now provides a redactional structure for several pieces of Abraham material, including the redactional structure of an additional extended piece of narration (→ Genesis 16; 18; 21). As a narrative unit, it presents Lot as a comic foil for Abraham, not a competitor who adds tension to the Abraham narratives, but a buffoon whose efforts to affect events produce only tragicomic consequences.

Bibliography
A. Jepsen, "Zur Überlieferungsgeschichte der Vätergestalten," *WZLeipzig* 3 (1953/54) 139-55; R. Kilian, *Die vorpriesterlichen Abrahamsüberlieferungen literarkritisch und traditionsgeschichtlich untersucht* (BBB 24; Bonn: Hanstein, 1966); idem, "Zur Überlieferungsgeschichte Lots," *BZ* 14 (1970) 23-37; A. Lods, "La caverne de Lot," *RHR* 95 (1927) 204-19.

TALE ABOUT THE ABRAM-LOT SEPARATION, 13:1-18

Structure

I. Itinerary	1
II. Narrative body	2-17
A. Exposition	2-6
1. Introduction of Abram	2
2. Change in location	3-4
3. Introduction of Lot	5
4. Problem	6
B. Complication	7
1. Strife	7a
2. Gloss	7b
C. Denouement	8-17
1. Abram's suit for peace	8-9
a. Appeal	8
b. Proposal for resolution	9
2. Execution of proposal	10-17
a. Lot	10-12
1) Description of the land	10
2) Lot's choice	11a
3) Conclusion	11b-12
b. Renewal of complication	13
c. Yahweh's promise to Abram	14-17
1) For land	14-15
2) For posterity	16
3) For land	17
III. Itinerary	18

This unit is framed by itinerary notices (vv. 1, 18), each somewhat extrinsic to the unity of the whole. V. 1 can function equally well with either the preceding unit or this one, in either case marking a movement of the patriarch as transition from the one unit of tradition to the other. V. 18 meshes relatively well with the instructions in v. 17; yet, the relationship is superficial and does not contribute substantially to the unity of the text. This itinerary notes simply departure and arrival without fundamental connection with the substance of the unit. The disunity is apparent even though the arrival site is marked as the oaks of Mamre and opens the unit to 18:1. Even the reference to an altar built at Mamre does not contribute to narrative tradition and thus remains somewhat on the periphery of the unit. The itinerary framework thus continues in form and tradition the pattern established by 12:6-9.

The unit can be described in terms of a plot line stretching from an introduction of the principals and the problem that characterizes their relationship to a resolution of the problem. Thus, exposition, vv. 2-6, and denouement, vv. 8-17, connect by means of a complication in v. 7. The problem in such an analysis is, of course, the disproportion in the various parts. Indeed, the denouement may be no genuine conclusion but only a respite. These points must be demonstrated by means of a more detailed examination. (1) V. 2 opens the exposition with inverted syntax (cf. the normal order of the itinerary in v. 1). This verse introduces Abram as a wealthy man, while vv. 3-4 connect the unit explicitly with the itinerary tradition of 12:6-9. V. 5 then returns to the inverted sentence order of v. 2 in order to introduce Lot, also described as a wealthy man. V. 6 follows by setting the problem for the following narrative unit: Abram and Lot could not dwell together; the land could not support them. (2) V. 7a compounds the problem by introducing strife as the primary characteristic in the relationship between the two families (→ 21:22-34). V. 7b is not a part of the complication but simply a gloss that introduces extraneous information into the course of the narration. (3) The denouement leads to separation between the family members, but not to a resolution of the tension. Abram's speech suggests a largessc toward Lot as a means for resolving the strife (cf. 21:25-32; 26:17-33). Lot may choose the area of land he wants for his own possession, but the choice involves institutionalizing the tension. The two agree on a permanent separation (vv. 9, 11). Lot exercises his choice. The good land in the Jordan Valley attracts his eye, and the problem would appear to be resolved. V. 10b foreshadows the following narration, however, and thus as a redactional bond prepares the way for ch. 19. The story itself concentrates on the strife within the family motivating the move. Vv. 11b-12 show the degree of separation that enables each party to pursue his own life.

The narrative doubles back on its complication, however. V. 13 sets the problem: The men of Sodom were wicked. The renewed complication does for the substance of the story what v. 10b does as a redactional addition—it foreshadows development of the tension in a new direction.

The complex character of the unit comes sharply to light in the remaining sections of the unit. Rather than developing the renewed tension, vv. 14-17 shift the pace of the unit to a traditional piece, a promise to Abram for possession of the land and for multiplication of descendants (→ Genesis 15). The promise speech moves from land (vv. 14-15) to descendants (v. 16) and back to land (v. 17), and with the promise the unit breaks off. Its narrative line is incomplete. (On tradition history and source relationships, → Genesis 13–14; 18–19. For consideration of the unit as a part of a larger whole, see van Seters, 222.)

Formulas and stereotyped expression include: the itinerary formulas (vv. 3, 18), the speech formula to mark speaker and addressee (vv. 8, 14), and the stereotyped nature of the promise speeches (vv. 14-15, 16).

Genre

The unit develops structural characteristics of a (→) tale, but breaks off before the tale can be completed. Genre identification thus cannot be established for this unit alone (→ Genesis 13–14; 18–19).

Setting

→ Genesis 13–14; 18–19.

Intention

The narrative depicts family strife leading to separation of family members. Ethnological elements may be reflected here. The family of Abram settles on land less attractive than the land settled by Lot's family, but profits in the final analysis.

117

For J, the unit depicts the tragedy associated with separation from the family of Abram.

Bibliography

→ Genesis 13–14; 18–19; B. Gemser, "The rîb- or Controversy-Pattern in Hebrew Mentality," in *Wisdom in Israel and in the Ancient Near East (Fest.* H. H. Rowley; ed. M. Noth and D. Winton Thomas; VTSup 3; Leiden: Brill, 1955) 120-37; G. W. Ramsey, "Speech Forms in Hebrew Law and Prophetic Oracles," *JBL* 96 (1977) 45-58.

REPORT OF HEROIC BATTLE, 14:1-24

Structure

I. Annals	1-16
A. Battle report	1-4
1. Date	1
2. Report	2-4
a. Statement of battle	2
b. Place	3
c. Source of rebellion	4
B. Battle report	5-12
1. Battle itinerary	5-7
2. Report	8-12
a. Event	8-9
b. Results	10
c. Spoil	11-12
1) Goods	11
2) Lot	12
C. Battle report	13-16
1. Messenger from the previous battle	13
2. Report	14-16
a. Event	14-15
b. Results: the freeing of Lot	16
II. Division of spoil	17-24
A. Confrontation: Abram and the king of Sodom	17
B. Tithe	18-20
1. Confrontation: Abram and the king of Salem	18
2. Blessing	19-20a
3. Conclusion	20b
C. Dialogue: Abram and the king of Sodom	21-24
1. Proposal for division of spoil	21
2. Response	22-24
a. Declaration of innocence	22-23
b. Renewed proposal	24

The unit (J) reveals its connection with the larger context only in the middle elements of its structure. At the beginning and end the connection is somewhat lame. Without reference to the principal figures of ch. 13, the first verses of ch. 14

(vv. 1-4) recount a battle report. At the end, Abram is the chief principal, but his act has nothing to do with chs. 13–14. These points contribute to the impression that the chapter is isolated. From the middle sections, however, the unit establishes its contact with the larger narrative theme connected with Abraham and Lot. In ch. 13, Lot separated from Abram in order to lay claim to the good land in the Jordan Valley. Lot is now separated from his land as a prisoner of war and must depend on Abram's heroic intervention to restore him to his rightful place. The unit can thus be understood properly as a part of the Abraham-Lot tradition, indeed, as a counterpart to the narrative about separation in ch. 13.

The narrative comprises two major elements: (1) a report of a battle and its consequences and (2) an account of disposition for spoil taken in the battle. The first element is essentially a unity (see van Seters, *Abraham*, 297-304). It unfolds as a series of battle reports, each related to the other in logical style but not always in chronological order. The first is a brief report of a battle, recounted in more detail by the second and reported by a messenger to a third party in the third. The report leads to a renewed battle with opposite results. The first segment includes a date (v. 1) and a general account of the battle depicting the conflict as a rebellion of vassals against overlords (vv. 2-4). Vv. 5-12 repeat the battle report with greater detail. First, an itinerary for the overlord recounts his victorious entry into Palestine. The entry follows the structural plan of a list, at least in vv. 5-6. The list is not quite an itinerary, noting departure from one site and arrival at another. Yet, its plan parallels the battle itinerary of royal annals (cf. the Annals of Shalmaneser III, *ANET*, 276-80) Moreover, vocabulary in vv. 6-7 parallels the itinerary vocabulary of Num 33:6-7 (see particularly *'al-hammidbar wayyašubu* [". . . on the border of the wilderness; then they turned back . . ."]). Vv. 8-9 repeat vv. 2-3, while vv. 10-12 report the results of the battle: in v. 10 the rout of the vassals, in vv. 11-12 the spoil for the victor come to the fore. Vv. 1-11 contain an annalistic report and fit properly in the structural framework of a battle itinerary. V. 12 also belongs to that structure, a part of the detail in the unit's description of spoil for the victor. Yet, the verse breaks the pattern by incorporating the personal names, Lot and Abram, from previous narrative units. With that break a point of tension appears.

Vv. 13-16 are a third report of the battle, though without the details of the second. A messenger relates to Abram the consequences of the battle, and the report leads to a new battle with contrasting results. The victors become the victims, and the spoil goes to Abram. Thus, the list structure in the earlier part of the unit gives way to report that merges into a span of tension for a narrative. One must be cautious here, however. The unit does not reveal characteristics of tale very easily. The reference to Abram and Lot in v. 12 depends on the larger context for identification. Without the context, v. 12 would suggest contact with narrative tradition, but it would not yet clarify the point of tension that would create a story line. It would at most be a foundation to explain the report in vv. 13-16. The point of tension is nonetheless established and resolved: Lot was taken captive as spoil in war; Abram's heroic response releases the captive from his fate.

The second major element in the unit, vv. 17-24, relates to the first as an account of disposition for the spoil gathered in the battle. Yet, it shifts its focus of narration entirely. There is no concern here for Lot, his family, or his goods.

The entire structure centers on Abram and his allies as possessors of spoil. But even in this shift a structural problem emerges (see van Seters, *Abraham,* 303). Vv. 17, 21-24 concern relationships between Abram and the king of Sodom, one of the victims who with Abram's help became victor. The subject of the account is division of spoil. To that end, v. 17 gives a general introduction to the encounter, v. 21 the proposal of the king of Sodom, and vv. 22-24 a declaration of innocence by Abram, who abandons any personal claim on the spoil. The proposal by the king of Sodom is in itself a denial of claim to physical goods taken in the battle in preference for possession of all persons taken as prisoners of war. The intention would be to reduce those persons to slavery.

Abram responds, however, as if the proposal suggests unjust appropriation of goods. This point appears in Abram's denial of claim to the goods as well as in an allusion to a boast from the king of Sodom. The citation implies that Abram might have taken more than his share of the spoil, thus suggesting the need for such a declaration of innocence. In v. 24, he claims only enough for the allies and that which the allies might have already consumed. Vv. 22-23 ground Abram's vow of innocence toward the spoil in an oath taken in the name of Yahweh El Elyon ("Lord God Most High"), and with that allusion an opening is established for the unit in vv. 18-20. In these verses, however, there is no reference to an oath. Rather, Abram and the priest of God Most High are associated with a ritual meal (v. 18). The meal (covenant?) leads to a blessing for Abram and payment of tithe from the spoil. The blessing, constructed in parallel lines, is rooted in God Most High, "creator" (*qōnēh*) of heaven and earth. The second line connects the Abram blessing with a blessing of El Elyon, the source of Abram's victory (*miggēn* ["who delivered . . ."]; cf. 15:1, *māgēn*). (See Towner; van Seters, *Abraham,* 302, 308.) It is significant, then, that Abram's appeal to an oath in v. 22 names the deity "Yahweh El Elyon" and secures some equation between this blessing for Abram and God and the blessing in 12:2-3 (→ Psalm 110). Yet, the blessing occurs after the defeat of the enemy. Abram is already blessed and stands as a source of blessing for his own people, a source of curse for his enemy. The blessing here thus appears the more to be a secondary attachment of Melchizedek tradition to the blessing pattern that roots primarily in the Abram/Abraham tradition. Moreover, the implication by the king of Sodom that Abram's blessing might have been unjustly appropriated hangs in the air and recalls the note in 13:13. The king of Elam and his allies could not endure against the blessed Abram. What, then, happened to the king of Sodom?

Thus, structure in the chapter encompasses diverse tradition. Indeed, it suggests a narrative tradition perhaps more extensive than that now preserved by the MT. The form of that tradition cannot be reconstructed, however, and remains only a specter of an oral past that suggests that the present form of the story should not be reduced too quickly to the results of a single level of writing process. The unit nonetheless displays some marked structural unity in the midst of its diversity. A battle, involving various peoples of the territory, leads to deportation of Sodom, including Lot. Abram, who gladly received the less fertile land in order to avoid further strife in the family, now comes to rescue his familial opponent. The juxtaposition does not, however, place Lot simply as the opposite of Abram. Lot remains a passive figure, taken as a slave by an overlord without explicitly being involved in the rebellion, then taken as a rescued kinsman by

Abram without explicitly being involved in the rescue. As a piece of a larger narrative unit (J), then, the chapter connects with chs. 13 and 18–19.

Genre

(On genre for the larger whole, → The Abraham Saga; → Abraham-Lot Novella.) The unit maintains its character as ANNAL, composed of battle REPORTS, particularly in the light of the successive encounters of the king of Elam along the way to his conflict with the coalition of kings in the Valley of Siddim. Its construction in third-person narrative contrasts with the first-person style of the annals of the Assyrian and Babylonian kings, however, and suggests that the annal structure merges with the narrative interests of third-person CHRONICLES. As battle report, the material has nothing in common with (→) tale (see van Seters, *Abraham*, 300). This point emphasizes the radical shift effected by the introduction of Lot and Abram (vv. 12-13): The chronicle structure merges with the design of a TALE (see van Seters, *Abraham*, 301). Indeed, the allusion places the unit into a larger narrative unit by virtue of its assumption about the relationship between Lot and Abram. It is possible to see the story simply as an account of rescue by a family member. But the story gains in depth if it is placed in the context of previous narrative accounts of the relationship. As an account of military conflict waged by a central figure on behalf of his family, the tale may reveal heroic motifs (see Emerton).

Setting

(On setting for the larger whole, → The Abraham Saga; Abraham-Lot Novella.) The tale is a part of the storyteller's repertoire and belongs to the popular context of the narrator's art. As an artistic process, the narrative may use forms from other settings, such as annal from the archives of the royal court.

Intention

As a part of a larger narrative unit concerned with Abram and Lot within the structures of a family, the unit contrasts with ch. 13 to depict Abram as the source of power in the family despite his relinquishing the fertile land to Lot. Lot has the choice of land but cannot defend it. This vignette incorporates battle reports as chronicles of an invasion from Mesopotamia. Since chronicles of an invasion should document the power of a king, the chronicle structure becomes a literary tool to emphasize by contrast the failure of the invasion when the blessed Abram moves into the conflict, a point that contrasts with the inability of Lot to do anything to affect the events.

Bibliography

M. C. Astour, "Political and Cosmic Symbolism in Genesis 14 and Its Babylonian Sources," in *Biblical Motifs: Origins and Transformations* (ed. A. Altmann; Cambridge: Harvard University Press, 1966) 65-112; J. Emerton, "The Riddle of Genesis XIV," *VT* 21 (1971) 403-39; W. Schatz, *Genesis 14. Eine Untersuchung* (Bern: Lang, 1972); J. van Seters, "The Conquest of Sihon's Kingdom: A Literary Examination," *JBL* 91 (1972) 187-89; W. S. Towner, " 'Blessed be YHWH' and 'Blessed Art Thou, YHWH': The Modulation of a Biblical Formula," *CBQ* 30 (1968) 386-99; W. Zimmerli, "Abraham und Melchisedek," in *Das ferne und nahe Wort* (*Fest.* L. Rost; ed. F. Maass; BZAW 105; Berlin: Töpelmann, 1967) 255-64.

PROMISE DIALOGUE, 15:1-21

Structure

I. Promise dialogue	1-6
A. Yahweh speech	1
1. Transition and word formula	1a
2. Self-revelation	1b
a. Reassurance formula	
b. Self-revelation formula	
c. Promise for reward	
B. Abram's request for surety	2
1. Speech formula	
2. Request	
C. Abram's complaint	3
1. Speech formula	
2. Complaint	
D. Yahweh's promise	4
1. Word formula	
2. Promise for a son	
E. Yahweh's instructions	5a
1. Speech formula	
2. Instructions for surety	
F. Promise speech	5b
1. Speech formula	
2. Promise for numerous descendants	
G. Conclusion	6
II. Promise dialogue	7-21
A. Yahweh speech	7
1. Speech formula	
2. Self-revelation	
a. Formula	
b. Land promise	
B. Abram's request for surety	8
1. Speech formula	
2. Request	
C. Yahweh's instructions	9
1. Speech formula	
2. Instructions for selection of animals	
D. Execution of instructions	10-11
E. Yahweh's promise	12-21
1. Circumstances	12
2. Promise speech	13-16
a. Speech formula	13aα
b. Promise	13aβb-16
1) Exodus	13aβb-14

	2) Abram's death	15
	3) Return to land	16
3.	Circumstances	17
4.	Promise speech	18-21
	a. Speech formula	18a
	b. Land promise	18b-21

Genesis 15 is distinct from the narrative context that surrounds it. The chapter, basically a part of the Yahwist tradition though perhaps expanded by the Elohist, does not represent the continuation of the narrative in Genesis 14, not even the narratives in Genesis 12–13. The governing structure in this unit is quite distinct (→ Genesis 13–14). It is necessary, nonetheless, to recognize a certain connection between Genesis 14 and 15 that may already have occurred before J gave the complex its current position (so, Lohfink, 84-86). The connection is attested not only by the opening formula, but also by key terms such as "possession" (*rěkūš*) in 14:11, 12, 16, 21 par. 15:14; "to go out" (*yāṣā'*) in 14:17, 18 par. 15:4, 5, 7, 14; and "to deliver" (*miggēn*) in 14:20 par. "shield" (*māgēn*) in 15:1. It would be possible to suggest, then, that the vague "reward" of v. 1 refers to the spoil of 14:20-24. Indeed, the connection suggests some intentional localization of the tradition in Jerusalem (→ Genesis 14). In contrast to Genesis 14–15, Genesis 16 moves in a direction more closely related to Genesis 12 and, by motif, Genesis 13. These narratives develop family relationships. Genesis 15 is quite different, however; this piece is isolated by structure and, perhaps with ch. 14, by content from its context.

The structure of the unit emphasizes its isolation. It does not develop the stages of a tale; it reveals no plot of a story; it is not narrative. (See Westermann, *Promises,* 15-16, who understands the chapter as essentially different from the usual tale that narrates a unique event, but describes the unit nonetheless as narrative. Lohfink, 33, describes the unit as "artificial narrative" [*nachgeahmte Erzählung*].) Rather, it is composed entirely of speeches. Moreover, even the speeches are arranged in a rather loose order. Nevertheless, one can recognize two segments of speeches that hang together, each as a dialogue between Yahweh and Abram. The two segments develop parallel lines and, though embracing quite diverse traditions, qualify as complements. With this loose order of speeches, the isolation from a context of narratives is apparent.

The parallel lines in the two segments can be described as follows: (1) self-revelation speech (v. 1 par. v. 7); (2) Abram's complaint ([2] 3 par. 8); (3) instructions speech (5a par. 9); and (4) promise speech (4, 5b par. 13-16, 18-21). The parallel lines are not evidence for two sources, however. They must be understood in a traditio-historical context, shaped from a relatively early point under the influence of a priestly oracle of salvation (see Westermann, *Promises*, 18; Kaiser). The first segment opens with a narrative formula, a transition from the preceding units: "After these things . . ." (*'aḥar hadděbārîm hā'ēlleh*). The presence of the formula does not, however, violate the observations about context noted above (see Lohfink, 33 n. 4; van Seters, *Abraham*, 253). Since the formula may be used as a transition between two closely related units (see 39:7; 40:1) or unrelated units (see 1 Kgs 13:33), it can build a context in some manner, but the context can be quite artificial (see Josh 24:29). Moreover, each of the speeches is marked with a speech formula ("He said to . . .") or a distinctive formula known more widely in the prophets ("The word of the Lord came to . . ."). The word formula (1 Sam 15:10; 2 Sam 7:4; 24:11; 1 Kgs 2:14; 6:11; 12:22; 13:20; 16:1, 7; 17:2, 8; 18:1, 31; 19:9; 21:17, 28; → Hos 1:1) tends to contribute to the isolation of the unit, however, since its appearance in 15:1 and 4 is unique in the Pentateuch and identifies the following speeches as a collection quite distinct from the narratives embracing it (see Westermann, *Promises,* 15; van Seters, *Abraham,* 253).

The self-revelation speech has two parts. The first, a self-introduction with its center in a nominal sentence, "I am your shield [*māgēn*]," identifies the speaker by name, or at least by attribute (see Zimmerli, "Ich bin Jahwe"). The preceding formula, admonishing Abram not to fear, does not presume response from the recipient but derives entirely from the sacred context of the revelation (cf. Exod 3:5-6). It does not itself represent the form of an oracle of salvation (see Begrich) but only an introduction to divine speech (see van Seters, *Abraham,* 255). The second part is a promise (cf. Exod 3:7-8). Perhaps the point of reference in the promise speech is military (see the comments of van Seters, *Abraham,* 254), but the content of the promise is vague: "Your reward shall be very great." The first response from Abram to the promise (v. 2) is strictly speaking not yet a complaint. It is a request, apparently, for a surety or sign related to the promise. The motivation for the request, however, anticipates a complaint. Abram is childless, and the absence of a child complicates the process of inheritance. With a new speech formula, v. 3 makes the complaint specific: "You have given me no offspring. . . ." The duplication of Abram speeches need not imply levels in the tradition. Yahweh's response to the complaint, however, encompasses three successive speeches. In these speeches lies the possibility for developing a tradition history, for the first and the second two speeches embrace slightly different traditions. The first speech, introduced by a word formula (v. 4), promises a son (see Westermann, *Promises,* 95-161): The slave shall not be the heir; rather, the *one* who comes from "your loins" shall be the heir. The second two speeches promise numerous descendants. The first of these delivers a sign (v. 5a); the second ties the sign to a promise. V. 6 then stands as a conclusion. Abram accepts the sign and the promise(s). The assertion in v. 6b derives from a formal, priestly designation of an act as appropriate and acceptable before God. The key term, "righteous" (*ṣĕdāqâ*), describes that relationship. There is, of course, no priest in the exchange here, no ritual. The dialogue unfolds between Yahweh and Abram. Yet, one should not attribute a theological individualism to the text (as von Rad, "Faith"). Rather, the cultic procedures that may in practice call for a priest (oracle of salvation, torah) have exerted formative influence on the shape of this dialogue (see Westermann, *Promises,* 15-17).

The second segment of speeches follows the same pattern. The first oracle (v. 7) is a self-revelation, introducing Yahweh not only by name but also by deed: "I am Yahweh who brought you out from Ur. . . ." The revelation thus anticipates the stereotyped form: "I am Yahweh your God who brought you out of the land of Egypt . . ." (Westermann, *Promises,* 23-24). Moreover, the formula is tied to a land promise: ". . . to give you this land to possess." The promise itself takes on a rather stereotyped structure (see Lohfink). Abram's response is now much less a complaint (Lohfink, 49) than a simple request for surety (cf. v. 2). The response, however, is more ritualistic in scope than the illustrative sign from nature in the first segment. Yahweh instructs Abram to "bring" or prepare a series of animals, and Abram prepares them in a specific fashion. Again, the act is not presented as cultic: There is neither priest nor sacrifice. Rather, a ritual stamps the development of the dialogue. Yahweh's two speeches, vv. 13-16 and 18-21, again embrace quite diverse traditions. The first contains a review of the coming oppression by foreigners and of the exodus, a note about Abram's death in a "good old age," and about the return of the descendants to the land. The review is cast as a promise, a qualification of the land promise already established in v. 7. The second speech is defined explicitly as a covenant, but there is no obligation laid on Abram. Rather, the covenant unfolds simply as a promise for the land, with a designation of boundaries.

The promise, vv. 9-11, 17, is presented in the context of an oath ritual (Lohfink). The ritual centers on the land promise, itself stereotyped and expanded in vv. 19-21 with a list that has parallels in the Deuteronomistic History but stems from a predeuteronomistic period, perhaps from the time of David. The list embraces regions of broad range, as the note in v. 18b as well as the list of names in vv. 19-21 readily shows (see Lohfink 65-78). At least it is clear that the formulaic structure of the unit is complemented by the list. Finally, the two Yahweh speeches are connected by descriptions of the circumstances in the confrontation (vv. 12, 17). The descriptions are themselves symbolic and highlight the occasion of intimacy between God and creature (cf. 2:21). Moreover, v. 17 builds on the ritual anticipated in vv. 9-11. But the character of the ritual cannot be illuminated in the scope of form-critical analysis of the pericope.

The structure of the unit is thus highly formulaic, overlaid with marked stages in the history of the promise to the patriarch. The promise for a son is extended to a promise for numerous descendants. The promise for land is extended from Abram's generation through four hundred years to a subsequent generation (cf. von Rad, *Genesis*, 21-23). The promise for land and the promise for a son are presented in distinct segments, combined by the complementary parallel that sets the segments together. In its present form, the unit reflects the theological operation that brought various traditions together. Whether this operation was the work of J or presented to J as a completed piece cannot be determined here (see Lohfink, 82).

Genre

The unit is not a narrative, although a narrative may lie in the background (so, Westermann, *Promises,* 18). In its present form, the unit is simply a DIALOGUE, structured on the basis of the ORACLE OF SALVATION (see Lohfink, 79: "a collection of different traditions about promises to Abraham"). As an oracle of salvation dialogue, several marked formulaic elements require comment. (1) A NARRATIVE formula opens the unit (see the comments above). (2) The word-event formula, so widely associated with the prophets, follows in vv. 1a, 4 (see Zimmerli, "Wortereignisformel"). (3) The admonition not to fear, v. 1b, commonly a part of an assistance formula (see Preuss), is here linked instead to a SELF-INTRODUCTION formula (Zimmerli, "Ich bin Jahwe"). Cf. also v. 7. (4) A priestly declaration of acceptance, v. 6, functions also as a conclusion for the segment. (5) The ORACLE OF SALVATION builds on a tradition of promise to the patriarch. The promise for a son is the content of the oracle of salvation. The promise for land, however, is embraced by the ritual in vv. 9-12, 17 and stands in the line of a series of OATHS (26:3) to the patriarch. (On the transformation of the oath to covenant, already prefigured in v. 18, which nevertheless remains simply a promise cast as an oath, → Genesis 17.) As a parallel to the collection of promises here, one might compare the oracles to Esarhaddon (*ANET,* 449-50) or Ashurbanipal (*ANET,* 450).

Setting

The unit plays an important role in the structure of J's patriarchal theme, for it now provides not a narrative unit, but a composition, in which a basic theological perspective from J emerges. In the tradition history, several elements of the unit were anchored firmly in the cult: self-revelation, oracle of salvation, and declaration of acceptance. The patriarchal traditions thus reflect not only a setting in the popular structures of the family (→ Genesis 16; 18), but also a setting in cultic structures (→ 28:10-22). It is significant that J employs forms that derive from the cult for his key composition, but one cannot deduce a setting for J from that fact. The land promise employs ritual that is not primarily cultic, but secular. The oath-taking ceremony, vv. 9-12, 17, captures the kernel of this setting.

Intention

The unit combines two traditions, originally independent, into a single crux. J is evident by the combination: (1) God's promise of land to the patriarch, (2) the delay in fulfilling the land promise, (3) the promise of a son (in itself subject of ancient narrative), and (4) extension of the promise to embrace numerous descendants. All elements of the promise thus stand for J as a single moment of commitment by God for Abram's future.

Bibliography

J. Begrich, "Das priesterliche Heilsorakel," *ZAW* 52 (1934) 81-92; A. Caquot, "L'alliance avec Abram (Genèse 15)," *Sem* 12 (1962) 51-66; H. Cazelles, "Connexions et structure de Gen. xv," *RB* 69 (1962) 321-49; W. M. Clark, "The Origin and the Development of the Land Promise Theme in the Old Testament" (Diss., Yale, 1964); R. Clements, *Abraham and David: Genesis XV and its Meaning for Israelite Tradition* (SBT 2/5; London: SCM, 1967); H. M. Dion, "The Patriarchal Traditions and the Literary Form of the 'Oracle of Salvation'," *CBQ* 29 (1967) 198-206; J. Hoftijzer, *Die Verheissungen an die drei Erzväter* (Leiden: Brill, 1956); O. Kaiser, "Traditionsgeschichtliche Untersuchung von Genesis 15," *ZAW* 70 (1958) 107-26; K. Koch, "Die Sohnesverheissung an den ugaritischen Daniel," *ZA* 58 (1967) 211-21; S. E. Loewenstamm, "Zur Traditionsgeschichte des Bundes zwischen den Stücken," *VT* 18 (1968) 500-6; N. Lohfink, *Die Landverheissung als Eid. Eine Studie zu Gen 15* (SBS 28; Stuttgart: Katholisches Bibelwerk, 1967); D. J. McCarthy, "*běrît* in Old Testament History and Theology," *Bib* 53 (1972) 110-21; idem, "Three Covenants in Genesis," *CBQ* 26 (1964) 179-89; H. D. Preuss, ". . . ich will mit dir sein!", *ZAW* 80 (1968) 139-73; G. von Rad, "Faith Reckoned as Righteousness," in *The Problem of the Hexateuch and Other Essays* (tr. E. W. Trueman Dicken; London: Oliver and Boyd, 1966) 125-30; H. Seebass, "Zu Genesis 15," *Wort und Dienst* 7 (1963) 132-49; L. A. Snijders, "Genesis xv. The Covenant with Abram," *OTS* 12 (1958) 261-79; W. Zimmerli, "Ich bin Jahwe," in *Geschichte und Altes Testament* (Fest. A. Alt; BHT 16; Tübingen: Siebeck,

1953) 179-209; idem, "Abraham und Melchisedek," in *Das ferne und nahe Wort (Fest.* L. Rost; ed. F. Maass; BZAW 105; Berlin: Töpelmann, 1967) 255-64.

SARAH-HAGAR NOVELLA, 16:1–21:21

Structure

I. Annunciation of Ishmael	16:1-16
II. Covenant	17:1-27
III. Annunciation of Isaac	18:1-15
IV. Sodom	18:16–19:38
V. Ancestress in danger	20:1-18
VI. Expulsion of Hagar	21:1-21

In Genesis 16–21, three narrative units constitute dependent elements which taken together form a connected narration. These three units, Genesis 16; 18:1-15; and 21:1-21, have been split apart in order to form a framework for three independent units, God's covenant with Abraham in 17 (P), the Sodom-Lot narrative in 18:16–19:38 (J), and an account of the ancestress in danger, ch. 20 (E or JE). Genesis 17 (P) has been inserted into this redactional unit since it follows P's note in 16:15 that Hagar bore Ishmael. Its position here is due to the redaction that brought JE and P together. The Sodom narrative appears to be an extension of the narrative unit involving Abraham's three visitors in 18:1-15 (so Westermann, *Promises*, 59-65). The unit about the ancestress in danger is rather isolated in this larger framework complex (→ 20:1-18). Moreover, a fourth unit, 21:22-34, hangs onto the conclusion of the framework by virtue of its association with the narrative account of Abraham's adventures in Gerar. It too is somewhat isolated in its context, not substantially drawn into the narrative framework and unrelated to the following unit.

In the redactional unity constituted by these various elements, the frame provided by the three units about Sarah and Hagar requires particular attention. In contrast to the narratives noted above, these three elements reveal a marked lack of independence. The first unit proffers an exposition, although 13:18 provides a distinct point of reference for its introduction; but it breaks off rather abruptly. The second has no clear beginning or ending. The third assumes previous narration but comes to an explicit point of conclusion. The transitions are not always smooth; one cannot set the three parts together as an unbroken narrative. Yet, the structure of each suggests its overarching contact with its counterparts.

The subject of narration supports the hypothesis of unity. The tension that gives substance to the plot is the struggle between wife and maid. This tension is set out fully in Genesis 16: The wife is barren; the maid conceives and is driven out. The problem abates somewhat in Genesis 18 with the announcement of impending birth to the wife and an accompanying threat to her safety (→ 18:1-15). Then it rises again in Genesis 21 to a negative conclusion: The maid and her son are expelled from the family. Despite the separation from the family, the exiles are rescued by an angel of God who reaffirms the annunciation promise. 21:21 constitutes a rounding off of the story line, a confirmation of the permanent residence of the maid and her son in the wilderness of Paran.

The narrative line can be divided between J (JE) and P. Thus, Gen 16:15-16 reports the birth of Ishmael; Genesis 17 carries the covenant oath to Abraham for a great dynasty of descendants who will possess a land as well as a promise for a son other than Ishmael; and 21:1b-5 reports the birth of Isaac. In this combination of J (JE) and P, the narrative in P is clearly a single scene, not a composition of elements. The narrative in J, by contrast, is much more complex, with interwoven scenes and crossing motifs. It would appear, therefore, that the redactional technique calling for a narrative line to serve as a framework belongs more readily to the older source structure.

Genre

In the present form of the text, these scenes are elements in the larger SAGA, a redactional piece used for embracing a distinct body of tradition. Behind the saga, however, the subtle interweaving of scenes, which makes the Sarah-Hagar story a convenient piece for redactional framing, identifies the whole as a NOVELLA (→ Genesis 37–50). In keeping with the style of a novella, the story depicts the subtle inner life of the maid who watches her son from a distance: "And she sat over against [the child? See 2:20]. And she lifted her voice and wept." Or it sets out the jealousy of the wife whose ire disturbs the husband: "The thing was very displeasing to Abraham on account of his son." The P parallel is not a narrative story; it does not develop a tension within a plot. There is no allusion to the competition in the family. It is simply a REPORT of annunciation and birth.

Setting

As a redactional piece, the unit presupposes the literary activity of P and J, if not the redactional overview of Rjep. The story itself belongs to the entertainment circles of the family.

Intention

(1) The unit provides context for a series of narratives originally independent of its frame. (2) It makes its own contribution to the traditions about the fathers by showing the promise for a son set in the midst of a narrative unit developed around strife in the family. Both motifs emerge as structurally significant for the patriarchal traditions as a whole. (3) In P, the tradition focuses on the promise in ch. 17, following simply with reports that show the initial fulfillment of the promise. (4) The J narrative presents its plot as narrative response to the promise in ch. 15. It is remarkable, then, that the tension in the plot does not develop around the question, "How will God fulfill the promise?" Rather, it develops around the crises within the family circle.

Bibliography

G. W. Coats, "The Curse in God's Blessing: Gen 12:1-4a in the Structure and Theology of the Yahwist," in *Die Botschaft und die Boten* (*Fest.* H. W. Wolff; ed. Jörg Jeremias and L. Perlitt; Neukirchen-Vluyn: Neukirchener Verlag, 1981) 31-41; F. C. Fensham, "The Son of a Handmaid in Northwest-Semitic," *VT* 19 (1969) 312-21; D. Irvin, *Mytharion: The Comparison of Tales From the Old Testament and the Ancient Near East* (AOAT 32; Neukirchen-Vluyn: Neukirchener Verlag, 1974); R. Kilian, *Die vorpriesterlichen Abrahams-Überlieferungen literarkritisch und traditionsgeschichtlich untersucht* (BBB 24; Bonn: Hanstein, 1966); S. E. McEvenue, "A Comparison of Narrative Styles in the Hagar Stories," in *Semeia* 3: *Classical Hebrew Narrative* (ed. R. C. Culley; Missoula, Montana: Scholars Press, 1975) 64-80; J. Magonet, "Die Söhne Abrahams," *BibLeb* 14 (1973) 204-10; R. W. Neff, "The Announcement in Old Testament Birth Stories" (Diss., Yale, 1969); idem, "The Annunciation in the Birth Narrative of Ishmael," *BR* 17 (1972) 51-60; idem, "The Birth and Election of Isaac in the Priestly Tradition," *BR* 15 (1970) 5-18; J. van Seters, "The Problem of Childlessness in Near Eastern Law and the Patriarchs of Israel," *JBL* 87 (1968) 401-8; H. C. White, "The Initiation Legend of Isaac," *ZAW* 91 (1979) 1-30; idem, "The Initiation Legend of Ishmael," *ZAW* 87 (1975) 267-305; P. Xella, "L'épisode de Dnil et Kothar et Gen 18:1-16," *VT* 28 (1978) 483-86.

ANNUNCIATION OF ISHMAEL, 16:1-16

Structure

I. Exposition	1
A. Problem	1a
B. Introduction of Hagar	1b
II. Complication	2-6
A. Sarai's plan	2-4a
1. Instructions	2a
a. Problem	
b. Plan for resolution	
2. Execution of instructions	2b-4a
a. General note	2b
b. Detailed description	3-4a
B. Tension	4b-6
1. New problem	4b
2. Sarai's accusation against Abram	5
a. Accusation	5a
b. Call for judgment	5b
3. Abram's response	6a
4. New problem	6b
III. Annunciation	7-12
A. New setting	7
B. Dialogue	8
1. Angel's interrogation	8a
2. Hagar's response	8b
C. Angel's speeches	9-12
1. Instructions to return to Sarai	9
2. Promise for descendants	10
3. Annunciation: promise for a son	11-12
a. Announcement of birth	11a
b. Name	11b
c. Destiny	12
IV. Conclusion	13-16
A. Etiology	13-14
1. Name of God	13
2. Name of place	14
B. Birth report	15-16

1. Birth	15a
2. Name	15b
3. Age of father	16

The context of this unit is significant (→ Gen 16:1–21:21). Immediately after the presentation of Yahweh's oath for Abram's son, descendants, and land, this chapter narrates the annunciation and birth of a son. The connection is only redactional, however. The story is separated from the promises of ch. 15 not only by the style of the exposition, but also by the content. Its subject is not developed out of the promise for posterity (contrast von Rad, *Genesis,* 191). The relationship between chs. 15–16 and ch. 17 is much closer, marked particularly by the notations of Abram's age in 16:16 and 17:1. Although the continuity of narration is supported by the two items of information, the distinction between the units is also marked by the same two verses. In the one, Abram is eighty-six years old; in the next, he is ninety-nine. On the function of these notations, see the comments below. Indeed, the continuity in the notations of age conceal the fact that, as the story now stands, it has no structural conclusion. It remains incomplete, open to the following narration (see von Rad, *Genesis,* 195). The closest point of contact is the Mamre story in Genesis 18 (see von Rad, *Genesis,* 193; cf. also 13:18).

The exposition features typical construction, first with a sentence in inverted order, and second with a nominal sentence. The first sentence names Sarai as the wife of Abram and notes her circumstances: "Sarai, Abram's wife, bore him no children." This note is crucial for the story, not to be broken away as a part of another source (see van Seters, *Abraham,* 193). The second introduces Hagar as Sarai's Egyptian maid. One may conclude that the story to follow centers primarily in the relationship between Sarai and her maid. The relationship is formulated in the crisis posed by Sarai's infertility, not in the promise given to Abram, a promise which remains at best only in the background.

The first major unit of narration confirms this judgment. V. 2a is a speech addressed by Sarai to her husband that designates the problem Sarai confronts. Indeed, it lays the blame for the problem on Yahweh (cf. 20:13; see also 3:12), a point which builds the contrast between this story and ch. 15. The center of the speech, however, suggests a resolution for Sarai's problem: She confers her maid on Abram as a means for obtaining a child for herself. The end of the speech designates the maid as a wife, but it is clear that the maid remains in the control of Sarai and only indirectly under the authority of Abram. Vv. 2b-4a then report the execution of Sarai's instructions. V. 2b is a general statement of execution: "Abram listened to the voice of Sarai." V. 4a reports the central event: "He went in to Hagar, and she conceived." V. 3 is considerably more verbose, with date and careful definition of relationship. In content, however, it adds little to the development of the story's plot. The point of tension unfolds rather in the second half of this element, vv. 4b-6. The problem for the story comes to light in v. 4b: "When she saw that she had conceived, she looked with contempt on [cursed] her mistress [*wattēqal gĕbirtāh bĕ'êneyhā*]" (→ 12:1-3). The reverse side of the problem is stated in v. 6b: "Then Sarai dealt harshly with her, and she fled from her." The problem, then, grows from the relationship between Sarai and Hagar. The two statements of the problem frame a vignette from the relationship between Sarai and Abram and show that the total structure of the family hinges on the conflict that lies at the story's central focus. Even though the maid belongs to Abram as wife, Abram appears somewhat passive. Moreover, Sarai's speech, v. 5, lays the problem on Abram. An initial accusation formula, "The wrong done me is on you" (see von Rad, *Genesis*, 192), and a call to judgment, "may Yahweh judge between you and me," carry her complaint: "I gave my maid to your embrace, and when she conceived, she looked on me with contempt." V. 6a is Abram's response to the complaint, a speech to Sarai setting Hagar completely under Sarai's control. It is the only speech from Abram to either of the women in the unit and, in itself, underlines the central focus on the relationship between the women.

The structure of the story is unfortunately disturbed by v. 7. One expects some resolution of the tension between the two women, and perhaps that occurs in v. 6b with Hagar's flight. One must be cautious in describing stories simply in terms of tension-resolution, however, since "resolution" of tension may not offer the kind or quality of resolution one might expect (→ Genesis 29–31). The story does not so much resolve the tension as drop the tension for new motifs.

A new element of structure opens in v. 7 with a new principal character, the angel of Yahweh. And the narration shows a change of locale. What occurs now will not involve Sarai and Abram. The locale is the wilderness: "The angel of Yahweh found her by a spring of water in the wilderness." Such changes in locale typically represent major structural divisions in OT narrative (cf. 37:12-14). The dialogue unfolds, nevertheless, around the Sarai-Hagar relationship. On interrogation, Hagar confesses that she is fleeing from her mistress. The angel bids her to return and submit to her oppressor, but no further word about the instructions appears. It is as if the initial dialogue functions as a bridge between the story developed in vv. 1-6 and the narratives to follow (→ Genesis 21). The story in effect shifts its structural line of development from the contention between Sarai and Hagar to an annunciation to Hagar that she would give birth to a son. The difficult structural pattern is highlighted by a renewal of the speech formula from v. 9 in vv. 10 and 11. V. 10 is a promise for great posterity for Hagar. Its content is doubtlessly influenced by the promise to Abram (see van Seters, *Abraham*, 194). Vv. 11-12 then present a promise for a son (cf. 15:4). This promise follows the stereotyped line of annunciation: announcement of birth of a son (v. 11a), the name (11b), and definition of his destiny (12). Moreover, the destiny speech has an interest in common with tribal sayings (→ Genesis 49). It does not, however, constitute a resolution of the tension between Hagar and Sarai; it relates directly to the son (contrast van Seters, *Abraham*, 193). The destiny it describes is one of strife and tension. The theme of the story in vv. 1-6 thus becomes institutionalized in the ethnological saying of a people.

The etiologies in vv. 13-14 do not develop out of the resolution of tension in the story, but out of the bridge between story and annunciation. The unit is thus not an etiology but has only an etiological appendix (see van Seters, *Abraham*, 193). The first, v. 13, grounds the name of God in the following saying: *'ēl ro'î hălōm rā'ûî 'aḥărê rō'î.* V. 14 uses the same saying to ground the name of a place: *bĕ'ēr laḥay rō'î.* These etiologies seem to be additions or intrusions into the story line. But the story line does not continue. Rather, v. 15 breaks the unit with a birth report and notice of the naming coupled in v. 16 with a note of Abram's age at the birth (cf. 5:6 and regularly throughout the genealogies).

The unit can be analyzed in terms of sources. Vv. 3 and 15 are structurally redundant and can be attributed to P. V. 1a is not so readily shunted off from the development of the story (see van Seters, *Abraham*, 193-94, who argues also for v. 3 as an intrinsic part of the unit). These verses constitute simply a report of conception and birth of Ishmael but prepare nonetheless for P in Genesis 17. The qualification of age for the central figure points particularly to unity in P's redaction, carried forward by 17:1. The remaining verses, J, nonetheless show evidence of growth in content: A story of conflict has been combined with the annunciation of Ishmael. J has no birth report for Ishmael. With these themes are traces of an etiological tradition concerned with theophany at a specific place. This growth may be understood in terms of a complex tradition history (see Neff, "Announcement," 108).

Genre
The unit is not complete as it stands; rather, a TALE of family strife (→ Genesis 21) shifts to an ANNUNCIATION OF BIRTH of a son.

Setting
The chapter derives from the Yahwist's literary construction (so, also P). The traditions that constitute the unit, both the story of conflict and the annunciation, derive from the interests of the family. They are family stories, preserved for the sake of understanding family roots (see Westermann, *Genesis,* 36-39). In addition, a local cultic etiology provides substance for presenting a crucial element in the story.

Intention
P simply reports the birth of Ishmael. J preserves the annunciation as a form that reports birth, although J has no explicit report of the birth of Ishmael. The birth announcement now sits in the middle of an account of family strife. The strife element is not resolved. It points, rather, beyond itself to further narrative elements (→ Genesis 21).

Bibliography
→ 16:1–21:21.

COVENANTAL OATH DIALOGUE, 17:1-27

Structure

I. Framework transition	1a
II. Dialogue	1b-21
A. God's speech	1b-2
1. Self-revelation formula	1bα
2. Instructions	1bβ
3. Promise for covenant and posterity	2
B. Abram's response	3a
C. God's speech	3b-8
1. Promise for covenant and posterity	3b-4
2. Name change	5

The context for this unit (P) is established by the Hagar-Ishmael tradition in Genesis 16 and the Sarah-Isaac tradition in Genesis 21 (on the different structure in J, → The Abraham Saga). It is not surprising, then, that this unit in contrast to the parallel in Genesis 15 (JE) subordinates the promise for land to the promise for great posterity.

The unit itself comprises an introductory phrase, noting the age of the patriarch, and a series of speeches addressed by God to Abram, with narrative notation of response. Two Abraham speeches round out the complex and give the final form of the pericope the appearance of dialogue. The one speech, v. 17, is a complaint; the other, v. 18, an appeal for Ishmael. Both are introduced by an etiology and a concluding narration.

The introduction consists entirely of a notation of Abram's age. The conclusion parallels the introduction, not only by the absence of speech, but also by repetition of age for the newly renamed patriarch (v. 24). These verses also function in relationship to the body of the unit. Thus, v. 22 marks the end of God's speeches to Abraham, the end of the dialogue: "When he had finished talking with him, God went up from Abraham." The remaining verses, vv. 23-27, contribute to the body of the unit by presenting the execution of the instructions given there in detail, first among the servants of the house (v. 23), then in the family with ages noted for both father and son (vv. 24-25), and finally as a general summary (vv. 26-27). With the summary the unit is nicely rounded off.

The series of oracles begins in vv. 1b-2 with a tie between a self-revelation formula, "I am El Shaddai," and a promise for numerous descendants. The promise is defined initially as covenant and recalls the parallel reference to divine promise as covenant in 15:18. The principal difference here is that for P, covenant does not come to expression in a land promise: "I will make my covenant between me and you and will multiply you exceedingly." The connection between the two elements is secured by an admonition to walk before God, so that God can make the patriarch complete (*tāmîm;* cf. 6:9, where Noah who walks before God is *ṣaddîq tāmîm*; see also 5:22).

V. 3a is a brief narrative statement of Abram's response, a stereotyped response to the presence of God (cf. 17:7; Lev 9:24; Num 17:10) or to the presence of a superior (cf. 44:14). The oracle in vv. 3b-8 renews the promise for a covenant that is given context in a promise for great descendants. V. 5 marks the name change for P. The act itself indicates lordship and suggests a shift in the understanding of covenant for this text (cf. 2 Kgs 24:17). To give a name is to express suzerainty (cf. the name change for Jacob in 32:28; MT does not preserve a name change for Abram in J). The name change does not control the development of the oracle, however. There is no law, no stipulation of relationship (on circumcision, see the comments below). To the contrary, here the name change is rooted in the divine promise: "Your name shall be Abraham, for I have made you father of a multitude ['*ab-ḥămôn*]." The sentence has elements of a name etiology but it is not spelled out in full.

The name change is followed in vv. 6-8 with a renewal of the promise: (1) multiplicity of descendants, with kings numbered among them; (2) covenant, labeled "everlasting" (*librît 'ôlām*; cf. 9:16), and identifying God with Abraham and his descendants; (3) land of Abraham's sojournings; and (4) identification of God with Abraham's descendants. It is important to note here that the promise is dominated by the designation "covenant," and the context of the covenant is an oath for descendants. The land enters the picture only as a place for the descendants to dwell, a transformation of a land for strangers (*mĕgūreykā*) into a permanent possession (*la'āḥuzzat 'ôlām*).

The details of the promise are followed in v. 9 by a renewed divine speech with a renewed speech formula. The new speech is first an admonition to keep the covenant. The statement is not covenant law; it is an admonition. But does the admonition to keep the covenant imply law that may be kept (cf. Exod 19:5)? V. 10 would open this implication further. V. 10a is an introduction which apparently intends to mark the content of the covenant: "This is my covenant which you shall keep between me and you and your descendants after you" (cf. Deut 28:69). The content would then be expressed by vv. 10b-11a. "Every male among you shall be circumcised. You shall circumcise [reflexive Niphal] the flesh of your foreskin." The content of the covenant would then be spelled out in detail in vv. 12-13a by defining the age for circumcision and the males subject to the sign (everyone, born or bought). V. 13b would appear to be a concluding formula to this stipulation: "So shall my covenant be in your flesh an everlasting covenant." And v. 14 designates the punishment for violating the law, a rather heavy penalty. How else can the punishment of v. 14 be understood than as the teeth of a circumcision law conceived as a restrictive condition of the covenant (contrast Clements, 73)? In the present form of the text, then, the everlasting covenant with Abraham, like the one with Noah, has no stipulation. It is a bond, an oath from God for the sake of the people. That the sign for the oath is something the people must do (contrast 9:12-16; 15:17) may indicate again a different conception of covenant. But as the story stands, the covenant is a divine oath, and its content is the promise for great posterity with a land to live in.

With a renewed speech formula, vv. 15-16 combine the subject of the promise for great posterity with a promise for a son. The speech, addressed to Abraham, opens with a name change for Sarai, and on the heels of the change comes a promise for blessing for her. That blessing is defined as a son for Abraham, combined with the promise for posterity and kings for Sarah. With the promise is a title to match the one given (with wordplay) to Abraham: "She shall be a mother of nations"/"I have made you the father of a multitude of nations."

A brief response narrated in v. 17a builds on a wordplay with the name Isaac in v. 19 (wayyiṣḥāq:yiṣḥāq), set into one of two distinct speeches from Abraham. The first speech is simply a complaint, capturing the incredulous character of the promise. The second is an appeal for Ishmael as the son of the promise (→ Genesis 16*). Its proximity to the first speech, though separated by the renewed speech formula, and its content suggest that it is an extension of the complaint. But the divine response is negative. The content of the response is an annunciation for the birth of a son to Sarah, thus picking up the speech in v. 16. The annunciation here comprises three stereotyped elements: birth, name, destiny: "Sarah your wife shall bear you a son. You shall call his name Isaac. I will establish my covenant with him as an everlasting covenant for his descendants after him." The content of the covenant is not specified here, although one may assume that v. 19b keys this covenant with the contextual focus on numerous descendants. V. 20 responds more directly to Abraham's complaint. God promises for Ishmael (1) blessing, (2) numerous descendants, (3) twelve princes, and (4) nationhood. But for Ishmael no covenant appears. The promise for posterity is thus of a different order from the one for Abraham-Isaac. V. 21 then returns to the promise of a covenant for Isaac and the announcement of the coming birth.

Thus, the unit in P shows something of the tradition's history, particularly in comparison with J in Genesis 15. The tradition no longer places such emphasis on God's oath for possession of land; here the promise seems more directly attached to multiplication of descendants. Moreover, the content of the everlasting covenant becomes explicitly the promise for a son by Sarah. This development can be seen in the structure of the unit. The first two divine speeches promise numerous descendants, the last two a son explicitly identified with Isaac, and the middle speech delivers instructions for the circumcision. Perhaps influenced by

9:1-17, this covenantal text resists embracing circumcision as covenantal law—it is but a sign of the covenant.

But behind this everlasting covenant and its sign are traces of a covenant which takes circumcision as the content of human commitment, what it means to "keep" the covenant God established with Abraham (contrast Clements, 73).

Genre

The unit is not narrative; it is not even (→) dialogue as Genesis 15 is. It is a series of SPEECHES providing promises, instructions for circumcision, and a formal ANNUNCIATION OF THE BIRTH of Isaac. The covenant structure of the unit suggests (→) oath rather than suzerainty bond, although circumcision may reflect an understanding of the Abraham covenant as commitment to the Lord. God's oath is his promise, and in that promise lies the generic character of the unit.

Setting

The unit is P's version of tradition also found in J. The setting is in the literary activity of the priestly writer. For earlier stages, → Genesis 15.

Intention

P connects the covenant with Abraham to the covenant with Noah. The relationship between God and Abraham's descendants is as firm as the relationship between God and the seasons and times of the year. P will connect that promise also to the birth of Isaac. For P, the patriarchal traditions depend heavily on the structural pattern of promise-fulfillment.

Bibliography

R. Clements, *Abraham and David: Genesis XV and its Meaning for Israelite Tradition* (SBT 2/5; London: SCM, 1967); S. McEvenue, *The Narrative Style of the Priestly Writer* (AnBib 50; Rome: Biblical Institute Press, 1971); R. Neff, "The Birth and Election of Isaac in the Priestly Tradition," *BR* 15 (1970) 5-18; J. G. Vink, *The Origin and Date of the Priestly Code* (Leiden: Brill, 1969); C. Westermann, "Genesis 17 und die Bedeutung von běrît," *TLZ* 101 (1976) 161-70; W. Zimmerli, "Sinaibund und Abrahambund. Ein Beitrag zum Verständnis der Priesterschrift," *TZ* 16 (1960) 268-80.

ANNUNCIATION OF ISAAC, 18:1-15

Structure

I. Exposition	1-2
II. Report of guests received	3-8
A. Opening dialogue	3-5
1. Abraham's host speech	3-5a
2. Guests' response	5b
B. Report of meal	6-8
1. Instructions to Sarah	6
2. Abraham's preparation	7-8a
3. Meal	8b
III. Annuciation dialogue	9-15
A. Interrogation	9a

B. Abraham's response 9b
C. Annunciation speech 10a
D. Sarah's response 10b-12
   1. Sarah's laugh 10b-12a
   2. Speech 12b
E. Annunciation speech 13-14
   1. Rebuke 13-14a
   2. Annunciation 14b
F. Sarah's denial 15a
G. Messenger's rebuke 15b

This narrative begins in midstream (see van Seters, *Abraham,* 203). This conclusion is substantiated by the unidentified suffix in v. 1aα: "The Lord appeared to *him.* . . ." The designation of vv. 1-2 as exposition does not vitiate this conclusion, since these verses serve as exposition in a limited section of narrative. Rather, they prepare for the impending interview between the unnamed principal figure and the three men, or perhaps Yahweh, named in the opening lines. In a manner parallel to 16:7, their function for the unit is to establish a relationship between the deity or his messengers and the one to receive the annunciation. Thus, the opening line suggests a theophany of Yahweh, but the continuation with three men places the narration not so much in theophany as in an encounter like 16:7. Moreover, the point of tension giving this narrative context is not stated (cf. 16:1a), but it is assumed. The dialogue that unfolds around an annunciation theme presupposes that the prospective mother is too old to bear children. This point appears in Yahweh's citation of Sarah's speech, v. 13: "Shall I indeed bear a child, now that I am old?" But the tension in this point is obscure. Is it simply a story about annunciation to a woman too old to bear a child? Or does the story not assume a point of tension from the context (→ Genesis 16)? (Von Rad, *Genesis,* 192, suggests that Genesis 16 assumes a Mamre locale. Van Seters, *Abraham,* 203, suggests 13:18 for the point of contact.)

The unit itself comprises two major parts. The first describes the occasion of hospitality offered by the principal figure, a sheik in the desert at home in his tent in the heat of the day, to three travelers. Vv. 3-5a present the host's invitation in all its extreme politeness. V. 5b is the acceptance speech. This exchange leads to a description of the meal, again in all its extreme politeness. Abraham, named for the first time in v. 6, instructs Sarah, introduced by name, to prepare cakes. He also makes preparation (vv. 7-8a). Then as host he watches while the guests eat. There is no narrative tension here; there is only the report of an event.

Narrative tension unfolds in the dialogue of vv. 9-15, however. The shift in speaker from plural to singular (vv. 9-10), from indefinite "they" to definite Yahweh, may suggest a problem in the development of the narrative. Perhaps the plural company of messengers can speak in the singular for Yahweh, or Yahweh was himself one of the visitors (→ 19:1). The first question to Abraham already forebodes the tension: "Where is Sarah your wife?" In v. 10, the quality of the narrative comes more sharply into focus. The speech formula names the speaker as Yahweh (contrast v. 9, where the same partner in the dialogue is designated only by a plural verb). Yahweh's speech announces the coming birth of a son, as well as the time. Vv. 10b-12 lay the foundation for a wordplay on the name of the son: Sarah laughed (→ 17:19). Yahweh's speech in vv. 13-14 responds to the laugh with a rebuke, formally an accusation but addressed to Abraham rather than Sarah. And the annunciation of the birth is repeated. The exchange in v. 15 again plays on the laugh, but surprisingly, no conclusion is drawn from the play. To the contrary, the exchange offers a threat to the safety of the prospective mother by virtue of the challenge Yahweh presents to her. The accusation addressed to Abraham in v. 13 calls for some kind of response. Sarah provides that response with a denial (v. 15a), and Yahweh rebukes the denial (v. 15b). But nothing comes of the threat, just as nothing develops from the wordplay. The momentary point of tension contributes nothing to structure for a plot.

The analysis can be extended by an additional step. If one compares this unit with another story dealing with a barren woman (2 Kgs 4:8-17), then some critical control in structure is possible. The expected pattern would be (1) recognition of the problem, (2) annunciation (birth, name, destiny, although this series may not be stated in full), (3) expression of doubt, and (4) fulfillment of the annunciation (see Neff, "Annunciation"). If the structure of the unit is properly understood in terms of patterns from an annunciation report, then we could expect an announcement of the birth, name, and destiny of the child. The annunciation of the birth of a son is, indeed, the center of the unit. The extensive play on the verb *ṣḥq* ("laugh") sets the basis for giving a name, but the name is not announced (cf. 17:19-21, P), and no reference to the destiny of the child can be found. This unit does not develop the pattern in full. Rather, it drops the birth motif in favor of the problems offered to the three men by Sodom (see van Seters, *Abraham*, 204). This narrative is thus not a distinct unit, but part of a larger narration in J (→ 16:1–21:1). It may, of course, properly be analyzed form-critically since it is an element of a larger whole. Indeed, it may hide evidence of an annunciation tale, originally quite distinct and independent. But in its current position as an element, it has no independent structural role.

Genre

The element is an ANNUNCIATION scene of a larger whole, characterized by an announcement of the coming birth of a child. As a scene of a larger whole, it loses its full pattern and serves the interests of a plot development that ranges beyond its scope. As evidence for a hypothetical original, it suggests the form of a TALE for an annunciation. It would fall particularly into a group of narratives concerned with healing a barren wife by a divine annunciation. Characteristic for the group is the narrative in 2 Kgs 4:8-17 (see Neff, "Announcement"), but it is now incomplete in the form defined by these patterns (→ 16:1–21:1).

Setting

On the setting of the whole, → 16:1–21:1. The hypothetical annunciation tale would also belong to the context of family traditions. See Neff, "Announcement."

Intention

The element sets out an annunciation of the birth of Isaac, and in the process it preserves a sense of foreboding, a threat posed by the three messengers to the prospective mother. Yet, in the annunciation, the unit intends to show the healing of the barren woman as a preface to the birth of the special son.

Bibliography

→ 16:1–21:21.

ABRAHAM'S INTERCESSION, 18:16-33

Structure

I. Transition	16
II. Yahweh's soliloquies	17-21
A. Plan for Abraham	17-19
1. Question	17-18
2. Answer	19
B. Plan for Sodom and Gomorrah	20-21
1. Reason	20
2. Plan	21a
3. Alternative	21b
III. Transition	22
IV. Dialogue	23-32
A. Opening petition	23-25
1. Leading question	23
2. Challenge	24
a. Hypothetical circumstances	
b. Leading question	
3. Petition	25
B. Concession	26
C. Petition	27-28a
1. Self-abasement formula	27
2. Challenge	28a
a. Hypothetical circumstances	
b. Leading question	
D. Concession	28b
E. Hypothetical circumstances	29a
F. Concession	29b
G. Petition	30a
1. Supplication formula	
2. Hypothetical circumstances	
H. Concession	30b
I. Petition	31a
1. Supplication formula	
2. Hypothetical circumstances	
J. Concession	31b
K. Petition	32a
1. Supplication formula	
2. Hypothetical circumstances	
L. Concession	32b
V. Conclusion	33

This unit is hardly an independent narrative. The transitions in vv. 16 and 22 (cf. also 19:1a) allude to the previous narrative unit, not only by means of an undefined adverb, "there" (*šām*), but also in the identity of the men who are at the center of the narration. V. 16b maintains the host's responsibility for guests characteristic of vv. 1-15 and implies that the men who move toward Sodom are the men who announced the coming birth of Isaac. Moreover, vv. 16a and 22a are virtually doublets in the structure of the unit, a feature of structural inclusion that binds vv. 17-21 with the following dialogue and sets both in the context of movement for the guests of Abraham toward Sodom. It should be noted, however, that the transition in v. 22 also creates a disjunction for vv. 23-33. The guests of Abraham continue toward Sodom, with Abraham remaining "before the Lord" (cf. Tiq soph). V. 33 concludes the interview of Abraham before the Lord with the notation that "the Lord went his way when he had finished speaking to Abraham, and Abraham returned to his place." The dialogue in vv. 23-33 thus wins a distinct position within a framework of movement for the guests of Abraham toward Sodom. The framework continues in 19:1a, although the number of the guests shifts from three to two, and they carry a specific title, "angel" (*šĕnê hammal'ākîm*). The shift might be explained by the note in 18:22 that Abraham and Yahweh remained behind. This explanation seems somewhat forced, however, since the context never suggests that the three visitors to Abraham are two angels and Yahweh himself. The visitors are described simply as three men (v. 2). The men leave Mamre for Sodom, with Abraham as their guide (v. 16). Finally, "the men" part company from Abraham, and Abraham stands before Yahweh. The note in 19:1a is simply different. Nonetheless, it seems probable that the visitors to Sodom are intended to be the same visitors moving toward Sodom in 18:16, 22, the same visitors who announced the coming birth of Isaac in 18:1-15. The shift would thus be some indication of a parallel tradition.

The initial soliloquies relate to each other as opposites. The first sets out the divine plan to reveal to Abraham intentions for future action. The largest part of the speech relates two reasons for the plan: (1) Abraham holds the divine promise to become a great nation and thereby to provide a blessing to all the nations of the earth, and (2) Abraham holds a special position before God ("I have known him" [*yĕda'tîw*]). The purpose of the position is to maintain righteousness and justice in coming generations. Particularly the second point contrasts with the description of the people in Sodom and Gomorrah in the second soliloquy: "The outcry against Sodom and Gomorrah is great and their sin is very grave." The contrast recalls the contrast between Noah and his neighbors preceding the destruction of the world in the flood (→ 6:1–9:17). The plan for destruction of Sodom and Gomorrah also mirrors the description of divine response to the construction of a tower (→ 11:1-17, cf. particularly the description of divine action in 18:21 par. 11:7).

The element of tradition in vv. 23-32 is structured as a dialogue between Abraham and Yahweh, a series of negotiations over the fate of the city. The focus here is limited to Sodom and thus ties more directly to the context. The speeches follow a rather predictable pattern. The first is the longest and thus establishes the sequence. It begins with a leading question that sets the subject for the exchange: "Will you destroy the righteous with the wicked?" The polar contrast reflected in the two soliloquies thus constitutes the theme of these speeches. V. 24 then sets up the character of Abraham's petition. He cites hypothetical circumstances: "Suppose there are fifty righteous within the city." Then the leading question is re-peated, the contrast heightened. A city of wicked people against fifty righteous constitutes the substance of the speech. On the basis of this contrast, Abraham presents his petition, v. 25, which wins a concession: For the sake of the fifty righteous, the wicked city will not be destroyed. But the interpreter must remain patient here, resisting the temptation to jump quickly to a theological conclusion. The exchange does not intend to set up a theory of vicarious redemption.

The following petitions are generally abbreviated to a display of the hypo-thetical circumstances. Only the second speech, v. 28a, combines the hypothesis, "suppose five of the fifty righteous are lacking," with a leading question: "Will you destroy the whole city for lack of five?" In four of the five speeches, the abbreviated petition nevertheless reveals its character as petition by combination with a supplication formula or self-abasement formula of some sort. Each petition wins its corresponding concession from Yahweh. Moreover, each one highlights the polar contrast between the wicked inhabitants of Sodom and the righteousness of Abraham noted in vv. 17-19. The negotiations break off at ten, but why should they stop there (see von Rad, *Genesis,* 214)? The point is not that Lot and his family are righteous. In the flood story, Noah survives the disaster in part because of his righteousness (7:1). But Lot is not labeled righteous, here or in ch. 19. In these negotiations, Lot never enters the discussion as a reason for appealing to the Lord for mercy. The issue is simply the contrast between wicked Sodom and the righteousness that cannot be found there (cf. 13:13). Moreover, the entire dialogue carries out the plan cited in v. 21. The grave sin is as grave as the depiction in v. 20. Thus, the negotiations constitute the probe of Yahweh into the character of the city, and the city proves void of righteousness. The unit sets the stage for ch. 19.

Scholars generally agree that this dialogue is the product of the Yahwist's imagination rather than the literary formulation of oral tradition. If it is properly understood as a Yahwistic creation, however, it would not be a piece designed to capture a central tenet of theology, but rather an introduction designed to set the stage for the following narrative.

Formulas and stereotyped language characteristic of speech appear fre-quently: (1) A self-abasement formula, v. 27, depicts the speaker in humble terms. (2) A supplication formula, vv. 30, 32a, casts a petition in negative jussive with *'al,* "Let the Lord not be angry." A different formulation of supplication appears in v. 31a, with key words for supplication: "Behold now . . ." (*hinnēh nā'*).

Genre

The element hangs together by virtue of the transitional framework in vv. 16 and 22 (cf. also 19:1a). It is not a complete unit in itself, however, and demands no genre identification as a whole. In its compass are two distinct genres of SPEECHES, soliloquy and negotiation (→ Gen 6:7; Exod 7:6–10:29).

Setting

The unit presupposes the larger context of the Abraham-Lot narratives in J. It derives from the literary redaction of the Yahwist.

Intention

As a part of J, the unit emphasizes the motif already known in J from 13:13 by depicting Sodom and Gomorrah, or in vv. 23-33 Sodom, as a wicked city devoid of even ten righteous people. It thus accomplishes for the following narrative what 6:1-4 accomplishes for the flood story. Its intention is not to propose a theological assertion about the redeeming value of the righteous in the midst of wicked surroundings (contrast von Rad, *Genesis*, 210-15), nor to propose a statement about God as one who will receive the righteousness of a few as credit for the wicked many. It is strictly to emphasize the wickedness of the city.

Bibliography

J. L. Crenshaw, "Popular Questioning of the Justice of God in Ancient Israel," *ZAW* 82 (1970) 380-95; K. Koch, "Gibt es ein Vergeltungsdogma im *Alten Testament*?" *ZTK* 52 (1955) 1-42; C. S. Rodd, "Shall Not the Judge of All the Earth Do What Is Just?" *ExpTim* 83 (1972) 137-39; L. Schmidt, *"De Deo": Studien zur Literarkritik und Theologie des Buches Jona, des Gesprächs zwischen Abraham und Jahwe in Gen 18:22ff. und von Hi 1* (BZAW 143; Berlin: Walter deGruyter, 1976) 131-64; A. Weiss, "Some Problems of the Biblical 'Doctrine of Retribution'," *Tarbiz* 31 (1961/62) 236-63.

TALE OF DESTRUCTION, 19:1-29

Structure

I. Transition	1a
II. Complication	1b-11
A. Opening encounter	1b
B. Dialogue	2
1. Host's speech	2a
2. Response	2b
C. Reception by host	3
D. Host's protection	4-11
1. Challenge	4-5
2. Defense	6-8
3. Challenge	9
4. Defense	10-11
III. Announcement of judgment	12-14
A. Announcement speech	12-13
1. Instructions for survival	12
2. Announcement for destruction	13
B. Lot's report to the family	14
1. Instructions speech	14a
2. Response of family	14b
IV. Survival	15-22
A. Instructions speech	15
B. Narration of event	16
C. Instructions speech	17
D. Objection speech	18-20
E. Concession and instructions speech	21-22a
F. Etiology	22b

Context for this unit is established by v. 1a, a transition piece that connects with at least 18:16, 22a, if not also 18:1-8. The context proffers a structural problem, however. In 18:1-8, the visitors are defined as three men, here as two angels. In 18:16 and 22a, the visitors are designated simply as "the men." It may be that 18:22 offers an answer to the context questions. The men departed from Abraham leaving Yahweh still standing with Abraham (see Tiq soph). Does the image not suggest that one of the figures who visited Abraham was Yahweh? Indeed, the shift in speaker in 18:9-15 might suggest the same image. Yet, one might be cautious here. The text might present a messenger's speech under the stamp of a plural, a collective, or simply as the speech of Yahweh, the act of the one who commissioned the message (cf. vv. 17, 21, 24-25). Moreover, the occasion of hospitality in this unit is not simply a copy of the same scene in ch. 18 (contrast van Seters, *Abraham*, 211). The parallel for this unit is to be sought more readily in Judges 19. Since a large structural issue hangs on the problem, however, resolution of the question can remain with the commentaries. In any case, it is clear that ch. 18 provides a necessary context for the narrative in ch. 19, although the narrative may well derive from older, originally independent tradition (see von Rad, *Genesis*, 216).

The unit has four principal structural elements: an elaborate narrative of hospitality in vv. 1b-11 (→ 18:1-8), an announcement of the coming destruction in vv. 12-14, an account of the efforts of the family to survive in vv. 15-22, and finally an account of the destruction with some description of the fate of those who escaped in vv. 23-26. The pattern suggests immediately some comparison with the flood narrative (→ 6:1-9:17). In the first element, Lot appears as the one who fulfills his duties as host for his two visitors. Like Abraham (18:1-8), Lot offers his guests what should be offered (vv. 1-3). But more than Abraham, Lot also defends his guests against the threat posed by the men of the city (vv. 4-11). Indeed, one has the impression that the crime threatened by the men of the city lies not so much with the demand for sexual license with the visitors as it does in the violation of the host's and even the city's hospitality. Lot's move to defend his visitors thus places him apart from his neighbors as one who attends to the responsibility of the host. Moreover, Lot's positive response to the threat, his consequential distinction from his (evil) neighbors, places him in the category of the righteous (see Kilian, "Zur Überlieferungsgeschichte Lots," 29). Lot thus does not contrast with Abraham in the same way that the men of Sodom contrast with him (→ 14:21-24). Indeed, in this position Lot would compare favorably with the righteous Noah. And as a righteous inhabitant Lot receives the invitation to escape the planned destruction.

Yet, Lot is never designated righteous. Indeed, the description of his defense for his guests places him in the category of a buffoon. Lot's contrast with Abraham is thus not one of opposition, in the manner of Ishmael and Isaac or Jacob and Esau (contrast Jepsen, 150). The contrast is one suggested by hero vis-à-vis buffoon. This point can be seen in two ways: (1) In an overdrawn defense of the guests, Lot offers his two daughters as alternatives to the men of the city for their pleasure (→ Judges 19). This act is perhaps little different from Abraham's defense of himself (→ 12:10-20; 20:1-18); yet, it contrasts with the intimacy that might be expected in a family (cf. Num 25:6). (2) Lot's efforts at defense lead to rejection as a foreigner by the very people whom he chose as neighbors (v. 9; contrast ch. 13). In the process of the rejection, Lot himself falls under threat from his neighbors and must be rescued by the guests he sought to protect (cf. ch. 14). Lot begins as an active principal in the narrative but becomes a passive, rather helpless object for the narrative's action. As a passive figure, Lot is virtually comic in his buffoonery (see von Rad, *Genesis,* 219). At least it is clear that his "righteousness" differs from that of Noah or Abraham.

The second major element in the story, vv. 12-14, announces the coming destruction of the city and the prospects for Lot's survival (→ 6:11-22). The announcement comes first in a speech by the visitors to Lot. One can assume that the announcement, built on the demonstration of wickedness by the men of Sodom in the first element, picks up the larger context (cf. v. 13b), particularly a demonstration of the city's character anticipated by 18:23-33. The point means, however, that 18:16-33 is dependent on ch. 19. Moreover, the announcement calls for Lot to save himself and his family (→ 7:1, 7). The comic effect of Lot's buffoonery comes again to the fore when he reports the announcement and its invitation to his family, v. 14. Contrary to Noah's experience in preparation for the tragedy, Lot is unable to convince his sons-in-law that the announcement was serious. They took him rather as a jester whose words had little effect: "He seemed to his sons-in-law to be jesting."

The position of Lot as a buffoon comes more sharply to the fore in the following dialogue. The third major section of the unit describes Lot on the next morning still in the condemned city, pressed by his guests to leave. V. 16a shows Lot's response. He could not take the urging seriously enough to leave the city. Thus, in v. 16b Lot and his family again appear as passive objects of the guests' intervention: "The men seized him and his wife and his two daughters by the hand, the Lord being merciful to him, and they brought him forth and set him outside the city."

But the buffoonery does not stop here. The visitors urge Lot and his family to flee to the hills (v. 17), lest they too should be caught in the destruction of the city. But Lot objects; he does not want to go so far and chooses another city instead (vv. 18-20). And to this suggestion the guests concede. The exchange leads to a brief etymological etiology of the city's name (v. 22b), but the etiology is peripheral and does not contribute to the controlling movement of the narrative. Rather, the unit element here centers on the dialogue. The dialogue thus emerges as a negotiation over Lot's salvation and the salvation of his family, a motif totally missing from the Noah counterpart.

The final element in the development of the narrative recounts the destruction event itself, a cosmic conflagration (→ 7:6-12). V. 23 notes the time for the event, vv. 24-25 the heavenly character of the destruction, with the total consequences of its rage. V. 26 then returns to the virtually comic, *Märchen*-like quality of the tradition. Lot's wife could not quite resist the temptation to look back, in contradiction to the explicit instructions of the visitors (v. 17). The motif must suggest resistance to leaving rather than mere curiosity about the event. In any case, as a consequence she becomes a pillar of salt. There is no etiological connection with a land formation here; there is only comic tragedy. The people chosen to escape the cosmic destruction in the role of the righteous cannot bear to leave their wicked city. They must be extracted from the destruction.

The conclusion to the unit appears in vv. 27-29. The narrative here shifts to Abraham, who returns to the place of his audience with Yahweh (18:22-33). From this perspective he can witness the full extent of the tragedy. There were no righteous people in the city, and even the ones chosen to escape the punishment hardly qualified for the category. Only the buffoon Lot and his two daughters escaped. V. 29 rounds off the narrative by suggesting that God exempted Lot for Abraham's sake. This verse recognizes the problems involved in suggesting in any manner that Lot might be righteous or for some other reason deserve his redemption. For this contrast, it is perhaps appropriate to recognize v. 29 as P in a J context. In any case, the contrast between righteous Abraham and foolish Lot appears rather sharply here.

Questions about oral antecedents come into play at this point. It is possible that this unit derives from a tradition originally primeval in character (see Westermann, *Promises,* 54). Its content would have described a worldwide destruction, just as Genesis 6–9 did (→ 19:30-38). One might ask whether the tradition of destruction at Sodom was originally connected with Lot at all (so, Kilian, "Zur Überlieferungsgeschichte Lots," 29). Is the focus of this tradition, particularly in the hypothetical oral stage, not entirely on the destruction of Sodom? Yet, the cosmic destruction needs some central figure as a carrier of human tradition beyond the judgment. Whether Lot or an unnamed principal, the story here describes such a figure. Its essential narration involves not simply the destruction of the city, but the characterization of the survivor. That the survivor is not quite righteous alters the character of the story with a marked irony. The figure of Lot as a cosmic buffoon would thus emphasize the structural focus of the unit on destruction, but it would also place the tradition in the larger context of the Lot tradition.

One formulaic expression deserves attention. In v. 22, a naming etiology begins with "therefore" (*'al-kēn*), employs the catchword verb "name" (*qārā'*), and identifies the name of the city in a wordplay on a key word in v. 20.

Genre

In its present form, the unit is a TALE of punishment and destruction in the larger context of the Abraham-Lot narration. The hypothesis that the tale was originally independent of the Lot tradition, with Lot as the buffoon a growth under the influence of 19:30-38, is plausible. In that case, the original tale would have reported the destruction of the city with a survivor, perhaps depicted as righteous. Whether antecedents can properly be classified as primeval (→) myth or primeval (→) saga remains too hypothetical to defend. An originally independent narrative about these events could be qualified at best simply as tale.

Setting

In its present form, the unit belongs to the literary process responsible for the Abraham saga, or perhaps the Abraham-Lot narrative. As an originally independent tale, the unit relates closely to primeval tradition.

Intention

The unit relates the destruction of Sodom as an indication of the fate that belongs to the wicked. The fate is anticipated by 13:13 as well as 14:21-24. But the intention of the unit falls not simply on the destruction of Sodom, but even more on the characterization of Lot in the process. In contrast to Abraham the hero, Lot is a buffoon, not wicked like the men of Sodom, but not righteous like Abraham.

An earlier independent tale would have reported this destruction as worldwide, God's response to the wickedness of his creation (→ 6:1–9:17), with Lot as the survivor parallel to Noah or Utnapishtim.

Bibliography

A. Jepsen, "Zur Überlieferungsgeschichte der Vätergestalten," *WZLeipzig* 3 (1953/54) 150; R. Kilian, "Zur Überlieferungsgeschichte Lots," *BZ* 14 (1970) 23-37; P. D. Miller, "Fire in the Mythology of Canaan and Israel," *CBQ* 27 (1965) 256-61; G. Wallis, "Die Stadt in den Überlieferungen der Genesis," *ZAW* 78 (1966) 133-48.

REPORT OF LOT'S INCEST, 19:30-38

Structure

I. Exposition	30
II. Description of events	31-36
A. Plan of daughters	31-33
1. Speech	31-32
2. Execution of plan	33
B. Plan of daughters	34-35
1. Speech	34
2. Execution of plan	35
C. Conclusion	36
III. Conclusion	37-38
A. Birth report: Moab	37
B. Birth report: Ben-ammi	38

The exposition in v. 30 establishes context for this small unit by creating a link with the narrative account of the destruction of Sodom, a link that assumes a connection with Zoar (vv. 18-23). Indeed, the designation of a dwelling for Lot and his two daughters as "the hills" or "a cave" represents an expansion of the motif from vv. 1-29, depicting Lot as a resister to the efforts of his guests to save him from destruction. In v. 17 the guests instruct him to flee to the hills. In vv. 18-20 Lot petitions for an alternative refuge in Zoar, since the hills bode a disaster. Now Lot is afraid of Zoar, and as an alternative to Zoar he flees to the hills.

The incest events depicted in vv. 31-36 do not appear to be tied directly to the place represented by the cave; tradition about a place is hardly the subject of the element. Rather, two speeches by the elder daughter set out a plan for seducing the father. In both speeches the plan involves inducing the father to drink so much wine that he would lose his senses and be quite unaware of his daughters' seductions (→ 9:20-27). There is no indication in the plot about the source of the wine (contrast 9:20-27). The reason for the seduction lies in the elder daughter's observation that there is no man available to give them children other than their old father, an allusion that perhaps assumes a worldwide tragedy. Thus, the plan rests on a "noble" concern to preserve posterity. Vv. 33 and 35 then recount the execution of the plan, with v. 36 a record of the results.

The "nobility" of the daughters' acts must certainly be qualified by the characterization of the father. If the story implies a severe judgment on the incestuous relationship (so, von Rad, *Genesis,* 224), the judgment on the act does not rise to an explicit element in the narration of the event. Yet, the description of the circumstances does little to present the plot of the daughters as noble. The impact of the unit focuses more directly on a characterization of the father. The one who offered his daughters for the sexual gratification of his wicked neighbors now becomes the object of his daughters' incestuous sexual relationship. If the story in 19:1-29 represents Lot as a buffoon, a passive object whose retardation in the movement of the story appears somewhat comic, then the same buffoonery certainly returns here. Lot not only reverses the direction of his fear, v. 30, but in the hills loses his sensibilities to the wiles of his daughters. To be seduced by one's own daughters into an incestuous relationship with pregnancy following is bad enough. Not to know that the seduction had occurred is worse. To fall prey to the whole plot a second time is worse than ever. The passive Lot, presented first in the account of the downfall of Sodom, remains equally passive here. In his passivity, he represents an ethnological foil for the righteous Abraham (chs. 13, 14).

The conclusion of the unit, vv. 37-38, contains two birth reports, with names that connect the sons of the daughters with national groups recognized by later generations. The ethnological element comes thus to the fore, with no explicit judgment on the incestuous origin of those people, but also with no explicit pride in the act that constituted their origin (contrast von Rad, *Genesis,* 224).

It may be possible to establish a tradition history that would account for the relationship between this unit and other items in the Lot-Abraham narratives. (1) It is possible that behind this narrative lies an account of a worldwide disaster, leaving Lot and his daughters as the sole human survivors (v. 31). The story would have dealt with the conception of humanity by a primeval man and two primeval mothers and stand in close proximity to the parallel in the flood story (so, Lods). The reconstruction remains somewhat hypothetical, however. At best, the story reveals elements of primeval tradition, parallel to Noah with his drunkenness following the flood as an occasion for violation of familial sexual taboo. From the parallel, one might deduce that Canaan's violation with Noah is related in some manner to incest, and that Noah's drunken stupor contrasts with his earlier righteousness, at least traditionally if not also morally. (2) It is possible that the kernel of the Lot tradition is centered in this account, connected as a local tradition to a particular cave (so, Lods; Kilian, "Zur Überlieferungsgeschichte Lots"). The tradition would have been originally independent of the destruction of Sodom, an account of the ancestor of the pre-Moabite inhabitants of the territory east of the Dead Sea. The connection with the downfall of Sodom, setting Lot up as the righteous inhabitant of an unrighteous city, as well as the identification of Lot as the ancestor of Moab and subsequently Ammon, would be secondary in the history of the tradition. It is important to note that relationship with Abraham would be the final stage in the tradition history, peripheral to the primary movement of this unit. Yet, the role of the cave is limited to the transition between the Sodom narrative and the report of incest. The report itself unfolds without reference to the cave, much less an indication of the cave as intrinsic for the narration. It may be that the traditio-historical kernel of the Lot tradition resides in this report of incest, with the passive, somewhat comic role of the father an intrinsic motif in the tradition. The traditio-historical origin would not tie so obviously to a place in that case, however. Rather, it would be simply a tale of buffoonery.

The naming etiologies at the conclusion of the unit use stereotyped formulations to establish the name-giving process for the two children.

Genre

The unit does not develop into a narrative story, although the substance of narrative is present. In its current form, it is but a REPORT, a part of a larger narration about Lot and his fate (→ Genesis 13–14; 18–19). Earlier forms of the tradition may have been primeval (→) saga or primeval (→) myth (see Lods). Ethnological elements enter the narrative and influence the character of the unit.

Setting

The narrative has a setting in the Abraham-Lot tradition, the literary activity of J. Prior to its literary structures, ethnological elements suggest a popular setting, but the setting definition cannot depend simply on such secondary items in the tradition history. The popular setting reflected in the storytelling merit of the subject would point to a wider circle of distribution than would be suggested by Moab or Amorite settings. Indeed, the depiction of Lot as a buffoon vis-à-vis Abraham suggests an Israelite popular setting. Moreover, the contact with family is strong here, reflecting some concern to depict for popular family circles the problems of life in a particular (primeval?) family (→ 9:20-27).

Intention

The unit depicts Lot's buffoonery, leading to an incestuous relationship with his daughters. As buffoon, Lot contrasts with the heroic Abraham. In the present form of the text, the tradition has an ethnological character. The buffoon was the father of Moab and Ammon, a point which speaks against labeling the unit as Moabite tradition. The ethnological character extends from this basic unit back to 19:1-29.

Bibliography

R. Kilian, "Zur Überlieferungsgeschichte Lots," *BZ* 14 (1979) 23-37; A. Lods, "La caverne de Lot," *RHR* 95 (1927) 204-19.

THREAT TO THE ANCESTRESS, 20:1-18

Structure

I. Itinerary	1
II. Complication	2
A. Abraham's plan	2a
B. Consequences	2b
III. Denouement	3-16
A. Divine intervention speech	3
B. Self-defense	4-5
C. Divine response	6-7
1. Acquittal	6
2. Instructions	7a
3. Threat	7b
D. Execution of instructions	8-16
1. Report to royal household	8
2. Abimelech's accusation	9-10
a. First accusation	9
b. Second accusation	10
3. Abraham's self-defense	11-13
a. Fear	11
b. Sister-brother	12
c. Explanation of plan	13
4. Restoration	14-16
a. General report	14
b. Abimelech's invitation to Abraham	15
c. Abimelech's explanation to Sarah	16
IV. Conclusion	17-18

This story has a loose relationship with its context (see Koch, 117-18). The relationship is established through an itinerary formula in v. 1 that looks back for locale to the previous narratives, without specifying what that locale was, and forward to the subject of this story. The itinerary recalls 12:9 in its notation of movement toward the Negeb and 12:10 in its wordplay between the verb "sojourned" (*wayyāgār*) and the place-name Gerar (*bigrār*). In addition, the common theme of the narrative and its counterpart in ch. 21 suggests contact with context: "The Lord had closed all the wombs of the house of Abimelech because of Sarah, Abraham's wife. The Lord visited Sarah as he had said." The inverted sentence structure in 21:1 would mark this line as the beginning of a new story, but it does not override the cohesion between the two chapters. Moreover, following the account of the birth of Isaac (21:1-21), the narrative again presupposes Abraham's presence with Abimelech (so, Gen 21:22-34; cf. 26:17-33). The end of the Abraham-Abimelech cycle is marked in 21:34, a general summary that repeats the wordplay verb, "sojourned" (*wayyāgār*).

Although the structure of this story follows the same pattern as the parallel in 12:10-20 (cf. also 26:1-16), its detailed narration develops particular characteristics. Following the itinerary, the complication of plot, v. 2, is crisp and short (contrast 12:11-13). Abraham's plan with his wife, structured as indirect speech, is blunt, and the consequence follows: "Abraham said of Sarah his wife, 'She is my sister.' So Abimelech, king of Gerar, sent and took Sarah." The denouement is, to the contrary, highly expanded. This point can be seen as early as the revelation to Abimelech of his crime, vv. 3-6. In contrast to Genesis 12, where no indication of the means the pharaoh used for finding the source of his problem appears, here God addresses Abimelech in a dream with an oracle of judgment: "Behold, you are a dead man [*hinnĕkā mēt*]." The reason for the judgment follows, introduced by causative *'al*, and Abimelech knows the cause of his crisis. Vv. 4-5 contain a protest of innocence (see van Seters, *Abraham*, 173-74), and vv. 6-7 are God's response in two parts. V. 6 declares Abimelech innocent by virtue of God's intervention, and v. 7 instructs Abimelech to restore the woman to her husband, with an appropriate warning formulated in the stereotype of apodictic law: "You and all which belongs to you shall surely die [*môt tāmût*]."

The warning marks the turning point in the story. Vv. 8-16 concentrate on the details that show that Abimelech heeded the warning and restored the woman to her husband. The pattern of the execution of divine instructions is much the same as in 12:18-19. The details, however, are considerably expanded: (1) Abimelech reports the crisis to his household, v. 8 (no parallel in ch. 12); (2) Abimelech confronts Abraham with accusation, v. 9, and, following a renewed speech formula, v. 10 (par. 12:18-19a); (3) Abraham's response, a self-defense built on an appeal that his wife really was his sister, vv. 11-13 (no parallel in ch. 12); and (4) an account of the restoration, vv. 14-16 (par. 12:20). Of particular importance in this expansion is first the allusion to Gerar as a place devoid of the "fear of God," a statement that assumes Abraham's fear and thus the motivation for his deed (v. 11). The allusion places Abraham in a questionable light since Abimelech's favorable response to God's warning shows him to be one who "fears" God. Second, in his self-defense speech Abraham pleads innocence in calling Sarah his sister (v. 12). But whether historically husbands might pass wives off as sisters or not, in this story Abraham's designation of Sarah as sister leads to the crisis. It is a deceptive deed, and as a consequence, the appeal is almost comic, at least lame. It bespeaks loss of relationship between Abraham and his wife. Indeed, the appeal to wandering from the protection of the father's house into various dangers wherever they might arise may suggest that Sarah warmed various beds. But the lame quality of the self-defense here is that, in Abraham's words, the cause of it all was God: "And when God caused me to wander . . . [*hit'û 'ōtî 'ĕlōhîm*]." Abraham's appeal in effect passes responsibility first to physical relationship with Sarah, then to relationship with God (→ Genesis 2–3). Third, the restoration involves not only returning Sarah to her rightful husband, but also payment of wealth. To Abraham the payment involves cattle and slaves, as well as an open invitation to settle anywhere in Abimelech's own land. To Sarah it involves an explanation: Abimelech made a payment of silver to Abraham in Sarah's name. Abraham is designated here as Sarah's brother, not her husband. The silver stands for Sarah's restoration as a woman of honor. Abraham thus escapes the consequences of his deed and emerges as a man of wealth if not also a man of honor. For his deed, contrary to the parallel in Genesis 12, Abraham is not deported; rather, he is invited to stay. Yet, even with these acts of good faith on the part of Abimelech, the health of his household is not restored automatically. In Genesis 12, restoration of the pharaoh is assumed, but here restoration depends on Abraham's role as intercessor. Only through his prayer was the plague on the royal house corrected (cf. v. 7). The plague itself now emerges in some detail. V. 7 suggested that if the adulterous marriage should be consummated, the king would die. V. 18 is not contradictory; even though consummation never occurred, precisely because consummation was potential (see Polzin), the king's harem was blighted with infertility. The righteous Abimelech must go to the hero of the story, even though the hero's righteousness is in question, and from him the righteous Abimelech must receive intercession for healing.

According to recent suggestions, this story, normally ascribed to E, is not independent of the J story in 12:10-20 (→ 26:1-17). It is, to the contrary, an expansion of J with details of narration that move the story out of its original folk structure into a more reflective form that serves the interest of theologizing (see van Seters, *Abraham*, 173; Polzin). A similar movement appears in Genesis 22. The complementary position of the story in the redactional structure of the patriarchal theme would tend to confirm that conclusion.

Stereotyped expressions and formulas appear in this tale. In addition to the common items of narrative such as speech formula, one should list an itinerary formula in v. 1, noting the direction of the journey and the point of station marking the end of the journey, and an accusation formula in vv. 9, 10, especially with the formula "What have you done to us?"

Genre

This unit loses the character of TALE noted for Gen 12:9–13:1 in its display of a theologizing tendency. Even though it focuses more directly on the persons of importance and their virtue or lack of it, it is not yet (→) legend (→ Genesis 22). (See Koch, 128, who suggests that the story here should be understood as a "legend about the prophets.") Since the structure is still dominated by a plot rather than a static repetition of Abraham's virtue as a husband, the story remains tale, but one should note that this tale has developed beyond its parallel in Genesis 12. It cannot be shunted aside from ch. 12 as a duplicate source or as an independent version (see van Seters, *Abraham*, 173).

Setting

The story here is more directly bound to a setting in the literary structure of JE than is Genesis 12 (see van Seters, *Abraham*, 173).

Intention

The story maintains its structure designed for capturing interest and thus entertaining an audience. But that intention is now submerged under an overarching narrative context that tends toward a theological reflection. How does the father of the family relate in the family? Here the audience hears a particular emphasis on God's protection of the family in spite of the fumbling efforts of the patriarch to protect himself. But the intention of the story is not to show how the promise for great descendants or even the promise for a son fell into danger (→ 26:1-17).

It depicts, rather, the fall of the family, the husband and wife, into danger. And the fall threatens the intimacy of the family unit.

Bibliography
→ 12:9–13:1.

BIRTH OF ISAAC, 21:1-21

Structure

The introduction to this story proffers a typical stylistic feature in v. 1a through its inverted sentence structure: "The Lord visited Sarah" (wĕyahweh pāqad 'et-śārâ). Yet, the introduction presupposes the context of a previous annunciation: ". . . just as he said." Thus, the introduction marks the unit as a distinct element but not as an independent element; to the contrary, it represents a continuation of narration from Genesis 16 and 18 (→ 16:1–21:21). The parallel line in v. 1b makes the same assumption of context even though stylistically it features normal sentence order, a natural continuation of v. 1a. Source analysis identifies this line as P, the context established by P in Genesis 17.

The unit then comprises three principal narrative elements and a conclusion that rounds off the narrative crises and resolution. The first element is simply a birth report. It does not join the development of tension between the two women in the family, set in motion by the narrative in Genesis 16, nor does it lay claim to the narrative crisis in the confrontation between God and Sarah in Genesis 18. It thus does not advance the narrative; it only reports an event. In P the event comprises an account of the birth, the naming, and the circumcision of the child, along with a notation of Abraham's age at the birth (cf. Genesis 5). In the J material, there is no birth report, only a combination of birth speeches from the mother. The event nonetheless presupposes the context. This point is clear in P in v. 2: "Sarah conceived and bore Abraham a son in his old age at the time of which God had spoken to him." In J this claim to context is more subtle. The wordplay developed in Genesis 18 (Sarah laughed) is renewed in the first birth speech: "God has made laughter for me. Every one who hears shall laugh at me." The speech has an ambiguous connotation. It is ironic that Sarah's great moment should produce people who would laugh at her (*lî*). The speech thus recalls the threat of 18:15, and it raises the specter of a parallel with the curse of Hagar in 16:4. But it is also good news—God's gift of laughter to Sarah is Isaac. The second speech also sets the unit here in the context of Genesis 18 by its reference to the birth of the child in Abraham's old age.

The crisis in the narrative, introduced in Genesis 16, is rejoined in 21:8-13, a continuation of the counterpart rather than a doublet. Here the conflict breaks out, not between a pregnant maid and a barren mistress, but rather between the same two women who have now borne sons to Abraham. V. 8 marks a high day for the young child of the primary wife—he is weaned. V. 9 marks the opposite pole. The explanation in the LXX obscures the point of the verse, a renewal of the wordplay on the verb "laugh." The MT reads: "Sarah saw the son of Hagar, the Egyptian, whom she had borne to Abraham, laughing." The threat of Ishmael throughout the narrative is that he would replace Sarah's son, or Sarah's lack of a son, as the heir of Abraham. Now the wordplay, so crucial for the whole story, sets out the weight of the conflict. It does not imply that Ishmael has done something amiss with Isaac. It suggests, to the contrary, that Sarah saw Ishmael *mĕṣaḥēq*, playing the role of Isaac. Indeed, the act implies some disdain on Ishmael's part, perhaps an equivalent to the curse of Hagar in 16:4. The immediate response to the scene is for Sarah to instruct Abraham to expel both Hagar and her son so that the son cannot take the place of Isaac or even share his place: "Cast out [*gārēš*; cf. 3:24] this slave woman and her son, for the son of this slave woman shall not be heir with my son Isaac." The tension in the family is clear not only in this audacious command to the master of the family, but also in his response, v. 11. At the very core of Abraham's family, through which all the families of the land will inherit blessing, lies a rift that threatens the family structure. Somewhat surprising, however, is the oracle in vv. 12-13, giving divine sanction to the instructions of Sarah. The sanction is rooted in two elements of tradition: (1) The promise for descendants will rest on Isaac. (2) The son of the slave woman will also become a nation (cf. 16:10).

Thus the crisis of the narrative reaches its peripeteia in v. 14. Abraham sent Hagar and her child away, and they entered the wilderness. The surprising factor in this verse, however, is that the tension breaks without achieving reconciliation between the warring principals. The conflict at the center of Abraham's divine promise becomes permanent. The element continues into vv. 15-16 with a renewal of tension (cf. the foreshadowing in 16:7-14). Hagar exhausts her provisions given her by her master and faces death from thirst. The pathos of this scene is captured in the description of her anxiety over the imminent death of her child. She sat "over against him" (*minneged*; cf. 2:20), a denotation of the intimacy in the relationship, and she wept (contrast LXX: "The child wept").

The final break in this tension then appears with the divine response and speech of the angel in vv. 17-19. The speech is constructed as an oracle of salvation. The admonition not to fear is here a part of the oracle of salvation, a response to Hagar's lament. It is followed by a clause (introduced with *kî*) that announces God's favorable hearing and thus parallels the assistance formula: "I am with you." V. 18 builds a promise for posterity in the form of a great nation (*gôy gādôl*) onto the oracle of salvation. The people of Ishmael, the son of Abraham, stand under God's promise just as the people of Isaac do. But significant for the speech is the absence of any reconciliation with the people of Isaac. The concluding verses in the unit (vv. 20-21) round this point off: God was with Ishmael; his life assumed normal channels—his mother found a wife for him among the Egyptians. But they remained in the wilderness; the family was broken. One can see here the outcome of the explicit statement in 16:12. V. 19 then resolves the crisis posed by Hagar's need for water.

With the exception of the P element in vv. 1b-5, these scenes belong to J or, better, to JE. On the larger structure and tradition history, → 16:1–21:21.

Stereotyped expressions in the unit include the formula from the oracle of salvation, "Fear not . . . for God has heard . . ." in v. 17. The formula "Fear not" (*'al-tîrĕ'î*) here functions in relationship to Hagar's lament (v. 16) rather than as the opening line of a self-revelation speech (contrast Gen 15:1b). It thus belongs to the salvation oracle. One should be careful, however, not to identify the formula wherever it occurs simply as salvation oracle.

Etiological wordplays enter this narrative, but they do not constitute an etiological genre. They belong rather to the particular style of the narrator.

Genre

The unit is not complete in itself. Genre observations must therefore relate to the larger whole (→ 16:1–21:21). The element is structured as a birth REPORT, particularly in P. For J, the birth report is present but hardly the whole structure (cf. vv. 6-7). Rather, the structure moves beyond the birth to the overarching plot of the unit. Behind the present form of the narrative lay perhaps a TALE of strife and separation. It would seem to be clear, however, that this hypothetical stage represents the antecedents for both chs. 16 and 21.

Setting

The element has a setting in the literature of J or P. On the tradition history, → 16:1–21:21.

Intention

The element in J brings the larger unit about Hagar and Sarah to a close (cf. the concluding verses, 21-22). It focuses on the conflict that existed from the opening element, pitches that conflict to a breaking point, then allows the relationships at the center of the conflict to break as a permanent resolution of the problem. That the narrative might be understood in an earlier oral form as an account of divine provisions for a person in need is possible (see Westermann, *Promises,* 13-15), but the pattern does not dominate the story as it now stands. It seems more likely that any oral stages of the tradition would have been focused in some manner on the conflict between the two factions within the family of Abraham.

Bibliography

→ 16:1–21:21.

BEER-SHEBA ETIOLOGY, 21:22-34

Structure

I. Oath		22-24
A. Request for oath		22-23
B. Response		24
II. Oath		25-30
A. Disputation		25-26
1. Complaint		25
2. Response		26
B. Resolution		27-30
1. Covenant ritual		27
2. Oath ritual		28-30
a. General description of the ritual		28
b. Ritual conversation		29-30
1) Question		29
2) Explanation of ritual		30
III. Conclusion		31-34
A. Etiology		31
B. Covenant ritual		32
1. Covenant proper		32a
2. Conclusion		32b
C. Planting a tree		33
D. Conclusion		34

This unit has no immediate contact with 21:1-21 or 22:1-19. Yet, it is not completely isolated in its present position. This point is established by the transition formula in v. 22aα: "At that time" (*wayĕhî bā'ēt hahiw'*). The formula presupposes some designation of common time in the preceding narration and thus functions as a bridge to this unit. Moreover, the unit connects with the account of the threat to the ancestress, 20:1-18, both by means of common principal figures and common locale. In 20:15 Abimelech invites Abraham to reside at will anywhere within the borders controlled by the Philistines, and in this unit Abraham's presence within those borders is a problem (cf. v. 34). Finally, 21:34 serves with 20:1 as a frame to bind the various traditions of the two chapters together. This unit would thus belong to the same narrative tradition that sets out 20:1-18 (E or JE).

Form in this unit involves movement from a general description of an oath (vv. 22-24) to a detailed display of the oath ritual (vv. 25-30). The final element (vv. 31-34) builds an etiology out of the narrative structure.

The first element is brief. After the transition formula in v. 22aα, this element contains Abimelech's suit for an agreement and Abraham's positive response. The suit is grounded in Abimelech's recognition of God's assistance for Abraham (v. 22b). It then appeals for an oath (see v. 23aα) that would establish a bond of mutual loyalty (ḥesed) between the two parties. To that end Abraham gives his oath (v. 24).

The second element contains more detail. It is not simply an elaboration of the first. Yet, the conflict it reports should not be taken as a contradiction of the first. Rather, it assumes the relationship established by the first and recounts a specific conflict that emerged within that relationship. The complaint is pressed, not by Abimelech, who brought the opening suit, but by Abraham. The issue is possession of water rights. On the basis of Abimelech's protest of innocence (v. 26), a ritual for a resolution of the quarrel unfolds. First, for a covenant (bĕrît) Abraham gives Abimelech cattle (vv. 28-31). In the second of these two parts, Abimelech asks a leading question: "What is the meaning of these. . . ?" The content of the oath follows: Abimelech will forego any claim for the well. The ritual is thus not a doublet of v. 27 but a more detailed description of the bond established by v. 27, in much the same manner as the entire element, vv. 25-30, depicts a particular example of the general bond established by vv. 22-24.

The conclusion for the unit reveals the same double reference to the bond. V. 31 is an etiological formula that connects the place-name explicitly with an act of swearing (nišbĕ'û). Yet, the narrative preparation for the etiology suggests an explanation of the place-name from the number seven. V. 32a then labels the ritual as a covenant (→ 26:26-33). But the shift need not demand division of the conclusion into two sources. The animals of vv. 28-30 constitute the substance for the oath ritual, suggesting again that the two items of tradition have grown together (for a division of the unit into two sources, see van Seters, Abraham, 186). Covenant here is defined as an oath undertaken in the context of ritual (→ Genesis 15). V. 32b would then mark the proper conclusion of the process: The participating parties separate. V. 33 is an isolated report, connected to the preceding narrative only by means of the common place-name. V. 33b should not lead to broader theologizing about the covenant. Even though it carries an epithet for Yahweh, it is not firmly anchored in the narrative tradition. V. 34 then appears to contradict v. 32b by suggesting that Abraham sojourned in the land of the Philistines. It should be seen as a redactional inclusion with 20:1.

Oral antecedents for this unit are difficult to reconstruct (see van Seters, Abraham). At most one can refer to tradition about quarrels over water rights and hypothesize that such tradition found expression in narrative forms such as this one, perhaps narrative forms primarily designed as etiology (→ 26:17-33). A tradition history would not necessarily define the relationship between this unit and its parallel as literary compilation (in contrast, see van Seters, Abraham). The common elements between this unit and 26:17-33 can be understood more readily as common tradition than as results of literary dependency. Indeed, one can consider seriously the suggestion that 26:17-33 is the older factor in the tradition history (→ 20:1-18; 26:1-16).

Genre

The unit suggests an etiological TALE. If these verses are no longer tale by virtue of their abbreviated development, they nonetheless reveal evidence of a plot with crisis—confrontation over a well—leading to resolution—the oath ritual. And the ETIOLOGY is rooted essentially in the plot.

Setting

The tradition derives from popular circles interested in narrating stories about patriarchal relationships. The unit belongs, not simply to the cult center of Beersheba (v. 33), but to a larger circle of narrative tradition, perhaps the tradition of the storyteller.

Intention

The unit recounts resolution of relationship between Abraham and Abimelech by means of an oath/covenant. But it also contributes to the larger scope of the Abraham tradition by depicting a point of tension between Abraham and his neighbors (→ 21:10-20; 20:1-18).

ABRAHAM LEGEND, 22:1-19

Structure

I. Exposition	1a
II. Description of Abraham's virtue	1b-18
A. Dialogue	1b-2
1. Yahweh's call to attention	
2. Abraham's response	
3. Yahweh's instructions	
B. Execution of instructions	3-10
1. Preparation for sacrifice	3-4
2. Abraham's instructions to the servant	5
3. Preparation for sacrifice	6-8
a. Narration: Abraham and son	6
b. Dialogue	7-8a
1) Isaac's call to attention	7aα
2) Abraham's response	7aβ
3) Isaac's request for information	7b
4) Abraham's response	8a
c. Narration: Abraham and son	8b
4. Presentation of Abraham's obedience	9-10
C. Confirmation of Abraham's sacrifice of faith	11-18
1. Dialogue	11-12
a. Angel's call to attention	11a
b. Abraham's response	11b
c. Angel's instructions	12
2. Execution of instructions	13
3. Etiology	14
4. Angel's speech	15-18
a. Speech formula	15

The context for the unit is important. It stands as a complement to the sacrifice of Ishmael that Abraham made in ch. 21. The relationship, however, is not simply one of common theme provided by the sacrifice of a son. In the final form of the text, this unit follows the report of the birth of Isaac and the corresponding expulsion of Hagar and Ishmael. The threat posed by Hagar and Ishmael to Sarah and thus to Isaac and the conclusion of the relationship without reconciliation stand as a sharp contrast to the narrative tradition of harmony between Abraham and his son in ch. 22. The contrast amplifies the complementary relationship with the foreshadowing of Abraham's obedience to God in 21:12-14.

The unit itself projects a recurring motif as its principal pattern of development: "Take your son, your only son whom you love, Isaac. . . ." In direct address to Abraham the phrase recurs in vv. 2, 12, 16, and in a concluding generalization, v. 18b. Moreover, third-person allusions to the motif can be seen in vv. 3, 6, 9, 10, always references to Isaac, *his son,* or simply *his son* (cf. also v. 7, where Isaac is not qualified by "his son," but the speech formula qualifies Abraham as his father, and the conversation addresses Isaac as "my son"). The point of the motif appears explicitly in vv. 16-18: "Because you have done this, and have not withheld your son, your only son, I will bless you . . . because you have obeyed my voice." Structure within the unit thus emphasizes Abraham's action in relationship to his son as obedience to God's command.

In v. 1a, the exposition defines the purpose of the events to be narrated as a test of Abraham. As v. 12 shows, the test would determine whether Abraham could demonstrate "fear of God" (*yĕrē' 'ĕlōhîm*) or, as in v. 18b, "obedience" (cf. Exod 20:20; Job 2:3). Thus, the exposition ties quite directly into the unifying motif and sets the stage for a presentation of Abraham's virtue (v. 18b). But at the same time, it undercuts the potential point of tension for developing a plot. The audience knows from the beginning that the threat to Isaac is not the subject of the narration. To the contrary, the subject of the narration is limited to a depiction of Abraham's faith.

The unit as a whole unfolds in a combination of dialogue and narrative. The first dialogue involves an exchange between God and Abraham, in effect an address to Abraham preceded by a call to attention and response. The address instructs Abraham to sacrifice his son, thus setting into motion the test of faith. Vv. 3-10 then spell out Abraham's obedient response. From vv. 3-4 it is clear that Abraham will obey the instructions. No doubt sets the narration in tension. Rather, the verses simply spin out the details of obedience already made clear by the exposition.

Vv. 3-10 involve a change of scene for the events of the narration. Vv. 3-4 depict the initial preparation for the sacrifice and the travel to the appointed locale (cf. 12:1-3). A brief speech to the servants accompanying them foreshadows the conclusion to the test. Then vv. 6-8 return to the details of preparation. Vv. 9-10 bring the details to a conclusion by describing the final moment of obedience: "When they came to the place . . . Abraham built an altar . . . and laid the wood . . . and bound Isaac his son. . . . And he took the knife to slay his son." The act of obedience is confirmed in vv. 11-18. A dialogue between Abraham and an angel in vv. 11-12 stops the slaughter and declares the act acceptable in the framework of the test. The dialogue begins with a stereotyped exchange of speech, a call to attention and response (par. vv. 1b-2). And it ends with an affirmation of Abraham's faith: "I know that you fear God, seeing you have not withheld your son, your only son, from me." V. 12 sets out new instructions, v. 13 their execution in an act of worship, and v. 14 an etiology built out of a following saying. The etiology would appear to be the end of the narrative, an appendix which does not derive from the dominant line of the narration, but depends only on the divine affirmation of the faith of the hero (cf. vv. 8, 14b). Despite the apparent ending, the etiological interlude leads to a second speech from the angel. In this more complicated speech, the angel cites first the oath of Yahweh (cf. Genesis 15) to multiply Abraham's descendants *because* Abraham did not withhold his son. The son-descendants pattern then leads to a promise that the descendants would possess the gate (territory) of the enemy (cf. 15:7, 8) and become a blessing for the nations (cf. 12:3). V. 18b parallels v. 16 as an inclusion, showing the successful conclusion of the test. The narrative then breaks off in v. 19 with an itinerary.

The regular recurrence of the son-obedience motif set in the context of a test of Abraham's faith reveals evidence of a plot, now compromised, which may have been behind the present form of this narrative. The plot could be reconstructed as follows:

I. Complication	1b-10
A. Instructions for sacrifice	1b-2
B. Execution	3-10
II. Resolution	11-14
A. Instructions for a stay of the sacrifice	11-12
B. Execution of the instructions	13
C. Etiology	14

The evidence for an older story does not permit reconstruction of an exposition. Rather, the outline opens with the complication: "Take your son . . . and offer him as a burnt offering. . . ." The narrative in the received text at this juncture is thus two-edged: (1) a call for obedience as a test for Abraham, with the patriarchal promise to Abraham at stake, and (2) a threat to the life of Abraham's firstborn. Vv. 3-10 heighten the tension with painstaking details of Abraham's obedience. With a combination of narration and speech, the storyteller paints a picture of father and son, moving slowly to a tragic destiny. The servants who accompany the central pair serve only to slow the pace of action and heighten the tension. Abraham must stop in the midst of his tragic odyssey to give his servants instructions; then the journey continues. Significantly, Abraham's speech in v. 5 foreshadows the good news of the story's climax, for in a series of first-person plural verbs, the coming set of events is announced: "I and the lad, we shall go there. We shall worship, and we shall return to you." And the tragic pair, unaware of the good news shared only by the storyteller and his audience, move off together. The transition narration in v. 6 captures the pathos of the scene: "So they went, both of them together."

Just at this point in the plot a problem in the structure of the story appears. The foreshadowing device suggests that the scope of the story encompasses Abraham's near sacrifice of Isaac (vv. 11-14). The point of tension in the story is now only the threat to Isaac's life. Obedience to the command is no longer at issue, for Abraham has already demonstrated that he would obey the command without a moment's hesitation. The arc of tension in the plot of the story thus does not open into the anticlimax in vv. 15-18, with its focus on the patriarchal promise and Abraham's exemplary obedience.

The dialogue in vv. 7-8 produces much the same image. In another poignant exchange of speeches, catching an awful destiny, yet a destiny that lies beyond the principals who share it, the son makes his request of the father. The wood and the fire are obvious. But what about a lamb? On the surface, Abraham's answer is an effort to dodge a straightforward reply. But again, the speech foreshadows the climax of the story, a climax involving the threat to Isaac without reference to the patriarchal promise and Abraham's obedience in vv. 15-18. Abraham prophesies that God will provide (rā'â) his own lamb.

A transition narration connects the dialogue with the climax of the plot. The transition, identical to the one in v. 6, picks up the poignant motif of unity between the father and his son. Following this transition, however, no further delays in the pace of narration appear. With rapid strokes, vv. 9-10 report construction of the altar, preparation of the wood, and final order for slaughter that would end the son's life in sacrifice: "Abraham put forth his hand and took the knife to slaughter his son." The story can now move no further. The tension must break with either the death of the son or his miraculous preservation. But again structural problems appear. The peak of tension in the story's plot does not involve Abraham's obedience; that obedience does not come into question. Rather, the breaking point centers on Isaac's life. This point belongs to the older tradition.

The dialogue in vv. 11-12, particularly the angel's speech in v. 12, marks the resolution of tension for the story. Just in time (see the similar sense of timing in Genesis 38), God stops the death blow. A substitution lamb appears (cf. the verb rā'â), caught in a thicket by his horns. The crisis ends in a burst of good news—the firstborn, the only son, Isaac, will not die. Vv. 13-14 then narrate the conclusion of the story, a brief reduction of the tension along less emotionally packed lines. Abraham offers the lamb in the place of his son, and an etiology plays on the verb rā'â as an explanation for the place-name.

The overall story builds on a test of Abraham's obedience, concluding with a reaffirmation of the patriarchal promise established in 12:1-3 and ch. 15 (→ The Patriarchal Theme). It thus shares in the theological emphasis provided by the larger context of Abraham traditions constructed under the programmatic stamp of J or JE. There is no reason to assume that traditions presenting Abraham as a man of obedience could not be constructed within the same framework with traditions presenting the same patriarch as a man of little faith, traditions such as

Gen 12:10-20, traditions given unity by the theology of the Yahwist. Behind this story lies an older story, developed around the tragic custom of child sacrifice, with its conclusion in a prohibition against this particular child's sacrifice and its corresponding etiology. That story would have reached its climax in v. 14. At that level, the story doubtlessly did not yet belong to one of the pentateuchal sources. Rather, the Yahwist has appropriated an ancient story of child sacrifice, altering it so that it becomes an example of Abraham's faith and an occasion for God's renewing the promise for great posterity, for possession of land, and for blessing open to all the nations of the earth. In the appropriation, the Yahwist creates an inclusion for his Abraham saga with the parallel in 12:1-3. Abraham, the man of faith, goes wherever God leads, and in the going, he proves himself obedient to the commandment of Yahweh.

Stereotyped expressions and formulas in this unit include the narrative transition in v. 1aα, speech formulas regularly constructed throughout the unit in order to indicate the speaker and addressee for speeches, formulas of conversation in vv. 1, 7, 11, with the vocative as a call to attention and the response constructed with the particle *hinnēh* plus suffix, and a naming formula in v. 14.

Genre

At the latest stage, the unit appears as a LEGEND (so, Coats, "Abraham's Sacrifice"). Structural emphasis on Abraham's obedience at each major stage in the movement of the narrative points to its identity as legend. Moreover, as is typical for the genre, the principal figure appears in superhuman, somewhat unrealistic dress. He never wavers from the course of his obedience. He never objects to the unreasonable, slightly insane commandment to sacrifice his son, as the Abraham of 12:10-20 or ch. 16 most certainly would have done. The text never raises questions about what kind of God would be asking such a horrifying confirmation of obedience and loyalty. In fact, the fate of Isaac is never in doubt for the legend. From the moment of the exposition, Isaac is relatively unimportant. The entire scope of the legend falls on a test of Abraham and a demonstration of his obedient faith.

The story behind the legend is a TALE of child sacrifice, with typical structure for the plot of a story. The tension of the plot is established by the command to sacrifice an only son, and the plot develops in an arc of tension from the initial complication to its resolution with God's provision for a substitute. Indeed, behind the present formulation of the tale may be a tradition about a theophany to confirm the change in requirement for firstborn sacrifice (note the Niphal *yērā'eh*). Moreover, though not the substance of the tale, the etiological elements alter the character of the unit (von Rad, *Opfer*). Its earliest stage thus may be identified as etiology, perhaps (→) *hieros logos*.

Setting

The legend seems to be the product of conscious adaptation from earlier tradition, designed to fit the story into the scope of the Yahwist's theology about Abraham and his promise. There is no firm evidence of a history of the legend prior to its incorporation into the literary construct of the Yahwist. The tale would have focused on sacrificial ritual, particularly the institution of a substitutionary sacrifice for the firstborn son. As a tale about ritual it would probably have been preserved within the cultic institutions.

Intention

The legend provides an edifying example of obedience for all subsequent devotees of Yahweh. Indeed, it emphasizes the importance of obedience for Israel by making the primary saint of obedience the father of Israel, the recipient of Yahweh's promise for posterity. This legend thus complements the picture of Abraham, the man of faith, in 12:1-3, both in content and in structure as the opposite pole of a literary inclusion. The legend functions, moreover, as an example of Abraham's faith in contrast to his lack of faith depicted in such stories as 12:10-20 or ch. 16. On the basis of this example, the promise for posterity, a slightly obscured promise for land, and a designation for blessing stand reaffirmed. The outcome of the faith test demonstrates that Abraham recognizes Yahweh as lord of the promise. Abraham does not control the life of the promise; he does not even control its death.

The tale maintains a plot line developed in the first order for suspense, thus for enjoyment. But its etiological character, both in establishing substitutionary sacrifice for the firstborn and in its foundation for a holy place, cannot be mistaken.

Bibliography

G. W. Coats, "Abraham's Sacrifice of Faith: A Form-Critical Study of Genesis 22," *Int* 27 (1973) 389-400; J. Crenshaw, "Journey into Oblivion: A Structural Analysis of Gen 22:1-19," *Soundings* 58 (1975) 243-56; P. R. Davies, "The Sacrifice of Isaac and Passover," in *Studia Biblica 1978, I. Papers on Old Testament and Related Themes* (JSOTSup 11; Sheffield: Sheffield University Press, 1979) 127-32; F. Golka, "Die theologischen Erzählungen im Abraham-Kreis," *ZAW* 90 (1978) 186-95; K. H. Gross, "Bedeutet die Opferung Isaaks das Ende der Menschenopfer?" *Katechetische Blätter* 82 (1957) 97-99; R. Kilian, *Isaaks Opferung. Zur Überlieferungsgeschichte von Gen 22* (SBS 44; Stuttgart: Katholisches Bibelwerk, 1970); R. Lack, "Le sacrifice d'Isaac—Analyse structurale de la couche élohiste dans Gen 22," *Bib* 56 (1975) 1-12; J. L. McKenzie, "The Sacrifice of Isaac," *Scr* 9 (1957) 79-84; I. Maybaum, "Die Opferung Isaaks," *EvT* 17 (1957) 249-64; D. Polish, "The Binding of Isaac," *Judaica* 6 (1957) 17-21; G. von Rad, *Das Opfer des Abraham* (Munich: Kaiser, 1971); H. Graf Reventlow, *Opfere deinen Sohn. Eine Auslegung von Genesis 22* (BibS[N] 53; Neukirchen-Vluyn: Neukirchener Verlag, 1968).

NAHOR GENEALOGY, 22:20-24

Structure

I. Transition	20aα
II. Genealogy: Nahor with Milcah	20aβb-23
A. First generation	20aβb-22
I. Introduction	20aβb
2. Name list	21-22
B. Second generation	23a
C. Conclusion	23b
III. Genealogy: Nahor with Reumah	24
A. Introduction	24a
B. Name list	24b

This unit (J) serves as a transition piece between 22:1-19 and ch. 24. Indeed, its allusion in v. 23 to the birth of Rebekah to Bethuel is an explicit preparation for 24:15. The transition thus places particular emphasis on the following traditions related to Nahor.

In its present form, the unit appears as two parallel genealogies, the roster of Nahor's sons born to two wives (→ Genesis 29–31). Each group employs the structure of a name list and thus appears as a linear genealogy. The first list opens in v. 20b by designating the mother of the persons who constitute the following list. The list itself contains eight names (vv. 21-22). The final name in the list provides the opening to the second generation, composed only of Rebekah. But the conclusion in v. 23b refers to the first-generation list, not to the second-generation Rebekah. It would appear, then, that the traditional form of linear genealogy has been adapted for structural focus on Rebekah. Moreover, the second list, introduced in v. 24a by reference to the mother of the persons constituting the list, contains four names but nothing more.

Thus, the name lists as they now stand introduce Rebekah, the second generation in a Nahor genealogy. But the name lists themselves reflect an older tradition. Nahor's sons constitute a twelve-member group, perhaps as an Aramean league of clans (see von Rad, *Genesis*, 245). The reason for including v. 24 derives from the structure of the name list, not from the introduction of Rebekah.

Finally, the narrative formula in v. 1aα presupposes the total narrative context, thus providing transition from the preceding unit (→ 22:1aα).

Genre

In its present form the unit can appropriately be understood as a linear GENEALOGY, composed of a diachronic line with a return in the movement of the line to its first level (→ 11:27-30). Behind the J genealogy lies a name LIST that describes the organization of a tribal league (→ Exod 1:1-7).

Setting

As a genealogy the unit derives from the redactional activity of J. As a linear genealogy built around a name list, the unit derives from the life of the family, expanded here into the form of a tribal league (→ Genesis 29–31).

Intention

In J, the unit functions as a bridge from ch. 22 to ch. 24. In the process, it introduces the central figure in Genesis 24, the daughter of Bethuel, the granddaughter of Nahor. As a name list, the earlier tradition defines the structure and thus the organization of the Aramean tribal league.

BURIAL REPORT FOR SARAH, 23:1-20

Structure

I. Death report	1-2
A. Summary of age	1
B. Death notice	2a
C. Mourning rite	2b
II. Business negotiation dialogue	3-16

This unit, a report of the death and burial of Sarah, is isolated from the form of the Abraham saga by its unique structure and content and by the absence of significant transition pieces. Thus, 22:20-24, a name list for the sons of Nahor, anticipates ch. 24 but not ch. 23. The structural isolation of ch. 23 is perhaps illuminated by the standard source analysis of the unit and its context: 22:20-24 and 24:1-67 are commonly assigned to J, while this chapter along with 25:7-17 belong to P. On the structural context for ch. 23 in P, → The Abraham Saga.

Vv. 1-2 constitute the introduction to the unit, a presentation of the circumstances that make the following events of negotiation necessary. The presentation is a death report, constructed in typical fashion with a designation of the subject's total years of life (v. 1), the death report itself, already implied by the reference to the total years of life (v. 2a), and a notice that proper mourning followed (cf. 47:27–50:14). Indeed, the parallel death report in 47:27–50:14 suggests that the structure should include a summary statement of years, the death report, mourning, and burial. Moreover, it is split at crucial places in order to allow inclusion of distinct traditional units as a part of the death report. Does this parallel not suggest that vv. 1-2 and 19 belong clearly together, with vv. 3-16 framed as a distinctive part of the death report?

In the light of this pattern, it is significant that vv. 3-16, along with the concluding vv. 17-18 and 20, report acquisition of land for the purposes of burial. The acquisition is not conquest, however, and indeed not a fulfillment of land promise. Divine promise and all other theological motifs of the patriarchal stories stand far removed from this unit (contrast von Rad, *Genesis*, 249-50). As far as this text is concerned, the land acquisition occurred strictly for purposes of burial. If that event is in itself theological, so much the better. But the unit itself draws no theological consequence from the acquisition.

The middle element of the unit unfolds as a dialogue of negotiations. Abraham and the local inhabitants negotiate over purchase of a burial place for Sarah. The dialogue is marked by a repeated show of polite overstatement. Thus, the first speech, vv. 3-4, is Abraham's request to the local inhabitants who are gathered in the gate of the city for the legal proceedings of their community (v. 10). Abraham wants burial ground placed at his disposal. The response, vv. 5-6, accepts the request and indeed offers burial space for Abraham's use. The speech has relatively little theological content even though Abraham is named a prince of God (*RSV* "a mighty prince among us" [*nĕśîʾ ʾĕlōhîm*]). There is no concern here to deny Abraham his request or to avoid the request. Abraham has not yet asked to buy a specific plot of land; he asks only for a burial piece ('*ăḥuzzat-qeber*). The local elders respond favorably to the request. The exchange simply opens the door to the next step in the negotiations, vv. 7-9, an Abraham speech with a specific proposal for purchase of land from a specific owner among the local elders. Abraham names the owner, place, its location in a field, and agrees to buy the place for the fair price. Again, one should note that no reference to this purchase as fulfillment of promise or any other theologically significant character appears. Its purpose is to acquire a possession so that "I should bring my dead out of my sight."

Vv. 10-11 contain the response of the owner, Ephron the Hittite, who agrees to Abraham's request for the land. The agreement is like the general statement in vv. 5-6. In a rather overdrawn gesture of courtesy, Ephron offers to give Abraham not only the burial place but the field as well. Abraham's response in vv. 12-13 asks for the price, and Ephron gives the price in a speech still marked by formal courtesy. With that, the negotiations end. V. 16 describes the payment. Vv. 17-18 then define the conclusion of the sale, as if in form of a deed for the legal action. The verses name the field and its location, the physical description of the field with cave and trees, the buyer, and the witnesses to the transaction.

Structurally, the unit hangs together with no breaks in the developing narrative. This P unit (vv. 17-20 in particular) reveals influence of business negotiations, even the formal pattern of a contract of sale (see G. Tucker). In the overall structure of P, the unit introduces a series concerned with the death and burial of principal patriarchal figures (→ 25:7-18).

Genre

The unit is a death REPORT, framing a DIALOGUE shaped by the patterns of business negotiations and contracts (see G. Tucker).

Setting

The unit has a setting in the literature of P. Death reports, thus the entire range of tradition in chs. 23–25, mark the transition from one narrative unit to the other. The form itself is related to genealogy, where death and burial may be reported. The business-contract form reflects the influence of the secular world of negotiations over legal contracts in the gate of the city.

Intention

The report notes the acquisition of land for the purpose of familial burial. It thus has contact with the larger familial narrations in the patriarchal traditions. But it does not develop theological intentions. It is simply a report of acquisition of burial property. Thus, as report of death and burial, it introduces and belongs to a group of narratives describing the death and burial of the principal patriarchal figures.

Bibliography

M. R. Lehmann, "Abraham's Purchase of Machpelah and Hittite Law," *BASOR* 129 (Feb. 1953) 15-18; H. Petschow, "Die neubabylonische Zwiegesprächsurkunde und Genesis 23," *JCS* 19 (1965) 103-20; G. M. Tucker, "The Legal Background of Genesis 23," *JBL* 85

(1966) 77-84; R. Westerbrook, "Purchase of the Cave of Machpelah," *Israel Law Review* 6 (1971) 29-38.

THE SERVANT OF ABRAHAM NOVELLA, 24:1-67

Structure

I. Exposition	1-9
A. Introduction of Abraham	1
B. Oath dialogue	2-8
1. Abraham's instructions to his servant	2-4
2. Servant's objection	5
3. Abraham's reassurance for the servant	6-8
C. Instructions executed	9
II. First panel	10-27
A. Exposition	10-11
B. Complication	12-21
1. Petition	12-14
a. General formula	12
b. Conditions for the sign	13-14
2. Execution of the petition	15-21
a. Description of the sign	15-20
b. Complication	21
C. Resolution	22-27
1. Presentation of gifts	22
2. Dialogue	23-25
a. Request by the servant	23
1) Identity of the subject	23a
2) Provisions for the night	23b
b. Rebekah's self-identification	24
c. Definition of familial provisions	25
3. Resolution of the complication	26-27
III. Second panel	28-54a
A. Exposition	28-29a
B. Complication	29b-49
1. Invitation	29b-31
2. Response	32-33aα
3. Explanation of the commission	33aβb-49
a. Servant's request	33aβ
b. Host's response	33b
c. Servant's explanation	34-49
1) Self-identification	34
2) Report of events	35-48
3) Complication	49
C. Resolution	50-54a
1. Acceptance	50-51
2. Response	52-54a
a. Worship	52

This story is relatively isolated in its J context. Although it appears in the overall structure of Genesis as one among the several units concerned with Abraham's last acts, a point made clear in the exposition of the story (see Roth), in fact it has relatively little to do with Abraham himself. And although the content of the story describes the discovery of a proper wife for Isaac, it has relatively little to do with Isaac. The story is rather about Abraham's servant, unnamed and without a role in the preceding or following narratives, yet the central figure in the development of this narrative. Indeed, even Rebekah plays a role subordinate to the servant, her only contribution simply a passive confirmation of the servant's major commission. To be sure, the final form of the text, indeed, the structure of the Yahwist, gives the story a context in relationship to the genealogy of Nahor (→ 22:20-24). And the blessing of Rebekah's family, 24:60, parallels the blessing to Abraham in the Yahwist, 22:17. Nevertheless, the story stands in obvious isolation, both in form and genre.

The story unfolds as a series of panels, each developed in some measure as parallel to the others, each introduced by its own exposition. The exposition in vv. 1-9 establishes the scope of the story's plot, and only here does the old Abraham appear. He addresses his servant with directions for an oath which amounts to a commission for a major responsibility. The servant is to go away from the Canaanites to Mesopotamia in order to seek out a wife for Isaac. In typical form (→ Exodus 3), the servant raises an objection to the commission: What should happen if the woman he finds refuses to come? The question focuses the major crisis of the plot, the point of unity for the story. The issue is not whether the servant can find someone to come to Isaac; the issue is whether something might happen to block the consummation of the marriage. Abraham's response, vv. 7-8, places the weight of the crisis on divine intervention. God will secure the proper wife in fulfillment of the commission. But it also highlights the genuine quality of the unit as story. If the woman should be unwilling to return with the servant, then the servant would be free of the oath. Successful execution of the oath is not a foregone conclusion. V. 9 concludes the exposition with a description of an ancient ritual for securing an oath by swearing on the genitals of the patriarch (see von Rad, *Genesis*). The servant thus executes the instructions given him by Abraham and the story is ready for narration.

The first panel recounts the servant's initial encounter with the future wife of his master's son, and at the same time it develops as a demonstration of God's designation of the proper choice. Vv. 10-11 set the scene. Laden with gifts from Abraham, the servant moves from Canaan to Mesopotamia and waits at a well (→ Genesis 29; Exodus 2). The encounter occurs, however, not by chance (→ Exodus 2) or by heroic display of strength (→ Genesis 29: Exodus 2), but by divine intervention. The servant prays, and in his prayer he outlines the specific circumstances that will serve him as a sign to identify the proper woman (cf. v. 14b; → Judg 6:36). Vv. 15-20 repeat the circumstances as narration of the event, although the repetition is not exact. V. 21 leaves the question of success for the commission open, dependent not so much on details in the sign as on the circumstances that develop around the major point of tension: Will the woman recognize the authority of the sign and go? Will her family permit such a trans-action? Vv. 22-27 resolve the initial question. The woman responds appropriately to all the questions that follow the sign. Since she is the right woman, the issue of the plot can be pressed further. Vv. 26-27 mark the end of the panel with a blessing that shows the first stage successfully established. God has demonstrated the proper resolution of the servant's commitment.

The second panel unfolds around the same pattern of structure, with the goal now recognition of the divine designation by the woman's family. The woman reports all the events to her mother's household, perhaps an allusion to the kind of familial (matriarchal?) structure in the period. The woman's brother then acts as spokesman for the interview to follow. He meets the servant at the public well and invites him to enjoy the hospitality of his family as a guest (cf. 29:13-14; Exod 2:19-20), and the servant accepts the hospitality. The pattern of the narrative, announcing a stage of the story and then narrating how the announcement was fulfilled, breaks in v. 33b with a speech from the servant. He intends to make clear the goal of his mission. Thus, by the permission of his host, the servant explains in a long speech, vv. 34-49, what he has come to Mesopotamia for. The explanation begins with a self-introduction that focuses on the family of Abraham and the events that brought him to the well, then moves to a report of the events at the well as a fulfillment of his request to God for a sign, and finally asserts the principal goal: "So now, if you are prepared to deal loyally and truthfully with my master, tell me; and if not, tell me so that I may turn to the right or to the left." The point of tension here is the same as in the first panel: Will the com-mission be successfully executed? Vv. 50-54a bring that question to a temporary resolution. The family of the chosen one agrees to the terms of the sign. With

168

that agreement, the gifts of Abraham to Laban, presumably the bridal price, are transferred, and celebration breaks out as the result of concluding the contract.

The third panel in the story, vv. 54b-61, raises the same point of tension: Will the commission be successfully executed? In this case, however, the focus of the question returns to the chosen woman. It begins with the request of the servant to be sent with his discovery back to his master. But v. 55, Laban's delay, raises the specter of foul play ($\rightarrow$ Genesis 29). The servant counters with pressure to be dismissed immediately. Laban then passes the ball in this game of wits to Rebekah. Thus, the issue for the panel appears forcefully in vv. 57-58a: "We will call the maiden and we will ask her opinion. . . . Will you go with this man?" The dialogue continues to v. 58b without a break. Yet, the distinction in the narrative movement between v. 58a and 58b cannot be overemphasized. In v. 58a the entire commission hangs in the air. Thus the verse constitutes the peripeteia of the narrative. V. 58b announces the results in one word: 'ēlēk ("I will go"). In that one word resides the entire resolution of the story. Vv. 59-61 then generalize on the basis of the resolution. There will be no further delay. Laban dispatches the company with a blessing for the fertility of the marriage. It should be noted that the content of the blessing corresponds to the content of the promise to Abraham. Indeed, the second facet of the blessing corresponds in content, although not in diction, to the reaffirmed promise to Abraham in 22:17: "Our sister! You shall become thousands of multitudes. And your seed shall possess the gate of those who hate them." Vv. 59 and 61 then frame the blessing with narrative generalizations. The servant and his party leave, and the scene closes.

The final panel in the narrative brings the arc of tension in the total plot to its proper conclusion. The physical location for the scene shifts from Mesopotamia to Canaan. Isaac enters the narration here for the first time, and the panel sets out the meeting between the two chosen people. The tension for the plot of the story as a whole was fundamentally resolved in v. 58b. Yet, here something of the tension returns, suggesting the intricate skill of the storyteller. What would happen if Isaac rejected the bride chosen for him by God? Or what would happen if Rebekah should now hesitate, contrary to her commitment in v. 58b? Vv. 64-65 suggest some element of reserve, not yet the intimacy that full commitment in the bond of marriage would involve. Yet, even this coy distance does not block the consummation of the commission. V. 67 brings the entire story to its conclusion with a report of the marriage. It is an intriguing sign of the culture that places the wedding night specifically in the tent of Isaac's mother, perhaps another sign of matriarchal tendencies in the society of the patriarchs. Moreover, v. 67b suggests that Rebekah now replaces Sarah as the matriarch of the clan, the one who gives aid to the new patriarch. Thus, the story has a quality, particularly in the final panel, that fits in the context of stories about death and succession of patriarchal-matriarchal figures.

The story as it now stands belongs to the Yahwist's narrative. This point emphasizes the connection between the blessing here and the blessing in the J context. Indeed, some parallel can also be seen between this story, with Rebekah leaving the land of her birth, and the J introduction to the Abraham saga in 12:1-4a, with Abraham leaving the land of his birth (so, Roth). Yet, it also seems clear that J did not create the story but rather adapted it for his purposes from an oral source. The prior form of the story would have focused directly on the role of the servant rather than the marriage agreement and blessing (see Roth).

Stereotyped expressions and formulas in the pericope include (1) the speech formula marking the speaker or both the speaker and addressee for a following speech; (2) a self-identification formula, composed of the pronoun "I" (*'ānōkî*) and the proper noun, used in this case in a quite secular setting (→ 15:1, 7); (3) a messenger formula, composed of the particle "thus" (*kōh*) plus a verb for speaking (in v. 30, *dibber*), plus a designation of the speaker who originated the message; and (4) a formula for releasing an oath in v. 41, marked especially by the adjective "innocent" (*nāqî*) (→ 44:10).

Genre

The story develops a complex plot with intricate speeches as keys for plot movement. This complexity marks the story as a NOVELLA (→ Genesis 37–47; Roth). Moreover, the novella can be more precisely defined as an EXAMPLE STORY, a narrative designed to show an ideal model for future generations. It is not, however, converted by that intention into a (→) legend. It remains a novella, with its corresponding structure, complexity, characterization, and plot movement (so, Roth).

Setting

The story now has a setting in the literature of J. Adapted from earlier stages, this novella is employed by that J story as a crucial part of the structure for the final days of Abraham. Behind the J story lies a story that derives from the storyteller's art. In this case, the family is not at center stage but in the background. The focus of the story falls here on the servant and suggests that the setting must have been in the institutional context that called for edification of officials and messengers. The royal court would have provided such a setting, with its interests in maintaining instruction for administrative officials (→ Genesis 37–47, particularly 39–41). Moreover, wisdom elements enter the narrative, suggesting some influence in the royal court from wisdom circles (→ Genesis 39–41; see Roth).

Intention

In J, the unit serves to round off the Abraham saga with an account from the last days of Abraham and to confirm the blessing to the patriarch for a new generation. A part of the blessing was to insure proper heritage in the wife of the heir, ordained not so much by her family ties as by the selection of Yahweh (see Roth). Behind the J adaptation was a story intended to cast a model of the servant-messenger. The ideal worked faithfully to complete the task of his commission in spite of various problems that presented themselves along the way. In addition, the story intends to affirm the importance of the right wife. The selection process, when brought to a successful conclusion, demonstrates the guidance of God.

Bibliography

L. Rabinowitz, "A Study of Midrash—Gen 24," *JQR* 58 (1967) 143-61; W. M. W. Roth, "The Wooing of Rebekah. A Tradition-Critical Study of Genesis 24," *CBQ* 34 (1972)

177-87; N. Tucker, "Gen 24. Der künstlerische Aufbau einer biblischen Erzählung," *Beth Mikra* 46 (1971) 326-38.

ABRAHAM GENEALOGY, 25:1-6

Structure

I. Sons of Abraham	1-4
A. Marriage report	1
B. Genealogical lists	2-4a
1. First-generation list	2
2. Second-generation list	3a
3. Third-generation list	3b
4. Second-generation list	4a
C. Concluding formula	4b
II. Inheritance lines	5-6
A. Primary line	5
B. Secondary line	6

This small unit (J) relates to its context in a rough manner, primarily because of the death-burial report in ch. 23 (P) and the longer but isolated narrative in ch. 24 (J). If these units can be taken as intervening pieces positioned here by a final redaction of the Abraham saga because of their relationship with things about the patriarch's last days, then 25:1-6 might correspond to 22:20-24 as a genealogical conclusion to the Abraham saga. The parallel with the Nahor genealogy might also suggest that the Abraham narrative tradition may have included a more extensive account of the relationship between Abraham and Nahor (→ Genesis 36 par. 37). The hypothesis might be further illuminated by reference to the Abraham-Lot tradition as a narrative depicting a similar inner-family relationship. A structural context is provided nonetheless by Genesis 23, with its purchase of a burial plot, and the Abraham death report in 25:7-11. This contact suggests that structurally the unit has as much contact with P as it does with J (→ 25:12-16; 17-18).

The unit builds primarily around a genealogical name list developed to the third generation on a linear plane, followed by a designation of inheritance lines. The genealogy is in itself a secondary line of familial development (cf. 22:24). It does not presuppose the death of Sarah, although the redactional position of the unit would underwrite such a presupposition. The name list begins simply with a report of Abraham's marriage to the woman named by the genealogy as the mother of the line. The genealogy itself sets out the productivity of that woman as a wife in Abraham's house. The line is established by (1) a marriage report, noting the name of the wife in question, (2) a series of name lists, recording the productivity of the new wife to the third generation with a return to the second (v. 4a), and (3) a concluding formula assigning the genealogy to the new wife. The name lists are not presented as a complete genealogy. Only two names from the first generation have a second-generation development, with one name from the second generation developed to the third generation and placed between the two second-generation lists. This genealogical tree then contrasts with the definition of inheritance lines in vv. 5-6. V. 5 makes Isaac the sole heir, while v. 6

describes a separation from Isaac imposed by Abraham on all the sons of the concubines. The connection with vv. 1-4 is thus not smooth, since v. 1 defines the mother of the sons in the genealogy as a wife, not a concubine. Yet, the designation of inheritance in v. 5 explicitly excludes the sons reported in vv. 1-4, and the note of expulsion in v. 6 at least recognizes that the division within the house of Abraham was a standing problem (→ Genesis 16; 18; 21). Whether this conflict is evidence for an Abraham narrative tradition no longer preserved is not clear.

Genre

The unit is a linear GENEALOGY. Perhaps it reveals evidence of an older narrative tradition in its reference to a conflict in the family over inheritance lines. It is not, however, a (→) tale. It is only a genealogy incorporating marriage or birth RE-PORTS. As a genealogy, it functions to establish inheritance lines and thus moves toward last-will characteristics. Behind the genealogy may be a (→) register for a six-member tribal confederation (see Noth, *History*, 149).

Setting

The unit has a setting in the literature of the Yahwist, a part of the collection of traditions about Abraham's last acts before his death. The genealogy denies a position in the primary inheritance lines for the sons of the new wife; it thus reflects struggle within the family to define itself. Narrative traditions that may lie behind this text also would belong to the social orders of family life (→ Genesis 16; 18; 21). Within the family the tradition would then belong to the storyteller. Here, however, the tradition describes the organizing of the family, not yet a part of the storyteller's art.

Intention

As a genealogy, the unit defines inheritance lines for the house of Abraham, the organization of the family. In J the unit concludes the Abraham saga with the list of his productivity through a second wife. Behind the J level of the unit lies an intention to describe the organization of a tribal confederation.

Bibliography

J. Magonet, "Die Söhne Abrahams," *BibLeb* 14 (1973) 204-10.

ABRAHAM DEATH REPORT, 25:7-11

Structure

I. Summary formula	7
II. Death notice	8
III. Burial notice	9-10
IV. Patriarchal succession	11
A. Blessing	
B. Dwelling place	

This unit marks the end of the Abraham narrative for P. It represents a natural continuation of the death-burial from ch. 23; indeed, v. 9 presupposes that unit. But the connection with ch. 23 is relatively loose, thus promoting the incorporation of ch. 24 and the brief report in 25:1-6. The loose bond with the P context facilitates the function of this unit as a conclusion in the Abraham narration for the final form of the MT.

Structure in the unit develops four distinct elements: (1) A summary formula of Abraham's life, v. 7a, concludes with the total number of years in the life, v. 7b (cf. the genealogical conclusion, 5:5, 8, 11, et al.). (2) A death notice, v. 8, marks the end of the patriarch's life (cf. the genealogical conclusions, Genesis 5). (3) A burial report, tied to the tradition in ch. 23, places Abraham's corpse in the familial burial site (cf. 50:4-14). (4) The final element defines the patriarchal succession by (a) God's blessing for Isaac, and (b) Isaac's residence at a site associated with a theophany. The two points in v. 11 foreshadow following narration (cf. 26:12). They are undeveloped here, however, and function only to shift the focus of the tradition from Abraham to Isaac. They suggest, therefore, that the total unit presupposes narration complexes about both Abraham and Isaac.

Genre
The unit is a death REPORT. But it is related closely to the death notices in a (→) genealogy (cf. 5:5).

Setting
The genre serves not so much a sociological function, such as a public obituary, but rather a literary function, a mark for the conclusion of a narrative unit of larger portions (→ Genesis 12–25). Death reports may have served an oral setting as well, such as family tradition, but here such an oral setting seems lost to the literary appropriation of the unit.

Intention
As a part of the priestly narration, the unit marks the conclusion of the Abraham story and parallels 11:10–12:9. As a unit associated with genealogy, it functions as a frame for the Abraham narration. It would then properly be understood as a continuation of 11:26, the tenth generation of the genealogy. Here it simply signals the end of the patriarch's life and thus the end of the saga.

ISHMAEL GENEALOGY, 25:12-16

Structure

I.	*Toledoth* formula	12
II.	Name list	13-16
	A. Introductory formula	13a
	B. List	13b-15
	C. Concluding formula	16

This small genealogy (P) for Ishmael belongs to the body of tradition gathered around the general structural category provided by Abraham's death. It parallels vv. 19-26 as genealogical tradition that belongs to one of Abraham's two sons (cf. Genesis 36 par. 37).

The structure opens with a *toledoth* formula, an intrinsic part of the parallel not to be dropped as a secondary imitation of the *toledoth* material (cf. v. 12 par. v. 19). To the contrary, the formula places the following genealogy in a context provided by the *toledoth* redactional series (→ 5:1). The formula then defines Ishmael explicitly in terms of the Sarah-Hagar tradition. V. 13a functions as a renewal of the introduction, suggesting that the tradition in the following list has an integrity of its own (see Noth, *History,* 17 n. 48). The list follows, vv. 13b-15, and the conclusion, v. 16, designates the list as a register of an Ishmaelite twelve-tribe system (Noth, *History*). That the list depends on old tradition, incorporated here as substance for the redactional patterns reporting the death of Abraham, seems probable (→ 22:20-24).

Genre

The unit is now cast as a GENEALOGY, the segment of only one generation. Earlier forms of the tradition, such as a (→) register of Ishmaelite tribes, may have had more in common with organizational (→) lists than with genealogies (→ Exod 1:1-6).

Setting

The unit belongs to the literary structure of P, a redactional element rounding off the narrative about Abraham and his sons. Earlier forms of the tradition, such as a register of Ishmaelite tribes, would have derived from the political institution concerned to define political structures.

Intention

The unit rounds off narration of traditions associated with Abraham's death by reporting genealogical structures of one successor in Abraham's family. The name list, vv. 13-16, may derive from a tribal register that defines political organization for a confederation of Ishmaelite tribes.

ISHMAEL DEATH REPORT, 25:17-18

Structure

I. Summary formula		17a
II. Death notice		17b
III. Patriarchal succession		18
	A. Dwelling place	18a
	B. Relationship to his people	18b

The death report for Ishmael belongs to the group of units organized around the theme of the patriarch's (Abraham's) death and burial. Its presence in the group underlines the tendency of this section to include death reports of various people associated with the patriarch. Moreover, this unit (P) connects with the Ishmaelite genealogy, vv. 12-16 (P), in the same manner that the Abraham death report, vv. 7-11, connects with an Abraham genealogy, vv. 1-6. It comprises a formulaic summary of Ishmael's life, constructed in tight parallel to vv. 7-8, and a designation of succession in the family, unfortunately somewhat obscure in its present form. The verse should not be defined simply as a gloss, however (contrast Noth, *History,* 17 n. 48). To the contrary, it has an intrinsic role to play in the structure of the unit. The reference for the third-person plural verb in v. 18a does not lie within the unit and must be assumed. If one can assume that the verb refers to the successors of Ishmael, however, the parallel with v. 11 might be established: (1) V. 18a designates the successor's dwelling place (cf. v. 11b). (2) V. 18b, with a singular verb, "he fell" (*nāpāl*), describes the relationship of Ishmael's successors to their brothers (cf. v. 11a). The assumption might also underwrite a suggestion that between vv. 17 and 18 some account of Ishmael's burial by his successors has fallen away (cf. vv. 9-10).

Genre

The unit is a death REPORT, incorporating stereotyped formulas such as the SUM-MARY of Ishmael's life, v. 17a (→ 5:5, 8, 11, 14, et al.), and the death notice itself, v. 17b (cf. 25:8).

Setting

The unit stands now in a literary setting, a part of the conclusion for the Abraham narrative that features accounts of relationships between Ishmael and Isaac (cf. 25:9). Its oral setting must be associated not only with storytelling as a form of story conclusion, but more directly with genealogy, a form set within the context of the larger family unit.

Intention

The death report marks the end of a longer narrative tradition, particularly when it is set within the context of 25:1-11, 12-16, and 19-20. As a genre particularly associated with genealogy, it functions to provide support for the genealogical framework in 11:26 and 25:7-11. As part of the Ishmaelite tradition, it closes the Ishmael-Isaac plot within the Abraham narrative.

CHAPTER 7

THE ISAAC SAGA

BIBLIOGRAPHY

H. Eising, "Formgeschichtliche Untersuchung zur Jakoberzählung der Genesis" (Diss., Münster, 1940); T. E. Fretheim, "The Jacob Traditions: Theology and Hermeneutic," *Int* 26 (1972) 419-36; W. Gross, "Jakob, der Mann des Segens. Zu Traditionsgeschichte und Theologie der priesterschriftlichen Jakobsüberlieferungen," *Bib* 49 (1968) 321-44; J. Lewis, "An Analysis of Literary Forms in the Jacob Narratives" (Diss., Southern Baptist, 1965); D. A. Lutz, "The Isaac Tradition in the Book of Genesis" (Diss., Drew University, 1969); J. G. Mitchell, "A Study of the Jacob Tradition in the Old Testament" (Diss., Southern Baptist, 1970); M. Noth, *A History of Pentateuchal Traditions* (tr. B. W. Anderson; Englewood Cliffs: Prentice-Hall, 1972); W. Richter, "Das Gelübde als theologische Rahmung der Jakobsüberlieferungen," *BZ* 11 (1967) 21-52; G. Wallis, "Die Geschichte der Jakobtradition," *WZHalle* 13 (1964) 427-40; idem, "Die Jakobtradition und Geschichte," in *Geschichte und Überlieferung. Gedanken über alttestamentliche Darstellungen der Frühgeschichte Israels und der Anfänge seines Königstums* (AzT 2/13; Stuttgart: Calwer, 1968) 13ff.; P. Weimar, "Aufbau und Struktur der priesterschriftlichen Jakobsgeschichte," *ZAW* 86 (1974) 174-203; W. Zimmerli, "Geschichte und Tradition von Beersheba im Alten Testament" (Diss., Göttingen, 1932).

THE ISAAC SAGA AS A WHOLE, 25:19–37:2

Structure

I. Narrative inclusion		25:19–35:15
A. Exposition		25:19-34
1. Birth report		19-26
2. Principals		27-28
3. Anecdote		29-34
B. Threat to the ancestress		26:1-33
C. Family strife		26:34–33:17
1. Marriage report		26:34-35
2. Tale of strife		27:1–28:5
a. Blessing		27:1-40
b. Jacob-Esau complication	(A)	27:41–28:5
3. Marriage report		28:6-9
4. Tale of strife continued		28:10–33:17
a. Bethel *hieros logos*	(B)	28:10-22
b. Jacob-Laban	(C)	29:1–32:1 (*RSV* 31:55)

c. Mahanaim	(B')	32:2-3 (*RSV* 32:1-2)
d. Resolution	(A')	32:4 (*RSV* 32:3)–33:17
D. Shechem *hieros logos*		33:18-20
E. Rape of Shechem tale		34:1-31
F. Shechem to Bethel		35:1-15
1. Pilgrimage report		1-7
2. Death of Deborah		8
3. Bethel *hieros logos*		9-15
II. Death reports		35:16–37:2
A. Rachel		35:16-20
B. Successive generations		35:21-26
1. Incest of Reuben		21-22a
2. Sons of Jacob		22b-26
C. Death of Isaac		35:27-29
D. Successive generations		36:1–37:2
1. Sons of Esau		36:1-43
2. Sons of Jacob		37:1-2

The Isaac saga relates to the Abraham saga by virtue of bonds established through the tradition about God's promises to the patriarchs (→ The Patriarchal Theme). As a narrative unit in itself, the Isaac saga reveals a diversity of structural patterns, suggesting a diverse tradition history (see Noth, *History,* 54-58). The elements in the structure of the saga are constructed in two major parts: (1) a narrative inclusion, developing an overarching plot to an explicit resolution (25:19–35:15), and (2) a looser collection of traditions about the patriarch's last days (35:16–37:2).

The diversity of tradition appears in the first element of the saga, 25:19-34. The element belongs basically to the Isaac tradition, even though it depicts the struggle that constitutes a major Jacob narrative (→ 26:34–33:17). Its compositional frame is completed in 35:27-29 with the report of Isaac's death and in 36:1–37:2 with the same kind of projection for future generations witnessed for the Abraham saga in 25:12-26. Indeed, one must suggest that for the latest redactional structure of this material no real distinction between Isaac saga and Jacob saga (the Joseph story) can be found. The successive generations link with each other, rather than drawing a radical distinction between each other. In contrast to the Isaac structure, introduced by 25:19-26, vv. 27-28 depict an opposition between Jacob and Esau, developed by the anecdote in vv. 29-34. This opposition functions as an introduction for a narrative display of the Jacob-Esau strife (→ 26:34–33:17). The Jacob-Esau narrative thus serves as the primary content for the Isaac saga, even though its core assumes Isaac in a deathbed setting (→ Genesis 24). It contributes its concentric structure as the dominant pattern of the larger unit.

The second major unit in the Isaac saga, a collection of traditions about the last days of the patriarch and his company, begins in 35:16, although 35:8 anticipates the theme. Moreover, an itinerary structure ties the two items together. Jacob flees Laban and Paddan-aram in order to return to Canaan and his father.

The traditions associated with that move, including the death of key members in the family, gain structural position within the framework of the itinerary.

I. Shechem	33:18–34:31
A. *Hieros logos*	33:18-20
B. Rape of Shechem tale	34:1-31
II. Bethel	35:1-15
A. Pilgrimage	1-7
B. Death report	8
C. *Hieros logos*	9-15
III. Death report: Ephrath	35:16-20
IV. Tower of Eder	35:21-26
A. Rebellion of Reuben	21-22a
B. Sons of Jacob	22b-26
V. Mamre	35:27-29
A. Arrival	27
B. Death report	28-29

The problem in structure suggested by this advanced allusion to death in the family derives from the combination of the earlier and later sources for the saga. Some consideration of the two parallel units is thus necessary.

Structure for the priestly Isaac saga is as follows:

I. Narrative saga	
A. Genealogy	25:12-26*
B. Family strife	
1. Dispatch of Jacob	26:34–28:9*
2. Itinerary	
a. Shechem	33:18a
b. Bethel	35:9-13
c. Mamre	35:27
II. Succession	
A. Death of Isaac	35:28-29
B. Esau	36:1-43*
C. Jacob	37–47*

The priestly framework for the Isaac saga shows a typical construction out of genealogical patterns. Thus, the introduction to the Isaac narrative doubles as the conclusion for the Abraham narrative, the genealogical succession following the death of the patriarch. It suggests that the entire structure of the Isaac narrative is not an independent unit but rather a distinct element of the Abraham narration. Moreover, the narrative unit ends in the same way. The *toledoth* formulas in 36:1 and 37:2 parallel the *toledoth* formulas in 25:12 and 19. The succession from Isaac is fixed by the generations of Esau and Jacob, just as the succession from Abraham was fixed by the generations of Ishmael and Isaac. For P, the patriarchal narration is essentially a unit, not to be divided into originally independent story segments.

The kernel of the narration for the Isaac tradition focuses on the contrast between Jacob and Esau (→ 26:34–28:9) and Jacob's itinerary for his return to Isaac. The final section reports the death of Isaac and a construction of generations that document succession to the patriarch.

The JE structure of this narrative unit is as follows:

I. Narrative inclusion
   A. Exposition   (A)   25:21-34
      1. Birth report   21-26
      2. Principals   27-28
      3. Anecdote   29-34
   B. Threat to the ancestress   (B)   26:1-33
   C. Family strife   27:1–33:20
      1. Blessing   (C)   27:1-40
      2. Jacob-Esau
         a. Complication   (D)   27:41-45
         b. Bethel *hieros logos*   (E)   28:10-22
         c. Jacob-Laban   (F)   29:1–32:1
         d. Mahanaim   (E')   32:2-3
         e. Resolution   (D')   32:4–33:17
      3. Shechem *hieros logos*   (C')   33:18-20
   D. Threat to the daughter   (B')   34:1-31
   E. From Shechem to Bethel   (A')   35:1-7
II. Death reports
   A. Deborah   35:8
   B. Rachel   35:16-20
   C. Reuben   35:21-22a

The Yahwist's narrative reveals a crisper structure than the one represented by the final form of the text. Two large elements again constitute the scope of the unit. First, a narrative inclusion develops a plot from exposition to resolution of the tension. 25:21-34 poses the tension between Jacob and Esau. 35:1-7 celebrates the successful passage through that crisis. Moreover, the structure of the element follows a concentric pattern, with the Jacob-Laban story at the center of the structure. The B and B' elements balance each other rather clearly. In both, an ancestress of Israel needs some kind of defense for her honor. In both, sexual abuse emerges as a problem. In both, the patriarch appears less concerned about the threat than other principals of the story. And in both, the narrative ends with some public demonstration of the woman's position (cf. 26:11; 34:31). Element C' parallels element C by its reference to the God of Israel, although the parallel is looser and more difficult to ground. The name Israel is of course associated with the blessing (→ 32:24-32) and suggests that the patriarchal blessing from 27:27-29 is constitutive for Israel. Elements D through D' belong, then, to the concentric patterns of the Jacob-Esau framework narrative (→ 27:41–33:17), and the center of that inclusion is the Jacob-Laban novella.

In the second element, three small units represent the interests of the death and burial segment in the composition of patriarchal traditions. 35:8 is now properly aligned in the composition of the whole. 35:16-20 reports the death and burial of Rachel in relation to the birth of Benjamin. 35:21-22a report the rebellion of

Reuben as an anecdote associated with the last days of Isaac. Perhaps J included a death of Isaac report parallel to P.

Questions about the history of the Isaac or the Jacob tradition are difficult to answer with certainty; yet, they open the growth dimension of the saga. It is relevant for this question to observe that embedded traditional units are more frequent in this narrative body than in the Abraham tradition. The traditio-historical rootage for the Isaac-Jacob tradition generally may be preserved in two, perhaps three, units: 25:23, perhaps also 27:27-29, and 28:13.

Genre

In the present narrative and the J source, the Isaac story appears to be a SAGA, a family narration composed of various episodic panels or even originally independent TALES. The P counterpart breaks the saga structure somewhat by imposing the patterns of GENEALOGY over this narrative and its Abraham and Jacob counterparts. For genre definitions in the smaller units, see the discussion below.

Setting

In the present narrative and the priestly parallel, evidence about the setting points clearly to a literary redactional context. The Yahwistic narrative also derives from such a redactional setting, although here the earlier forms of the tradition still exert their influence. J is much more strongly influenced by storytelling concerns. Earlier stages of the tradition as a whole derive from the storytelling institution of the family, broken only on occasion by the interests of a larger national scope.

Intention

The Isaac saga preserves the tradition about strife in the family and suggests that blessing or renewal of the promise is possible through commitment to the God of the promise as the source of Jacob's protection.

CHAPTER 8

The Individual Units

BIBLIOGRAPHY

J. P. Fokkelman, *Narrative Art in Genesis: Specimens of Stylistic and Structural Analysis* (Amsterdam: Van Gorcum, 1975); M. Noth, *A History of Pentateuchal Traditions* (tr. B. W. Anderson; Englewood Cliffs: Prentice-Hall, 1972); G. von Rad, *Genesis, a Commentary* (tr. J. H. Marks; rev. ed.; OTL; Philadelphia: Westminster, 1972); J. van Seters, *Abraham in History and Tradition* (New Haven: Yale University Press, 1975); C. Westermann, *The Promises to the Fathers: Studies on the Patriarchal Narratives* (tr. D. E. Green; Philadelphia: Fortress, 1980) 1-94.

JACOB-ESAU BIRTH REPORT, 25:19-26

Structure

I. *Toledoth* formula	19a
II. Birth report: Isaac	19b
III. Marriage report	20
IV. Birth report	21-26a
A. Intercession	21a
B. Response	21b
C. Report of birth oracle	22-23
1. General statement of strife	22aα
2. Complaint	22aβ
3. Request for oracle	22b
4. Oracle	23
D. Birth	24-26a
1. Notice of twins to be born	24
2. Birth report: Esau	25
3. Birth report: Jacob	26a
V. Age of Isaac	26b

This unit parallels 25:12-16 as a part of the concluding segments of the Abraham narration. Like 25:12-16, its basic framework is P (vv. 19-20, 26b), although the P narration must have contained some account of the birth of Jacob and Esau. Evidence for this point in the structural elements for the P report would include a *toledoth* formula (cf. v. 12) and the notation of Isaac's age at the birth of the children, an allusion that assumes some greater detail than now preserved in P, perhaps simply the core of the birth report in vv. 21-26a (J). The birth report would then parallel the name list in vv. 13-14.

The distinction between the parallel units, vv. 12-16 and 19-26, lies primarily in the tendency of the latter toward narrative tradition. Thus, the *toledoth* formula is followed not by an account of birth of Isaac's sons, but by a report of Isaac's own birth (v. 19b; → 21:1-21). The notation is of course undeveloped and resembles the genealogical construct (cf. 5:3), but the notation does contrast with the opening formula. Moreover, the birth report is followed by a marriage report (→ 24:1-67). Again, the notation is undeveloped, but again, the contrast with the simple structure of vv. 12-16 is significant.

The significance of the contrast emerges more fully when one considers the juxtaposition of the Ishmaelite genealogy, vv. 12-16, with the Ishmaelite death report, vv. 17-18. An Isaac death report appears in 35:27-29. The gap between this unit and its counterpart in ch. 35 suggests that for P the tradition serves as a larger framework for narrative units (→ 27:46–28:9). Indeed, the framework function of this material serves not only priestly narrative tradition but also Yahwistic narrative, and it is precisely this structuring function that accounts for the Yahwistic birth report now incorporated into the priestly frame. But the frame also serves a larger function for the priestly narrative—it represents the conclusion of the Abraham-Isaac narrative by exposing the successors of Abraham. This exposure is the function of the *toledoth* formula. At the same time, it sets the stage for the Jacob story by noting (v. 26b) that the successors of Isaac are plural. The comment assumes for P some notice of the birth of Jacob and Esau. (On the conflict element, → 26:34-35.) But it does not assume a major structural division in P. Rather, it connects Jacob narrative with Abraham narrative through Isaac, as if the narrative units belong to one basic narration (→ The Patriarchal Theme), and that narrative now addresses Isaac as the subject.

The birth report itself, vv. 21-26a (J), appears as the center of the unit, simply supported by the frame in vv. 19-20, 26b. The report begins not with an exposition for a narrative (contrast 16:1), but with an account of Isaac's intercession vis-à-vis the problem his wife suffered and an account of Yahweh's response. Technical terms appear here not as "healing" but as cultic categories for intercession and favorable response (see the verb *'ātar*, Qal and Niphal ["pray"]). Vv. 22-23 introduce an oracle into the birth report. Because of the struggle in her womb, Rebekah presents a complaint. V. 22b marks the complaint as a formal request for an oracle (see the verb *dāraš* ["seek"]). The oracle itself comprises two couplets, each in parallel construction, each announcing the division in the family of Isaac. At the center of the birth report, then, an annunciation of twins anticipates a fate for the twins marked by competition, service of the one to the other, and strife (→ 16:12).

These motifs continue into the birth report itself, vv. 24-26a, with its corresponding etiology for the names of the twins. Esau, the firstborn, has no clear name play. Rather, the description of the child as "red" (*'admonî*) plays on the connection between Esau and Edom, while the description of the child as "a hairy mantle" (*kĕ'adderet śē'ār*) plays on the connection between Esau and Seir. The motif of strife develops in the account of the birth of Jacob, for here the wordplay emerges in the description of Jacob holding the heel of his brother (*ba'ăqēb 'ēśāw*). In his name, Jacob is one who struggles with his brother.

The birth report thus serves not only to provide genealogical content for the total unit in vv. 19-26, the redactional structure of the Abraham narrative, but also to foreshadow the coming accounts (in J) of the struggle between Jacob and Esau (→ 33:1–17). The oracle in the birth report is perhaps the kernel of ancient Isaac tradition embedded in the unit. If so, it points to the motif of strife and division as the center of the old tradition, not a promise for a son. It functions more in this context as a part of the Jacob narrative, an exposition for the coming story (von Rad, *Genesis*, 265).

Genre

The unit as a whole is a birth REPORT, dominated now by the birth report in vv. 21-26a. The priestly form of the tradition is more likely to be understood as a GENEALOGY, parallel to the Ishmaelite genealogy in vv. 12-16. The Yahwistic counterpart is in contrast only a birth REPORT. At the center of the birth report is an ORACLE, a birth saying that defines the character of the children who constitute its subject (→ 16:11-12; 49:2-27).

Setting

The redaction gives the unit a setting in the final literary pattern of the Abraham narrative. Its character as a genealogy would fit into this setting (→ 25:12-16). As a birth report, the tradition derives from the traditional patterns of the family, concerned with birth and death. The birth oracle would also reflect the traditions of the family (→ 16:11-12; 49:2-27).

Intention

The unit records the birth of Isaac's children, Jacob and Esau, already under the stamp of strife. As a part of the final redaction, the birth report is the center of an Isaac genealogy, an element in traditions about the death of Abraham and his people. As a birth report, an element of older (J) tradition, the unit foreshadows narration in the coming Jacob story. The unit thus qualifies both as a conclusion for the Abraham-Isaac narration and as an introduction for the Jacob-Esau narration. It is in effect the transition that binds both major units together. As the kernel of the older Jacob tradition, it sets the tone for the entire scope of the Jacob story as an account of strife in the family.

Bibliography

G. W. Coats, "Strife without Reconciliation—a Narrative Theme in the Jacob Traditions," in *Werden und Wirken des Alten Testaments* (*Fest*. C. Westermann; ed. R. Albertz et al.; Göttingen: Vandenhoeck und Ruprecht, 1979) 82-106; M. R. Hauge, "The Struggles of the Blessed in Estrangement," *ST* 29 (1975) 1-30, 113-46; V. Maag, "Jakob—Esau—Edom," *TZ* 13 (1957) 418-29; J. Murtagh, "Jacob and Esau—Horus and Seth: A Parallel," *Bible Today* 53 (1971) 357-66.

JACOB-ESAU EXPOSITION, 25:27-28

Structure

I. Transition	27aα
II. Introduction of principals	27aβb
III. Point of tension	28

This brief unit functions as an introduction to the entire Jacob-Esau narration. The transition in v. 27aα binds the unit with the previous section and suggests that, at least for J, the introduction to the Jacob narration appears not simply in vv. 27-28, but in vv. 21-26 as well (→ 25:19-26).

After the transition piece, v. 27aα, the unit introduces the chief figures for the coming narration by presenting a contrasting characterization. Typical for expositions is the beginning construction, with an indefinite *wayĕhî* and a following active participle: "Esau was a man who knew hunting, a man of the field." Moreover, v. 27b employs nominal construction, with a following active participle: "Jacob was a quiet man [a complete man] who dwelt in tents." The contrast is already enough to place Jacob and Esau in competition. But v. 28 increases the force of the tension by showing parental preferences; indeed, it suggests that the competition involves a point of tension not only between Jacob and Esau, but also between Isaac and Rebekah: "Isaac loved Esau, because he ate of his game; but Rebekah loved Jacob." Such contrasts offer not only evidence for divisions in the family (cf. also v. 23), but also the subject for narrative traditions.

Genre

These verses are exposition for a larger narrative context. They do not therefore represent an independent unit subject to genre definition.

Setting

Exposition belongs to the art of the storyteller. The setting is thus literary, the process of redaction that organized the narration about Jacob and Esau.

Intention

These verses function for the larger unit of Jacob-Esau traditions as an introduction of the principals. In addition, they indicate the problem that holds the principals together as the subjects of a story.

Bibliography

→ 25:19-26.

JACOB-ESAU ANECDOTE, 25:29-34

Structure

I. Exposition	29
II. Complication	30-34b
A. Business negotiations dialogue	30-33a
1. Esau's request	30
2. Jacob's price	31
3. Esau's agreement	32
4. Jacob's price	33a
B. Transaction	33b-34a
1. Payment	33b
2. Results	34a
C. Point of tension	34b

This unit (J) is a brief narration, not yet a tale, designed to set out the dominant point of tension characteristic for the following narration. On the basis of this exposition of tension, one can project that the Jacob narration involves the relationship between Jacob and Esau, and that it will reach a resolution when it can narrate how the Jacob-Esau tension can be resolved (→ 33:15-20; 35:1-8). But the resolution does not appear here.

The unit has its own exposition, a verse designed to set out the circumstances necessary for clear communication in the following report. It shows what the two competitors were doing: "Once when Jacob was boiling pottage, Esau came in from the field, and he was famished." Again the contrast is crucial: Jacob has food; Esau has none. But in the contrast, Esau also appears somewhat foolish. The man who has a traditional reputation as a skillful hunter (→ vv. 27-28) comes in from the field empty.

Vv. 30-33a contain a dialogue cast as a business negotiation (→ Genesis 38): Esau wants food; Jacob has food. Thus, Esau's speech in v. 30 is a request to buy what he needs. It also has a wordplay on red and Esau-Edom (*hā'ādōm / 'ĕdôm*). But the etiological element with a typical naming formula is peripheral to the narrative and arises simply because of the traditional association of Esau with Edom. In v. 31 Jacob names his price; in v. 32 Esau accepts the price. V. 33a adds to this exchange a note that Jacob seeks a surety for the price (cf. also 38:17), and with that exchange the negotiations close. The transaction itself is detailed in vv. 33b-34a with a statement of payment and exchange of goods. The birthright of Esau, Isaac's firstborn, passes to Jacob. The conclusion, v. 33b, does not focus on Jacob's success, however; it focuses rather on Esau's failure to honor his birthright. With this notation, the position of the narrator becomes clear. The competition is no longer a neutral question for the tradition, even though Isaac's preference is for Esau (contrast the Joseph story). Rather, Esau now appears as the less-favored son of the tradition, a distinct foreshadowing of the coming narration.

The unit as it stands is a part of the Yahwist's narration. Older forms of the tradition may lie behind the unit. The motif of strife between Jacob and Esau is certainly a viable subject for such tradition. Concrete observations about structure are not possible, however.

Stereotyped expressions in this unit include the naming formula in v. 30, introduced by the resultative "therefore" (*'al-kēn*), built with a 3rd m.s. Qal form of the verb "name" (*qārā'*), and drawn from a wordplay in the preceding sentence.

Genre

An ancient (→) tale may lie behind the unit (see Fokkelman, 95-97), but in its present form, the unit is not a developed tale with a structured plot; it is simply an ANECDOTE (see Westermann, *Promises,* 78-79). Indeed, it is not in itself complete. It sets out a point of tension, but it does not offer any sign of resolution for that point. The narration thus is simply an anecdote, a report of an incident in the life story of the two principals.

Setting

The unit in its present form presupposes the literary construction of the Yahwist. If oral tradition lies behind this construction, either as a developed tale or simply as a narrative anecdote, it must surely have been preserved in the context of the family.

Intention

In its present form, the unit introduces the principals for the coming narration; it thus functions as a part of the exposition for the Jacob-Esau tradition. Moreover, it establishes a characterization for the plot. Esau appears impulsive, and in his thoughtless act, he "despised his birthright." The following narrative will in some manner develop the competition between Jacob and Esau under the note that Esau played lightly with his familial position. As anecdote, it simply reports an occasion of strife between the two brothers.

Bibliography

→ 25:19-26.

THREAT TO THE ANCESTRESS, 26:1-17

Structure

I. Exposition	1
II. Theophany	2-6
A. Speech	2-5
1. Instructions	2-3aα
2. Promise	3aβb-4
a. Blessing	3aβ
b. Land promise (oath)	3b
c. Posterity/land	4a
d. Blessing	4b
3. Reason for the promise	5
B. Execution of instructions	6
III. Complication	7
A. Isaac's plan	7a
B. Reason for the plan	7b
IV. Denouement	8-11
A. Discovery	8-10
1. Narrative account	8
2. Accusation speech	9a
3. Self-defense	9b
4. Accusation speech	10
B. Warning to the people of Gerar	11
V. Conclusion	12-17
A. Blessing on Isaac	12-16
1. Description of Isaac's blessing	12-14
2. Well problem	15
3. Deportation speech	16
B. Itinerary	17

This story parallels 12:10-20 and 20:1-18. Moreover, its relationship to its context is similar to the context relationship of 12:10-20 and, even more, 20:1-18 (see Koch, 118). The opening of the story is a break from the preceding narrative line, almost an isolation from its context. Indeed, this unit lays claim to 12:10-20 by an explicit allusion: "There was a famine in the land, besides the former famine that was in the days of Abraham." The relationship to the following narration is paralleled in Genesis 20 and constitutes a cycle of narrative tradition concerning relationship with the king of Gerar (→ Genesis 21).

The structure of this story reveals the same basic pattern already familiar from 12:10-20 and 20:1-18. An exposition relates the circumstances that motivate Isaac (no reference to Rebekah) to leave home for a foreign land: A famine was in the land, just as in 12:10-20. V. 1b then introduces the two principal figures of the story, Isaac and Abimelech, and sets them in a particular relationship. Isaac went to Abimelech (because of the famine). Vv. 2-5 have no parallel in the two counterparts and no primary connection with the story that unfolds here. They contain an oracle of promise to Isaac, transferring the tradition associated with Abraham to the second generation. The promise opens with a command to Isaac: "Do not go down to Egypt. Dwell in the land of which I shall tell you. Sojourn in this land." In the command is perhaps a connection with the exposition. Since in the first famine Abraham went to Egypt, and the exposition ties this story to the first famine, one may assume that Isaac would also go to Egypt. The connection is rather artificial, since v. 1b has already explained where Isaac went. It suggests therefore that the promise tradition is secondary to the basic development of this story, certainly to the outline of the traditional story (› 12:10-20; 20:1-18). The instructions continue in v. 3 with a key verb that represents a play on the place-name (gĕrārâ): "Sojourn in this land . . ." (gûr bā'āreṣ hazzō't). The play is somewhat forced here, however. V. 3aα doubles v. 2b; perhaps the wordplay picks up the tradition associated with a nominal form from this verb in 15:13 (gēr). The following elements of the promise would support this suggestion. The promise itself begins with an assistance formula, a promise for God's presence. The formula is constructed, however, not in its usual nominal pattern, but in a verbal sentence that is reminiscent of Exodus 3:12-14. Moreover, v. 3aβ connects a blessing to the promise for divine presence. The content of the blessing is filled out by the following promise. V. 3b is a land promise (cf. Gen. 15:18) adapted in this case to the setting of the story in Gerar. The adaptation is reflected in the plural construction of the noun (hā'ăwarāṣōt hā'ēl) but paralleled perhaps in the breadth of land described in 15:18-21. V. 3bβ then identifies the promise explicitly with the oath to Abraham in 15:18-21. Vv. 4-5 shift the promise from land to descendants, and again the allusion is to the formulation of the tradition in 15:5. This promise then connects to the land promise (cf. 15:18), with the appropriate shift in the key word (v. 4) to a plural. In this text, then, as in Gen. 22:15-18, the promise of numerous descendants and the promise of possession of land have grown together. Immediately after the two promises, the blessing recurs. The blessing here, however, orients to the nations (gôyê hā'āreṣ) rather than to Isaac, as in v. 3. The pattern follows 22:17-18, both recalling 12:3 with its reference to the blessing for all the families of the earth. V. 5 then offers the basis for the promise: "because Abraham obeyed my voice and kept my charge, my commandments, my statutes, and my laws." The allusion must refer to Genesis

22, and appropriately, the promise and blessing from there grounds in Abraham's obedience: "because you have obeyed my voice."

V. 6 reports that Isaac obeyed the instructions. With the execution of the command, the narration establishes a transition to the primary subject of the story. The complication for the story comes in v. 7, duplicating the complication in 12:11-12 and 20:2. In this case, however, the complication does not appear so much as a "plan" worked out in advance, but as an *ad hoc* explanation from a person confronted with a threatening situation. It reports a conversation, without actually setting the conversation out. The report notes the same pattern, however, as the one revealed by the complication and self-defense in Genesis 20. Isaac does not ask his wife to say "sister." As Abraham does in Genesis 20, so here Isaac says it for her. And as in the other two, so here the motivation lies in the patriarch's fear for his life because of the hosts' lust for his wife's beauty. The patriarch's involvement in the complication here is thus the same as in the two counterparts. The consequences, however, are not. The king does not take the beautiful woman for his harem. The complication ends simply with Isaac's offer of his wife as his sister.

The denouement unfolds here as in the two other stories. The king discovers that Rebekah is really Isaac's wife. The source of his discovery is not divine, as in 20:3-7, or implicit as in 12:17. Rather, he observes Isaac playing with her (note the wordplay on the name: *wĕhinnēh yiṣḥāq mĕṣaḥēq*). The confrontation that follows is somewhat overdrawn, however, given the honor of the beauty who had not yet entered the foreign harem. Does the confrontation not imply an actual adulterous marriage, as in both chs. 12 and 20? But if the implication is present, and the event a matter of fact in the counterpart (12:10-20), here it does not come to the surface. The problem is left dangling as a "blind motif" (see van Seters, *Abraham*, 180). Nonetheless, the confrontation follows the same line as in the counterparts. Accused of foul play (vv. 9a, 11), Isaac offers his self-defense. Thus, in this story the intimacy between husband and wife is never broken by the husband's foul deed, though the potential is there. Isaac offered, but no one took up his offer, and the family remains intact. V. 11 marks the conclusion of the element with a warning that keeps the marriage intact. Isaac has not acted with the integrity of his house in mind. He acted for himself and thereby shows himself as an individualist. It is, to the contrary, the king of Gerar who acts with the integrity of Isaac's family in mind.

The conclusion in vv. 12-17 can be considered a part of the story in a very loose manner (see Koch, 118). Yet, the content is essential to the story in its tradition history. Thus, the description of Isaac's blessing in vv. 12-14 relates how Isaac became a wealthy man. But here, contrary to the two counterparts, the process has nothing to do with payment for taking the beautiful wife into the harem or payment as restoration to her rightful place. She never left her husband's side. Now, the gathering of wealth derives from Yahweh's blessing. Moreover, the strife between Isaac and his hosts has nothing to do with the beautiful wife. Rather, the subjects of Abimelech envy the wealth Isaac gained. The comment in v. 15 must represent an example of the strife the Philistine envy caused. It is an allusion to 21:25-34, but it also serves as an allusion for a coming narration (see 26:18), and it captures the quality of strife at the basis of the tradition. Finally, v. 16 reports the deportation of Isaac (singular). But the cause for the deportation is not the confrontation over Isaac's wife; it is the (economic?) power Isaac represents in the community: "For you are much mightier than we" (*kî 'āṣamtā mimmennû mĕ'ōd*). Thus, the story fails to develop the character the counterparts display. The broken relationship with the hosts arises because of the hosts' lack of trust, not from the patriarch's guilt. The wealth derives from God's blessing, not the night's labor of the patriarch's wife. And there is no broken relationship between patriarch and wife. V. 17 then brings the story to a firm conclusion with an itinerary note. Isaac departed in keeping with the expulsion and settled in the valley of Gerar. The relationship of vv. 12-16 to the plot of the narrative is not readily apparent, however. That the acquisition of wealth follows the removal of potential for an adulterous relationship is clear. But that the removal is the motivation for the acquisition does not seem as clear (against Polzin). The structure of the story is too loose to support conclusions of a causal nature (see Koch, 124). It is virtually an appendix to the story rather than an intrinsic element of the story's narration (→ 26:17-33).

In the tradition's history, this story represents the latest stage (J) of development. It is doubtlessly more extensively redacted than 12:10-20, and its loose structure contrasts sharply with 20:1-18 (see Koch, 125-27). But this judgment should be balanced by the recognition that ancient tradition still makes its presence known in just this story (Noth, *History*, 102-9; see the critical comments by van Seters, *Abraham*, 168). It may be correct to suggest that the Isaac story is the third step in the relationship of the three parallels (so, van Seters, *Abraham*, 168). But that the third step must be a literary revision of the first two, indeed, that the second step can be only a literary revision of the first, seems questionable methodologically. The evidence points to revisions and relationships. That the relationships were literary rather than oral cannot, however, be substantiated from the evidence without first assuming that oral preservation of stories was rare. To reconstruct three early sources (so, van Seters, *Abraham*) stretches the evidence as far as does the reconstruction of oral stages. Traditio-historical layers can thus be recognized in vv. 2-6, the promise; vv. 7-11, the narrative of a threat to the ancestress; vv. 12-14, the expulsion of Isaac; and v. 15, an allusion to the coming narrative.

Genre

The story maintains its character as TALE (→ 12:9–13:1; 20:1-18).

Setting

In J, the story belongs to a setting in literary structure. For earlier settings, → 12:9–13:1.

Intention

This story describes relationships with people outside the tribal group. The relationship is broken, but not by what the patriarch does. The broken relationship, which ends in a somewhat friendly manner with the patriarch farming enough land to make him wealthy, nevertheless characterizes the life of the principals.

Bibliography

G. Schmidt, "Zu Gen 26:1-14," *ZAW* 85 (1973) 143-56; for other items, → 12:9–13:1.

WELL ITINERARY, 26:17-33

Structure

I. First stage		17-21
A. Itinerary formula		17
B. Report of well naming		18
1. Completion of wells		
2. Naming		
C. Well etiology		19-20
1. Completion of well		19
2. Complaint		20a
3. Etiology		20b
D. Well Etiology		21
1. Completion of well		21aα
2. Complaint		21aβ
3. Etiology		21b
II. Second stage		22
A. Itinerary formula		22aα
B. Well etiology		22aβb
1. Completion of well		
2. Report of no complaint		
3. Etiology		
III. Third stage		23-33
A. Itinerary formula		23
B. Theophany		24-25a
1. Speech		24
a. Self-introduction		
b. Assistance formula		
c. Promise for descendants		
2. Response: construction of an altar		25a
C. Well etiology		25b-33
1. Completion of well		25b
2. Complaint		26-29
a. Confrontation		26
b. Isaac's disputation		27
c. Initiation for oath		28-29
3. Oath ritual		30-31
a. Common meal		30
b. Oath		31a
c. Conclusion		31b
4. Completion of well		32
5. Etiology		33

This unit connects with the preceding narrative by means of common principal characters, Isaac and Abimelech, and a common place, Gerar. It makes a natural continuation of the closing command of Abimelech in v. 16, "Go away from us," by using an itinerary as a structural framework, thus depicting details of Isaac's departure. Indeed, the substance of the event associated with the third itinerary station assumes knowledge of the expulsion reported in vv. 12-16 (cf. vv. 15, 18). Thus, although this unit is distinct from the narrative about a threat to the ancestress (→ 26:1-16), its connection as a part of tradition about Abimelech and the patriarch provides its essential context (→ 20:1-18; 21:22-34). Vv. 12-16 function in effect as the introduction to this itinerary as well as the conclusion to the narrative about a threat to the ancestress.

The context created by 26:12-16 depicts a power struggle between Isaac and Abimelech. The focal point in the struggle is possession of water (cf. 26:15). In this case, however, the details of the power struggle fall away. The unit unfolds by means of a series of three itinerary formulas, each noting departure from a particular place and arrival at another, each embracing one or more well etiologies. The recurrent pattern of structure in the etiologies comprises a notation that a well had been established, a problem had or had not arisen over claims for possession of the well, and a name had been given the place. The first stage of the itinerary embraces three well etiologies. The first, v. 18, notes restoration of wells established by Abraham and thus refers to v. 15 as well as 21:22-34. The etiological format, however, is not complete—there is no reference to possession of the wells. Rather, the notation alludes to the quarrel at the time of Abraham, and the naming process is simply an allusion to the naming that occurred at that time. This element is thus completely dependent on the Abraham text with its description of a quarrel and its naming and hardly deserves designation as an etiology, at least not as an independent one. Vv. 19-21 present two examples of the complete pattern. The first etiology draws on a following clause, introduced by kî ("because"), and is rooted essentially in a quarrel over the water. The second one has no clear wordplay but suggests by its structure that an etiology may have been involved at one time. Indeed, one might ask whether these allusions to wells that sparked conflict may hide fragments of a narrative tradition that once was more extensive than the present text. Would these allusions provide a clue to the character of the Isaac tradition, now reduced to a minimum by the Abraham saga?

The second stage of the itinerary, v. 22, embraces only one etiological scheme, developed with a report of a well completed without a quarrel. Moreover, the rootage of the etiology arises from a saying that emphasizes the peaceful respite associated with the new locale. The tradition is thus quite the opposite of that embraced by the first stage, even though the form is identical. The third stage expands the form markedly by introducing a report of theophany, vv. 24-25a, and greater narrative detail for the etiology, vv. 26-33. The theophany comprises an oracle, highly formulaic in structure, which can be divided into three parts. (a) A self-revelation formula introduces the name of the God who addresses Isaac by reference to Abraham. (b) An assistance formula begins with the admonition not to fear. (c) The promise guarantees blessing and great descendants, again rooted explicitly in the Abraham tradition (→ Genesis 15).

The theophany report marks its conclusion with a notation that Isaac built an altar, v. 25a. Vv. 25b-33 then attach the theophany report to a well etiology. The etiology here follows the same basic pattern as the ones in stages one and two. A notation that a well was completed (v. 25b) leads to an account of a quarrel over the well (vv. 26-29). The quarrel occurs in the structure of a pre-official legal confrontation. V. 26 narrates the arrival of the Philistines before Isaac, leaving one to assume an initial challenge over the rights to the well. V. 27 contains Isaac's counter accusation. The Philistines respond with a suit for resolution of the quarrel in a covenant (oath, → Genesis 15). The speech, vv. 28-29, unfolds first with a recognition of Yahweh's assistance (→ Genesis 39–41), second with an appeal for an oath qualified as a covenant, and third with a statement of purpose for the oath. The oath does not establish reconciliation between Isaac and the Philistines. To the contrary, it is cast as a negative. It secures an agreement for nonaggression. V. 29 alludes to the peace (*raq-ṭôb . . . bĕšālôm*). But the peace is ironic here, since Isaac is recognized by Abimelech as the blessed of the Lord but in the covenant oath can have no further intimate contact with the natives of the land (→ Genesis 29–31). This peace is thus not reconciliation, but rather an absence of violence. The Philistines appeal for the right to live without attack from Isaac. They want an oath that would guarantee their right and, indeed, the right of Isaac, to live separate lives without encroaching on each other's privileges. To that end a ritual feast is celebrated (v. 30) and the oath is established (v. 31). The element thus delivers greater detail in the tradition about quarrels over water rights. It concludes in vv. 32-33 with a renewed report of a completed well and an etiological formula, which is rooted essentially in the substance of the narrative. The oath is the basis for the name.

The unit belongs to the J source, a part of the narrative tradition about Isaac and Abimelech. It presupposes Isaac's wealth, gained in this case not by the position of the patriarch's wife in the harem of his host, but by his ability to wrest wealth from the land. Behind the connection of the tradition to the threat to the ancestress lies a tradition of animosity between Isaac and Abimelech. This tradition may have been rooted in the narrative of 26:1-16. Yet, this unit suggests that the animosity arose over jealousy and fear from the Philistine hosts for the wealth and power represented by Isaac's house. Indeed, one might hypothesize that more extensive narrative tradition than that preserved here lies behind the several etiologies. Perhaps these etiological elements were originally more substantial pieces.

Genre

The unit is an itinerary LIST embracing a series of ETIOLOGIES. The etiologies unfold generally according to a pattern in which the name of the place is rooted in a preceding or following saying (see Long). The etiologies may be understood as distinct genre units incorporated into the present text by means of the itinerary list. The final etiology expands the pattern with a clause introduced by "therefore" (*'al-kēn*) and completed with an etiological formula, "until this day" (*'ad hayyôm hazzeh*). The etiological units may also support some reconstruction of earlier forms of the tradition. Toward that end, they could be described as brief statements of originally longer etiological narrative. Evidence for such longer narrative TALES is to be found in vv. 25b-33. These verses preserve some evidence of a plot line with crisis and resolution still apparent. A conflict between Abraham and Abimelech leads to a covenant-oath ritual that resolves the conflict, and the etiology is rooted in the resolution of the plot. If these verses are no longer tale in themselves, they nevertheless point to a stage in the tradition history when they were constructed as a distinct tale. V. 18, in contrast, no longer preserves the characteristics of etiology; it is now simply an allusion to a previous text unit.

Setting

The itinerary list is redactional, a means for connecting the various well etiologies with the context, particularly with the account of the threat to the ancestress. (On itinerary lists in general, → Genesis 14; Numbers 33.) The theophany report, vv. 24-25, is also redactional, a point of connection between the Isaac narrative and the narrative motif of promise so common for Abraham (see also v. 18). The etiologies would derive from the sphere of popular tradition connected with the southern wilderness. The recurrent quarrel motif connects this series with narrative tradition more broadly. The longer etiological narrative would reveal evidence of such broad narrative tradition and suggest a setting not simply in Beer-sheba as local tradition, but in a wider range of storytelling.

Intention

In the final form of the text, the itinerary shows Isaac's departure from Abimelech, indeed, his final break with the king of Gerar. It thus functions as a part of the larger narrative context, particularly the context composed of ch. 26. Narrative tradition also places Isaac in the midst of strife (so, vv. 12-16), a strife that leads finally to an arrangement that shows the goodwill of the patriarch toward his hostile opponents. The popular tradition thus maintains an element of political propaganda (see van Seters, *Abraham*, 190).

Bibliography

B. O. Long, *The Problem of Etiological Narrative in the Old Testament* (BZAW 108; Berlin: Töpelmann, 1968).

JACOB-ESAU STRIFE NOVELLA, 26:34 – 33:20

Structure

I. Marriage report			26:34-35
II. Jacob-Esau			27:1–33:20
A. Blessing	(A)		27:1-40
B. Strife	(B)		27:41–33:17
1. Complication		(a)	27:41–28:5
a. Rebekah's dispatch			27:41-45
b. Isaac's dispatch			27:46–28:5
2. Marriage report			28:6-9
3. Bethel *hieros logos*		(b)	28:10-22
4. Jacob-Laban		(c)	29:1–32:1 (*RSV* 31:55)
5. Mahanaim		(b')	32:2-3 (*RSV* 32:1-2)
6. Resolution		(a')	32:4 (*RSV* 3)–33:17
C. Shechem *hieros logos*	(A')		33:18-20

In the span of these several chapters an expansive narrative structure emerges. It follows on the heels of the threat to the ancestress but develops none of the themes opened there. Rather, its point of narration derives from the motifs introduced by 25:19-34, particularly those associated with the theme of strife without reconciliation. Jacob competes with Esau, and because of his competition, he must flee Canaan and assume residence with an uncle in Haran in Paddan-aram. Competition also flowers between Jacob and Laban, and Jacob must therefore flee from Laban back to Esau.

The narrative is composed of several distinct layers. The most apparent layer is the priestly version of the separation of the brothers:

I. Marriage report		26:34-35
II. Dispatch of Jacob		27:46–28:5
III. Marriage report		28:6-9

In this version of the tradition, Jacob leaves Canaan with his father's blessing, given him under the pressure of his mother, but in full recognition of the circumstances. He flees to Laban in order to find a proper wife and avoid the mistakes of Esau. The blessing in the name of El Shaddai carries with it a bestowal of the promise for great posterity and possession of a great land. (For details, → 26:34–28:9.)

The Yahwistic structure that emerges from the priestly framework is also complex, including a new framework narrative:

I. Blessing	(A)		27:1-40
II. Strife	(B)		27:41–33:17
A. Complication: Jacob leaves Canaan		(a)	27:41-45
B. Bethel *hieros logos*		(b)	28:10-22
C. Jacob-Laban		(c)	29:1–32:1
D. Mahanaim etiology		(b')	32:2-3
E. Resolution		(a')	32:4–33:17
III. Shechem, possession of land	(A')		33:18-20

Each of the three Yahwistic elements can be analyzed for itself. The first focuses on the patriarchal blessing which becomes a source of division in the family. The second develops the motif of strife without reconciliation as the subject of its narration. But the narration is split in order to embrace cultic traditions about Bethel and Mahanaim and the Jacob-Laban strife story. Finally, the third element reports the successful acquisition of land in Canaan, a prerequisite for the blessing. The concentric structure of this element from the Yahwist is apparent. The Jacob-Laban story is at the center, two elements of cultic tradition frame it, and the Jacob-Esau narrative embraces the whole. Moreover, the combination of the three units of tradition is distinctive for the patriarchal traditions as a whole. In this narrative inclusion is a combination of the strife without reconciliation, the east-Jordan Jacob, with the promise for land and posterity apparent in the Bethel *hieros logos*, the so-called west-Jordan Jacob. The combination makes the absence of the promise in 29:1–32:1 all the more striking since the combined structure in no way becomes an illustration for promise stories. The combined structure remains a story of strife without reconciliation, and that tradition appears to be the most substantial content of the patriarchal theme, at least of the Jacob tradition.

Genre

As a combination of narrative elements, this unit is a redactional composition. Its individual parts will be considered below. As a composition, it functions as a NOVELLA (→ Abraham-Lot Novella).

Setting

Literary activity in organizing and transmitting extensive narrative traditions produced this complex. It has a setting in the literary activity of the Yahwist.

Intention

The unit as it stands combines various items of tradition in a meaningful whole, showing in the process two major themes in the patriarchal traditions: promise to the fathers (Bethel) and strife without reconciliation.

Bibliography

→ 25:19-26.

TALE OF STRIFE, 26:34 – 28:9

Structure

I. Marriage report	26:34-35
A. Event	34
B. Results	35
II. Tale of strife	27:1 – 28:5
A. Exposition	27:1a
B. Complication	27:1b-40
1. Plans for Isaac and Esau	1b-4
a. Summons	1bα
b. Response	1bβ
c. Instructions	2-4
2. Plans for Rebekah and Jacob	5-17
a. Transition	5
b. Dialogue	6-13
1) Instructions	6-10
2) Jacob's objections	11-12
3) Rebekah's reassurance	13
c. Execution of instructions	14-17
1) By Jacob	14a
2) By Rebekah	14b-17
3. Execution of plans: Isaac and Jacob	18-29
a. Transition	18aα
b. Dialogue	18aβb-22
1) Jacob's greeting	18aβ
2) Isaac's challenge	18b
3) Jacob's address	19

a. Instructions	1-2
b. Blessing	3-4
4. Execution of instructions	5
III. Marriage report	28:6-9
A. Exposition	6-8
1. Jacob's experience	6-7
2. Esau's observation	8
B. Event	9

The unit as it now stands is the first fully developed narration of events resulting from the struggle exposed by 25:19-26 and 27-34. Moreover, 27:41-45 presupposes continuation in chs. 32–33. It is not in itself complete (→ The Jacob Saga); as it appears now, it is but an expansion of the story line in vv. 1-40. The unity of the pericope is problematic, however. Details of the structure in this unit show that as the text now stands, two quite different versions of the tale have been combined, with no clear narrative advantage gained by the combination other than preservation of the two versions at the same point in the narration of the whole (but see Fokkelman, 100-2). It is appropriate, then, to mark the distinctions in the two.

In P, the structure of the unit is as follows:

I. Marriage report	26:34-35
A. Event	34
B. Results	35
II. Dispatch of Jacob	27:46–28:5
A. Rebekah's instructions to Isaac	27:46
B. Isaac's dispatch of Jacob	28:1-4
1. Instructions	1-2
2. Blessing	3-4
C. Execution of instructions	28:5
III. Marriage report	28:6-9
A. Exposition	6-8
1. Jacob's experience	6-7
2. Esau's observation	8
B. Event	9

For this priestly narrative, context is provided by 25:19-26. Yet, in the priestly context there is no sign of conflict between the two sons of Isaac. To be sure, the birth report itself is assumed (25:26a) but not preserved. Perhaps P introduced the theme of struggle in a birth report that has not survived. In the text material now identified as P, however, no notation of conflict prepares the way for this unit.

The tradition of conflict between the two brothers lies nonetheless at the heart of this narration. Structure here develops clearly around an ABA' chiasm. Two units describing Esau's marriages, 26:34-35 and 28:6-9, complement each other and frame the dispatch of Jacob to Paddan-aram. Moreover, the marriage reports lay the blame for the conflict in the family on Esau. In the first report, v.

34 provides nothing more than information about the marriage. V. 35 in contrast makes an evaluation, and in the evaluation lies the conflict so central for the tradition: "They [the wives of Esau] made life bitter for Isaac and Rebekah." At this point, however, the conflict does not fall so centrally on Esau. The problem in fact resides in the Hittite women (note the feminine verb form in v. 35). The parallel in 28:6-9 makes Esau's involvement in the problem quite clear, however. Given the brevity of the report, vv. 6-9, the explanation for Esau's involvement, vv. 6-8, is quite lengthy. It sets out Esau's intent to do the opposite of what Jacob did, an act that will explicitly add to the divisions in the family (cf. v. 8). It is significant that the tradition portrays the principal in the conflict here as a daughter of Ishmael, a point of contact with the conflict tradition in the Abraham narrative.

The middle element in the P unit unfolds from the problem posed for Rebekah by the Hittite wives of Esau. Her speech to Jacob thus opens with an allusion to the problem and poses in contrast a complaint, anticipating the consequences should Jacob also take a Hittite wife. Isaac's response carries both instructions for a proper marriage and the patriarchal blessing establishing the line of succession in terms of the traditional promise. The blessing itself does not tie explicitly to the instructions for a proper marriage, although the juxtaposition suggests that finding a proper wife is fundamental to fulfillment of the promise. Rather, the blessing opens with a formulaic introduction citing El Shaddai as the source of its power (→ 17:1-27). The content of the blessing then falls on two major points: (1) numerous descendants, cast under the stamp of fruitful productivity as a sign of God's blessing, and (2) blessing that would result in possession of the land given Abraham by God. The possession of the land appears here dependent on the promise for descendants, the results of God's blessing that issues into fruitful productivity.

With the patriarchal succession established, the blessing in the hands of Jacob rather than Esau, v. 5 then notes the consequences. Jacob departs for Paddan-aram in obedient execution of Isaac's instructions. There is no deception of Isaac, no trick against Esau. There is only obedient execution of fatherly instruction. Such an image for Jacob builds the contrast with Esau the more sharply, and it highlights the contentious character of Esau in the family by setting up vv. 6-7. The break in the family is for P clearly the result of Esau's deeds.

In J, the structure of the unit is now clarified, and the story is quite different:

I. Exposition	27:1a
II. Complication	1b-40
A. Isaac and Esau	1b-4
B. Rebekah and Jacob	5-17
C. Isaac and Jacob	18-29
D. Isaac and Esau	30-40
III. Transition	41-45
A. Renewed complication	41-42a
B. Dispatch of Jacob	42b-45

The exposition in 25:27-34 sets the immediate context for this J narrative. A conflict in the family of Isaac pits brother against brother, wife against husband. 27:1a makes no reference to that conflict. Rather, it depicts the old patriarch, ready for death, ready thus to establish proper succession in his family and to impart the traditional blessing to his chosen heir (→ Genesis 24). This element functions as exposition, then, in order to set the particular scene, a scene that requires Isaac to be old and blind, unable to move beyond his bed. Structurally, the scene assumes the second major body of narrative in an Isaac tradition, the body of traditions concerned with the death of the patriarch and his associates. But the story as a whole assumes contact with the larger structure describing conflict between Isaac and Rebekah over the sons Esau and Jacob. It is the more appropriate analysis, then, to depict the following story as a story about the Jacob-Esau conflict. Moreover, the unit does not develop a proper ending. It exhibits a major plot, a span of tension that underwrites the plot, but it does not offer resolution of that tension. Rather, the tension is renewed (27:41-42a), then postponed by removing Jacob from the scene of the tension in the family (→ The Jacob Saga).

After 27:1a sets the scene in the larger context of deathbed tradition, the complication of the plot appears quite complex, a structure of four highly developed scenes (see also von Rad, *Genesis*). The first two center on instructions given by the competing parents to the competing sons. The second two note how the instructions were carried out. Moreover, the four scenes depend heavily on sensual allusions for the development of plot: The old man cannot see, but he can hear, feel, taste, and smell. All constitute motifs for the narrative, and all contribute to the dramatic involvement of the story's plot.

The first scene emphasizes taste. It describes the instructions of the old patriarch to his favored son Esau for preparation of the patriarch's favorite food. The scene thus recalls the exposition in 25:28 where Isaac's preference for Esau is related explicitly to the food Esau could prepare for him. Structure in the scene between Isaac and Esau features first the vocative exchange that introduces a confrontation between two figures (→ Exod 3:4), and second a commission from Isaac to Esau (→ Exod 3:5). The commission reveals Isaac's plan to send his son for food. Moreover, the plan for eating issues immediately into a plan for patriarchal blessing, the patriarch's deathbed designation of succession.

The second scene connects with the first by means of a transition piece, v. 5a. The transition establishes how Rebekah happened to gain access to the plan. But at the same time, it highlights the tension in the relationship between Rebekah and Isaac. Rebekah was not privileged to the conversation between Isaac and Esau—the address is explicitly from Isaac to Esau; yet, she heard (v. 5a). The audience can already sense some urgency in the scene. Whatever Rebekah does with her information, she must do it quickly. Vv. 6-10 set out Rebekah's plan as a speech to her favorite. Vv. 6-7 contain a report of the Isaac-Esau scene. Following v. 8, an appeal to Jacob for obedience, vv. 9-10a pose the alternative plan, the plan for deception. V. 10b makes the purpose of this deception quite clear: Jacob would be able to obtain Isaac's blessing, a blessing Isaac intends for Esau (so, v. 4). The plan again emphasizes taste. Rebekah will use a kid from the flock to prepare "savory" food, the kind Isaac loves. But the scene does more. Jacob objects to the plan, vv. 11-12, not on moral grounds, not out of a concern for family loyalty, but from a practical necessity. There is an obvious difference between Jacob and Esau. If the blind father should discover the deception, Jacob might win a patriarchal curse for himself, not the blessing. And how might Isaac uncover the deception? "Perhaps my father will feel me. . . ." Rebekah overrides the objection by assuming the potential curse on herself and urges Jacob to obey. Vv. 14-17 then describe in detail how those instructions were carried out, first by Jacob, then by Rebekah.

The third scene of the complication sets Jacob, ready for the ploy to obtain the blessing, before Isaac. The scene begins with a brief transition, v. 18aα, then a dialogue between the principals. The first stage of the dialogue is the opening vocative (see v. 1b). But coupled to the traditional response to the vocative, "here am I" (*hinnennî*), is an initial challenge: "Who are you, my son?" The response captures the tension of the scene. Isaac knows the figure to be a son, but which one is he? The exchange thus depicts the doubt Isaac nurses that the speaker could be Esau. Jacob's response is brash: "I am Esau, your firstborn." The purpose of his lie makes the response the more premeditated and deceptive: "I have done as you told me. Now sit up and eat of my game, in order that you may bless me." But the deception only increases. The next round renews Isaac's doubt: "How is it that you have found it so quickly, my son?" Then Jacob's lie becomes blasphemous: "Because Yahweh your God granted me success." On a third occasion, Isaac expresses his doubt. The challenge in v. 21 moves beyond words of assurance and even reference to Yahweh's involvement to a probe by touch. Although the probe produces a form of agreement, it is a form still beset by doubt. The senses conflict with each other. Hearing and touching confuse the blind man: "The voice is Jacob's voice, but the hands are the hands of Esau." The competition and conflict of the family thus come sharply to expression. The blind Isaac doubts the claims of his son but cannot establish the weight of the evidence for himself. Thus, the door to the blessing opens for Jacob (v. 23). The probing exchange does not end here, however. V. 24 renews Isaac's challenge and Jacob's lie. With that exchange the feast occurs, a sensuous moment in itself: "He ate . . . and he drank." But the probe goes farther: The father calls for a kiss. With the kiss comes the smell of the garments, and with the smell comes the blessing.

The blessing has four parts. (1) A metaphor builds on the sense of smell, the new element in the scene. The smell of the son is the smell of the field (Esau's territory). The smell of the field is then the sign of Yahweh's blessing, and the point of the sign is fertility. (2) Fertility dominates v. 28. (3) V. 29a shifts the focus from the wealth associated with fertility to power structures in the family and in the world. (4) Blessing and curse are available for all by virtue of their relationship with this blessed one (→ 12:1-3).

The fourth scene shifts the pattern of tension, as well as the structure of sensual motifs. The deception is complete; the blessing has passed from Isaac to Jacob. Now the threat of discovery that might have produced curse for Jacob becomes a tragic note of poor timing. Esau comes in with his feast of savory food just as Jacob exits with the blessing. He petitions his father, fresh from Jacob's feast of savory kid, to eat a feast of savory game. And again the purpose is a blessing. Then Isaac's probe begins again: "Who are you?" "I am your son, your firstborn, Esau." Isaac needs no further evidence about Esau. His doubt and confusion still center on the previous encounter: "Who was it. . . ?" But the answer is no mystery. How can a father eat when he has already eaten? How can he bless when he has already blessed? Isaac's emotional response is in itself sensual but, like having too much savory food, not pleasant: He trembled violently. It is surpassed, however, by the unrestrained cry of Esau: "When Esau heard . . . he cried out with an exceedingly great and bitter cry."

Esau's response is not simply sensual, however. He petitions Isaac for his own blessing. The following exchange, v. 35, recognizes Jacob as the cause for the family's problem (contrast P). V. 36a plays on the name Jacob (*ya'ăqōb*) and the verb "supplant" (*'āqab*). The play assumes 25:29-34 and may be judged as secondary in this unit. Certainly it does not suggest that the structure of the entire unit is designed to support the wordplay. The point is supported by a second Esau speech with its own speech formula, v. 36b. This second speech renews Esau's petition for his own blessing as a natural development from the initial request. Isaac's response, v. 37, reconfirms Jacob's blessing, however. The mistake cannot be corrected; Isaac cannot give his favorite the blessing now held by Rebekah's favorite.

A new plea from Esau leads to the substitute in vv. 39-40. Four elements make up this saying: (1) a denial of fertility; (2) commitment to a life of strife by the sword (→ 25:23); (3) servitude to the brother (→ 25:23); and (4) the promise for an end to the servitude. Basically the opposite of the blessing for Jacob in vv. 27-29, this speech casts Esau's future under a cloud of dominance by his younger twin. The exception is, of course, v. 40b, a reversal of the antiblessing that has no real preparation in the story itself. The reversal is perhaps to be understood not so much from unity with the story as from development of the tradition over some period of time.

Vv. 41-45 now appear as the final element of the Yahwist's story. However, they are not so much a part of this unit as a transition to the next element of the narrative. They introduce a quite new point of tension and anticipate a corresponding resolution. The issue is not now blessing or curse but whether Esau will indeed kill Jacob as he desires. The transition nonetheless connects with the narrative in vv. 1-40. It does not open with an exposition; it assumes the plot of its predecessor. This point of contact is of course reflected by the priestly parallel, which duplicates this transition rather than Jacob's duplicity over the blessing.

The plot of this story reaches its climax, then, in the dispensation of the blessing to Jacob and the antiblessing to Esau. In its narration and in the structure of its blessing speeches, it develops the strife between the brothers. Morever, the strife is as permanent as the blessing that cannot be recalled. It is strife without reconciliation. The traditio-historical rootage of the unit is crucial. One might expect the bestowal of blessing to be formulated under the stamp of the promise to the patriarch. That motif is perhaps latent here, but the formulative kernel is strife in the family. For traditio-historical antecedents, → 25:23.

Stereotyped expressions in this story include the formulas for beginning a dialogue, vv. 1, 18; the blessing construction from the Abraham tradition, v. 29 (→ 12:3); and a variety of speech formulas indicating the speaker and addressee.

Genre

The final form of the text is a composition of two narrative parallels. In P, the unit is not yet a (→) story; it is a narrative element in the larger P presentation of the Jacob tradition. In J, the unit develops a plot and thus can be classified as a story. Perhaps the earliest form of the story was simply a TALE, but the tale functioned to support the SAYING (→ 9:20-27). Since an APOPHTHEGM normally appears in brief compass, and this unit is expansive, it should most appropriately be categorized as a novella. The sayings themselves qualify as BLESSING and ANTIBLESSING. The one transmits the quality of fertility and authority that belongs to the dying patriarch. The other is more of an absence of blessing, not yet a curse. It simply plays the opposition to the initial blessing.

Setting

As a part of a larger complex whole, the unit has a setting in the literature of P and JE. Earlier stages in the history of the tradition would place the story in the storytelling treasure of the family. The blessing would of course reflect the familial institution carried forward by the patriarch in his bestowal of deathbed blessing on a favorite son.

Intention

The final form of the text combines the narrative conceptions from P and J. P reports how Esau's marriages cause divisions in the family, with the parents' decision to dispatch Jacob to Paddan-aram in order to seek a wife there among relatives. With the dispatch goes the patriarchal blessing. J describes the division in the family as competition between Jacob and Esau, complicated by the deception of Jacob and Rebekah. Because of the deception, the blessing falls on the wrong son. It has nothing to do with the dispatch to Haran. The transition then introduces the flight of Jacob under the influence of the mother. But the primary intention of the unit lies in the bestowal of blessing.

JACOB-ESAU COMPLICATION, 27:41–33:17

Structure

I. Complication	27:41-45
A. Strife	41
1. Transition	41a
2. Esau's plan	41b
B. Rebekah's response	42-45
1. Report to Rebekah	42a
2. Instructions to Jacob	42b-45
a. Report to Jacob	42b
b. Instructions	43-45a
c. Reason for the instructions	45b
II. Bethel *hieros logos*	28:10-22
III. Digression: Jacob-Laban	29:1–32:1 (*RSV* 31:55)
IV. Mahanaim	32:2-3 (*RSV* 32:1-2)
V. Resolution	32:4 (*RSV* 32:3)–33:17
A. Complication renewed	32:4 (*RSV* 32:3)–33:3
B. Denouement	33:4-11
C. Conclusion	33:12-17

This complex unit from JE functions not only to develop its own intrinsic plot, but also to frame a series of distinct traditions. The priestly form of the tradition also frames a distinct series, but it appears in a different context (→ 26:34–28:9). The story is thus present only in the frame, element I (27:41-45) and element V (32:4–33:17; *RSV* 32:3–33:17). The intervening elements represent digression or totally distinct traditional elements.

The first framing element in the story appears in 27:41-45. The narration begins *in medias res* and thus demonstrates the role of the element not as exposition, but as transition between the preceding unit and the framing narration. V. 41a captures the strife motif with the sharp opposition of the feuding brothers, and the opposition is related explicitly to the preceding unit. That the narration begins here rather than simply extending the plot of the previous unit can be sustained in the following elements, however. V. 41b stipulates a new point of tension. The issue is not the patriarchal blessing and the hierarchy of family structure. The issue is, rather, Esau's plan to kill his brother. The tension introduced by Esau's emotional rejection of Jacob develops more fully in Rebekah's speech, vv. 42-45. Esau's plan is reported to her in some unexplained manner. Thus, she formulates a new set of instructions for her beloved son: she dispatches him to Haran. The results of the tension here duplicate the results of the tension in P—the family is divided. The cause, however, is unique. It has nothing to do with marriage. That Jacob eventually returns with a family is somewhat incidental. The cause is Jacob's violation of Esau and Esau's resulting hatred (v. 45a). Rebekah again takes the initiative rather than appealing to Isaac as she does in P. Her justification is her concern not to lose two sons in one day, doubtlessly an allusion to blood revenge that would follow should Esau succeed in his plan (see von Rad, *Genesis,* 279). The family is broken, and the cause is the Jacob-Esau conflict. The element thus develops the theme of 25:20-34, but it does not reach a resolution until the narration of the brothers' reunion in 32:4–33:17.

Genre

The final form of the text is a composition comprising two narrative lines parallel to each other in form and function, but contrasted to each other in content. Both depend on larger narrative contexts and thus call for genre definition in terms of structural elements rather than independent units. In both P and J, the parallel elements function in the larger whole as complication of plot. Both presuppose an exposition that introduces the principals. Both set out an arc of tension that builds a plot around the principals. For P, this complication is relatively brief. Fault for tension in the family belongs to Esau, and it results in the patriarchal blessing for Jacob. In J, the narrative is complex. Jacob appears as the deceiver under the tutelage of his mother. Yet, he wins the patriarchal blessing and its designation as successor in the familial line and, because of the emotional response of his brother, must flee. When the tension breaks the family apart, the broken pieces strain against each other for some kind of resolution, either by death or by reconciliation (→ Jacob-Esau Strife Resolution).

Setting

As a part of a larger complex whole, the unit has a setting in the literature of its context: Rjep or P or JE. Earlier stages in the history of the tradition would have reflected the oral storytelling of the family.

Intention

The final form of the text combines narratives from P and J (on P, → 26:34–28:9). J describes the division in the family as competition between Jacob and Esau, complicated by Jacob's and Rebekah's deception. The family is broken. The narrative tension anticipating either the death of Jacob at the hands of Esau or some adjustment that will allow the family to return to its normal structures of life establishes the substance of the Jacob-Esau tradition.

Bibliography

→ 25:19-26.

BETHEL *HIEROS LOGOS*, 28:10-22

Structure

I. Itinerary	10
II. Dream report	11-19
A. Exposition	11
1. Arrival at an unnamed place	11aα
2. Preparation for the dream	11aβb
B. Dream	12-15
1. Vision	12-13aα
2. Oracle	13aβb-15
a. Self-revelation formula	13aβ
b. Promise	13b-14
1) Land	13b
2) Posterity	14a
3) Blessing	14b
c. Assistance formula	15
C. Etiology	16-19
1. First saying	16
2. Second saying	17-19
a. Jacob's speech	17
b. Construction of sacred pillar	18
c. Naming	19
III. Vow	20-22
A. Conditions	20-21a
B. Conclusion	21b-22

This unit is relatively isolated in its context. It does not represent an intrinsic part of the narration opened in the preceding unit. Rather, it is extrinsic to the narrative line, a well-defined unit with a clear beginning and ending. Moreover, as an isolated unit, it fits into this position by virtue of the structural break in the context occasioned by Jacob's journey (→ Exod 4:24-26, 27-31). The break provides context for the occasion, but it does not contribute one way or the other to the arc of tension in the larger narrative.

The structure of the unit employs three major elements: (1) an itinerary formula, v. 10; (2) a dream report, vv. 11-19; and (3) a vow, vv. 20-22. The itinerary formula follows a widely dispersed pattern for such formulaic pieces

($\rightarrow$ Exod 12:37) and functions here to cement the unit into the context occasioned by Jacob's flight from Beer-sheba to Haran ($\rightarrow$ 33:18). The formula thus reflects a transitional, redactional function and is not intrinsic to the movement of the unit.

The dream report, vv. 11-19, carries the weight of the unit. Again, three elements constitute the substance of these verses. The first is an exposition, v. 11. V. 11aα sets the dream report into the movement of Jacob's flight by noting his arrival at a certain place for the night; v. 11aβb then recounts his preparations for sleeping but reveals no contact of substance with the itinerary. The dream itself comprises a narrative description of the vision, vv. 12-13aα, and an oracle in the following verses. The weight of the dream falls thus on the oracle, with the vision functioning simply as the context which accounts for the oracle. The description of the vision is nonetheless typical ($\rightarrow$ 37:6-7). The narration is introduced by the standard verb: "He dreamed" (*wayyaḥǎlōm*). Then each major segment in the narration begins with "behold" (*wěhinnēh*), with verbal construction in participial forms. Here, three stages make up the vision: (1) a ladder was set up, (2) messengers of God were going up and down, and (3) Yahweh stood on it.

The oracle then develops three parts. (1) A self-revelation formula identifies the deity as Yahweh and combines the name with the patriarchal formulations: "The God of Abraham your father, and the God of Isaac." (2) A promise to Jacob guarantees a land, descendants as numerous as the dust and spread out over the land, and a blessing for all the nations through Jacob and the descendants. It is possible that the traditio-historical place of origin for the promise is located just here ($\rightarrow$ 35:1-7 as fulfillment of the promise; but see de Pury). (3) An assistance formula, v. 15, with its guarantee for divine presence in Jacob's journey until he returns to this place and for divine faithfulness to the promise, connects the oracle again to the context in Jacob's flight ($\rightarrow$ 35:1). Parts one and two relate to the third part in a rather wooden fashion and suggest the isolation from the context noted above. The kernel of tradition in the oracle would, in that case, be the promise for land and descendants.

Vv. 16-17 conclude the dream report itself with two sayings. The first does not underwrite an etiology. It does, however, mark the place as holy, the site of divine presence. In that manner, it points not so much to a naming etiology as to an account for founding a sanctuary ($\rightarrow$ Exod 3:1-6). The second, v. 17, is clearly a key for a naming etiology. The saying labels the place as the house of God. V. 17bβ does not figure into the naming as clearly as the reference in v. 17bα, although both doubtlessly support the etiology in some manner. The naming itself occurs in v. 19a, with v. 19b a gloss to account for the prior name. The wordplay moves, then, from "house of God" (*bêt 'ělōhîm*) to Bethel (*bêt-'ēl*). Intervening between the saying and the act of naming is v. 18, a narrative account of the founding of the sacred pillar as a memorial of the sacred revelation during Jacob's sleep. Its point of reference would thus be more nearly the saying in v. 16. The results suggest two etiological conclusions for the unit, an account of the founding of a sanctuary at Bethel and an account of the name.

The unit concludes in vv. 20-22 with a sacred vow. The conditions of the vow relate the unit to the larger context of Jacob's flight from Isaac's house. They call for God's presence with Jacob in the whole of his journey until he returns to his father's house ($\rightarrow$ 35:27-29). The consequences of the vow will be Jacob's embracing Yahweh as his God, the place where he stands as sanctuary, and the wealth God gives him as a source of support for the sanctuary. The support is conceived particularly in terms of a tithe (→ 14:20b). The vow thus focuses on the function of the unit as a foundation story for a sanctuary, but it incorporates the naming etiology by declaring the sanctuary to be the house of God.

As it now stands, the unit is a part of the Yahwist's work, expanded at points by the Elohist. The tradition history emerges from this final form of the text. (1) The tradition has been incorporated into the context of J's narrative about Jacob's flight from his father's house and anticipates his return. (2) The narration of a dream supports a naming etiology. (3) The kernel of the tradition, however, recounts the founding of a sanctuary and thus relates the unit to local tradition. Could it be that the promise was located originally at this point in the patriarchal tradition? (See de Pury.)

Genre

As a part of the larger narrative about Jacob, the unit has nonetheless a marked generic integrity. It is an episode in Jacob's ITINERARY (Westermann, *Promises,* 85-86). In its earlier levels, it must be defined as a naming ETIOLOGY which has been imposed secondarily on a HIEROS LOGOS for the sanctuary at Bethel (Westermann, *Promises,* 85-86).

Setting

As an episode in Jacob's itinerary, the unit has a setting in the literature of J. The earlier stages of the tradition relate the unit to a naming etiology, but no clear conclusions can be drawn here concerning setting. The oldest stage would appear to be a *hieros logos* for the sanctuary at Bethel and thus a part of local cultic tradition.

Intention

The unit accounts first for Jacob's protection in his journey to and from Haran. It anticipates a parallel episode to account for Jacob's return to Bethel to pay his vow. Earlier stages include a naming etiology that connects the local name to Jacob's dream, a secondary development in the tradition, and a narrative account of the founding of a sanctuary, the original intention of the unit. In this level, the unit reports how the sanctity of the place came to light and thus accounted for the foundation of a place of worship. This level, moreover, attaches a promise for land and descendants to the local tradition.

Bibliography

O. Eissfeldt, "Jakobs Begegnung mit El und Moses' Begegnung mit Jahwe," *OLZ* 58 (1963) 325-31; F. O. Garcia, "Bethel: The History of an Israelite Sanctuary" (Diss., Princeton, 1967); W. Gross, "Jakob, der Mann des Segens. Zu Traditionsgeschichte und Theologie der priesterschriftlichen Jakobsüberlieferungen," *Bib* 49 (1968) 321-44; C. Houtman, "What Did Jacob See in His Dream at Bethel? Some Remarks on Genesis xxviii 10-22," *VT* 27 (1977) 337-51; C. A. Keller, "Über einige alttestamentliche Heiligtumslegenden," *ZAW* 67 (1955) 141-68; 68 (1956) 85-97; V. Maag, "Zum *Hieros Logos* von Beth-El," *Arsberättelese* (Göteborgs Stadtsbibliotek) ¾ (1951) 122-33; E. Otto, "Jakob in Bethel. Ein Beitrag zur Geschichte der Jakobüberlieferung," *ZAW* 88 (1976) 165-90; A. de Pury, *Promesse divine et légende cultuelle dans le cycle de Jacob. Genèse 28 et les traditions patriarcales* (Paris: Gabalda, 1975).

JACOB-LABAN NOVELLA, 29:1– 32:1 (*RSV* 31:55)

Structure

I. Exposition	29:1-14
A. Transition	1
B. Introduction of Rachel	2-12
1. Heroic setting	2-3
2. Dialogue	4-8
a. Introduction of Rachel	4-6
b. Explanation of the well's stone	7-8
3. Heroic meeting	9-12
C. Invitation to Laban's hospitality	13-14
1. Meeting between Laban and Jacob	13
2. Formula of kinship	14
II. Complication	29:15-30
A. Business negotiations	15-19
1. Laban's offer to negotiate	15
2. Designation of wages	16-18
a. Introduction of two women	16-17
b. Specification of wages	18
3. Laban's agreement	19
B. Business transaction	20-30
1. Jacob's payment	20
2. Marriage	21-25a
a. Request for the bride	21
b. Description of feast	22-24
c. Results	25a
3. Jacob's accusation against Laban	25b
4. Laban's defense	26-27
a. Appeal to custom	26
b. Negotiation for wages	27
5. Marriage	28-30a
a. Event	28-30aα
b. Conflict	30aβ
6. Jacob's payment	30b
III. Digression	29:31– 30:24
A. Conflict	29:31
B. Leah's birth reports	29:32-35
1. Reuben	32
2. Simeon	33
3. Levi	34
4. Judah	35

This story has no intrinsic contacts with its context. Even 29:1, a transition piece that functions effectively as a bridge between this unit and the preceding description of Jacob's dispatch from Canaan, has no intrinsic rootage in the context. To be sure, there are allusions to the context. Laban is identified as the brother of Jacob's mother (29:10), an allusion to Genesis 24, and 29:12-13 assumes the same relationship. But the comment is general, hardly intrinsic for the substance of the narrative. The story itself assumes at most that Jacob and Laban are kinsmen (for comparison of characterization between Genesis 24 and this unit, see the discussion below). Moreover, v. 13b is also general and cannot be taken as an allusion to the substance of the narrative context. There is no reference to the struggle between the brothers, the blessing that promoted Jacob's flight. The unit shows no impact from the general narrative motifs of divine promises for a son, descendants, land, or blessing. Even the occasional references to God as the God of Abraham or Isaac reveal no dependency of the story on the context. It presupposes only that Jacob was traveling toward the land of the eastern people. The isolation of the unit suggests that the story derives from an independent tradition and functions as a kernel for the growth of the larger Jacob saga (see Noth, *History,* on the east-Jordan Jacob). It is in effect a story within a story (→ Genesis 39–41). On the traditio-historical dimension of this observation, see the comments below.

The structure of this story includes an exposition in developed narrative style, remarkably free of conflict and characterized by heroic dimensions, followed by a series of elements that interact in a complex exchange between complication and resolution. The contrast between the exposition and its following series constitutes the fulcrum for the development of a plot in the story.

The exposition places a major emphasis on Jacob as a principal in the story by casting him in the role of a heroic figure. But in the same process, the element emphasizes Rachel, the complement of the heroic figure. Jacob-Rachel thus constitutes a major narrative axis for the unit as a whole. The setting for the narration is a community well, a pastoral scene that leads to heroic demonstration (→ Exod 2:15b-22). The demonstration of heroic strength develops here, however, not by a defense of a hapless woman, but by an unusual deed as a gesture of help for a shepherdess. Vv. 2-3 set the stage for Jacob's show of strength by describing the well as a source of water for several flocks, protected from indiscriminate use by a large stone. The initial description (v. 2a) places three flocks waiting at the well, while the continuation (v. 3) shows that all the flocks would have to gather before the shepherds could remove the stone. The impact of the description is that the stone was so large that moving it required all the shepherds. This point is confirmed by vv. 7-8. Here Jacob admonishes the shepherds that they should be about their business. But the shepherds respond by admitting that they were not able (*lō' nûkal*) to water their sheep and return to the pasture; they must wait for all the flocks to gather before the stone could be rolled from the well (contrast von Rad, *Genesis*, 288-89). The point is not that the shepherds were lazy; it is that the stone was too heavy. Vv. 4-6 develop a dialogue between Jacob and the shepherds that (1) elicits an identification of the shepherds as citizens of Haran, the goal of Jacob's flight; (2) recognizes Laban, the uncle Jacob sought; and (3) as a response to Jacob's inquiry about his uncle's well-being, introduces Rachel, the daughter of the uncle.

The goal of the element appears clearly, then, in vv. 9-12. Rachel enters the scene, and in response to her, Jacob removes the stone alone and waters the sheep she has brought. Vv. 11-12 conclude the meeting with contact between the two principal figures. Jacob introduces himself to Rachel with a kiss, a cry, and an explanation, and Rachel responds by running away to report to her father (→ Exod 2:17-18; cf. also Gen 24:28). Rachel's response thus also serves as a transition from Jacob-Rachel to Jacob-Laban. The final element in the exposition, vv. 13-14, contains the second major narrative axis for the unit as a whole. These verses stand, nonetheless, as a contrast to the development of the complements in the narrative. Here Laban is hospitable: he embraces Jacob, kisses him, and takes him into his house. He hears the affairs of Jacob's past (no details), and then he declares Jacob a relative (→ 2:23). The principal figures of the story thus appear without conflict. The scene merits its pastoral setting.

The first unit of complication for the story appears in 29:15-30, a point of tension in the relationship between Jacob and Laban. Vv. 15-19 can be designated as business negotiations, a dialogue aimed at defining the working relationship between Jacob and Laban. The dialogue itself shows no sign of the coming problem that constitutes the conflict of this element. Laban's speech in v. 15 invites Jacob to name his wages for his work in Laban's house. And although words such as "serve me" (*wa'ăbadtanî*) and "your wages" (*maśkurtekā*) now control the relationship, the invitation is not in itself negative (contrast Fokkelman). Jacob responds to the invitation, v. 18, a movement that meshes with the invitation and shows no sign of the coming conflict. V. 19, Laban's agreement to the deal, follows suit. The dialogue appears to be straightforward, negative only if one assumes that business relationships should not qualify life among relatives. The exception to the positive relationships in the element appears in a parenthetical comment inserted into the midst of the dialogue, vv. 16-17. The story has already introduced Rachel in a fashion that suggests a narrative axis composed of the Jacob-Rachel complement. Now the narrator sets Rachel opposite a sister, and the opposition is characterized by a conflict: Leah-Rachel; older-younger; weak eyes-beautiful and lovely. The structure of the element does not, however, imply that a new narrative axis enters the scene. Rather, the opposition precedes Jacob's specification of his wages as the beautiful daughter Rachel and qualifies the Jacob-Rachel axis. Moreover, it suggests that the apparently very friendly negotiation between Jacob and his kinsman Laban, the first narrative axis, is colored by the conflict in the second. Vv. 16-17 thus constitute a foreshadowing of the conflict that emerges explicitly in the second part of the element.

Vv. 20-30 describe the transaction based on the negotiations between Jacob and Laban. V. 20 constitutes Jacob's payment for his bride, a comment that reserves conflict for subsequent elements. For seven years Jacob lived with Laban and his family without a problem. The first sign of conflict appears in vv. 21-25a, an account of Laban's response to his contract. Jacob must first request his wife, a point that may suggest reluctance to keep commitments (→ 24:54-59). The characterization of Laban here is different from the one that appears in Genesis 24, however. There Laban agreed to the arrangement after some hesitancy. Here the hesitancy produces major conflict. Vv. 22-24 constitute the marriage report itself. Laban throws a stag party for Jacob. (The word for "party" here, *mišteh,* is derived from the verb "drink.") After the party Laban gave his daughter to Jacob as a wife, and Jacob accepted her. But in the morning, when Jacob's head was clearer and he could see who was in his bed, he discovered Laban's deception—he had accepted the wrong sister (v. 23b; cf. 19:31-38, where Lot was so drunk that he did not know he was sleeping with his daughters).

Jacob's response to Laban is understandably irate. V. 25b is an accusation, a stereotyped, preofficial formula that requires formal response. Laban responds with a defense that appeals to popular custom. The defense should be recognized as rather lame, however. The continuation of the same Laban speech offers Jacob a new contract for obtaining the second daughter. The move assumes not simply the popular custom, but the acceptance by Jacob of Leah as a wife. Although Laban changed his end of the contract, Jacob expended his seven years of work on an initial wedding, and a second wedding would cost another seven years. Vv. 28-30aα represent the second event. No feast celebrates the wedding here. Jacob receives the right bride. Moreover, both brides receive maids from their father. Vv. 24 and 29 are not intrinsic to the narrative scene. Rather, they prepare for the following one. Yet, with the two brides and their maids, Jacob's household is complete. The more important comment for the structure of this element is v. 30aβ: "He loved Rachel more than Leah." The element presents a major conflict: Jacob-Laban. But a second conflict is also present: Jacob-Rachel qualified by Rachel-Leah. Both points merit development in the following narrative. Thus the second period of seven years (v. 30b) concludes the element.

The next element is not simply a collection of individual units (contrast von Rad, *Genesis,* 293-94). It is, rather, a birth report organized around the narrative theme of the whole. It functions to set a conflict in the relationship between Rachel and Jacob, as well as to establish an order or hierarchy in the line of sons (→ 35:22b-26). 29:31 sets the point of tension for the element: Leah was hated but fertile; Rachel, in contrast, was loved but barren. The element will develop the tension between the two sisters into a major parallel plot for the unit. Yet, if the element is to be integrated into the whole, the tension should in some manner qualify the Rachel-Jacob axis rather than unfolding a completely new parallel. The narrative focus would not be Leah-Jacob, or even Leah-Rachel, but Rachel-Jacob colored by the Rachel-Leah complement. It is just this pattern of narrative that transforms the element from a collection of units into an integral part of the whole.

The point of v. 31, then, is not that Jacob hates Leah. Jacob remains relatively passive in this element (→ 16:1-6; 21:1-14; for the only exception, see 30:1-2). He is present as an influence in the scene; he fathers children for the wives. Indeed, the names of the Leah children reflect Jacob's failure to love her. But the narrative depicts no relationship between Jacob and Leah. The point is rather that Rachel hates Leah. The barren-fertile opposition highlights the tension posed by the hate. Jacob's failure to love Leah is then a minor reflection of Rachel's hate. And when the explanation of Simeon's name alludes to hate, the hate is not simply Jacob's, but Rachel's also. This narrative theme constitutes the framework for the series of twelve birth reports at the center of the unit. Its span reaches resolution in 30:22-24, not by reconciliation of the two sisters, but by removal of Rachel's barrenness, a factor in the Rachel-Jacob axis. Framework elements can also be seen in 30:1-4, 9, and 14-16. In 30:1-4, the hatred between Rachel and Leah prompts a desperate complaint by Rachel to Jacob: "Give me children or I shall die." Jacob's response, however, is not comfort for the distraught wife, but a rebuke. The relationship represented by the Jacob-Rachel axis is thus fractured, and out of that tension comes Rachel's gift to Jacob of Bilhah as a (secondary) wife. In v. 9 Leah appears in a parallel position. Now suffering from infertility, she gives Zilpah to Jacob as another secondary wife.

The complication intimated by this point, particularly the relationship between Leah and Rachel presupposed by the gift of Zilpah, is not developed, as it is in 30:1-4. Rather, the point comes to narrative expression in 30:14-16, an element cast primarily by the Rachel-Jacob span. Leah's firstborn son brings his mother "mandrakes," an apparent remedy for infertility. But Rachel petitions Leah for them, and the petition provokes Leah's rebuke (cf. the parallel with 30:1-4). The rebuke is set in the context of a struggle between the women, each afflicted now with infertility. It implies, however, that Leah's infertility derives from an absence of Jacob. Moreover, Rachel's negotiation for the mandrakes makes the same point. If Leah will sell her mandrakes, then she may have Jacob for the night. The transaction is completed. Jacob sleeps with Leah, and Leah's infertility is cured. That leaves Rachel with the mandrakes and, after the night of hire, her husband. The span of tension is resolved, however, not by the potency of the mandrakes nor even by the potency of Jacob, but by God: in v. 22, "God remembered Rachel and harkened to her and opened her womb." The divine intervention is somewhat wooden for the narrative. The tension of the plot has not prepared the audience for its move (contrast 8:1). It would have been smoother if perhaps Yahweh had worked through the mandrakes. Yet, for the Yahwist, birth for the patriarchal family lies in Yahweh's hands (→ 25:21; see also 21:1a). This move, however, does not constitute the conclusion of the narrative. The strife is not resolved. The tension and its resolution produce children, not reconciliation.

This narrative frame now embraces twelve birth reports. The reports develop popular etymologies for the names of the children. They develop as might be expected in birth reports. On the basis of a saying, the mother gives the child a name. They are not isolated from the frame narrative, however. To the contrary, they carry forward the narrative motif of strife in the family, in some cases bending the etymologies in order to meet the motif. So, in the first entry, the name Reuben is explained not in terms of Yahweh's seeing a son, as might be expected, but rather as Yahweh's seeing Leah's affliction: rā'â yahweh bĕ'onyî. The series breaks readily into three groups of four reports. The first group, 29:32-35, is united. Leah bears four sons, and three bear names that reflect in some manner her struggle with Rachel for Jacob: "Because Yahweh has looked upon my affliction [from Rachel], now my husband will love me." "Because Yahweh heard that I am hated, he gave me this one." "Now this time my husband will be joined to me, because I have borne him three sons." The fourth is obviously neutral: "This time I will praise Yahweh."

The second set of four birth reports comprises two groups of two, each from one of the secondary wives. The names are nonetheless given and explained by the primary wife. So, Rachel names Bilhah's children. The first is an allusion to her appeal for justice, perhaps her struggle with Jacob, perhaps her struggle with Leah. The second, however, is clearly a play on her struggle with Leah: "With mighty wrestlings I have wrestled with my sister and have prevailed." In contrast, Leah's names for Zilpah's children are all positive and say nothing about the struggle: "Good fortune," "I am happy."

The final set of four birth reports is somewhat more broken. It comprises two reports of Leah's sons, one report of a Leah daughter, and one report of Rachel's son. The first report bends the narrative to meet the explanation of the name. The narrative assumes that the name, Issachar, should be explained from Leah's sale of mandrakes to Rachel. She thereby hired her husband for the night. The explanation sets out the name, however, by reference to Leah's gift of Zilpah to Jacob. And the final name calls on Leah's hope that relations with Jacob would be possible. The report of the daughter's birth has no name explanation. The short form breaks the established pattern of structure for the unit and marks the verse as secondary. The report depends on the narrative context for the unit, not simply the unit. Thus, it foreshadows Genesis 34. Moreover, the number twelve is structurally important for the list. Leah has six sons, perhaps a six-tribe confederation in themselves. The secondary wives have four. Rachel should have two, but Benjamin is missing. The Benjamin birth report is associated rather with the death of Rachel, but it may have originally belonged to this unit (see Noth, *History*, 100 n. 292). In order to replace the missing Benjamin and hold the number of Jacob's children to twelve, this unit presupposes a report of the death of Rachel at a coming moment in the larger narrative. And in its place, the birth report for the daughter holds the number at twelve.

It is interesting, then, that even though the list of Jacob's sons is relatively late in the tradition's history, it has no allusion to the promise tradition. The point is the more surprising since in just this element of the unit, the promise for great posterity achieves substantial fulfillment. Abraham's descendants, Jacob's sons, are the twelve tribal fathers. Rather than the promise tradition as the narrative motif that gives structure to the whole, the unit develops strife in the family as its structuring key. And strife is also the point of unity in 29:1-30.

The next unit of complication, 30:25-43, returns to the point of tension that qualifies the Jacob-Laban axis (→ 29:15-30). V. 25a is a transition from the previous element, noting that the conclusion to the element can properly be defined as Rachel's bearing Joseph. Now the narrative is ready for a new event. Two major elements follow. The first depicts Jacob and Laban again at the negotiations table. Vv. 25b-34 constitute the negotiation's dialogue that defines a new relationship between the two contrasting figures. Jacob opens the dialogue with a request to return to Canaan. Vv. 25b and 26 constitute a certain duplication. Yet, structurally they are not redundant and cannot qualify as doublets. They represent, rather, a stylistic duplication for the sake of emphasis. Moreover, v. 26b is an assertion of quality in the work Jacob has undertaken. The assertion undergirds his appeal for dismissal. He has paid the proper price for his wives. Vv. 27-28 counter Jacob's request to leave with Laban's proposal that he stay. The proposal is rooted in Laban's conviction, established by divination, that his wealth derives from Yahweh's blessing because of Jacob's work. There is thus some reflection here of blessing by virtue of association with Yahweh's blessed (→ 39:1-6). When Laban offers generous payment for continued service, Jacob responds with a question, vv. 29-30. But the question is subtle. It asserts Laban's recognition of Jacob's service, indeed, of Yahweh's blessing because of Jacob's service, and it poses the necessity Jacob faces for building his own wealth. The position is apparently an objection to the proposal. In fact, it anticipates a request for high wages. Laban responds, v. 31a, by repeating his offer to provide a suitable wage. Jacob's proposal, vv. 31b-33, then designates his wages. He will take speckled, spotted sheep and goats and black lambs for his wages. One might anticipate here that Jacob must be working on some kind of deception. Marked animals are not rare, but neither are they plentiful. Is the magic described in vv. 37-42 presupposed in the very request, not simply the response to Laban's deceit? The story sets two cheats in opposition, each competing for supremacy over the other. And each must suspect the moves of the other. V. 33 assumes the strained relationship. It will be necessary for Jacob to demonstrate his honesty; thus, the marked sheep and goats apparently serve the cause of Jacob's demonstration of fair division of the herds. V. 34 then sets out Laban's agreement and the dialogue closes.

The relationship is strained, however. Laban had previously negotiated with Jacob and revealed there his tendency to cheat. So here too he cheats. Vv. 35-36 describe this deception not only as an effort to remove all marked animals before Jacob could collect his wages, but also as an effort to put distance between Jacob and the animals. Jacob would never know. But Jacob did know, and his response, vv. 37-42, describes his magical skill (cf. Laban's divination skill, v. 27). By proper procedure, Jacob can stimulate birth of marked animals. Moreover, he controlled the breeding, so that the stronger animals became his, and the weaker strain remained for Laban. The results are clearly marked in v. 43: Jacob becomes rich, and Laban pays the price. Thus the conflict increases.

A resolution of the tension in the plot of the story appears in 31:1-21. The transition, v. 1-2, sets out an intensification of the conflict. The sons of Laban have grown hostile to Jacob because of his accumulated wealth (→ 26:16). The reason for their hostility lies in the observation that the wealth in question derives from Laban. It implies at least a reduction in inheritance for them, if not some suspicion that Jacob obtained the wealth by some (magical) play. V. 2, a classical example of understatement, carries Jacob's response to the conflict. The transition thus connects with the preceding element of complication, and it anticipates some kind of marked change in direction of the plot. Further intensification is not really possible.

The body of this element appears in vv. 3-21. Vv. 3-16 contain Yahweh's instructions to Jacob to leave Laban and the response this intervention merits. V. 3 is the divine speech, the instructions and a promise for presence expressed by means of an assistance formula. Jacob then delivers the instructions to his wives. Following an expanded speech formula noting Jacob's summons of his wives to the field where he kept his flock (v. 4-5aα), Jacob builds his case for leaving. The rest of v. 5 is a general observation about the situation: Laban is hostile to Jacob; the God of Abraham-Isaac is with him. Then the details appear. Vv. 6-10 describe the events that have led to this crisis, including reference to divine intervention (vv. 7, 9), all under an introduction that assumes recognition and agreement from the wives: "You know that . . . my claim is just." Vv. 11-13 cite an oracle delivered by an angel to Jacob. It is in some manner a justification for Jacob's description of the events leading to the moment. The knowledge Jacob exercised in order to control the birth of the flock did not derive from magic—it derived from God. The growth of Jacob's wealth at the expense of Laban resulted, according to Jacob, not from manipulation, but from divine intervention. But the citation does not function to support an appeal for legal recognition from the wives, at least not directly. Rather, it refers to the instructions that Jacob must return to his home, v. 3. The self-identification formula in v. 13a underwrites the authority of the instructions in v. 13b (→ Lev 18:2). It is not Jacob's idea that just now the family should leave for Canaan. The idea really derives from the God of Bethel to whom Jacob made a vow (→ 28:20). The identification of the deity does not, however, establish an intrinsic union between the story and the unit in 28:10-22. The vow and, indeed, the reference to Bethel are incidental to the structural function of the formula as an assertion of authority for the instructions to leave Laban. The instructions themselves, vv. 3, 13b, regularly pass over Bethel for a general statement, "the land of your birth." The instructions assume, then, only that Jacob is not a native of the land of Laban. There is no reference to the problem with Esau, no reference to the competition for the blessing. There is only reference to the land of his birth. Under pressure from Laban, Jacob must leave for home. The implication for the wives is, of course, an appeal for recognition of justice in Jacob's case. Will they obey the instructions and go to Jacob's land? Or will they refuse to recognize the justice of the instructions?

Vv. 14-16 must count as a key text in the story. It is crucial because here the wives recognize the justice of Jacob's case against Laban. But even more, here the wives act together. The tension from the preceding element has disappeared with the birth of Rachel's son. Now, the two women stand as a single unit in the events of the narrative. The opposition in the Rachel-Leah parallel now merges into a single pole that complements Jacob. Thus, in this unit, as in 29:15-30, the narrative assumes two poles: Jacob-Laban, with Laban in the back stage, and Jacob–Rachel-Leah. The narrative movement occurs through the action of the Jacob–Rachel-Leah pole, cast as a reaction to the Jacob-Laban pole.

Vv. 17-21 contain no speech. They describe, rather, the event of separation that constitutes the resolution of the crisis. Jacob takes his family and his wealth across the river, and the crossing itself marks the division (cf. the role of the Jordan as a division in the journey of Israel; → Joshua 3–4). The element is not the conclusion of the story, however. It breaks one point of tension, but at the same time it foreshadows a second point. Vv. 19-20 report that Laban was not present at the moment of Jacob's departure and that Jacob's flight without telling Laban constituted a victory: "Jacob stole the heart of Laban the Aramean because he did not tell him that he was fleeing" (→ Exod 12:33-36). Should not one victory merit another challenge, in good narrative style? The foreshadowing of a new conflict receives a second prong, however. Without explanation, v. 19b reports that Rachel stole her father's household gods (hattĕrāpîm). There is no effort to associate this act with Rachel's complaint that inheritance in the father's house for her has evaporated. There is no narrative role for this allusion in the conflict between Jacob and Laban's sons. As an element in the narrative, it stands only as anticipation for the conflict in the following unit. Thus, denouement recedes and the stage is set for a new confrontation.

Vv. 22-24 combine a new element of conflict with the major break in the development of the story's plot. The first part of the element, vv. 22-25, controls the character of the conflict. Vv. 22-23 contain the conflict anticipated by v. 20. When Laban heard that Jacob had fled, he took his own kinsmen (note the implied division between the two family groups) and pursued Jacob into the hill country of Gilead. The conflict is captured sharply by the juxtaposition of the two hostile camps, v. 25. In contrast, however, v. 24 compromises the conflict with a report of divine intervention. The conflict can produce no problems because God instructed Laban to say nothing to Jacob, good or bad. Laban has simply been defeated. If the element is to develop a genuine position in the structure of the story, then it must look beyond the competition between Jacob and Laban over Jacob's unannounced flight to a new problem.

The dialogue in vv. 26-44, styled as a disputation between Jacob and Laban, accomplishes just this goal. Laban opens this dispute with a long list of grievances against Jacob, vv. 26-28a. The introduction in v. 26, "What have you done?", makes the list an accusation, and the formulation of the question in vv. 27 and 28a under the control of the interrogative particle "Why?" carries the same point. Vv. 28b-29a follow the accusation with a threat. Thus, the first prong of the conflict comes sharply to expression. V. 29b defuses the conflict with the divine intervention introduced by v. 24: The threat can have no consequences. But v. 30 opens the second prong of the conflict. A new accusation shifts the focus from Jacob-Laban to Rachel. Yet, the shift is only implied. Laban's accusation assumes the problem still to be Jacob-Laban: "Why did you steal my gods?" The form of the accusation calls for Jacob's defense to each point. Thus, in Jacob's speech in vv. 31-32a, he answers the first accusation with a rather lame confession of fear in the face of the conflict with Laban (v. 31). The narrative requires no more than that, since by virtue of the divine intervention the Jacob-Laban axis has already been resolved. The second accusation provokes a stronger response (v. 31a) since, in his ignorance of Rachel's deed, Jacob assumes the innocence of his family: "Any one with whom you find your gods shall not live." His strong response thus places Rachel in danger and shifts the conflict of the element from Jacob-Laban to Jacob-Rachel.

Vv. 32b-35 reverse the direction of the narrative. V. 32b opens the element with the complication in the Jacob-Rachel axis. Jacob did not know that Rachel had stolen the gods; thus, he exposed her to the danger of discovery and death without knowing the full scope of his decision. Vv. 33-34 recount Laban's search for the gods, and thus for the fate of Jacob-Rachel, in painstaking detail. Step by step he searches each tent of the family. V. 34a reveals Rachel's advanced preparation, v. 34b the results of his search of her tent. The only alternative open to Laban now is to search the animals. V. 35a captures Rachel's defense: She had hidden the gods in her saddle, and now she sits on them. When Laban comes to search her animal, she turns him aside: "Let not my lord be angry that I cannot rise before you, for the way of women is upon me." So Laban searched, but he did not find the gods so well hidden by Rachel.

Thus, the Jacob-Rachel axis is preserved. By her own cunning, Rachel resolves the danger Jacob brought on her. Moreover, the foresight exhibited by

Rachel turns the tables on Laban. Laban entered Jacob's camp with an accusation against Jacob. Jacob was on the defensive, the object of Laban's attack. Now Laban has failed to prove his case against Jacob. That failure comes not through the cunning of Jacob, but first through divine intervention, then through the cunning of Rachel. It seems to be clear, then, that for the story the gods do not represent legal or theological interests but rather a device for showing the downfall of Laban. Rachel sits on the gods during her menstrual period not to cast theological discredit on the gods of the Mesopotamian patriarch, but rather to cast discredit on the patriarch himself. Laban was defeated by Rachel's (claim to be in her) menstrual cycle. The denouement of the Jacob-Rachel axis thus becomes the denouement of the Jacob-Laban axis.

Vv. 36-42 exploit the results of the denouement. Laban came to Jacob with a formal accusation, and before his kinsmen he failed. His charges could not be substantiated, even though the audience knows that they were based on a just cause. Vv. 36-37 focus on Jacob's complaint about the apparently unwarranted search and his appeal to the kinsmen for a judgment. Vv. 38-41 shift the complaint to the long history of conflict with Laban, while v. 42 claims judgment against that violation already rendered by God. The conflict thus doubles back on its course: The accuser becomes the accused; the cheater has been cheated out of his justice. The conflict is over, although the family members have gained no reconciliation. The conflict, both on the Jacob-Rachel and on the Jacob-Laban axes, simply breaks in Jacob's favor. Vv. 43-44 make the break official. Laban concedes defeat, while claiming the justice of his cause, and he must now formalize his concession in a covenant with Jacob.

The final element in the story, vv. 45-54, extends the denouement into formal bonds that define the relationships. The story thus does not break off suddenly with the denouement, but now relaxes more gradually. (1) Jacob and his kinsmen erect stones. (a) V. 45 reports Jacob's construction of a pillar (*maṣṣēbâ*). (b) V. 46 describes the construction of a heap of stones by the kinsmen, with a meal, celebrated only by the Jacob people, or according to the OL, the Laban people. (2) V. 47 is virtually an aside, a reference to the name of the construction given by both Laban (an Aramaic name) and Jacob (a Hebrew name). Laban's response to the construction is also captured by vv. 48-53a. Here the naming process belongs only to Laban, cast in the typical structure of an etymological etiology.

Yet, there is a problem in the structure of these verses that makes the element somewhat ambiguous. (a) Laban's name for the heap of stones is in v. 48 the same Hebrew name given the heap by Jacob in v. 47. But here the name functions as a witness between Laban and Jacob. Would not the point of the name rest in the juridical resolution of the relationship? Since in the story the judgment goes against Laban, one must ask here which principal in the conflict the naming originally belongs to. If the naming belongs to Laban, would it not reflect his continuing appeal for recognition of justice in this claim? The OL reference to Laban in the place of Jacob in v. 46 would support this point (see von Rad, *Genesis,* 312-13). It seems probable nonetheless that the structure of the naming section originally represented the pile of Jacob's witness to the relationship, named by Jacob. In that case, the etiology for the heap of stones would be associated with Jacob, the one for the pillar with Laban. If the OL reading in v. 46 should then be correct, each party of the conflict would appear as the namer of the opposition's construction. (b) Laban's name for the pillar, v. 49aα, leads to the nonaggression pact and a guarantee for rights for the daughters, vv. 49aβb-50. The point reflects the relatively weaker position of Laban in the denouement, a concern to insure that Jacob would do him no further harm (v. 49) or to insure that his daughters would receive no disadvantage in future relationships Jacob might establish (v. 50). In vv. 51-53a this element is expressed in a speech by Laban to Jacob. It is sealed by an appeal for judgment to the patriarchal gods of both figures. Nonaggression is the formal resolution of the conflict at the center of the story, and Jacob accepts that state. He formalizes the pact by an oath in the name of his patriarchal god, a point that increases the impression that covenant and oath stand closely together in popular conceptualization. The oath ritual includes a sacrifice and a meal with the kinsmen. The allusion to participants in the meal as *his* kinsmen carries an exclusive ring. Perhaps it alludes to the role of the kinsmen as witnesses in the struggle.

The final response, 32:1 (*RSV* 31:55) leaves no doubt, however, about the mood of the conclusion. When Laban parts company the defeated and weaker, he kisses his grandchildren and daughters and blesses them, but there is no word for Jacob, a marked contrast with 29:13. The resolution of the story thus defines the relationship between Jacob and Laban without a sign of reconciliation. The two kinsmen remain competitors and enemies.

The unit as it now stands is basically the work of the Yahwist. Some Elohistic elements may appear (see Noth, *History*, n. 94), but generally this definition is not supported by structural observations. The narrative framework for the naming elements in ch. 30 and the report to the wives and their response in ch. 31 functions well within the body of the unit. It is not possible to siphon them off as an independent narrative element. If Elohistic fragments appear here, they have no recognizable form-critical integrity. At most, the material provides expansive tradition for the Yahwistic narrative. Signs of growth in the history of tradition also appear here, particularly around the naming of the pillar and heap of stones. Perhaps the story is rooted in a memory of traditions about conflict between the Israelites and the Arameans with strong connections to particular places where these conflicts might have been settled by treaty and oath rituals.

One may ask a traditio-historical question about the relationship of this story to the general theme of the patriarchal tradition. The question is important since in this story lies an account of the growth of the patriarch Jacob into a tribal unit of twelve. Yet, there is no allusion here to the promise for a land or great posterity. The motif that carries the story is strife. Does this conflict, even though the story is relatively late in the history of the patriarchal traditions, suggest anything about the character of the tradition (→ The Patriarchal Theme)?

Stereotyped expressions and formulas call first for a consideration of the name list for the sons born to the wives of Jacob. The name list itself is relatively constant in comparison to other examples of the list, altered only by the insertion of the concubines' sons into the middle of the Leah series. This point is governed by narration interests, however, not by a problem in the history of the list (→ 35:22b-26). Others include the speech formula so central for Hebrew narrative (vv. 4 et al.), questions of polite conversation (vv. 5, 6; note the use of *šālôm*), a formula for describing kinship (29:14), a formula for preofficial legal accusation

(29:25; 31:26-27, 30), formulas for naming etiologies (31:48-49 and passim in chs. 29–30).

Genre

The story must be categorized as NOVELLA, comparable to the Joseph story (→ Genesis 24). Its structure is complex, an interweaving of plot elements to create various patterns of narration. The Jacob-Rachel and Jacob-Laban axes illustrate the point. The subtle characterization of the principals, including the psychological probing of relationships between Rachel and Leah, fits the concerns of the novella. Resolution of narrative tension by reference to divine intervention is a point of difference from the Joseph story. Indeed, one has the impression that the plot development is weakened markedly by the ploy. The narrator paints the hero into a corner, then extracts him by an interruption in the narration rather than by development of narration lines out of the substance of the story. But this point does not deny the genre classification. It suggests only that the storyteller has not worked through the subject with the same skill as the creator of the Joseph story. For both the Joseph story and this account of conflict, vocabulary patterns avoid stereotyped categories for the genre. Formulas from the legal world appear, but those formulas represent narrative material for the storyteller, not a qualification of the genre. The same point applies for the typical formulas for storytelling, such as SPEECH formula. The point is that theological stereotyping does not seem to have exerted influence on this narrative. There is, for example, no stereotypical allusion to the promise for land or for posterity.

Setting

The novella here derives from the composition of an artist, not from the social structures of a functioning institution. Although the artist takes formulas from legal or cultic settings, such as the accusation or the ritual for the oath and covenant, he transforms that material into his own creation. Setting here can be described only in terms of the artist at work.

Intention

The novella was told for the pleasure of its audience (→ Genesis 24; 37–47); yet, it develops at the same time its own internal goals. (1) It describes the growth of Jacob's family under the narrative motif of strife. The promise for posterity or land does not appear. (2) The relationship between Jacob and Laban is resolved without elimination of the strife. Jacob and Laban agree to be enemies. (3) The relationship between Jacob and Rachel is resolved with the birth of Joseph. But strife remains latent, at least between Rachel and Leah, if not also between Rachel and Jacob (→ Genesis 27). Perhaps the primary intention of the novella is to depict the family that continues to live despite the strife that threatens to break it apart. Is that not a statement about the character of Israel's history?

Bibliography

D. Amin, "The Tradition Concerning the Birth of Jacob's Children" (Hebr., Eng. summary), *Beth Mikra* 49 (1972) 220-24; M. Burrows, "The Complaint of Laban's Daughters," *JAOS* 57 (1937) 259-76; H. Cazelles, "Laban change dix fois le salaire de Jacob," *Recherches bibliques* 8 (1967) 29-34; G. W. Coats, "Strife Without Reconciliation—a

Narrative Theme in the Jacob Traditions," in *Werden und Wirken des Alten Testaments* (*Fest.* C. Westermann; ed. R. Albertz et al.; Göttingen: Vandenhoeck und Ruprecht, 1980) 82-106; D. Daube and R. Yaron, "Jacob's Reception by Laban," *JSS* 1 (1956) 60-62; O. Eissfeldt, "Stammessage und Novelle in den Geschichten von Jacob und seinen Söhnen," in *EUCHARISTĒRION. Studien zur Religion und Literatur des Alten und Neuen Testaments* (ed. H. Schmidt; FRLANT 36; Göttingen: Vandenhoeck und Ruprecht, 1923) 56-77; J. J. Finkelstein, "An Old Babylonian Herding Contract and Genesis 31:38," *JAOS* 88 (1968) 30-36; R. Frankena, "Some Remarks on the Semitic Background of Chapters xxix-xxxi of the Book of Genesis," *OTS* 17 (ed. A. S. van der Woude; Leiden: Brill, 1972) 53-64; F. Garcia-Treto, "Genesis 31 and Gilead," *Trinity University Studies in Religion* 9 (1967/68) 13-17; idem, "Gen 31:44 and 'Gilead'," *ZAW* 79 (1967) 13-17; C. Gordon, "The Story of Jacob and Laban in the Light of the Nuzi Tablets," *BASOR* 66 (1937) 25-27; S. Lehming, "Zur Erzählung von der Geburt der Jacobssöhne," *VT* 13 (1963) 74-81; S. Mowinckel, " 'Rahelstämme' und 'Leastämme'," in *Von Ugarit nach Qumran. Beiträge zur alttestamentlichen und altorientalischen Forschung* (*Fest.* O. Eissfeldt; ed. J. Hempel et al.; BZAW 77; Berlin: Töpelmann, 1961) 129-50; J. van Seters, "Jacob's Marriages and Ancient Near Eastern Customs: A Reexamination," *HTR* 62 (1969) 377-95.

MAHANAIM ETIOLOGY, 32:2-3 (*RSV* 32:1-2)

Structure

I. Description of theophany		2
II. Naming etiology		3
A. Jacob's speech		3a
B. Etiological formula		3b

For the overall structure of the Yahwist, this unit stands in a parallel position to 28:10-22, an episode in the itinerary of Jacob from Paddan-aram to Canaan (see Westermann, *Promises,* 86). It is in the same manner rather isolated from the Jacob-Laban narrative preceding it and the Jacob-Esau narrative following. Moreover, though briefer, the structure is similar. It describes, first, a theophany that confronts Jacob in the course of his travel. The unexpected quality of the theophany suggests a discovery of a holy place ($\rightarrow$ 28:10-22). The theophany would then undergird some reference to a sanctuary. Indeed, the reference might have involved a more extended narrative. But these items are no longer preserved. The unit is not a narrative; it has no plot. It simply describes an event and moves to a conclusion based on the event. The conclusion is a formula for naming a place. Jacob speaks in reaction to the theophany: "This is God's army," and from the speech, the name draws its explanation (on the discrepancy between *maḥănēh* and *maḥănāyim*, see Westermann, *Promises,* 86).

Genre

The unit is now simply a naming ETIOLOGY. If an old narrative tradition lies behind this etiology, perhaps it was fully a ($\rightarrow$) *hieros logos* such as 28:10-22.

Setting

As a part of itinerary tradition, an element from Jacob's travels back to Canaan, the etiology may belong more properly to popular lore than to a particular cultic institution. If *hieros logos* lies behind the unit, it would have derived from the sanctuary whose founding it recounts. In its present form it belongs to the setting in the literary construction of the Yahwist, the redaction that constructs tradition into a larger narration.

Intention

The unit explains the origin of a place-name in terms of an episode from Jacob's travels. For the Yahwist as a whole, it balances the Bethel tradition as an account of a complementary experience of theophany to show the character of Jacob's travel.

Bibliography

C. Houtmann, "Jacob at Mahanaim. Some Remarks on Genesis xxxii 2-3," *VT* 28 (1978) 37-44.

JACOB-ESAU STRIFE RESOLUTION, 32:4 (*RSV* 32:3) – 33:17

Structure

A. Complication	32:4–33:3
1. Messenger commission	32:4-7
a. Commission speech	4-6
1) Formulas	4-5bα
2) Message	5bβ-6
b. Messengers' report	7
2. Jacob's response	32:8-21
a. Preparations	8-9
b. Intercession	10-13
1) Invocation	10
2) Self-abasement	11
3) Petition	12a
4) Reason	12b-13
a) Jacob's fear	12b
b) Promise	13
c. Preparation of gift	14-21
1) Description of gift	14-16
2) Instructions	17-21a
3) Purpose	21b
3. Confrontation	32:22–33:3
a. Description of circumstances	32:22-25a
b. Jacob and the wrestler	32:25b-33
c. Description of circumstances	33:1-3
B. Denouement	33:4-11
1. Esau	4
2. Jacob	5-11a
a. Presentation of family	5-7
1) Esau's question	5a
2) Introduction of family	5b

There is a clear distinction between the unit in 32:2-3 and the one beginning in 32:4. The one unit displays structural characteristics of an etiology for a place-name (→ 32:2-3). The etiology comes to its conclusion without continuation into the following narrative, even though the audience might expect some further development of the theme, such as a *hieros logos*. V. 4 shifts the subject completely from the event that constitutes the basis for the etiology. Yet, vv. 4-7 do not constitute a beginning. Rather, these verses suggest narration *in medias res,* and thereby remind the audience that 32:4–33:17 is the concluding segment of a framework narrative that began properly in 27:41-45. As a piece of the Yahwistic narration, it frames not only its priestly parallel in 27:46–28:9, but the Jacob-Laban novella in 29:1–32:1 and the Bethel *hieros logos* in 28:10-22 with its parallel in the Mahanaim etiology, 32:2-3.

The corresponding element in 27:41-45, however, functions not so much to mark the exposition of the narrative theme as it does to provide a bridge from the preceding unit to the framing narration. It presupposes the tension from the preceding unit, strife between the brothers, concluded without elimination of the tension only by awarding the patriarchal blessing to the hero of the story. 27:41-45 opens, then, with an intensification of that tension, and the tension motivates Jacob's flight from Canaan to Haran. That movement forms a natural frame with this section—flight of Jacob from Haran to Canaan. In both framing elements, the complication for the narrative is the same. It is not the pressure of Laban to expel Jacob or prevent his flight. In both cases, it is Esau who hates Jacob and seeks to kill him. How can Jacob escape?

The point of tension developed in 32:4–33:3 sets Jacob at the border, ready to enter Esau's territory. The structure of the element heightens the tension to its peripeteia by describing the inevitable confrontation between the two antagonists. Jacob anticipates the confrontation by sending messengers to prepare the way. Two formulas associated with messenger speech introduce the message to be delivered to Esau. (1) The message commission formula, "Thus you shall say to my lord Esau," addresses the messengers directly with a commission to act for the sender as bearers of a message (→ Exod 7:15-16; et al.). (2) The messenger formula, "Thus says your servant Jacob," is a part of the speech commissioned by the sender for delivery to the recipient. It functions to identify the sender for the recipient, if not also to claim the authority of the sender for the message. Both formulas appear here in a secular context, suggesting that although both appear frequently among the prophets, they are not simply "prophetic" formulas. They are speech forms from common life used simply to establish identity, if not also authority, for messages delivered by duly appointed representatives.

Jacob's message to Esau shows the height of tension in the scene. The tricker must seek the favor of the slower wit. This he does initially with an explanation of his years with Laban: "I have sent to explain to my lord in order to find favor in your eyes." The messengers return, however, with news that seals the confrontation: "We came to your brother Esau, and he is coming to meet you, and four hundred men with him."

The next element, 32:8-21, paints Jacob's response to the news with diverse motifs. (1) Jacob is afraid. (2) He divides his family into two companies on the theory that, should Esau attack one, the other could escape. 33:1-3 shows, however, that the division represents a hierarchy of value in the family and thus confirms a continuing division among the people who form the substance of Israel. The motif may be connected in some manner with the etiology in 32:2-3. In v. 8, Jacob divides his house into "two companies" (*lišnê mahănôt*). (Cf. also v. 10.) The connection is undeveloped, however. The two companies would explain the dual ending in the place-name more readily than the general company of God in v. 2. But even here dual endings do not appear. If some connection was originally a part of this narrative, it has lost its impact. The story now uses the motif simply to describe a division in the family. (3) The prayer in vv. 10-13 also exhibits such motifs. The substance of the prayer is a petition for delivery from the hand of the enemy. It begins, however, with an invocation that places responsibility for the conflict on God. The invocation first connects the name Yahweh with the God of the patriarchs, then expands the name with a participial clause citing God's command to Jacob to return to Canaan. It was God's command that brought Jacob to this conflict, just as God's command led Abraham here. Indeed, the citation refers in a general way to God's promise, constructed as purpose dependent on fulfillment of the command: "Return to your land and to your kindred, so that I may do good with you" (→ 12:1). The citation functions implicitly as the foundation for the petition in the prayer: "Because you said. . . , now please save. . . ." Between the foundation and the petition is a self-abasement, not constructed with stereotyped formulas, but rather developed out of the substance of the story. V. 12a sets out the petition in the substance of the story. V. 13 then returns to the theme of the invocation, a citation of God's promise. Indeed, here the promise tradition is explicit: God had promised Jacob great posterity, as numerous as the sand of the sea. The impact of the citation is again only implicit, however: "Because you promised, then please save. . . ." The undeveloped relationship of the promise to the petition, both here and in v. 10, and its implicit duplication of the grounding for the petition in v. 12b suggest that the promise here is secondary. The promise tradition does not enter this strife story at a substantial level.

Jacob's response to the news of an impending confrontation with Esau also includes preparation of a gift to buy off the expected tragedy (vv. 14-22). V. 21

is a key for the element. Not only does it explain the dynamics in Jacob's preparation as an attempt to sway the emotions of the offended brother by a sizable gift, but it also anticipates coming confrontation by introducing the motif "I shall see his face" (cf. 32:31; 33:10). The ground is set for the confrontation.

The confrontation has three distinct parts. (1) 32:22-25a describes the scene. The present was dispatched; Jacob's family was deployed; and Jacob remained alone, on the wrong side of the stream. (2) 32:25b-33 sets out a confrontation (→ 32:25b-32). (3) 33:1-3 then describes the breaking point of the narrative: Jacob presents himself to Esau. The confrontation forebodes conflict: "Esau was coming and four hundred men with him." It forces Jacob to arrange his family according to its divisions. But even more, it forces Jacob to present himself to Esau in an inferior position. A subject who knows his guilt bows seven times before the king (see von Rad, *Genesis,* 327), and so does Jacob. Jacob announces the kind of reception he expects and, in effect, accepts responsibility for the guilt he incurred.

The break in the tension of the narrative appears clearly in v. 4. Esau, the innocent sufferer at least for J, the offended who sought Jacob's life, now greets Jacob with reconciliation: "But Esau ran to meet him and embraced him, and fell on his neck and kissed him. And they wept" (→ 45:14-15). This element radically alters the direction of the plot. The offended brother does not bite or kill the tricker—he embraces him (cf. von Rad, *Genesis,* 327). And with that move from Esau, reconciliation is possible. Vv. 5-11 show Jacob's public response to the offer. He presents his family, vv. 5-7, then his gift, vv. 8-11a. The presentation employs motifs developed at earlier points in the narrative. Jacob still wants to secure Esau's favor. Indeed, the exchange between the two is marked by polite jousting reminiscent of business negotiations. In the polite process, Jacob appeals to Esau with the "face of God" motif. "To see your face is like seeing the face of God." The allusion, however, does not tie the unit directly to the Penuel tradition (→ 32:25b-33). It accounts at most for a catchword context for ordering originally diverse material. V. 11b should then cement the reconciliation between the brothers: Esau accepts the gifts offered by Jacob. The denouement is completed.

Yet, the conclusion to the story, 33:12-17, poses a slightly different image. In vv. 12-15 a dialogue between the brothers demonstrates Esau's continuing interest in restoring the familial relationships. V. 12 poses an invitation for common activity, virtually an assumption for reconciled family structures. Vv. 13-14 contain Jacob's counterproposal, a rejection of Esau's invitation to travel together, but a promise to join Esau in Seir as soon as the pace of the cattle and the children would allow. Esau then offers to leave servants to help, and again Jacob refuses. The brothers must therefore separate: "So Esau returned that day on his way to Seir" (v. 16). The reconciliation and restored family unity anticipated by the audience since Jacob promised his imminent arrival in Seir remain in jeopardy, however. V. 17 shows the break: "But Jacob journeyed to Succoth and built himself a house and made booths for his cattle." There is thus no reconciliation, no restored unity in the family. Jacob and Esau remain as divided as the birth oracle in 25:23 suggests.

This framework narrative from the Yahwist has the entire story of Jacob and Esau, with the digression about the Jacob-Laban relationship as a major interlude, in view. The tradition history that precedes this framework from J relates in some manner to the Jacob-Esau tradition represented by 25:20-26, 27-28, 29-34;

26:34–28:9. The dominant motif in the construction of this tradition is not the promise to the fathers, but strife without reconciliation.

Genre

This unit functions as complication and resolution for a larger whole. The entire narrative, 27:41–33:13, is complex in structure, even beyond its redactional role as a framework. As it now stands, it is dependent on 27:1-40. Yet, it develops its own structural plot to a resolution of the tension that motivates its opening patterns. Its insight into the psychological process of fear in Jacob, as well as other such probes, suggests that while the story derives from oral tradition, it has been formulated with a conscious and expansive style. The genre for the framework as it stands should thus be recognized as no longer (→) tale but NOVELLA. Earlier stages may have been tale.

Setting

In J, the framework structure of the story reflects the redactional setting for collecting traditions of various types and ordering them for extensive narration. The story itself would capture the theological interests of J. As a story about strife, the tradition develops initially from the treasures of the storyteller in the family.

Intention

In J, the story provides a framework for several items of tradition. In addition, it exposes sharply the problems of a divided family. Brother hates brother, and the result is a division in familial structures that becomes permanent. In the process of depicting ethnological reality in terms of a story, however, several additional elements in human experience appear. How can one incorporate strife as a part of familial life into a system that seeks intimacy for family life? In painting such human experience, the story recognizes the reality of strife without reconciliation, and indeed attributes this tragedy, not to Esau, but to Jacob.

Bibliography

→ 25:19-26.

TALE OF JACOB'S STRIFE AT JABBOK, 32:25-33 (*RSV* 32:24-32)

Structure

I. Exposition	25
A. Transition	25a
B. Description of the event	25b
II. Negotiations	26-30
A. Report of progress in the event	26
B. Dialogue	27-30
1. The man's petition	27a
2. Jacob's request for blessing	27b
3. The man's inquiry for name	28a
4. Jacob's response	28b

In the received text, this unit is but an element in a larger story (→ 32:4–33:17). It functions there as a part of the description of Jacob's confrontation experience, an intensification of the crisis that gives plot to the story. The context does not imply, however, that the mysterious man who wrestles with Jacob is Esau, not even by the play on the face motif in 33:10. It might be argued that Jacob's successful struggle with the man here would explain Esau's unexpected willingness to seek reconciliation in 33:5. If the man here were Esau or in some manner his representative, his loss here would lead to his desire for reconciliation there. But the two confrontations do not lend themselves to simple equations. Indeed, such an argument would miss J's characterization of both Esau and Jacob. The struggle in this scene is thus not the Jacob-Esau struggle. Rather, this story appears as a story within a story in order to heighten the tension of the larger narrative context. Jacob must confront Esau. As a foreshadowing of that central confrontation, he confronts the mysterious man, wrestles with him, and wins. This unit then complements the context, but it does not duplicate it.

The story itself reveals a duplicity in its structure. V. 25 sets the context. V. 25a is in some manner a transition from the previous element, Jacob's preparation to meet Esau. After arranging all of his house for the encounter, Jacob was left alone. The point is nonetheless intrinsic for the story. It names the protagonist as Jacob and places him in isolation, appropriate for the mysterious character of the following struggle. V. 25b then sets the circumstances: "A man wrestled with him until the breaking of the day." The duplicity appears, then, in v. 26. V. 26aα reports the progress of the struggle: The mysterious man could not prevail. Vv. 27-30 presuppose this state of the struggle: The mysterious man appeals to Jacob to let him go. The assumption is that he must be away before day fully dawns, a motif at home in various mythological contexts (see von Rad, *Genesis,* 321). But the appeal does not assume v. 26aβb, the blow that leaves Jacob lame. Indeed, the lame motif remains under the surface of the entire dialogue and does not return to the narrative until vv. 32-33. The duplicity would appear to be a complication in the history of the tradition designed to support an etiological conclusion, not an original element in the story.

The dialogue, vv. 27-30, turns not on Jacob's success in the struggle, but on the petition and counter-petition. Jacob's success is the point of departure in that dialogue. The man must petition Jacob for release; then Jacob responds with a request for blessing (v. 27b). To meet the request, the man asks Jacob his name (v. 28a). When Jacob gives it, the man changes it: No longer Jacob, he is now Israel (cf. 33:18-20, the name El Elohe-Israel as a possible root more closely connected to this tradition than Peniel). And the explanation for the name is rooted in the story, not in a scientific etymology: "You have striven with God and with men and have prevailed." The explanation sets God and men as the object of the key verb, a point that cannot be justified in an analysis of the name. The name suggests that the story should be interpreted as a struggle between Jacob and God, but that point alone does not do justice to the explanation. Israel is by nature, by name, the one who struggles with both God and man. Moreover, that essence of struggle is in some manner the blessing. It stands as the response to the request for blessing.

The parallelism in the dialogue is continued into v. 30. Jacob asks the man his name, just as the man asked for Jacob's name. The man, however, does not volunteer his name. He responds with a rhetorical question: "Why is it that you ask my name?" Then, rather than waiting for an answer, the text reports immediately that the man blessed him. The blessing here stands in parallel with the name change and shows that the focal interest of the unit, the blessing itself, is the change in name from Jacob to Israel. Behind this element is perhaps the recognition that to possess the name of God, or of God's messengers, is to possess power to manipulate God or messenger. But that motif is not developed here. The focus is not on God's name, but on God's blessing, and the blessing introduces the new name of the patriarch.

Vv. 31-33 conclude the narrative with two etiologies, both of which appear somewhat extrinsic to the unit. V. 31 explains the name Peniel: "For I have seen God face to face, and yet my life is preserved." But the story makes no reference to the face-to-face motif, the one possible exception being the allusion to the face of God in 33:10. Vv. 32-33 pick up the motif from V. 26b, but both the etiology and its foreshadowing in v. 26b seem disruptive in the context.

The story is Yahwistic, a part of the larger Yahwistic context. Some indication of tradition history is nonetheless preserved. Behind the present focus on the change of name lies an account of struggle between patriarch and god, ending in success for the patriarch. A later stage in the history of this tradition appears in 35:9-11. This tradition history suggests that the alternation between the names Jacob and Israel cannot be used simply as evidence for two different literary sources but represents instead a significant traditio-historical problem.

Genre

In the J context, the unit is but a description of Jacob's confrontation with a mysterious man, a complement to the following description of his confrontation with Esau. As a distinct unit, it is an ETIOLOGY for the name change. The etiological elements in vv. 31-33 attach to the primary unit and do not affect its genre classification. Earlier stages of the tradition were probably etiological MYTH (→ 6:1-4; Exod 4:24-26). The etiology cannot be defined, however, as an explanation for Peniel, either as a name etiology or as a *hieros logos*. The Peniel element, as well as the reference to the ford of Jabbok, seems extraneous to the generic structure of the unit. The myth would have focused rather on "blessing" as a crucial element in patriarchal tradition.

Setting

The J literary setting is apparent. The etiology for the name Israel as a replacement for Jacob reflects the interests of a people united under a common name. The setting here witnesses a move in tradition from familial saga to nationalistic history.

The hypothetical myth cannot be defined as Penial etiology and attributed to the place as a *hieros logos*. Since its exact character remains obscure, its setting cannot be tied down.

Intention

The J unit constitutes a complementary parallel for Jacob's confrontation with Esau. It depicts Jacob's struggle as a source of his blessing and suggests by its play on the name Israel that the patriarch is in essence a man of strife. It accounts, then, for the shift in the patriarch's name from Jacob to Israel, a shift that is not carried out consistently in the redaction of following material. Its etiological character allows for the addition of two etiological endings, an explanation of the place-name Peniel and the dietary custom that prohibits eating the sinew on the hip. The hypothetical reconstruction of earlier forms suggests that from the earliest period the tradition concentrates on the divine blessing for the patriarch.

Bibliography

B. W. Anderson, "An Exposition of Genesis XXXII 22-32. The Traveller Unknown," *AusBR* 17 (1969) 21-26; R. Barthes, "The Struggle with the Angel: Textual Analysis of Genesis 32:23-33," in *Structural Analysis and Biblical Exegesis: Interpretational Essays* (tr. A. M. Johnson; PTMS 3; Pittsburgh: Pickwick, 1974) 21-33; W. Dommerhausen, "Gott Kämpft. Ein neuer Deutungsversuch zu Gen 32:23-33," *TTZ* 78 (1969) 321-34; K. Elliger, "Der Jakobskampf am Jabbok. Gen 32:23ff als hermeneutisches Problem," *ZTK* 48 (1951) 1-31; H.-J. Hermisson, "Jakobs Kampf am Jabbok (Gen 32:23-33)," *ZTK* 71 (1974) 239-61; J. E. Lewis, "Gen 32:23-33: Seeing a Hidden God," in SBLASP (ed. L. C. McGaughey; Missoula: Scholars Press, 1974) 34-56; F. van Trigt, "La signification de la lutte de Jacob près du Yabboq, Genèse xxxii 23-33," OTS 12 (1958) 280-309; H. C. White, "French Structuralism and OT Narrative Analysis: Roland Barthes," in *Semeia* 3: *Classical Hebrew Narrative* (ed. R. C. Culley; Missoula, Montana: Scholars Press, 1975) 99-127.

SHECHEM *HIEROS LOGOS*, 33:18-20

Structure

I. Itinerary	18
II. Description of sanctuary foundation	19-20
A. Business transaction	19
B. Construction of altar	20

This unit establishes its relationship to the context through an itinerary notation. There is no note of departure site. Rather, the verse opens with a designation of arrival in peace at Shechem. The clause defining the arrival site nonetheless exposes the opposition of the itinerary formula by setting Shechem, a city in Canaan, in opposition to Jacob's departure from Paddan-aram. The itinerary formula has thus been adapted for this particular context. The event at Shechem described here is a part of Jacob's flight from Laban. The flight does not necessarily presuppose the reunion with Esau, although it does not exclude that pericope. It presupposes, rather, Jacob's intention to return to his home—and his father (so, 31:30). The itinerary would also attach to 35:27, a framework that incorporates distinct traditions about the last days of the patriarchs with themes from the primary saga (→ Genesis 25–35). But it also suggests that for the overall structure of the saga this *hieros logos* stands in parallel with the *hieros logos* for Bethel (→ 28:10-22).

V. 18 is the itinerary. Vv. 19-20 contain no tale. They report an event that has two facets: (1) A business deal leads to Jacob's purchase of land. The land itself was defined by Jacob's itinerary station (cf. 28:10-22). (2) On the land he builds an altar. The altar then receives a name. The key verb is the characteristic verb from naming etiologies. Yet, no etiological formulas suggest that the naming occupies the center of the unit. No discovery of holiness in the land appears here. No wordplays emerge. The structure of the unit remains simply a narration of an event. Nevertheless, the structure marks a special theme with the report that Jacob built an altar. Does this point not assume some discovery of holiness in the place? Behind the narration may lie a more extensive tradition history. The definition of the land purchased by Jacob as land where he had pitched his tent may allude to some such tradition of Jacob spending the night and thus discovering the holiness at a particular place (→ 28:10-22). Indeed, the connection between Jacob and this holy place may represent the oldest point of attachment for the Jacob tradition, a location that would make possession of land a crucial element in the tradition (see Noth, *History,* 80-81). The tradition may reflect a memory of a connection between Shechem and a distinct patriarch named Israel (so, Seebass). The connection points also to a pilgrimage (35:1-7), attached originally to a tree sanctuary in Shechem (Noth, *History,* 80-81). As a complementary part of the structure in the whole saga, the unit now appears to be a part of the Yahwist (contrast Noth, *History,* 35).

Genre

As a narration of an event, the unit can be classified as REPORT, not (→) tale. The report has a particular tendency. It attests not simply to the origin of the name (cf. 32:2-3), but to the foundation of a cultic center (cf. 28:10-22). Characteristic is the report of construction of an altar (cf. 28:18). The genre may thus be more precisely defined as HIEROS LOGOS.

Setting

Hieros logos belongs to the cult, an account of the founding of the cult at a particular place.

Intention

Hieros logos describes the initial moment of cultic activity at a place as the moment that gives sanction to the subsequent cultic activity at the place. Shechem was a center for cultic events in Israel. Its origin as a center from which its cultic procedures draw authority is described.

As a part of the Yahwistic saga as a whole, this *hieros logos* stands in parallel with the Bethel *hieros logos,* 28:10-22, just as does the etiology for Mahanaim. In position, however, it balances the patriarchal blessing for Jacob in ch. 27. At this level, the intention of the pericope is not to account for the founding of a sanctuary at Shechem, but rather to account for Jacob's possession of land, an initial prerequisite for fulfillment of the blessing (→ 27:27-28).

232

Bibliography

C. A. Keller, "Über einige alttestamentliche Heiligtumslegenden," *ZAW* 67 (1955) 141-68; 68 (1956) 85-97; H. Seebass, *Der Erzvater Israel und die Einführung der Jahweverehrung in Kanaan* (BZAW 98; Berlin: Töpelmann, 1966).

RAPE OF SHECHEM, 34:1-31

Structure

The story in this unit is isolated from its context as far as its content is concerned. It shares at best a catchword contact on the basis of the role Shechem plays here and in both 33:18-20 and 35:1-7. Indeed, the contact is weak by virtue of Shechem's personification as hero of the story here, while in the context Shechem is a place-name. The context also reveals a concern to account for Israelite occupation of Shechemite territory ($\rightarrow$ 33:18-20). 34:1-31 may be understood as an allusion to Israelite occupation of Shechemite territory, the city of Shechem the hero. Yet, the story in the unit does not develop such a theme in any intrinsic way. Plunder leads to complication in the relationship between Israel and Shechem, not to occupation of the land. Thus, the story remains isolated in its context, with at best a common allusion to Shechem as a proper name. Would its position as a structural element in the Yahwistic saga about Isaac, a balance for the tale about a threat to the ancestress, provide sufficient weight to clarify the context?

The story unfolds a simple plot focused not on the rape of Dinah by Shechem, but on the rape of Shechem by the brothers of Dinah. The elements in the structure thus comprise an exposition, a complication, a denouement, and a conclusion. The exposition introduces the antagonists of the story: Dinah-Shechem, Hamor-Jacob, and the brothers of Dinah. Dinah and Jacob remain rather passive in the action of the story. Dinah is raped, and her future negotiated and committed in a scene of deceit with her filling no substantial role in developing the plot. Jacob waits for his sons to negotiate the problem and recedes behind their decision to barter deceitfully. Even his rebuke in v. 30 leads to the stronger response of Simeon and Levi in v. 31. The main figures in the story are thus the brothers, principally Simeon and Levi, and the opposition, Shechem with his father Hamor. The story does not display a tribal history accounting for the demise of Simeon and Levi, then. It shows these characters as primary contributors whose action is in some manner confirmed.

The exposition introduces not only the principal figures, but also the problem that brings them together. Shechem rapes Dinah but also loves her. The problem is thus how to convert the strained relationship into a permanent one. Shechem seeks one direction; Simeon and Levi establish its opposite (v. 7). Indeed, the exposition suggests the direction of the plot by citing a rule of the land: What Shechem did ought not be done (v. 7). In the exposition, Shechem is in the wrong, the sons of Jacob in the right.

The complication of the story unfolds from the exposition, not focused directly on the rape of Dinah, but rather setting out the manner of justice rendered against Shechem for his folly. The element appears as a dialogue, cast as business negotiation. Shechem will seek to make Dinah his wife, thus formalizing the relationship he established by force. His intentions constitute the subject of the negotiations of Shechem and his father Hamor with the brothers. Both Hamor and Shechem appear to negotiate in trust. The brothers, however, develop their end of the negotiations explicitly as deceit (v. 13). Their appeal is for circumcision among the men of Shechem, so that intermarriage may take place. The announced purpose of the connubium is to create one people (v. 16). Circumcision would make all the people a single unit, thus implying inclusion in the covenant of Abraham with Yahweh. It is remarkable, then, that the negotiation over such covenantal relationship is itself marked as deceit, not simply the outcome, but the intention of the negotiation from the start.

Vv. 18-24 develop the complication to its crisis. The Shechemites respond to the negotiations in trust. Shechem himself is the first to submit to the circumcision. Then on the basis of his own reputation with his people, both in deed (vv. 18-19a) and in character (v. 19b), the appeal is made to the people of the city, and the agreement is executed in apparent good faith. It is significant, nevertheless, that the appeal reveals an element of deceit in its own right (v. 23a). The commitment between the two negotiating parties rests on weak ground. Neither party has any basis for trust of the other.

The denouement falls with swift strokes. Vv. 25-26 report the attack by the brothers against the hapless men of Shechem. Vv. 27-29 note that the consequences of the attack must be understood in terms of the victor in the battle. The brothers win spoil from the opposition. The conclusion itself focuses on the saying propounded by the brothers as defense against Jacob's rebuke. Jacob observes that the deceit will make him and his family odious in the eyes of the Canaanites and the Perizzites. But that is hardly a rebuke, given the relationship traditionally cited as the order of the day (→ Deut 20:10-17). The sons' defense in v. 31 should be taken then as the structural goal, the principal element in the unit. It explains the action undertaken in contradiction to the agreement between the opposition parties.

In its present form the story belongs to the Yahwistic narrative, a balance for the threat to the ancestress in Genesis 26. Earlier forms of the tradition may have provided an explanation for the demise of Simeon and Levi as viable tribes in the organization of Israel.

Genre

The unit displays the SAYING, not only by making the saying the decisive piece of defense against the rebuke of the father, but also by the allusion to the saying in preparation for the deceit (so, v. 13). The unit thus has much in common with an APOPHTHEGM (→ 9:20-27). But it is more than a sayings narrative. Its plot structured over a span of tension suggests a TALE, designed to support the saying as a part of its denouement.

Setting

In J, the unit develops from a setting in the literary construction of the source. Strife in the pattern of relationship that defines Israel vis-à-vis its neighbors remains the hallmark of the literary construct. Behind the J construct is a tale derived from the family's store of tradition, a part of customary law in the tribal unit that becomes the basis for heroic storytelling.

Intention

In J, the story shows the relationship between Israel and neighbors under the stamp of strife. There is no concern for reconciliation. There is only the curse that brings death or slavery to Israel's opposition. It thus appears as a balancing element to the tale about a threat to the ancestress. The tale also preserves a saying that undergirds customary law.

Bibliography

R. E. Clements, "Baal-berith of Shechem," *JSS* 13 (1968) 21-32; M. Kessler, "Genesis 34—An Interpretation," *The Reformed Review* 19 (1965) 3-8; S. Lehming, "Zur Überlieferungsgeschichte von Gen 34," *ZAW* 70 (1958) 228-50; W. In der Smitten, "Genesis 34—Ausdruck der Volksmeinung," *BO* 30 (1973) 7-9; L. Wächter, "Die Bedeutung Sichems bei der Landnahme der Israeliten," *WZRostock* 17 (1968) 411-19.

BETHEL *HIEROS LOGOS* (J), 35:1-7

Structure

I. God's instructions	1
A. Pilgrimage	1a
B. Construction of altar	1b
II. Jacob's instructions	2-3
A. Preparation	2
B. Pilgrimage	3
1. For the event	3a
2. Construction of altar	3b
III. Instructions executed	4-7
A. Preparation	4
B. Pilgrimage	5-6
C. Construction of altar	7

This unit (J) presupposes a context associated with Shechem, but not an explicit context with the narration of a slaughter or of strained relationships in ch. 34. This point increases the impression of isolation for the tale in ch. 34. Moreover, if the context is simply Shechem narration, not the particular narration in ch. 34, then the point of contact for this unit would be 33:18-20, a *hieros logos* for the cultic center at Shechem. The point of connection between the two might be described as more than unity of locale or common genre. In some degree, 35:1-7 represents a continuation of the narrative present in 33:18-20.

The structure of the unit develops three distinct elements, each with at least two principal subunits that give content to the scope of the tradition. The first is a speech of God to Jacob, setting out instructions for (1) a pilgrimage from Shechem to Bethel, and (2) construction of an altar, i.e., a sanctuary in Bethel. The definition of holiness for the sanctuary presupposes a past theophany and, indeed, alludes specifically to 28:10-22. The allusion is not in itself essential to the development of the unit and cannot serve as evidence that the whole unit is dependent on 28:10-22. Nor does it suggest that this unit is a literary doublet of 28:10-22. The report about founding the sanctuary at Bethel here is distinct from its parallel precisely in the connection of the foundation with the pilgrimage, as well as its redactional position as a frame around the Jacob-Laban events. It can thus be defined as J.

The second element is Jacob's speech to his people, setting out the instructions of God for (1) preparation for a holy celebration by rejection of foreign gods (not explicitly, or even implicitly, an allusion to the teraphim stolen from Laban by Rachel), by purification such as abstinence from sexual relations, and by purification of garments, and (2) a pilgrimage to Bethel in order to construct an altar there. The altar construction is subordinated syntactically as a purpose clause to the pilgrimage itself, but the two items are nonetheless central for the instructions. Indeed, the purpose clause is perhaps better understood, as far as the content of the sentence is concerned, as the dominant factor.

The third element presents the execution of all three items, all in narration. (1) The people prepare for the holy occasion by rejecting foreign paraphernalia which Jacob buries under the oak near Shechem. The act is only part of the series anticipated in v. 2; yet, it functions clearly as purification. It represents not only rejection but also proper disposal of the foreign gods as the act of loyalty necessary for the new cultic event. (2) The pilgrimage is associated with a corresponding terror of the Canaanite cities that witnessed the event. This motif is a foreshadowing of the conquest (→ Josh 5:1) and reminds the audience of the connection between the Bethel *hieros logos* and the land promise (→ Gen 28:13). On the relationship between the land promise and Shechem-Bethel, see Noth, *History*, 80-81. (3) The results of the pilgrimage can be seen in the construction of an altar at Bethel. The altar is not subordinated to the pilgrimage. It stands as the final event in the series, the goal of the process. The naming emphasizes the event (33:20), a point that underwrites the goal of the unit in accounting for the altar in Bethel.

Tradition history can place this structure in a sacred pilgrimage from Shechem to Bethel (see Alt). If such a cultic event accounts for the origin and growth of the unit, it would support the thesis noted above that this unit stands close to the unit in 33:18-20. Indeed, it may be evidence of a shift in cultic order: Bethel replaces Shechem (→ 28:10-22). V. 7b shows the place to be holy and connects the unit to the parallel in 28:10-22 (see also v. 1)

Genre

Structurally, the unit is but a REPORT of an event. Yet, the event is particular, the construction of an altar as the result of a sacred pilgrimage. The generic quality can thus be specified as HIEROS LOGOS for the sanctuary at Bethel. *Hieros logos* also has an interest in naming (→ 33:20), but the unit is not etiology for the name (contrast 32:2-3).

Setting

In J, the unit parallels the introduction of Jacob in ch. 25 and thus has a literary setting in the total scope of the Yahwistic saga. *Hieros logos* belongs to the cultic institution which it justifies. The institution is centered in the altar (or sanctuary) at Bethel. It is also related to a pilgrimage from Shechem to Bethel, perhaps a sign that the sacred center for Israel shifted from Shechem to Bethel.

Intention

In J, the unit parallels the exposition in ch. 25 as an account of the beginning and ending of the struggle between Jacob and Esau. The event reports the foundation of the sanctuary in Bethel (→ 28:10-22). The foundation is associated with a pilgrimage from Shechem to Bethel. Perhaps in this association one can detect evidence of cultic power passing from one center to the other (see Alt). Also here is an allusion to possession of the land as a fulfillment of the land promise.

Bibliography

A. Alt, "Die Wallfahrt von Sichem nach Bethel," in *In piam memoriam Alexander von Bulmerincq. Abhandlungen der Herder-Gesellschaft und des Herder-Instituts* (Riga: Plates,

1938) 218-30; O. Keel, "Das Vergraben der 'fremden Götter' in Genesis 4b," *VT* 23 (1973) 305-36; C. A. Keller, "Zwei umstrittene Stellen aus dem überlieferungskreis um Schechem," *ZAW* 73 (1961) 78-87; R. Tamisier, "L'itineraire spirituel de Jacob," *BTS* 47 (1962) 4-5.

DEBORAH DEATH REPORT, 35:8

Structure

I. Report	8a
A. Death	8aα
B. Burial	8aβ
II. Place-name	8b

This little unit connects with the context on the basis of a catchword organization. The context concerns Bethel. The burial site at the center of this tradition is Bethel. Yet, beyond catchword organization, the unit has no contact with its context. In the redaction of the patriarchal narratives as a whole, it may be taken as an introduction to the section of narratives dealing with death and burial of patriarchal figures and their associates. The following unit (P) interrupts that organization with a parallel to the Bethel tradition in 28:10-22 and 35:1-7. But the theme of death and burial or succession returns in 35:16 (J). It should be noted, however, that this unit has more contact with an Isaac narrative than with Jacob. Deborah has played no role in the narrative frame. There is no connection between her death and the pilgrimage from Shechem to Bethel described in 35:1-7. Rather, one has the impression that with this verse J shifts the organization of the Jacob tradition from the narrative inclusion to the narratives about the last days and death of the patriarch and his family (→ 35:16-20).

The unit itself comprises a report of Deborah's death and burial at a particular site in Bethel, as well as an account of the place-name (→ 50:1-14). It may be that behind this death report a more extensive narrative tradition reported the importance of this nurse for the family of Isaac and Jacob. Why was she present in Bethel with Jacob rather than in Mamre with Isaac (→ 35:27-29)? Perhaps the association with Rachel is simply a secondary element in the history, designed to bring the allusion into the Jacob stories (see Noth, *History,* 85-86). If this death report does hide a more extensive narrative tradition, however, its shape and content cannot be determined now.

Stereotyped expressions here include the formulaic sentence reporting the naming of the place, v. 8b.

Genre

The unit is a death REPORT.

Setting

Death reports belong to the traditional lore of a family.

Intention

The unit reports the death of a member of Jacob's (Isaac's) family. That the nurse was Rebekah's attendant, yet apparently present at Bethel with Jacob rather than with Isaac at Mamre, warrants no comment from the text.

BETHEL *HIEROS LOGOS* (P), 35:9-15

Structure

I. Theophany report	9-12
A. Description of the appearance	9
B. Name change speech	10abα
C. Results	10bβ
D. Self-revelation speech	11-12
1. Self-revelation formula	11aα
2. Admonition	11aβ
3. Promise	11aβb-12
a. Posterity	11aβb
b. Land	12
II. Construction of sanctuary	13-15
A. Description of departure	13
B. Construction	14
1. Pillar	14a
2. Dedication	14b
C. Naming	15

This unit breaks the context established by v. 8, the death and burial of members in the patriarch's family, in order to return to an account of the foundation of the sanctuary at Bethel. It is thus a doublet of 28:10-22 (not 35:1-7). This point is confirmed by style, as well as by the disruption of the new context, and argues for definition of the unit as a part of the priestly narrative.

The unit comprises two principal elements. The first reports a theophany, although v. 9 does not explicitly show the holiness of the place (cf. v. 13). But the theophany also associates the sanctuary with the promise for posterity and land, a consistent element within the Bethel tradition (see de Pury). The promise speech appears as an extension of a self-revelation formula defining the God of the promise as El Shaddai ($\rightarrow$ 17:1-2). The process is defined in v. 9 as blessing. The definition of the locale as holy thus lays claim to a larger tradition of promise and blessing cast in a fashion typical for P.

The oracle in vv. 11-12 is connected to another speech of God in v. 10. At this point, the Jacob-Israel name change occurs (cf. 17:5). There is no interpretation of the new name (contrast 32:28). Rather, the name change is fully a part of the covenant, promise tradition for P ($\rightarrow$ 17:1-8). The theophany in vv. 9-12 serves, then, to extend the traditions about the covenant associated with Abraham to Jacob.

The second element in the unit assumes the theophany as a demonstration of holiness in the place. V. 13 attaches the theophany explicitly to "the place where he had spoken with him." The consequence of the demonstration of holiness in the place can be described in two points: (1) Jacob constructed a pillar and then dedicated it. (2) A designation of the name of the holy place opens the door to continuity in the authority of the place as a sanctuary in the cult of Israel.

Tradition history can be followed by reference to the J parallels in 28:10-22 and 35:1-7. Stereotyped formulas and expressions include a self-revelation formula in v. 11aα, constructed with the first-person pronoun "I" (*'ănî*) plus the proper

noun, and a naming formula in v. 15, featuring the typical verb "called the name
. . ." (*wayyiqrā'* . . . *'et-šēm*) and the proper name (cf. v. 10).

Genre
The unit is a HIEROS LOGOS.

Setting
The unit has a setting in the literature of P. Its earlier stages share points in
common with the genre. *Hieros logos* belongs to the cult which draws its legitimation from the patterns of its structure (→ 28:10-22).

Intention
In P, the unit attaches the promises and blessings in the covenant with Abraham
to Jacob and shows in the process the relationship between Jacob as a patriarch
of the promise and Bethel. *Hieros logos* should normally show the foundation of
a sanctuary at a site of past theophany. In this text, the foundation is also con-
ditioned by the promise and blessing to Jacob.

Bibliography
→ 28:10-22.

RACHEL DEATH REPORT, 35:16-20

Structure

I. Itinerary	16a
II. Birth report	16b-18
A. Crisis	16b
B. Announcement of birth	17
C. Name	18
1. Mother	18a
2. Father	18b
III. Death report	19-20
A. Death event	19a
B. Burial	19b-20
1. Location	19b
2. Marker	20
a. Construction	20a
b. Formula	20b

The report in these verses does not appear as a continuation of the preceding
narrative. The narrative context, for example, gives no indication that Rachel is
pregnant. No explicit structural element establishes this unit as a sequel to
29:31–30:24. There Rachel's desire for a child consumes her life. Here her delivery represents her death. And there is no connection drawn by the tradition.
The two units are distinct traditio-historically.

The report is given context by the itinerary in v. 16a, a formula adapted to
the purpose of the unit. The first part of an itinerary formula can be recognized
in v. 16aα: "They departed from Bethel" (→ Numbers 33). The second part,

240

however, does not note arrival at a site, but rather an approach to a site. In fact, it is just that adaptation that opens the report unit. But the context is secondary to the content of the unit. Structure and genre are self-contained, a part of the collection of traditions introduced by 35:8 concerning the death of the patriarch or his household.

The unit itself comprises two elements, a birth report in vv. 16b-18 that functions as context for the death report in vv. 19-20. The focus of the unit thus falls on the death report. The first element opens in v. 16b with a report of crisis: Rachel enters a difficult labor. The birth report itself is contained in the midwife's speech, an announcement of the birth of a son (not simply an annunciation of coming birth). The admonition against fear is set in the context of Rachel's complaint over the pain of her birth and her imminent death. It thus corresponds to the priestly oracle of salvation, given here however not by a priest, nor in a cultic process. It is but a means for comfort. Moreover, the oracle precedes the naming of the child. First the mother, then the father attach names to the child. The first derives from the unit's context. Rachel dies, and in the process she gives her son an ominous name, the mark of her death. The second name remains the traditional name for the son, a factor that points to the distinction between this name and the naming events in chs. 29–30, where the mothers' names stick.

Vv. 19-20 constitute the formal death report with an account of Rachel's death and burial. The burial element is somewhat expanded with a name for the place and an account of a pillar at the grave. The name, Ephrath, is explained by a gloss that equates Ephrath with Bethlehem. But the equation is doubtlessly secondary (von Rad, *Genesis,* 340), though a significant secondary insertion. Perhaps it alludes to a site in Bethlehem that was considered holy (so, the pillar [*maṣṣēbâ*]). If the pillar marks the site as holy, a place for worship, however, the point is not explicit. The pillar now functions simply as a marker for the tomb. V. 20b designates the pillar as a site of importance; the final formula, "which is there to this day," gives the definition the authority of the narrator. But its importance lies in its role as marker for Rachel's tomb.

The unit is a part of the Yahwist's final collection of items about the death and burial of patriarchal figures and associates. Stereotyped expressions include the elements of an itinerary formula in v. 16, marking departure from a site with the key verb "journeyed" (*wayyis'û*), and the naming formula, v. 18, with its typical verb "name" or "call the name" (*wattiqrā' šĕmô*).

Genre
The unit uses a birth REPORT as cause of death for a death REPORT.

Setting
In J, the unit is one of the small pieces of tradition that constitute the final section of narration about the patriarch and his family. As birth-death report, it represents the tradition of the family.

Intention
The unit accounts for the death and burial of Rachel in a common human experience, thereby denying sacred significance to the pillar of her tomb. In the process, the unit also reports the birth of the last son among the twelve.

Bibliography

D. Daube, "The Night of Death," *HTR* 61 (1968) 629-32; J. Muilenburg, "The Birth of Benjamin," *JBL* 75 (1956) 194-201; J. A. Soggin, "Die Geburt Benjamins, Genesis 35:16-20 (21)" *VT* 11 (1961) 432-40.

REBELLION REPORT, 35:21-22a

Structure

I. Itinerary	21
II. Report	22a
A. Event	
B. Report to Jacob	

The itinerary in v. 21 does not name the point of departure for this station segment, although the typical verb for the first part of the formula appears here (→ Numbers 33). The second segment of the itinerary appears quite in order. It is significant that the name of the subject is here Israel rather than Jacob (cf. v. 20). The shift in name may reflect some adjustment in the tradition in the light of Gen 32:28 and 35:10. If so, this is the first adjustment in the narrative to attempt such a change (contrast the consistent redaction following the change in the name Abram to Abraham). Would it not be more probable that the name in the itinerary derives from the report that follows?

The report itself comprises two events: (1) Reuben's violation of his father's concubine, and (2) the report to Israel. No plot unfolds here. No conclusion is drawn from the report of Reuben's rebellion. The unit as it stands is simply a report.

One can imagine, nonetheless, that a more complex tradition lies behind the unit. When an oldest son violates his father's concubine, particularly when the event is in some manner public knowledge, he stakes his claim to the authority of the father's leadership (→ 2 Sam 3:7; 16:21). Would such a rebellion not reflect Reuben's demise in the structure of Israel's tribal confederacy even though tradition held him in the position of the eldest son (cf. v. 23)? Would the place of the report in traditions about death and burial for the patriarch not point in the same direction? The unit unfortunately gives no direction for such a reconstruction. Its structure is simply that of a report.

The report derives from the traditions of the Yahwist. Stereotyped expressions include the typical elements of the itinerary formulas in v. 21.

Genre

The unit is simply a REPORT. As a brief report from the experiences of the patriarch Israel, the report may be more precisely defined as an ANECDOTE.

Setting

The unit derives from the lore of the family.

Intention

In the present form, the unit simply reports an event in Israel's household. No judgment is drawn; no consequence is stated. Its position as a part of J's traditions about Israel's last days suggests that the report has something to do with succession in the patriarchal family. But precisely what it accomplishes is not stated. The unit intends now simply to report (see Fokkelman, 235).

Bibliography

S. Gevirtz, "The Reprimand of Reuben," *JNES* 30 (1971) 87-98.

NAME LIST: SONS OF JACOB, 35:22b-26

Structure

I. Introduction		22b
II. Name list		23-26a
A. Sons of Leah		23
1. Reuben		
2. Simeon		
3. Levi		
4. Judah		
5. Issachar		
6. Zebulun		
B. Sons of Rachel		24
1. Joseph		
2. Benjamin		
C. Sons of Bilhah		25
1. Dan		
2. Naphtali		
D. Sons of Zilpah		26a
1. Gad		
2. Asher		
III. Conclusion		26b

This unit is totally isolated in its context. No itinerary formula binds it to its surroundings. No apparent logic calls for a list of the sons of Jacob at just this point, unless it should be to show that Reuben, the subject of vv. 21-22a, is properly ordered as the firstborn in the series. The group of twelve is not in itself the subject of traditions in the context, and no tradition explicitly attacks the order or stability of the series or the organization represented by the series. Its function in this position is implicit by virtue of the themes implied in vv. 21-22a (see the comments on the priestly source below).

The unit is framed by a clear introduction and a stereotyped formula for a conclusion. The introduction designates the number of items constituting the following list and thus ties the unit more directly to organizational pieces (→ 46:27; Exod 1:5). Num 13:2 does not define the total number of entries in the list, but it implies the number by calling for one man from each of the items in the following list. The definition of number is not necessarily an introduction, however. It might also appear as a conclusion (→ 46:27). The stereotyped formula at the conclusion can function as a traditional introduction (→ 46:8; but see also Num 13:16). It begins characteristically with a demonstrative pronoun, "these" ('*ēlleh*), and a definition of the items in the list: "All the sons of Jacob who were born to him in Paddan-aram." (Cf. 46:8: "These are the names of the sons of Israel who came into Egypt. . . .")

The list itself is traditional, the order of the sons of Jacob. Some variations in the list can be documented, although standing patterns of structure clearly control major elements. The sons of Leah appear regularly in the first position. Indeed, in the history of the list the order of the six sons is relatively constant, altered only by the eventual demise of Levi (→ Num 13:1-16), and possibly reflects the organization of an early six-tribe league (see Noth, *System*). The position of the last two sons in the list is less stable than the first four (cf. Num 13:1-16). In this list, the Rachel tribes follow the Leah tribes (cf. also Exod 1:1-17), with the sons of the concubines ordered after the sons of the primary wives. They may, however, appear at almost any junction in the list after the Leah entry (in Numbers 13 after the first four Leah entries). The concubine tribes appear at any position following the Leah series and in any order. The inner structure is normally Dan-Naphtali and Gad-Asher, although in Numbers 13 even this factor falls away. The stability of the list in the course of its tradition history derives thus from the Leah series, with the other sons in some manner related to it. In this list, the presence of Levi in the Leah list and the cohesion of the four groups suggest a relatively early point in the tradition history.

It may be, nonetheless, that the list is now preserved in P, the fulfillment of the promise to Jacob in 35:11-12 (so, von Rad, *Genesis*, 342). No form-critical evidence supports this conclusion (see, however, the stylistic evidence such as the place-name Paddan-aram; cf. 35:9).

Genre

The unit is a name LIST. It is to be distinguished from (→) genealogy in that its structure does not depend on the development of a family history. It is simply a list that arranges entries in a particular order. The list is related traditio-historically to genealogy. It embraces the same tradition that appears, e.g., in Exodus 6 as genealogy. But structure and intention are distinct (→ Gen 46:8-27; Exod 1:1-7; Num 13:2-16).

Setting

The name list derives from the literary interests of P to show fulfillment of the promise in 35:11-12. As an older tradition, the list derives from the institutional needs to show organization in a group defined by the scope of the list.

Intention

The list organizes the items included in the scope of its structure. As a part of P, the organization shows how God fulfilled his promise in 35:11-12. As an older tradition, the list shows the political structure of the tribes that make up the Israelite confederacy. Indeed, the order of the Leah tribes may intend to describe the organization of an earlier six-unit confederacy.

Bibliography

M. Noth, *Das System der zwölf Stämme Israels* (Stuttgart: Kohlhammer, 1930).

ISAAC DEATH REPORT, 35:27-29

Structure

I. Itinerary	27
II. Death report	28-29
A. Summary formula	28
B. Death notice	29a
C. Burial notice	29b

V. 27 sets the context for this unit within the framework of the itinerary structure. Indeed, this entry in the itinerary, without notation of departure site, marks the goal of the series. Jacob leaves Laban in order to go to his home (30:25) and to his father (31:30). Now he arrives at Mamre or Kiriath-arba (Hebron), where Isaac was. The site is the traditional home for Abraham and Isaac, according to this entry. The itinerary thus assumes the union of all three patriarchal figures and represents a late stage in the history of the patriarchal traditions.

The death report itself comprises three typical elements. (1) V. 28 is a summary formula of the patriarch's life, the total number of years he lived (→ 9:29). (2) V. 29a is the report of the death itself. Typical formulation for the death report is: "He was gathered to his people, old and full of days" (cf. 25:8). Typical vocabulary for the report appears in the verbs "breathe his last" (*gw'*), "die" (*mwt*), and "be gathered" (*'sp* [Niphal]). (3) V. 29b notes the burial, curiously combining the traditional foes as the agents for the burial (but see 50:13-14). The tradition of the unit thus has no trace of the conflict or the promise that dominates the narrative elements in the patriarchal sagas.

One might then ask if the unit should properly be interpreted as a fragment of a distinct Isaac tradition (→ 25:19-26). Would the unit not mark the conclusion to the scope of an Isaac narrative that began at least in 25:19-26? This interpretation must remain a plausible hypothesis. If the unit does derive from an original Isaac saga, the saga has not extended its own structure into the present form of the tradition (→ The Isaac Saga). The final form of the text preserves the lines of the Isaac saga, but the tradition seems to be dominated by the power of the Jacob tradition. As this unit now stands, however, it may be taken as a kernel for death-burial traditions associated with Isaac (→ 35:8). Indeed, the death of Rachel with the birth of Benjamin (→ 35:16-21) need not contradict this hypothesis since the "last days" theme involves members of the patriarch's larger family (→ 24:1-67).

Genre

The unit is a death REPORT.

Setting

In J, the unit belongs to that literary collection of traditions associated with the last days of the patriarch. As a tradition about the patriarch, the report belongs to family or tribal treasures.

Intention

The unit reports the death and burial of Isaac in the context of several distinct units about death and burial of patriarchal figures. As a part of family tradition, the unit attests to the death of a family patriarch and his burial in the traditional family plot.

ESAU BIRTH REPORTS, 36:1-5

Structure

I. Introduction	1
II. Marriage report	2-3
A. Introduction	2a
B. List of wives	2b-3
1. Adah	2bα
2. Oholibamah	2bβ
3. Basemath	3
III. Birth reports	4-5
A. Lists of births	4-5a
1. By Adah	4a
2. By Basemath	4b
3. By Oholibamah	5a
B. Conclusion	5b

V. 1 gives this unit its proper context in a collection of traditions about the last days of Isaac (→ 25:12-18, 19-26). Part of the concern for the collection is to demonstrate the line of succession from the patriarchal office. The *toledoth* formula here thus parallels the *toledoth* formula in 37:2 in the same manner that the *toledoth* formula in 25:12-18 parallels the formula in 25:19-26. Indeed, in both cases the older but less important son precedes the younger son whose generation represents the proper succession.

The *toledoth* formula introduces the descendants of Esau (note the definition of Esau as Edom in v. 1b, a gloss that nevertheless represents a common motif in traditions about Esau; → 25:29-34). The body of the unit does not develop explicitly as a genealogy, however. Rather, the elements forming the unit orient around the theme of marriage and birth.

Vv. 2-3 thus report the marriages of Esau, first with a general statement of Esau's marriages among the Canaanites (→ 26:34–28:9 [P]), then with a simple list of the Canaanite wives. The list defines each wife by reference to father and people. The three wives are Hittite, Hivite, and Ishmaelite; yet, all three carry a general qualification as Canaanite (→ 28:1). One might ask also whether the order represents a hierarchy in the harem. Such a possibility is not probable, however. This point is suggested first within the confines of this unit. The birth reports in vv. 4-5a reverse the order of the second two wives. One might deduce from the consistency of order represented by the position of the first wife that her descendant would stand as a strong factor within the structure of Esau's descendants (→ Sons of Leah, 35:23). The birth report itself comprises a list of sons borne by each wife. Adah and Basemath have only one son. The last wife carries a list of three. But again no value judgment is established by the list. It is simply a representation of the productivity of the wives.

The point about hierarchy among the wives of Esau is also suggested by comparing the name list with the names of the wives noted in 26:34–28:9. There

246

Esau also has three Canaanite wives, two Hittites and a daughter of Ishmael. But only one name—Basemath—corresponds with names in this list. Moreover, the familial identification for that name is quite contrary to the data in this list. Here Basemath is the daughter of Ishmael. There she is the daughter of Elon the Hittite. Here Adah is the daughter of Elon the Hittite. The absence of a consistent pattern in the name list militates against conclusions about hierarchy in the harem.

The list is concluded in v. 5b by a stereotyped formula ($\rightarrow$ 46:8). This definition of the list pinpoints the unit primarily as a birth report ($\rightarrow$ 46:26-27). The unit derives from P. Whether older Esau tradition lies behind the report, either involving the wives and the birth of the sons ($\rightarrow$ 29:31–30:24) or developing priority in a league of Esau descendants, cannot be determined with certainty.

Genre

The unit builds on structural patterns provided by name LISTS. But the lists are qualified as marriage REPORT and birth REPORT. Moreover, for this unit the marriage report supports the birth report. The unit itself can thus be classified as a birth REPORT. As a birth report, the unit should be distinguished from ($\rightarrow$) genealogy ($\rightarrow$ 35:9-14). The concern here is not to trace the lineage through successive or segmented generations, but to account for the births in the first generation. The point of comparison would thus be 29:31–30:24.

Setting

In P, the unit shows the line of succession from Isaac. Esau was also fruitful, but in contrast to the Jacob succession, Esau does not carry the patriarchal succession forward. The tradition itself shows the process of a shift in setting. It doubtlessly still reflects the life of the family, but it is moving toward the larger familial institution, anticipating the interests of national political structure ($\rightarrow$ 25:12-18).

Intention

For P, the birth report records the succession of Isaac through Esau, and it does so without narrative development. There is no negative judgment on this branch of Isaac's family, just as 25:12-18 implies no negative judgment. Rather, there is simply the report that the family in Canaan developed through births of sons to Esau.

REPORT OF ESAU'S MOVE, 36:6-8

Structure

I. Esau's move	6-7
A. Description of his company	6a
B. Description of the event	6b-7
1. The move	6b
2. The reason	7
II. Conclusion	8
A. Site	8a
B. Gloss	8b

This unit (P), focused on Esau and ordered within a collection of Esau tradition, fails to develop the structure of a plot, although the substance for a plot obviously appears. Esau took all his possessions and family members out of Canaan, away from Jacob because he had too much for the land to support both him and his brother (→ 13:1-18). Vv. 6-7 thus duplicate 32:4–33:17 (J) by accounting for the permanent division between the brothers. This element is confirmed by the conclusion in v. 8a, marking the permanent residence for Esau as Seir. The gloss in v. 8b duplicates the gloss in 35:1 (→ 25:29-34). The point is that the brothers are divided: Esau is in Seir; Jacob remains in Canaan. It is significant, then, that for P the one who initiates the division, contrary to the J counterpart, is Esau (→ 27:46–28:9).

The unit belongs in the traditio-historical context represented by the strife between the brothers (→ 26:34–33:17). It develops its distinctive contribution to that tradition by shifting the cause for the division from Jacob to Esau.

Genre
The unit is a REPORT, developed as an ANECDOTE. It describes simply the move from Canaan to Seir that constitutes the division between the brothers.

Setting
In P, the unit is an episode in the story about Isaac and his family. As a traditional piece, the episode derives from the family narratives that comprise the patriarchal theme under the general rubric of strife without reconciliation.

Intention
For P, the unit depicts the consequences of Esau's contentious relationship with his family, already introduced in 27:46–28:9. The intention of the traditional episode is to account for the permanent division between the brothers.

ESAU GENEALOGY, 36:9-14

Structure

I. Introduction	9
II. First generation	10
A. Introduction	10a
B. List	10b
1. Son of Adah, Eliphaz	
2. Son of Basemath, Reuel	
III. Second generation	11-13
A. Sons of Eliphaz, son of Adah	11-12
1. Introduction	11a
2. List	11b-12a
a. Primary sons	11b
b. Son of concubine	12a
3. Conclusion	12b
B. Sons of Reuel, son of Basemath	13
1. Introduction	13aα
2. Name list	13aβ

This unit duplicates the structure and tradition of 35:1-5, adding to it a development of Esau's family into the second generation. Thus, as an introduction, v. 9a is again the *toledoth* formula, and again the formula connects Esau and Edom (cf. 35:1). In this case, however, the connection does not appear as a gloss added to explicate the name by reference to a more commonly known figure. In 35:1, the name is qualified by reference to familial relationships: Esau is the father of Edom. V. 9b then makes the connection to the region of Seir, and the tradition contacts for Esau are complete.

Elements II and IV comprise the first generation of Esau's sons, broken apart in order to insert element III, the second generation developed from only two of Esau's wives. The unit has nothing to do with Esau's selection of wives. It simply assumes the family structure and concentrates on developing the lineage, marking the series in segments of the generations. The position of the wives here corresponds nevertheless to the series named in vv. 1-5. Adah appears first. The second two wives alter the order noted in vv. 2-3 but follow the order of vv. 4-5. Moreover, the names of the sons in the first generation, vv. 10, 14, correspond exactly with the names in vv. 1-5. The new element in the unit, highlighted by a loss of focus on the wives, is the development of the list to the second generation.

Each entry comprises a stereotyped introduction, a name list, and a conclusion. The introductory formula shifts, however, when the structure moves from the first to the second generation. In the first generation, the formula is introduced by a demonstrative pronoun, "these" ('*ēlleh*), and develops in nominal sentence structure (v. 10) or inversion (v. 14). The second generation, v. 11, breaks the pattern with normal narrative style, the sentence introduced by a 3rd m. plur. imperfect of the verb "be" (*hāyâ*). The second stage of the second generation returns nevertheless to the formula beginning with '*ēlleh* and constructed in inversion.

Conclusions in the unit do not appear regularly (vv. 12b, 13b), and when they do appear, they are apparently simply repetitions of the stereotyped introductory formula, constructed as nominal (v. 12b) or inverted (v. 13b) sentences.

The lists themselves may comprise traditions about tribal leagues. Thus, Eliphaz, a son of Esau, has six sons (including Amalek the son of a concubine; → vv. 15-16). The other two entries show four and three together and constitute no clear, functional number. Yet, they recall the births of Bilhah, Zilpah, and Rachel, each with two sons, and suggest that numbers may vary according to the patterns of distinct leagues (→ vv. 17-18).

The unit appears as an extension of the tradition in vv. 1-5. This unit would thus be a part of P's demonstration of Esau's family succession following Isaac's death.

Genre

The unit is related to vv. 1-5 but no longer shows the limited perspective of a birth (→) report. It is thus properly GENEALOGY, segmented into stages for the generations.

Setting

The genealogy still shows the interests of familial tradition. The move toward political constitution is nevertheless apparent simply in the ordering of sons (→ 22:20-24).

Intention

The genealogy sets out the succession in familial lineage from the house of Isaac. It shows the pattern of Esau's line, but it does not develop that line with narrative tradition. Rather, it breaks off the tradition in order to prepare for the succession represented by Jacob.

Bibliography

R. R. Wilson, *Genealogy and History in the Biblical World* (New Haven: Yale University Press, 1977).

ESAU NAME LIST, 36:15-19

Structure

I. Introduction	15a
II. Second generation	15b-17
A. Sons of Eliphaz	15b-16
1. Introduction	15bα
2. Name list	15bβ-16a
3. Conclusion	16b
a. Chiefs of Eliphaz	16bα
b. Sons of Adah	16bβ
B. Sons of Reuel	17
1. Introduction	17aα
2. Name list	17aβ
3. Conclusion	17b
a. Chiefs of Reuel	17bα
b. Sons of Basemath	17bβ
III. First generation: sons of Oholibamah	18
A. Introduction	18aα
B. Name list	18aβ
C. Conclusion: chiefs of Oholibamah	18b
IV. Conclusion	19
A. Sons	19a
B. Chiefs	19b

This name list belongs to the collection of traditions about Esau, 36:1-43. It is distinguished from the preceding unit not only by the stereotyped formula for introducing a list in v. 15a, "These [*'ēlleh*] are. . . ," but also by the introduction of a key term in the definition of the list: "These are the *chiefs* [*'allûpê*] of the sons of Esau." The list thus moves farther away from the structural characteristics of genealogy to the characteristics of political organization. Moreover, the introduction to the unit must be distinguished from the introductory formula in v. 15bα, a nominal sentence without the typical demonstrative. The second introduction stands at the head of a particular name list and thus marks the beginning of one segment in the total unit. It is significant for a definition of structure in the unit that this introductory element defines the segment of the list here not as a first generation, the sons of Esau (v. 15a), but as a second generation, the sons of Eliphaz, who was the son of Esau.

The list itself comprises seven names, including Amalek, each name qualified by the title "chief" (*'allûp*). It thus fails to correspond to the six-member list in vv. 11-12, a fact that breaks the pattern of a six-tribe structure one might expect from such political lists. The name unique to this list is Korah. One might conclude that Korah has fallen out of the list in vv. 11-12, thus the need to insert Amalek as a special entry, the son of a concubine. Or one might assume that Korah is an example of dittography in the history of the list, introduced here from the name list in v. 18aβ. The problem cannot be resolved on formal grounds, however. One might just as well argue for an original seven-member list which would balance the seven chiefs in vv. 17-18. The conclusion in v. 16b is composed of two parts, a designation of the list as the chiefs of Eliphaz and associated with the land of Edom, thus a duplication of the introduction, and a designation of the list as the sons of Adah, a wife of Esau. The one conclusion reflects a political structure, the other more closely attached to the genealogical interests of familial structure. V. 17 builds on the same pattern. An introductory formula follows the more common structure, a nominal sentence with the demonstrative pronoun "these" (*'ēlleh*). The subject of the formula is again a second generation, "the sons of Reuel." Following the formula, the list qualifies each entry by the title "chief." The list itself has only four entries. The concluding formula, v. 17b, follows the pattern of the conclusion from the first element: V. 17bα, introduced with the demonstrative, functions as a conclusion to the political list, and associates the list with Edom. V. 17bβ then concludes the list with the sons of Basemath, a wife of Esau, and the ties of the unit to a tradition set within the family structure emerge.

The third element, v. 18, is markedly different in structure from the first two. It is not a second-generation list, the grandsons of Esau, but a first-generation list, the sons of Oholibamah, a wife of Esau. The introductory formula recognizes this shift in content. Yet, in form the same pattern appears. The introductory formula precedes a list of three names, each qualified by the title "chief" (*'allûp*), and the conclusion rounds off the element. But the double style of the conclusion apparent in the first two lists fails to appear here, perhaps because it is not necessary to relate the list to familial structures.

The conclusion reveals the same double edge apparent in the body of the unit. Two formulas appear, each introduced with a demonstrative "these" (*'ēlleh*) and each constructed as a nominal sentence. The first orients toward the familial interests of the unit: "These are the sons of Esau." The second draws on the political structures represented by the list: "These are their chiefs." The final element is the gloss that frequently accompanies the Esau lists: "He is Edom" (→ 35:31-39).

The structure of the list shows the tendency of the tradition to shift away from genealogical patterns to patterns qualified by the term *'allûp* ("chiefs"). The origin of the tradition has not been clearly defined, although the unit itself can be attributed to P or a supplement to P.

251

Genre

The unit is a name LIST. It reflects a particular pattern of organization. It is thus not simply a list, but a system for organizing the tradition contained by the list. It is not a (→) genealogy, although some relationship with genealogy can be assumed. Indeed, a shift from genealogy to organizational name list can clearly be seen here.

Setting

In P, the list represents tradition that demonstrates priestly redactional interests. The list itself derives from the institutional concerns for tribal organization. Such a setting reveals a shift from the familial interests in genealogy to the national interests in leadership organization.

Intention

In P, the list shows the development of Esau's descendants as one branch of the sons of Isaac. The list itself organizes those descendants according to leadership groups. The organizational system still reflects the concerns of structure in the family, but it suggests that the intention shifts from familial grounding to the interests of national political organization.

SEIR GENEALOGY, 36:20-30

Structure

I. First generation	20-21
A. Introduction	20a
B. Name list	20b-21a
C. Conclusion	21b
II. Second generation	22-28
A. Sons of Lotan	22
1. Introduction	22aα
2. Name list	22aβ
3. Sister	22b
B. Sons of Shobal	23
1. Introduction	23aα
2. Name list	23aβb
C. Sons of Zibeon	24
1. Introduction	24aα
2. Name list	24aβ
3. Gloss on Anah	24b
D. Sons of Anah	25
1. Introduction	25aα
2. Name list	25aβb
E. Sons of Disbon	26
1. Introduction	26a
2. Name list	26b
F. Sons of Ezer	27
1. Introduction	27a
2. Name list	27b

This unit derives its context from the traditional association between Seir and Esau. The association is not developed, however, by explicit references to Esau. At most, the Seir clan is placed in the land of Edom, just as Esau's clan was (v. 21; cf. vv. 16, 17, or the glosses in vv. 1, 8, 19).

The unit itself follows structural patterns typical for the entire chapter. Its three major elements list the first generation of Seir twice (vv. 20-21, 29-30) as a frame around the second generation (vv. 22-28; → 36:9-14). This kind of structure employs segments of distinct generations as typical structural elements.

The first-generation lists have three elements: (1) an introduction, (2) a name list, and (3) a conclusion. The introductions are constructed in the same form, each a nominal sentence introduced by the demonstrative "these" (*'ēlleh*). V. 20 defines the list as the sons of Seir who dwell in the land. One may suspect that the definition might have included the name of the land, as it does at other points where "the land" functions to qualify items in the list (v. 21). It is nonetheless clear that the introduction in v. 20 places emphasis on familial ties: "These are the sons of Seir." The introduction in v. 29, however, shifts the pattern to the office of leadership: "These are the chiefs [*'allûpê*] of the Horites" (→ 36:15-19).

The lists are formally identical. The conclusions, however, offer additional data for the tradition's history. Both employ the stereotyped formula for lists, the nominal sentence introduced by the demonstrative. Both define the list by reference to the office of leadership: "These are the chiefs of the Horites. . . ." The first formula combines that designation with the more familial "sons of Seir" (cf. v. 20, the introduction) and places the list "in the land of Edom." The second duplicates reference to the office in an abstract plural: "according to their leadership clans" (*lĕ'allupêhem*), and places the list in the land of Seir. For this unit, there is an equation between the land of Edom and the land of Seir, and the equation brings the unit into contact with the Esau tradition, also placed in the land of Edom.

The second-generation list follows the structure dictated by the order of names in the first-generation list. Each name thus has its own entry. Each entry has at least two elements, an introduction and a name list. Vv. 22b and 24b also contain glosses on the entry, v. 22b by noting the name, not of a daughter, but of a sister of the father in the entry. V. 24b explains who one son in the entry is in order to distinguish him from the father in the next entry. Otherwise, each of the seven entries is identical in form to all other members in the series. The introduction is the common form, with one exception. A nominal sentence introduced by a demonstrative names the content of the list: "These are the sons of Shobal" (*wĕ'ēlleh bĕnê šôbāl*). The exception in v. 22 is a verbal sentence with the subject properly identified: "The sons of Lotan were . . ." (*wayyihyû bĕnê lôṭān*).

Traditio-historical background for this list is difficult to reconstruct beyond general comments about association with Esau as an indication of succession from Isaac. Perhaps the unit is to be associated with P, at least as a supplement to P's structure (see Noth, *History*). Further penetration of the tradition is not now possible.

Genre

The unit appears closer to GENEALOGY ($\rightarrow$ 36:9-14) than to political organizational ($\rightarrow$) lists ($\rightarrow$ 36:15-19). The framing element in vv. 29-30 suggests, however, that the genre (and thus the tradition) is moving in the direction of such organizing systems.

Setting

For P, the unit demonstrates the literary redaction interests represented by the construction of the final form of the text. The unit itself may still reflect the interests of familial tradition, although a shift in setting from the narrower concerns of family to the broader concerns of tribal political organization appears to be exerting its influence.

Intention

For P, the unit constitutes one in a series of traditional elements, designed to show what Esau's future, or the future of his associates, was. The list itself develops the familial heritage from Seir the Horite through the second generation. The unit reveals a shift in intention, however, from its genealogical patterns to the patterns of organizational systems. The new intention focuses on organizational units.

Bibliography

J. R. Bartlett, "The Land of Seir and the Brotherhood of Edom," *JTS* 20 (1969) 1-20; R. R. Wilson, *Genealogy and History in the Biblical World* (New Haven: Yale University Press, 1977).

EDOMITE KING LIST, 36:31-39

Structure

I. Introduction	31
II. List	32-39
A. Bela	32-33a
1. Enthronement	32
a. Event	
b. Identification	
1) Father	
2) City	
2. Death	33a
B. Jobab	33b-34a
1. Succession to the throne	33b
a. Event	
b. Identification	
1) Father	
2) Place-name	

    2. Death   34a
 C. Husham   34b-35a
    1. Succession to the throne   34b
      a. Event
      b. Identification: land
    2. Death   35a
 D. Hadad   35b-36a
    1. Succession to the throne   35b
      a. Event
      b. Identification
        1) Father
        2) Military record
        3) City
    2. Death   36a
 E. Samlah   36b-37a
    1. Succession to the throne   36b
      a. Event
      b. Identification: land
    2. Death   37a
 F. Shaul   37b-38a
    1. Succession to the throne   37b
      a. Event
      b. Identification: land
    2. Death   38a
 G. Baal-hanan   38b-39a
    1. Succession to the throne   38b
      a. Event
      b. Identification: father
    2. Death   39a
 H. Hadar   39b
    1. Succession to the throne
    2. Identification
      a. City
      b. Wife

Examination of the context for this unit uncovers a degree of isolation. The unit has a common point with the preceding units: the land of Edom. But beyond the catchword, at best a broad interest in the traditions associated with the land, there is no connection between this list and the surrounding material.

The unit has a stereotypical formula for an introduction. A nominal sentence beginning with the demonstrative "these" (*'ēlleh*) defines the subject of the list: "These are the kings who ruled in the land of Edom before a king ruled the sons of Israel."

The list itself is defined by the succession of eight kings. But the kings do not succeed each other as a series in a genealogy; there is no dynasty here. Rather, each king appears to be deposed by his successor. Each entry thus merits certain data to identify the subject. But the structure itself is a uniform list.

The tradition history of the list is difficult to reconstruct. The unit belongs, perhaps, to P or a secondary supplement of P.

Genre
The unit is a king LIST.

Setting
The unit reflects the interests of political structures, the monarchy of Edom.

Intention
For P, the unit provides additional material for detailing Esau's history in Edom. The goal is achieved, however, only by virtue of the common place-name. No reference to Esau ties the king list to the Esau tradition.

The list organizes the history of Edom by reference to the succession of kings who ruled the territory. It is possible, however, that the list contains independent Edomite kings, some ruling at the same time as others (see de Vaux, 517).

Bibliography
J. R. Bartlett, "The Edomite King-list of Genesis XXXVI 31-39 and I Chron I 43-50," *JTS* 16 (1965) 301-14, R. de Vaux, *The Early History of Israel* (tr. D. Smith; Philadelphia: Fortress, 1978).

ESAU NAME LIST, 36:40-43

Structure

I. Introduction	40a
II. Name list	40b-43a
III. Conclusion	43b

This unit gains its contact with the context by virtue of the reference in v. 40a to Esau. It provides data about Esau's future (→ 36:1-5, 6-8, 9-14, 15-19). It does not, however, develop substantial contact with the traditions embraced by the context.

The introduction, v. 40a, is the stereotype commonly expected for lists. A nominal sentence beginning with a demonstrative "these" (*'ēlleh*) defines the following list as the names of the chiefs (*'allûpê*) of Esau according to their families, their dwelling places, their names (→ 36:30). Each entry in the list is then qualified by the title "chief" (*'allûp*). The conclusion then duplicates the introduction with a nominal sentence beginning with a demonstrative and a qualification of the list as "chiefs of Edom according to their dwelling places in the land of their possession." One should note here also the gloss that identifies Esau and Edom (cf. vv. 1, 8, 19).

The tradition embraced by the list shows no clear connection with preceding name lists. Some of the names from preceding units appear here also. But the patterns of appearance do not permit a tradition history. Indeed, one name, Oholibamah, is here a chief among the sons of Esau, while in the context (vv. 2, 5), she is a wife of Esau. It would appear, then, that the list is a creation *ad hoc*.

The unit can be associated only provisionally with P.

Genre

The unit is simply a name LIST.

Setting

For P, or the supplement to P, the unit demonstrates the redactional setting that draws various items of tradition together under a common catchword. Behind P, the unit derives from the organizational interests of political structure (→ 36:15-19, 31-39).

Intention

For P, the unit appears among other traditional items to demonstrate the organization of Esau's descendants as a segment of the succession to Isaac. As an organizational list, the unit establishes the system of leadership (→ 36:30).

CHAPTER 9
THE JACOB SAGA

BIBLIOGRAPHY

G. W. Coats, "Redactional Unity in Genesis 37–50," *JBL* 93 (1974) 15-21.

THE JACOB SAGA AS A WHOLE, 37:1– 50:26

Structure

I. The Joseph story	37:1-36
A. Exposition	1-4
B. Complication	5-36
II. The Judah-Tamar story	38:1-30
III. The continuation of the Joseph story	39:1–47:27
A. Digression	39:1–41:57
B. Complication	42:1-38
C. Denouement	43:1–45:28
D. Conclusion	46:1–47:27
IV. Jacob's death report: a redactional framework	47:28–50:14
V. Recapitulation of the Joseph story denouement	50:15-21
VI. Joseph's death report	50:22-26

The redactional framework in Genesis 37–50 contrasts sharply with the patriarchal traditions in Genesis 12–36. No series of independent tales, this composition adopts the Joseph story (I and III) as a central structural trunk, then hangs an independent (II) and two dependent but distinct (IV, VI) narrations onto its framework. Moreover, one of those narrations (IV) is structured into the Joseph story by means of an inclusion (V). Despite the obvious distinctions in all categories, the collection of traditions in this composition cannot be divorced completely from the patriarchal theme (→ Genesis 12–50). It concludes the patriarchal traditions with a narration of a deathbed scene for the last principal patriarch, as well as one for his son Joseph. Both anchor firmly in the promise to the patriarchs for great progeny and possession of a great land (→ Gen 35:9-15; Josh 24:32). Moreover, the collection opens the door for the exodus theme, with its exposition developed around Egyptian oppression against the Israelites by a pharaoh who did not know Joseph (see Exod 1:1-14).

The point of unity in this composition derives from a common subject— Jacob and his sons. The Joseph story provides a useful point of structural cohesion for this motif since its subject is not simply Joseph, but Joseph and his brothers.

Indeed, within the scope of the Joseph story itself, the interplay between Joseph and his brothers consistently holds Jacob, the father, as a foil. Structure in the collection thus grows out of structure in the Joseph story, with the remaining elements dependent on the Joseph plot. Thus, the exposition in 37:1-4 belongs primarily to the Joseph story; yet, the opening sentence defines one principal as Jacob and thus serves the larger collection of traditions as well. Moreover, the expression in v. 2a, a *toledoth* formula for Jacob, functions obscurely in the exposition of the Joseph story and should be defined as a part of an inclusion framework in connection with 47:28–50:14 (→ 37:1-4).

At the crucial point of transition between the complication and a retardation in the plot's movement produced by the digression, the narration breaks, and a distinct story about Judah and Tamar is inserted. The Judah-Tamar story, secured in its position by recapitulation of a transition sentence (37:36 and 39:1), develops none of the narration motifs from the Joseph story, although it fits into the unity of the overall collection as a story about one of Jacob's sons. (For details about the points of unity with the Joseph story, → Genesis 38.) For the collection as a whole, the Judah-Tamar story functions as an intensification of the digression.

A similar interpolation can be seen at the end of the collection. 47:28–50:14 (IV) is in itself a composition of traditions centered on Jacob's deathbed scene and used as a redactional framework for distinct units of tradition. Cast as a continuation of the traditions about Jacob and his sons in Egypt, this narration was bound into the Joseph story by recapitulation of the Joseph story denouement (V). The deathbed narration completes the composition focused on Jacob and his sons, giving the collection as a whole a last-days-of-Jacob stamp. The final element (VI), a narration of Joseph's last days, along with his last testament to his successors, imitates the structure and intention of the Jacob deathbed scene. Thus, Jacob and his sons complete their course.

The latest stage in the growth of this collection exhibits secondary elements. Some can be attributed to P or a priestly redactor: 37:2a; 46:8-27b; 48:3-7; 50:22-26. In addition, comments like 41:45-46a, 50-52, and the specification of Joseph's age in 37:2a might be attributed to a priestly redaction. But in none of these cases does a complete, self-contained priestly tradition about Jacob and his sons appear. The priestly elements are relatively well integrated into the structure of the framework and do not suggest earlier stages of the unit as a redactional framework. They suggest, rather, that the latest stage appears as a redactional framework constructed from a collection of diverse traditions.

Genre

This unit is a redactional composition and thus resists a single genre definition. It appears as an expansion of the Joseph story, itself a (→) novella, but the expansion is not a novella. The expansion broke the generic identity of the Joseph story into a collection of several genres. On the genre of the distinct units, see the individual units below. The composition follows the fundamental pattern of the patriarchal sagas, however. It features tradition about the patriarch plus some account of his last days. It might be identified therefore as a Jacob SAGA.

Setting

The collection of traditions in Genesis 37–50 reflects a writing process, a redaction of diverse tradition units under a common theme (→ 25:19–50:26).

Intention

As a redactional framework, Genesis 37–50 provides necessary unity for including diverse traditions about the last days of Jacob in the overall narration about the patriarchs. The collection thus intends to close the large segment of Jacob traditions. In addition, it opens the door for the exodus traditions by accounting for the shift from Jacob in Canaan to Israel in Egypt. The unit thus functions as a bridge between the patriarchal traditions (Genesis 12–50) and the exodus traditions (Exodus 1–12 [13:1-16]).

CHAPTER 10
The Individual Units

BIBLIOGRAPHY

G. W. Coats, *From Canaan to Egypt: Structural and Theological Context for the Joseph Story* (CBQMS 4; Washington: Catholic Biblical Association, 1975); idem, "The Joseph Story and Wisdom: a Reappraisal," *CBQ* 35 (1973) 285-97; J. L. Crenshaw, "Method in Determining Wisdom Influence Upon 'Historical' Literature," *JBL* 88 (1969) 129-42; H. Donner, *Die literarische Gestalt der alttestamentlichen Josephsgeschichte* (Heidelberg: Winter, 1976); H. Gressmann, "Ursprung und Entwicklung der Joseph-Sage," in *EU-CHARISTĒRION. Studien zur Religion und Literatur des Alten und Neuen Testaments* (FRLANT 36; Göttingen: Vandenhoeck und Ruprecht, 1964); idem, "Die Komposition der Joseph-Geschichten," *ZDMG* 77 (1922) 55-71; W. Lee Humphreys, "The Motif of the Wise Courtier in the Old Testament" (Diss., Union [N.Y.], 1970); O. Kaiser, "Stammesgeschichtliche Hintergründe der Josephsgeschichte," *VT* 10 (1960) 1-15; R. Kessler, "Die Querverweisse im Pentateuch. Überlieferungsgeschichtliche Untersuchung der expliziten Querverbindungen innerhalb des vorpriestlichen Pentateuchs" (Diss., Heidelberg, 1972); B. O. Long, *The Problem of Etiological Narrative in the Old Testament* (BZAW 108; Berlin: Töpelmann, 1968); H. G. May, "The Evolution of the Joseph Story," *AJSL* 47 (1930/31) 83-93; idem, "Die Geschichte des Sinuhe und die alttestamentliche Diasporanovelle," *WZGreifswald* 20 (1971) 277-81; A. Meinhold, "Die Gattung der Josephsgeschichte und des Esterbuches: Diasporanovelle I," *ZAW* 87 (1975) 306-24; M. Noth, *A History of Pentateuchal Traditions* (tr. B. W. Anderson; Englewood Cliffs: Prentice-Hall, 1971); G. von Rad, *Die Josephsgeschichte* (BibS[N] 5; Neukirchen: Neukirchener Verlag, 1964); idem, "The Joseph Narrative and Ancient Wisdom," in *The Problem of the Hexateuch and Other Essays* (tr. E. W. Trueman Dicken; London: Boyd, 1966) 292-300; idem, *Genesis, a Commentary* (tr. J. Marks; rev. ed.; OTL; Philadelphia: Westminster, 1972); D. B. Redford, *A Study of the Biblical Story of Joseph (Genesis 37–50)* (VTSup 20; Leiden: Brill, 1970); W. Richter, "Traum und Traumdeutung im AT," *BZ* 7 (1963) 202-20; H. Schulte, *Die Entstehung der Geschichtsschreibung im Alten Israel* (BZAW 128; Berlin: Walter deGruyter, 1972); H. Seebass, *Geschichtliche Zeit und theonome Tradition in der Joseph-Erzählung* (Gerd Mohn: Gütersloher Verlagshaus, 1978); D. A. Seybold, "Paradox and Symmetry in the Joseph Narrative," in *Literary Interpretations of Biblical Narratives* (ed. K. R. R. Gros Louis, J. S. Ackermann, Th. S. Warshaw; Nashville: Abingdon, 1974) 59-73; C. Westermann, "Die Joseph-Erzählung," in *Calwer Predigthilfen 5* (Stuttgart: Calwer, 1970) 45-118.

THE JOSEPH STORY, 37:1-36; 39:1 – 47:27

Structure

I. Exposition: introduction of principals   37:1-4

    The Joseph story has been structured into a larger collection of tradition about Jacob and his sons by means of a redactional framework (→ Genesis 37–50). The story itself comprises six major structural elements. The span of tension holding these elements together as a single unit develops two contrasting themes. The first runs from an initial breach in family relationships, apparent in the exposition, developed to a peak in the narration of crisis (II), and broadened by a reversal of roles in a repetition of the crisis (IV), to a reconciliation of the family members, established in the plot's denouement and carried to its conclusion in the final element. The second magnifies the alienation-reconciliation theme with a closely related point of tension, focused on Joseph's use of power. The power theme opens in the exposition, heightens by a challenge to Joseph's power in the narration of crisis, and develops as the major subject of the digression. The theme is also substantial in the reversal of roles depicted by the repetition of the crisis (IV) and, in fact, functions as a means for effecting the reconciliation of the family in the final elements.

    Both the breach in family relationships and the development of Joseph's power facilitate a structural dialectic. The opening and closing sentences of the Joseph story define the dialectic as an interaction between Jacob in Canaan and Israel in Egypt (see Coats, *From Canaan*). These poles provide not only unity in the story's plot, but contact with a larger context of pentateuchal traditions. In Egypt, Jacob the patriarch becomes Israel the people, subject to the pharaoh's power administered by Joseph (cf. 45:3-13; 47:27b). It is thus significant that the exodus theme begins with an emphasis on Egyptian oppression by a pharaoh who did not know Joseph (→ Exod 1:1-14).

    From 37:1 to 47:27, with the exception of ch. 38, the Joseph story is basically a unit, composed in a single narration. Some secondary elements can be seen, such as the theophany report in 46:1-4, the name list in 46:8-27, the data about Joseph's wife and family in 41:45-46a, 50-52, the *toledoth* formula in 37:2a. These additions reflect a priestly redaction of the Joseph story, set in the larger context of pentateuchal traditions. Moreover, some additions such as the Midianite parallel to the Ishmaelite figures in ch. 37 may reflect an Elohistic expansion (see Coats, *From Canaan*). Beyond these points, no clear evidence for successive literary editions of the Joseph story (against Redford) or for multiple literary sources (against von Rad, *Josephsgeschichte*) can be detected. Repetitions do appear in the structure of the story (cf. 45:3 and 4-13), but the repetitions belong to the story's stylistic repertoire and do not serve source distinctions or value judgments on successive editions (so, Coats, *From Canaan*). In addition to repetition, the unitary style of the story features symmetry in structure, plot retardation, wordplays, irony, and embellishments (see Seybold, 59-73). Divested of its priestly redaction and an occasional Elohistic commentary, the story appears to be from one source, preserved now in J (cf. the emphasis on blessing for the pharaoh connected with Jacob's arrival in Egypt in 47:7, 10 as a point of contact with J in 12:1-3).

It is difficult to reconstruct a kernel of earlier tradition out of all the structural elements in the Joseph story. If the present story grew from an earlier one about Joseph and his brothers (so, Schulte, 24-28), that story has been transformed completely, and efforts to reconstruct the earlier stages seem hopelessly hypothetical. The uniformity in structure preserved by the present text suggests the creation of a single hand rather than various stages of production in oral transmission. Moreover, the firmest conclusions about traditio-historical background for the Joseph story point to sources available to the author rather than earlier stages of growth. The digression in element III (Genesis 39–41) may derive from an earlier tradition (cf. Gunkel, "Komposition," 62-66; Humphreys, 208-16). If this element were a kernel story, however, it would not represent an earlier edition of the Joseph story. Rather, it would be a distinct story incorporated into the Joseph narration to account for Joseph's rise to power in Egypt.

Genre

The Joseph story is a NOVELLA (so, Gunkel, *Genesis,* 397). Like a (→) tale, it narrates a plot from a point of crisis to its conclusion. The plot focuses on an event or a series of events constructed in sequence. The sequence is dictated, however, not by a cause-effect relationship among the events in the sequence, but by the artistic design of the plot moving to a dramatic resolution of tension. The perspective of the story is centered on the real world. The events described occur at a specific point in time, at a specific place. To be sure, the point in time is not dated. Yet, the events are not generalized, as if they might belong equally well in any point of time. To the contrary, they occurred during the reign of *the* pharaoh who faced seven years of famine, preceded by seven years of fertility.

The plot line in the Joseph novella develops its narration in a series of scenes, structured as distinct movements toward the resolution of the story's basic crisis. Each scene unfolds with a limited number of principals and a specific arrangement of events. And each scene is dependent on its context, with perhaps the single exception of the digression. Taken as a whole, then, the intricate series of scenes constitutes the unity of action in the whole, a unity which combines a large cast of actors in a step-by-step display of relationships. Moreover, this novella interweaves several subplots in a fashion consistent with the genre. These include, among others, Joseph's rise to power, the brothers' deception as a way of life, and a mysterious fate controlling both the brothers and the father (see also Ruth, Jonah).

If the digression is defined as a germinal story adapted as a central narration to describe Joseph's rise to power in Egypt, it may be classified as LEGEND (so, Coats, "Joseph Story," 288-91). A series of three scenes serves a single line of development. None of the scenes is complete in itself. Each supports the climax of the whole in the last scene. The succession of events occurs within a specific, although undated, time, in a specific place. In each case, the narration focuses not on events, but on the central figure as an ideal who exemplifies particular characteristics.

265

Setting

A novella must be seen as the work of an artist, not the product of oral tradition. The artist can employ older material, but his work is essentially the product of his careful construction. At its latest stage, the Joseph story is a part of a larger redactional collection. As a single story, it has been preserved by J and thus fits into J's theological and structural scheme. But it has a distinct character of its own, as the product of an artist whose work J incorporated for structural and theological bridging. As a masterpiece, it would thus appear to be the creative product of a single hand.

But the setting can be more specific. The artist has roots in Israel's theological traditions and constructs his work as a theological link between two major themes of those traditions. Yet, he does not depend heavily on stereotyped formulas established within Israel's oral traditions. To the contrary, he stands removed from commitments to specific formulations. This kind of enlightenment would come into the scope of Israel's experience at a relatively late point, perhaps the product of the royal court. If the digression stands as a distinct element, it may also belong to the royal court. Moreover, its distinctive character points to a context within royal wisdom tradition, the product of reflection about characteristics for a wise administrator of power (von Rad, "Joseph Narrative").

Intention

Three points can be identified: (1) The Joseph story functions as a bridge, theologically and structurally, between the patriarchs and the exodus (Noth, *History*, 208-18). The story's dialectic between Jacob in Canaan and Israel in Egypt serves this function. (2) The plot develops around a family crisis. By interaction between an impetuous Joseph and treacherous brothers, the family breaks apart. The novella then displays a process of reconciliation for the broken family. Indeed, just here is the reconciliation of the patriarchal family cast by the entire theme of patriarchal traditions under the pale of strife and broken intimacy. But the point of the story is that reconciliation does not occur because of merit in any single member of the family. Rather, the reconciliation constitutes a genuine peripeteia, the result of commitment from all members of the family toward a common future. (3) The digression presents a wise administrator as a man whose characteristics can edify future generations. Execution of responsibilities in the office shows wisdom and discretion and orients the office toward the benefit of the people whom the administrator serves, not simply his own constituents, but all the people of the world. The Joseph story at large picks up this theme, but with a negative twist. Joseph in element IV and the first part of element V represents the opposite of a wise and discreet administrator. With the peripeteia, his use of power changes for the benefit of the family and preservation of life in the family for the sake of future generations.

I. EXPOSITION, 37:1-4

Structure

A. Statement of location	1
B. Introduction of principal characters	2-4
1. Introductory formula	2aα

2. Definition of characters   2aβ-4
  a. Joseph   2aβb
    1) Biographical data   2aβ
    2) Crisis   2b
  b. Israel   3
    1) Relationship with Joseph 3a
    2) Crisis   3b
  c. Brothers   4
    1) Response to the father 4aα
    2) Crisis   4aβb

The first element in the exposition for the Joseph story designates the location for the opening events: "Jacob dwelt in the land of his fathers' sojournings, in the land of Canaan." This sentence contrasts exactly with the last statement of the Joseph story (Gen 47:27): "Israel dwelt in the land of Egypt, in the land of Goshen." Thus, the scope of the Joseph story, as suggested by the opening and closing verses, lies in a shift of location from Jacob in Canaan to Israel in Egypt.

In the second element, a *toledoth* formula places the Joseph narration into a larger collection of Jacob traditions (→ Genesis 37–50). Then the following verses set out the dramatis personae for the narration. In a sentence constructed in nominal order, v. 2aα (following the *toledoth* formula) lists important biographical data about Joseph. V. 2b then suggests the crisis: Joseph brought bad tales about his brothers to his father. Israel is the second principal to appear. V. 3a, also constructed in nominal order, notes only one biographical datum, the father's relationship with Joseph vis-à-vis his other sons. V. 3b, like v. 2b, suggests the crisis of the story. Israel made a special coat for Joseph, a visible sign of his preferential love. Finally, the brothers react (v. 4). They were, in fact, introduced in subordination to Joseph in v. 2aβ. Thus, no additional biographical data about them are now necessary. The only goal of this element is to specify their relationship to the father and his favored son: "When his brothers saw that their father loved him more than his brothers, they hated him. And they were not able to speak to him in peace [*lĕšālōm*]."

The exposition shows at least two stages of development. It exposes the characters for the coming narration and thus relates integrally to the Joseph story. The *toledoth* formula corresponds, moreover, with the conclusion in 47:28–50:14, especially the formula in 47:28, as part of an inclusion (see McEvenue, 36-41). It thus reflects a stage of development when the Joseph story was incorporated into a larger context of traditions about Jacob and his sons. The *toledoth* formula is not an element of the larger *Toledoth* Book (see the unit on P, above), but an imitation of the priestly formulas (so, Noth, *History*, 18 n. 53).

Genre

These verses qualify in all respects as an exposition for a larger story. An exposition commonly employs nominal sentence order as a stylistic device (Richter, *Die sogenannten*, 30-31). The statement of location in v. 1 has parallels in 4:16; 13:18; 19:30; 20:1; 21:20, 21; 22:19; 26:6, 17; 36:8; 50:22; et al., each showing the statement as a part of a transition of exposition. The *toledoth* formula in v. 2 can introduce a (→) genealogy, but it can also be used simply as an introduction to a (→) story (2:4; 6:9; 25:19). In this text, it is simply an introduction for a larger collection of traditions about Jacob and his family. Its position in the exposition does not alter the identity of the unit as a specific genre element. Even as an expanded unit, these verses retain their character as exposition.

Setting

An exposition has no setting apart from the story it introduces. The expanded exposition points to a change in setting from the literary context of the Joseph story to the redaction context of Genesis 37–50.

Intention

An exposition provides the information necessary for narrating a story. Here it exposes the principal characters of the story by specifying their relationships and the place and circumstances for playing out those relationships. In addition, it suggests the scope of the story's plot. (1) The opening sentence, functioning in parallel with 47:27, shows that the story intends to justify the shift from Jacob in Canaan to Israel in Egypt (see Coats, *From Canaan*). (2) Joseph's preferred position with his father, symbolized by the coat of authority, suggests his power. The power position is highlighted in the dreams of the next element. (3) The closing sentence, functioning in contrast with Gen 45:15, points to a controlling arc of tension ranging from a breach in family relationships to an eventual reconciliation among all members.

As an exposition expanded to include a larger scope of traditions about Jacob and his family, the unit constitutes part of a framework for a major segment of material about Jacob.

Bibliography

S. McEvenue, *The Narrative Style of the Priestly Writer* (AnBib 50; Rome: Biblical Institute Press, 1971); W. Richter, *Die sogenannten vorprophetischen Berufungsberichte. Eine Literaturwissenschaftliche Studie zu 1 Sam 9:1-10, 16, Ex 3f. und Ri 6:11b-17* (FRLANT 102; Göttingen: Vandenhoeck und Ruprecht, 1970).

II. COMPLICATION, 37:5-36

Structure

A. Dream report		5-11
1. First dream		5-8
a. Introduction		5
b. Dream speech		6-7
c. Response: brothers to Joseph		8a
d. Narration of consequences		8b
2. Second dream		9-11
a. Introduction		9a
b. Dream speech		9b
c. Response: father to Joseph		10
d. Narration of consequences		11
B. Development of the crisis		12-33
1. Joseph and Jacob		12-14a

The first major unit of narration in the Joseph story contains three basic structural elements. The first opens the narration with two dream reports. The first one, vv. 5-8, employs four elements of structure: a general introduction, a dream speech, a speech in response to the dream, and a final narration of the consequences arising from the dream report. The general formula of introduction is constructed with the verb "dream" (*ḥlm*), joined with a noun from the same root (*ḥălôm*). This introduction should be understood as a third-person narration parallel to the first-person call to attention in vv. 6 and 9b. The call to attention, moreover, is constructed typically with the verb *ḥlm*. The dream report continues in vv. 6-7 with a speech from Joseph to his brothers detailing the dream, thus specifying the general note in v. 5aα. The speech uses the particle *hinnēh* ("behold"), a typical element in reporting dreams. The unit concludes with a speech from the brothers, two rhetorical questions, and a narration describing the brothers' response, a specification of v. 5b. This dream foreshadows the plot development in Genesis 42.

The second dream report is constructed in parallel with the first. It opens with a narrated introduction, v. 9a, constructed like v. 5a with a general statement that Joseph dreamed a dream (cf. the verb and noun from *ḥlm*) and reported it to his brothers (cf. the particle *hinnēh*). The dream speech itself, v. 9b, details the dream with a call to attention and a description of the dream's content. The dream report ends in v. 10, like v. 8, with two rhetorical questions (from the father rather than the brothers) and a narration describing the brothers' response, v. 11. This dream foreshadows the denouement in Genesis 43–45 and demonstrates the use of symmetry as a basic element of structuring.

Since the dreams foreshadow major elements in the total scope of the story, they might legitimately stand as part of the exposition. Yet, they represent a distinct movement vis-à-vis the content of vv. 1-4. Even though they foreshadow other parts of the story, they relate structurally to the following verses.

In the second element of the unit, the tension between Joseph and his brothers, apparent in the dream reports, develops into the major crisis of the entire Joseph story: Joseph's dreams and his insensitive narration of his superior role in them motivate the brothers' treachery. Structure in this element builds on a series of dialogues, marked off by narrated interludes as well as explicit notations of change in physical location. In the first dialogue series, Jacob commissions Joseph for an errand to the brothers. The word *šĕlôm* ("welfare") in v. 14 echoes the same word in v. 4 with an ironic twist: Joseph must check on the *šĕlôm* of the brothers who could not speak to him in *šĕlôm*. Moreover, characteristic vocabulary for commission appears here: "Go, that I may send you to them" (*lĕkâ wĕ'ešlāḥăkā 'ălêhem*). "Go, see . . ." (*lek-nā' rĕ'ēh*). It is significant that, contrary to a common pattern in commission dialogues (cf. Gen 43:3; Exod 3:11), Joseph offers no objection to the commission.

V. 14b changes the location of the scene, with the dialogue series in vv. 15-17a introduced by a brief exposition, v. 15a. The dialogue itself is constructed as an exchange of questions, designed to elicit information. This facet of the scene does not duplicate the following one. To the contrary, it functions intrinsically in the scene as a retardation in the pace of action. V. 17b again changes the location. In the subsequent exchange of speeches, the brothers plot Joseph's death. Two speeches from Reuben, back to back, suggest a composite structure of the dialogue, however, The first one, v. 21, reflects Reuben's role in the conspiracy. The second, v. 22, breaks the pattern by setting out details for an alternative plot: Reuben removes himself from the plan to kill Joseph. And a parenthetical note in v. 22b explains that Reuben really intends to deliver Joseph from the plot.

Vv. 23-24 change the location again in that Joseph arrives and Reuben's alternative plot is carried out. An exposition in v. 25 sets the stage for development of a new plan. When Ishmaelite merchants happen by, Judah recommends selling Joseph for a profit (v. 26). With the execution of the new plot, vv. 27b-28, Joseph's disposition for the principal scope of the story is set. He will be taken *to Egypt* as a slave, and the gravity of the act dislocates the family. Not only has the family been broken by treachery, with a member removed from the circle, but also the removal is the result of a serious violation: Men have sold a brother (cf. Exod 21:16). Finally, the location changes again. A dialogue between sons and father, vv. 32aβ-33, calls for a legal recognition of the prepared evidence, the coat of Joseph's preferential position which the brothers had dipped in a goat's blood. The irony is completed when the coat Jacob presented to Joseph as a sign of his love leads him to affirm, legally, the loss of his beloved (see Daube for the character of the move as a narrative element formed under influence of legal process).

The conclusion in vv. 34-35 is cast as a dirge. The father considers Joseph dead. The only alleviation for the despair, a privilege for the audience but not for Jacob and the brothers, lies in the implication of the scene that Joseph, now in the hands of the Ishmaelite caravan, would not die there. The transition note in v. 35 makes the point explicit. Joseph was sold to an Egyptian and thus maintains the prospect for fulfilling his dreams. The plot of the Joseph story thus exposes the prospect for reconciliation in a divided family (so, Westermann). But it also involves a movement, first of Joseph, and then of other members in the family, from Canaan to Egypt.

The narration in 37:5-36 is basically a unit, not to be divided into two parallel literary sources or even two widely separated editions of the same scene. The dreams heighten the tension introduced in the exposition of the story in vv. 1-4. Moreover, Joseph's privileged life at home while the brothers are away with the sheep does not deny the exposition note about his profession as a shepherd. On the contrary, it too heightens the distinction between the antagonists, not a distinction between parallel sources. The double speech by Reuben derives from a stylistic convention for emphasis at crucial turning points of the story. Even the Midianite-Ishmaelite parallel does not necessarily deny the integrity of the chapter. The variation between the transition in 37:36 and the point of reference in 39:1 suggests that the parallel is a traditio-historical problem. The note functions as a primary part of the story in 39:1, with the parallel in 37:36 identified as a secondary duplication designed to secure the position of ch. 38 in the final form of the text. Moreover, the Midianite-Ishmaelite parallel in v. 28 can be understood as a gloss, with the Midianite motif introduced in order to alleviate the shame involved in casting Judah as the man who suggested selling his brother into slavery, and the brothers as the men who accomplished the deed (see Coats, *From Canaan*). That gloss may reflect the concerns of an Elohistic commentary, but it does not derive from a second, parallel narration of the scene.

Genre

In a story, the complication element expands the basis of tension established by the exposition into the principal focus of the plot. It thus provides a key to the unity of the entire story. This element in the Joseph story clearly fulfills that function and qualifies as the complication of plot.

The dream REPORTS show stereotyped structure patterns, typical of dream narration (cf. Genesis 40; Judges 7; Daniel 8; 10). The stereotyped pattern appears especially in the dream speeches, with a CALL TO ATTENTION featuring verbs and nouns from ḥlm ("dream"), and the detail of the dream punctuated by the particle hinnēh ("behold") (see Richter). The dialogue in vv. 13-14a is stamped with the characteristics of COMMISSION SPEECHES. The one in vv. 32-33 has patterns drawn from legal procedures. Finally, the speech in v. 35 (cf. also v. 30) is a DIRGE (see 2 Sam 19:1 [*RSV* 18:33]).

Setting

This element has no setting apart from the Joseph story as a whole.

Intention

The unit develops the major crisis of the Joseph story. The tension between the brothers and Joseph shifts into overt violence. Joseph is removed from the family circle, but he is not dead. The plot cannot reach its climax until the disrupted family is reconciled and the brothers' deception removed. The alienation-reconciliation scope of the plot also suggests that the Joseph story centers on the shift, first of Joseph, then of other members of the family, from Canaan to Egypt (→ Genesis 37, 39–47). The dream reports serve as the foundation for the crisis, the immediate motivation for the brothers' violence. But they also have a larger role in the scope of the story. The first dream foreshadows the humble submission of the brothers to Joseph in ch. 42, while the second anticipates Jacob's move from Canaan to Egypt under the protective care of Joseph in 43:1–47:27. The dreams thus suggest that the crisis of the Joseph story cannot be separated from Joseph's rise to power (chs. 39–41). And that position of power as foreshadowed in the dreams undergirds a basic intention in the story to describe how Jacob and his family moved from Canaan to Egypt.

Bibliography

D. Daube, "Law in the Narratives," in *Studies in Biblical Law* (New York: KTAV, 1969) 1-74.

THE JUDAH-TAMAR NOVELLA, 38:1-30

Structure

I. Exposition		1-6
A. Judah		1-5
1. Statement of location		1
2. Marriage and birth of sons		2-5
B. Tamar		6
II. Complication		7-11
A. Narration of Er's death		7
B. Speech: Judah's instructions for levirate		8
C. Narration of Onan's death		9-10
D. Speech: instructions for the widow		11
III. Digression		12-23
A. Statement of change in location		12-14
1. Judah		12
2. Tamar		13-14
a. Speech: report of Judah's move		13
b. Narration of Tamar's plot		14
B. Business negotiations		15-18a
1. Speech: Judah's request for business relationship		15-16a
2. Speech: Tamar's request for price specification		16b
3. Speech: Judah's offer		17a
4. Speech: Tamar's counter-request		17b
5. Speech: Judah's call for clarification		18aα

6. Speech: Tamar's specification of price   18aβ
C. Narration of business transaction   18b-19
D. Conclusion for the digression   20-23
    1. Narration of efforts to redeem pledge   20
    2. Dialogue: friend and men of the place   21
    3. Dialogue: friend and Judah   22-23
IV. Denouement   24-26
   A. Statement of change in time   24aα
   B. Legal process   24aβb-26a
    1. Speech: Report of Tamar's pregnancy   24aβ
    2. Speech: Judah's judgment statement   24b
    3. Speech: Tamar's response   25
      a. Presentation of evidence   25a
      b. Call for recognition   25b
    4. Speech: Judah's statement of acquittal   26a
   C. Concluding narration   26b
V. Etiology   27-30
   A. Statement of time   27
   B. Speech   28
    1. Speech formula   28abα
    2. Saying   28bβ
   C. Speech   29a
    1. Speech formula   29aα
    2. Saying   29aβ
   D. Etiological conclusion   29b
   E. Etiological conclusion   30

The Judah-Tamar narrative breaks into a firm unity in the Joseph story (cf. Gen 37:36 and 39:1) and thus delays the pace of action in the Joseph story plot. Reasons for its disruptive position are: (1) The narrative has a rough similarity in structure and genre to the Joseph story. (2) The two share a common motif in that both Judah and Jacob are deceived and subsequently forced to give formal recognition to a piece of evidence (Redford, 17-18). (3) The Judah-Tamar story shares catchwords with the Joseph story (Redford, 17-18). (4) Chronologically, the story could come only here, since in ch. 37 Judah is a boy among his brothers, here he is away from home, and in ch. 46 he brings his family, including Tamar's sons, to Egypt (Redford, 17-18). These points are superficial, however. In contrast to the unity provided by context in the patriarchal narratives, this story is completely isolated from the Joseph story (→ Genesis 37–50).

The exposition introduces the major characters of the story, Judah and Tamar. Judah's wife and three sons, along with the Adullamite friend, play incidental roles and drop from the plot when their roles have been fulfilled. The point of tension in the plot builds on the family order introduced in vv. 1-6. But it comes to full light only in the interplay of family responsibility described in element II. Tamar's husband, Judah's oldest son, offends God in some unexplained manner (v. 7a) and dies (v. 7b). Judah then instructs his second son to fulfill his responsibility as a brother-in-law, an allusion to the levirate custom (cf. Deut 25:5-10). The second son also offends God, in violation of the levirate (v. 9), and dies

(v. 10). The complication ends with the widow, still without child, dispatched to her father's house to await the third son's maturity. But the tension now is clear: Judah does not intend to subject his third son to the dangers of the levirate with Tamar (v. 11). The issue, however, is not whether the third son will also die, or whether Tamar will remain a widow, but whether she will remain a *barren* widow in her father's house (cf. Ruth 3).

The digression changes the scene of action for both Judah (v. 12) and Tamar (vv. 13-14). The statement of change also reveals part of Tamar's plan. She exchanges her widow's garments for a veil, the costume of a prostitute (cf. v. 15). The goal of her plan is to secure her right in the levirate. That right is not marriage, but the conception of a child (see Coats, "Widow's Rights"). The purpose was not simply to have a son who carries the name of the dead husband, but to secure inheritance rights for the woman (see Thompson and Thompson). In order to accomplish her plan, Tamar enters into a dialogue (vv. 15-18a) with Judah, structured as a business negotiation. Thus, Judah closes the business arrangement with Tamar without knowing that she is his daughter-in-law. And Tamar is pregnant, the right of the levirate fulfilled by her father-in-law.

The denouement in element IV (vv. 24-26) brings the narrative to a rapid climax. Judah hears of Tamar's pregnancy and without a formal trial sentences her to death. Tamar then presents her evidence, requests formal recognition of its significance, and wins a reversal of the judgment. The story recounts no marriage between the third son and Tamar. Judah does not marry Tamar himself (contrary to the plot in Ruth). The point of the denouement is simply Judah's recognition of Tamar's legitimate claim to her life and her child, thus her dead husband's inheritance (see Belkin). In an exchange of speeches, structured as a legal process, that right is secured.

The final element, an etiology for Tamar's twins, is an appendix to the narrative. The etiology for the first son (v. 29b) is an explanation for the name derived from assonance with the second saying of the midwife (v. 29a). The etiology for the second son is built on the order of birth (v. 30; cf. v. 28). But neither is drawn from the development of the narrative itself.

The only break in unity in the narrative appears in the shift from the topic of the widow's right to the etiology. The doublet speech from Tamar to Judah, vv. 25a and 25b, serves to emphasize the developing tension. It thus does not break the unity and cannot constitute evidence for identifying two parallel sources. The narrative comes entirely from J (so, von Rad, *Genesis*). Evidence in the story does not justify reconstructing an earlier form of the tradition with Judah providing marriage for Tamar (contrast von Rad, *Genesis,* 361) or with Tamar cast as a sacred prostitute prohibited by law from having children (against Astour, see Coats, "Widow's Rights"). It is possible that earlier forms of the story treated Judah harshly for his refusal to complete the levirate obligation (so, Gunkel). The stage of tradition in this story seems to suggest, however, that the levirate responsibility was not obligatory (so, Thompson and Thompson).

Genre

This pericope should not be too easily cast as a ($\rightarrow$) saga, again a point of similarity with the Joseph narrative context (against Gunkel, 362). It is relatively brief. Only two characters play major roles in the plot, with supporting characters dropped from the scene. It focuses on Tamar, with motifs from heroic tradition: a woman accused of a capital crime who wins her freedom at the last possible moment. Indeed, the heroine is declared righteous vis-à-vis the principal male figure. The story also has ethnological characteristics (cf. 17:30-38). Thus, the emphasis falls on Tamar's future through her children, and the etiological appendix picks up this interest by offering an explanation of the names the two sons carry (cf. 17:37-38). Subsequent genealogies and name lists emphasize Perez over Zerah and consider both the sons of Judah, not the sons of the dead husband (cf. Gen 46:12; Num 26:21; Ruth 4:12, 18; 1 Chr 2:4; 9:4). Additional ethnological elements can be seen in the patriarch of the family, Judah. He moves away from his family to Adullam and lives among the Canaanites, perhaps a reflection of tribal history in Judah. Yet, the story cannot be identified clearly as heroic (→) saga or family saga. Its artistic conception argues for categorizing it as NOVELLA, but even this position remains tentative. In any case, the addition of the etiological appendix does not alter the genre, creating an (→) etiology, but appears simply as an appendix to the story.

The opening formula in 38:1, "It happened at that time," is a refrain in the repertoire of narrative introductions (cf. Gen 21:22; 1 Kgs 11:29). The negotiation dialogue reflects the patterns of a business relationship designed to produce a contract (cf. Genesis 23). Thus, Judah begins by defining the purpose of the relationship (note the polite introduction, hābâ-nā' ["come, now"]), and the discussion of price ensues. Judah's first offer is not in itself satisfactory, a typical element in the business world. When Tamar asks for more, Judah gives her a chance to set her own price, a surety on the first offer. Once the price has been settled by the seller (v. 18a), the business deal can be concluded (see Tucker). A second exchange of speeches, vv. 24-26, is not precisely a dialogue, but the development forms around the legal process. The formulaic character of the sentence with hakker-nā ("mark, now") belongs particularly to the legal world, a technical term for identifying evidence (see Daube).

Setting

It is difficult to maintain that this story was preserved by circles primarily interested in the genealogy of David (against Thompson and Thompson). Ruth picks up the genealogy of David with Perez, the son of Judah and Tamar (cf. Ruth 4:18-22). The story in Genesis 38 thus has contact with Davidic interests, but the contact is thin. No reference to either Judah or Tamar appears in the Davidic genealogy in Ruth, and no firm evidence supports the suggestion that the story itself circulated within Davidic circles.

If the story is properly ethnological, it might have circulated within the popular setting of the tribe (Judah? Perez?). But difficulties still appear. Judah is not the focal character; he is virtually the villain of the story. Perez plays no role in the story as a principal figure. Even the etiological element seems to be a secondary development in the structure of the unit. The focal character is the heroine, Tamar, but she is not the matriarch of a tribe, at least not in the same sense as Rachel, Sarah, or even Rebekah.

In the final analysis, the setting for the story remains obscure. One could guess that the story circulated in some kind of popular setting, perhaps in the family, since it is the kind of Cinderella story that delights a general audience. If the story is novella, perhaps it came from a particular artist. In that case, nothing more would need to be said than that the story derives from an institution open for storytelling.

Intention

The story intends to *entertain* by describing a basic injustice against a helpless widow, rectified by the heroic efforts of the widow herself. The injustice is a violation of the widow's right (whether by law or by custom) to have a child and thus secure her position within the inheritance scheme of her dead husband. The issue is not marriage. The implication of this position is that the levirate relationship at this point in its history was concerned only with conception of a child for the widow, not with her marriage (cf. Ruth).

Moreover, an entertaining story affects the moral fabric of the society. To present a helpless widow whose just claim eventually receives a hearing from a judge who has the power of life and death over her casts a model for any audience. The entertaining story reveals at least some intention to edify.

Bibliography

M. C. Astour, "Tamar the Hierodule," *JBL* 85 (1966) 185-96; S. Belkin, "Levirate and Agnate Marriage in Rabbinic and Cognate Literature," *JQR* 60 (1969-1970) 275-329; G. Coats, "Widow's Rights; A Crux in the Plot of Genesis 38," *CBQ* 34 (1972) 461-66; D. Daube, "Law in the Narratives," in *Studies in Biblical Law* (New York: KTAV, 1969) 1-74; T. Thompson and D. Thompson, "Some Legal Problems in the Book of Ruth," *VT* 18 (1968) 79-99; G. M. Tucker, "The Legal Background of Genesis 23," *JBL* 35 (1966) 77-84.

III. DIGRESSION, 39:1 – 41:57

Structure

A. Joseph with Potiphar's wife		39:1-20a
1. Exposition		1-6
a. Statement of location		1
1) Joseph		1a
2) Potiphar		1b
b. Joseph's elevation to power		2-6a
c. Physical data about Joseph		6b
2. Narration of the scene		7-20a
a. Transition formula		7aα
b. Dialogue		7aβ-9
1) Speech: the invitation to Joseph		7aβb
2) Speech: Joseph's refusal		8-9
c. Transition passage of time		10
d. Continuation of dialogue		11-12
1) Exposition		11
2) Speech: the invitation to Joseph		12a
3) Narration of the refusal		12b
e. Speech: recitation of events to servants		13-15
f. Transition passage of time		16

The digression is fully integrated with the preceding and following elements in the Joseph story. Thus, 39:1 picks up the transition from 37:36 and signals the digression as an explanation of Joseph's fate in Egypt. 40:15 alludes to the brothers' treachery in 37:25-28, without, however, incorporating an explicit reference to the brothers or the tension that divided the family. Moreover, the final elements in the plot of the Joseph story presuppose Joseph's position of power in Egypt as it is described in the digression. The digression thus retards development of the major point of tension in the story and contributes thereby to the overall pattern of structure.

The digression has three principal scenes, with each developing an intricate plot of its own. The first two scenes, however, offer no resolution of the tension. Rather, the tension introduced in the first is transferred through the second and into the third. Thus, the first two scenes lead necessarily beyond their own structure to the point of climax in the final one. Moreover, structural symmetry marks a style of unity in the whole and suggests that neither the first nor the second can stand in isolation.

The first scene opens with a lengthy exposition. The first part of the exposition, v. 1, notes the disposition of Joseph in Egypt and introduces a new character, Potiphar. Data about this character include his identity by name, his relationship with the pharaoh, position, nationality, and his relationship with Joseph (cf. also 37:36). Since the sentence functions clearly as a part of the exposition, its primary position in the Joseph story must have been here rather than in 37:36. The parallel in ch. 37, including the description of the merchants as Midianites, would thus be secondary, an imitation designed to provide transition around the Judah-Tamar story in Genesis 38 (→ 37:36). The second part of the exposition defines Joseph's relationship with Potiphar. Vv. 2-6a adapt an assistance formula for the narration, then report that on the basis of God's assistance Joseph was elevated to a position of power in Potiphar's house second only to Potiphar himself. It is significant to note that elevation to power is not the primary focus of the scene, but a part of the exposition. V. 6b then closes the exposition with an essential fact about Joseph, the foundation for the principal tension of the scene as developed in vv. 7-20a.

Transition from the exposition to the principal body of the scene is accomplished by a stereotyped formula, v. 7aα (see also 40:1). The body of narration develops around a series of dialogue speeches, marked off by narrated transitions (see also 37:12-33). The first dialogue, vv. 7aβ-9, occurs between Potiphar's wife and Joseph, introducing the point of crisis for the scene: The woman invites Joseph to her bed. Joseph's refusal speech is constructed in two parts: (1) a longer statement of reasons for the refusal, vv. 8-9a, and (2) the refusal itself, v. 9b. Significantly, the reasons for the refusal do not derive from a theological moralization. Reference to a sin against God is a part of the refusal, not a part of the reason. It thus plays no crucial role in the scene. The reasons for the refusal lie rather in an enlightened sense of responsibility Joseph owes to his master.

Following a transition passage of time, v. 10, a repetition of the encounter heightens the crisis. In an initial speech, vv. 11-12a, the woman repeats her invitation to Joseph. The response parallels the speech in vv. 8-9, although here it appears in narration rather than speech (v. 12b). And the narration accomplishes a transition from the dialogue between the woman and Joseph to a new stage of crisis. The speech in vv. 13-15, directed by the woman to the servants of the house, shows the woman's intention to accuse Joseph falsely. After another transition passage of time, she gives the same speech to her husband, who obviously can punish Joseph severely without public trial. The punishment comes, but not as a resolution of the crisis: Joseph is transferred to prison, but his fate is unclear. The punishment simply leads to the second scene, a retardation rather than a resolution of the tension. The first scene thus is an integral part of the digression. Without its preparation, the second and third scenes would have Joseph inexplicably in prison, not simply as a servant of the captain of the guard (contrast 41:12 with 41:14), but as an inmate (see Coats, *From Canaan*).

In 39:20b-23, an exposition for the second scene parallels the exposition for the first scene. The statement of location in v. 20b, like the introduction of Potiphar in 39:1, establishes Joseph's disposition for the scene. In addition, it anticipates the major development of the scene by defining Joseph's prison as a place for the king's prisoners. Then vv. 21-23, like vv. 2-6a, describe Joseph's elevation to a position of power in the prison, second only to the keeper of the prison. Like vv. 2-3, so v. 21a narrates Joseph's fortune in the prison by means of an adaptation of the assistance formula. And like vv. 4-6a, vv. 21b-23 describe Joseph's elevation to power (compare the similar wording in the two elements). The symmetry with the first scene is thus apparent.

The major body of narration begins in 40:1aα with the same transition formula found in the same position as in the first scene (39:7aα). Vv. 1aβ-4a are problematic in the structure of the scene since they introduce two new figures as principals in the scene's narration. Their function lies not only in presentation of data for identifying the principals (vv. 1aβ-2), but also in establishing the contact between the new figures and Joseph (vv. 3-4a). Significantly, Joseph now serves the new figures, not the captain of the guard. His position with them is parallel to his position with Potiphar (compare 39:4 and 40:4). Yet, the transition in v. 1aα denies these verses to the exposition. They relate to the preceding exposition and the following narration in much the same way as 37:5-11 relate to the preceding and following verses.

In vv. 5-19, the structural pattern derives from a dream dialogue and suggests that the point of symmetry for the scene shifts from the preceding scene to the following one (cf. also the elements in ch. 37). The dialogue begins in vv. 5-6 with a brief exposition of the circumstances, parallel in structure and function to the introductory formulas in 37:5 and 9a. The initial exchange in vv. 7-8 sets the stage for the following dream speeches. But it also shows that, contrary to 37:5-11, where Joseph recites his own dreams without recourse to interpretations, here the dreams will be recited to Joseph and Joseph will provide the interpretations.

The speeches in vv. 9-11 and 16-17 stand in the scene structurally as the execution of Joseph's instructions. Structure within the speeches, however, follows the pattern of the dream speeches in Genesis 37 (cf. also ch. 41). The call to attention in the first speech has been reduced to a single phrase: "In my dream" (*baḥălômî*). But the phrase is marked off from the dream narration by a typical *wĕhinnēh* ("and behold"). The call to attention thus maintains its function in the speech as a distinct element despite its brevity. The dream narration develops, following the introductory particle, with a wide range of syntactical variations. The second speech, vv. 16-17, follows the same pattern. The call to attention is again "in my dream." The dream narration is again marked off from the call to attention by the particle *wĕhinnēh*. And, as in vv. 9-11, so here the narration develops around a wide variety of syntactical patterns (see Richter).

In each case, an interpretation speech follows recitation of the dream, vv. 12-15 and 16-17. In each case the speech begins with a specialized headline (vv. 12aβ and 18). And in each case the interpretation allegorizes on the motifs of the dream narration. In the first interpretation speech, Joseph sets up a request to the addressee, as if building on the positive character of the interpretation (vv. 14-15). The second speech has no corresponding request, perhaps a result of the negative interpretation.

Vv. 20-23 round off the scene with a notation that the dream interpretations were fulfilled, just as Joseph specified. One might expect a note of hope for a resolution of Joseph's plight since the interpretations prove accurate. But the request attached to the first interpretation is forgotten. Joseph remains in prison; his fate remains unclear. Thus, like the first scene, the second one does not have a clear conclusion. To the contrary, its ambiguous ending retards the tension and leads beyond its own structure to the third scene.

The second scene constitutes an integral segment of the digression and cannot readily be separated from the first as a doublet. The symmetry of construction, not only with the first scene, but also in anticipation of the third scene, argues for the integrity of the digression.

There is no exposition for the third scene. It is distinguished from the second one only by a brief transition formula, a note about passage of time (cf. 40:1). The point of reference for the formula, "at the end of two years," is the first and second scenes, particularly the conclusion of the second scene that leaves Joseph forgotten in prison (cf. 41:14). Following the transition is a narration of two dreams (vv. 1b-7). Structure in this movement follows the same pattern as the dream speeches in 40:9-11 and 16-17, dispite the shift from first-person speech to third-person narration. Thus, the introductions in vv. 1bα and 5a fill the same position as the call to attention in a dream speech (cf. 37:5a, 9a). And the dream narrations in vv. 1b-4a and 5b-7a fill the same position as the dream recitation in a first-person speech. Moreover, the narration here, as in 37:7, 9 and 40:9-11, 16-17, begins with the particle *hinnēh*. The conclusions in vv. 4b and 7b function simply to mark the end of narration for each dream (cf. 41:21b).

The next element introduces Joseph into the scene, an interlude in the pharaoh's drive to resolve the mystery posed by his dreams (vv. 8-14). The pharaoh's servants fail in their efforts to interpret the dreams (cf. Dan 2:10-11), and in the following frustration, pharaoh's servant who forgot Joseph remembered his error. One should note here that the pharaoh summons Joseph from the dungeon (*min-habbôr*), not from service to the prison keeper.

The dialogue series in vv. 15-36 is constructed in parallel with the dialogue in 40:5-19. The opening exchange in vv. 15-16, like the opening exchange in 40:7-8, sets the stage for the pharaoh's recitation. And like 40:7-8, Joseph's part alludes to a theological rootage for dream interpretations (cf. also 41:25, 28). Yet, there is no direct reference here or in the earlier parallels in the Joseph story to divine intervention in the interpretation process (contrast Dan 2:19). Joseph depends here, as in Genesis 40, on his own skill, even though that skill derives finally from God. The same point would apply for the assistance formula structure

281

in the first two scenes. Joseph rises to a position of power with the help of God, but he does so because he is a skillful administrator.

The dream speech itself can be divided into two parts, each structured on the same pattern (vv. 17-21 and 22-24). With the exception of the shift from third-person narration to first-person speech, this section is virtually identical to the section in 41:1b-7. Joseph's interpretation speech is introduced with a headline longer and more complex than the ones in ch. 40, but the same function is obvious. Moreover, the interpretation allegorizes on the motifs of the dream narration, the same method of procedure as the one in ch. 40. Then, perhaps on the basis of the advantage Joseph holds by interpreting the pharaoh's dreams with positive consequences, Joseph offers counsel—in effect, a request to the king. The request is structured as an exhortation for founding an office with responsibility for accumulating grain in the years of coming fertility and dispensing it in the years of coming famine. Moreover, the man to head such an office would be "discreet and wise" (*nābôn wĕḥākām*). These virtues belong to an ideal administrator of power (see 1 Kgs 3:12). The final part of the speech specifies reasons that call for the office.

Vv. 37-46, like 40:23, note the response to the request, while vv. 47-57, like 40:20-22, report fulfillment of the interpretation. In the first section, a general introduction (v. 37) shows that the pharaoh will execute the counsel as Joseph formulated it, with the rhetorical question to the servants (v. 38) hinting of Joseph's role in the new administration. Then a series of pharaoh speeches to Joseph establishes the new office. The first two speeches (vv. 39-40 and 41) are not doublets. To the contrary, they are complements, the one promoting Joseph to a position over the pharaoh's house and the other extending his power over all the land. Vv. 42-43 then narrate the execution of the king's proclamation. The speech in v. 44, with the narration in vv. 45-46, would appear to duplicate that movement. Indeed, the narration in vv. 45-46 is itself a combination of duplicate elements. Conclusions about the significance of these duplications should, however, reflect the tendency for duplication noted above in 37:21-22. Moreover, contrary to the pattern of the first two scenes, in this section Joseph's elevation to high office comes at the peak of the narration. It constitutes the resolution of tension in the digression. But the narrative is not simply a rags-to-riches tale. It moves beyond the elevation to power to a second stage.

In the second part of this concluding element, vv. 47-57, a report of Joseph's administration over the periods of fertility and famine carries the fulfillment of the interpretation. The first period includes a comment about the fertility of the land (vv. 47-49) as well as a comment about Joseph's own fertility, the birth of two sons (vv. 50-52). The two etiologies in the birth report assert the names of the sons first, then explain them from assonance with a key word in the following dependent clause. The second period of Joseph's administration is introduced in vv. 53-54 with a transition passage of time. The primary substance of this element is a report of the people's complaint about hunger (cf. Num 11:13). And the pharaoh's response places the people under the authority of Joseph. Finally, the scene notes that Joseph executed his office for the benefit of the Egyptians and all the earth.

The third scene develops roots out of the first and second ones. Thus, the digression in Genesis 39–41 stands together, tightly structured with symmetry, plot pace control, and extended development of motifs from one scene to the next. Some structural duplication appears in the elevation speeches, recalling the stylistic duplication of Reuben's speech at a crucial point in the movement of the plot. But these speeches do not constitute sufficient evidence for reconstructing parallel sources (Coats, *From Canaan*). As far as structure in the digression is concerned, no piece is out of place. Even the items commonly isolated as P additions, like 41:45-46 or 50-52, fulfill a consistent, although not indispensable, role for the unit. They may well be priestly additions. But if they are, they do not violate the integrity of structure in the whole. (For a discussion of sources and tradition history in the Joseph story, → Genesis 37; 39–47.) At an earlier stage in tradition history, the digression may have circulated as an independent story, quite unrelated to the Joseph and Israel context it now occupies (so, Gunkel, "Die Komposition"; Humphrey, 208-16).

Genre

As an integrated element in the Joseph story, this unit is a digression, a delay in developing the principal movement of the plot in the overall story. If the unit had a life of its own before being incorporated into the Joseph story, it would be subject to its own distinct genre characteristics. The unit's emphasis on the virtues of Joseph as an administrator suggests that as an originally independent story the digression functioned as a LEGEND (so, Coats, "Joseph Story").

Formulas and stereotyped structures within the digression include the AS-SISTANCE formula, adapted here for narration (39:2-3, 21). The TRANSITION formula in 39:7 and 40:1 has parallels in Gen 22:1; 1 Kgs 13:33; 17:17; 21:1; Esth 2:1; 3:1. In each case, it serves to provide transition from one item to the next, either within the structure of a single pericope or as a bridge between two independent units. A second transition formula appears in 41:1, with parallels in Gen 4:3; 8:6; Exod 12:41; Deut 9:11; Judg 11:39; 15:7; 1 Kgs 2:29; 17:7; Jer 13:6; 42:7; 2 Chr 8:1. Again, the formula can appear within a single unit (cf. Gen 4:3) or as transition between two units (cf. 2 Chr 8:1). The dream DIALOGUE (Gen 40:9-19; 41:15-36) includes DREAM SPEECHES, INTERPRETATION SPEECHES, and some notice of fulfillment for the interpretation (see Richter). Whether the combination reflects a genre or simply the results of narrative construction from distinct, generic speeches is not yet clear (cf. Coats, *From Canaan*). The dream SPEECH and the interpretation SPEECH appear nonetheless as generic units. The authorization formula in 41:44 has parallels in legal material (cf. Lev 18:5). Finally, the etiologies follow a prescribed pattern for naming ETIOLOGY (see Long).

Setting

As a part of the Joseph story, the digression has no distinct setting. If it had a life of its own, an independent story within the larger Joseph story plot, it would have been drawn from the traditions of the royal court. Particularly in view of its intention, that setting might be specified as the wisdom schools of the royal court (so, von Rad, "The Joseph Narrative").

Intention

As digression in the Joseph story, the unit accounts for Joseph's fate in Egypt. His rise to power within the pharaoh's court enables the narrative to move from the crisis casting Joseph as powerless in ch. 37 to the crisis and denouement with Joseph as a powerful administrator in chs. 42–45. As an independent story, the unit depicts an ideal power figure whose characteristics enable him to execute his office with discretion and wisdom, first in the household of Potiphar, then in the prison, and finally in the kingdom. The focus of intention does not fall on how a prospective administrator might rise to a position, although structure in the denouement, ch. 41, highlights Joseph's elevation. Rather, the focus demonstrates proper use of power within the office. Joseph stands as an administrator whose work exemplifies wisdom and perception as virtues that should be characteristic for any administrator. The story as legend would thus edify the members of the institution from which it derives.

IV. COMPLICATION, 42:1-38

Structure

A. Transition	1a
B. Development of the crisis	1b-38
1. The brothers and Jacob in Canaan	1b-5
a. Jacob's accusation	1b
b. Jacob's commission	2
c. Execution of instructions	3-5
2. The brothers before Joseph in Egypt	6-26
a. Change of location	6a
b. Dialogue between the brothers and Joseph	6b-16
1) General introduction	6b
2) Joseph's request for information	7abα
3) The brothers' response	7bβ
4) Joseph's accusation	8-9
5) The brothers' self-defense	10-11
6) Joseph's renewed accusation	12
7) The brothers' renewed self-defense	13
8) Joseph's conclusion	14-16
a) Renewed accusation	14
b) Test	15-16
(1) Preface to the test	15a
(2) Oath	15b
(3) Instructions for the test	16a
(4) Oath	16b
c. Transition passage of time	17
d. Joseph's change in the test	18-20a
1) Reasons for the change	18
2) New instructions	19-20a
e. Execution of instructions	20b
f. Dialogue among the brothers	21-22
1) Common confession of guilt	21
2) Reuben's self-vindication	22
g. Concluding narration	23-26

This scene complements the complication of plot in ch. 37 by establishing an antithetical parallel: The oppressed becomes the oppressor. It begins with an implicit transition in location from the digression of chs. 39–41. Contrary to the digression, the principals of action are once again the father, the brother, and, after v. 5, Joseph. The location is not Egypt, but Canaan. Yet, the transition presupposes the events in Egypt described by the digression. The explicit transition uses a report of Jacob that grain is available in Egypt.

The crisis develops through a series of four panels, each marked by a change in location. The first one sets the brothers before Jacob in Canaan. Jacob's opening question to the brothers, although somewhat general in nature, sets a mood of tension for the scene since it has an accusing character: "Why do you look at one another?" The second speech is more explicitly a commission cast against the background of the famine. Jacob instructs the sons for a trip to Egypt in order to buy grain and thus protect the family against the threat of death. The brothers respond to the instructions without question (cf. 37:13-14). The allusion to Benjamin's preferred role, v. 4, significantly does not open a new source of tension in the family, in contrast to ch. 37. Rather, it lays a foundation for Joseph's demands regarding Benjamin in vv. 14-16 and 18-20. Yet, the tensions within the family are implicit. The point can be seen in Jacob's accusing question. But even more, vv. 3-5 note that Jacob's instructions were carried out. And the process brings the brothers to Egypt and a new confrontation with Joseph.

The next panel opens with a transition from Jacob and his sons in Canaan to Joseph in Egypt, the ruler of the land. Structure in this element employs a dialogue series between the brothers and Joseph, with the speeches marked off by more extensive narration than usual for the Joseph story. The function of the narration framework is to comment on the role Joseph maintains in the dialogue.

V. 6b establishes the context for the dialogue, the point of fulfillment for the dream in 37:5-8. The exchange begins in v. 7 with a request for information: "Where do you come from?" But the commentary with the speech emphasizes that Joseph knows who the men are. His question is qualified by harsh behavior, a construction designed to establish an artificial relationship.

In the following exchange, vv. 8-11, the point of the harsh behavior becomes clear. Joseph's speech is again introduced with a long commentary that shows Joseph's advantage. For a second time, the text notes that Joseph recognized the brothers. But they do not know who he is. Joseph's speech is thus the more pointed: "You are spies. You have come to see the weakness of the land." The accusation is serious—Joseph has the power to confine the men to an uncertain fate on the spot (vv. 14-16). The relationship is thus similar to the one in 37:12-35, with the roles reversed. Moreover, the accusation is obviously false. It is thus reminiscent of 39:13-18, with Joseph in the accuser's role.

The brothers' self-defense (vv. 10-11, 13) does not give the impression of a carefully constructed discourse. It rambles without logical progression from a denial of the charges to a statement of the brothers' purpose in Egypt, an identification of their relationship with each other, an affirmation of their honesty, and a renewed denial of the charges. The rambling effectively serves the scene, however, since it paints an image of total surprise, a lack of preparation for defense against such charges. Joseph renews the accusation (v. 12), and the brothers respond with more details about their family (v. 13). The details were not elicited directly by the accusation; they flow from the brothers' panic. But the panic is the more poignant in the light of vv. 29-38.

Joseph's speech in vv. 14-16 concludes the first series by setting up a test for determining the validity of the brothers' claim to innocence. The preface to the test is vague: "In this you shall be tested" (*bĕzō't tibbāḥēnû*). But the point of reference is made clear in the following verses, instructions to the brothers for bringing the younger brother to Egypt. And the pressure of the test is sealed with a pair of oaths. The function of the test structure is made more explicit in the brothers' citation of the speech to Jacob, vv. 33-34.

After a transition passage of time, Joseph addresses a new speech to the brothers, changing the content of the test (vv. 18-20a). Rather than confining all the brothers in prison except one who would return for Benjamin, now all the brothers would return with food except one who would remain in prison. That brother can be redeemed and more food purchased if the nine free men would return with Benjamin. V. 20b is a brief, typical statement for noting execution of instructions.

But the scene does not change. A dialogue among the brothers relates the plight they now face to the guilt they suffer (v. 21), although Reuben protests his innocence (v. 22). Moreover, Joseph's response is noted. The anonymity of his position emphasizes the kind of control he has over his prey. The brothers did not know that Joseph understood their confession. He then weeps. But the cause for the weeping is obviously not the confession. The motif carries, to the contrary, a structural function for the entire plot of the Joseph story. He weeps again in response to Benjamin (43:30-31a), and again as he reveals himself to his brothers (45:2). Each case occurs at the peak of tension in audiences between Joseph and his brothers. And in each case, the weeping breaks the tension with progressing signs of hope for a full reconciliation. Yet, despite the break in tension represented by the motif in this scene, Joseph turns immediately to the details of the test. Simeon is imprisoned and the remaining brothers are sent away with their grain and, unknown to them, their money.

Vv. 27-28 constitute an interlude (cf. 37:14b-17a). After an exposition places the brothers at an inn en route to Canaan, one brother opens his grain to feed his animal, only to discover his money. The man reports the discovery to his brothers. But the report brings lamentation, not joy. Moreover, there is no reference here to their guilt. Rather, an air of mystery surrounds the event. It is completely beyond the understanding of the men involved, a foreboding sense of fate. Thus, the confrontation between Joseph and the brothers is complete. But the victory comes without resolution of the tension in the family. To the contrary, now the tension is more severe: Another brother is lost; a demand lies on Benjamin's head; and the brothers cannot understand. Moreover, the victory belongs to Joseph. It completes the foreshadowing of the initial dream in ch. 37 and reverses the power struggle from ch. 39. The family seems intent on tearing itself apart.

The severity of the crisis comes to expression in the final panel of the scene (vv. 29-38). The brothers return to Canaan and report to their father. Their speech recites the accusation (vv. 29b-30) as well as their self-defense (vv. 31-32) and Joseph's test. The test itself, particularly the preface (v. 33a), is made more explicit by associating the vague formula from v. 15a with the knowledge formula (see Zimmerli, 90-91). To bring Benjamin back will validate their claim, will enable Joseph "to know" that the brothers are innocent. Jacob then participates in discovering the money (v. 35), with the money now a sign of a cruel fate. In keeping with the omen, Jacob laments over the loss of Joseph and Simeon as well as the threat to Benjamin. Reuben responds to the lamentation with an oath to guarantee Benjamin's safe return. But Jacob refuses to give his permission. The brothers cannot return to Egypt with Benjamin, even to free Simeon.

The chapter maintains integrity from the beginning to the end. The one sign of duplication in structure is in the first panel, with two speeches addressed back to back by Jacob to his sons. But a doubling of speeches at crucial transitions appears at other places in the Joseph story (cf. 37:21-22; 41:37-45) and can be taken as a stylistic device. Moreover, no clear evidence suggests that any part of the scene might have been lost in transmission (see the comments on ch. 43). It seems more satisfactory, in view of the artistic structure of the unit, to attribute the whole to one source.

Genre

The scene has no independence of its own. It derives naturally from the preceding section of the narrative and lays a crucial foundation for the following ones. Thus, genre questions about the element must be limited to the functional characteristics it reveals in relationship to the whole. As a part of the Joseph story, it is a complication of plot. It parallels ch. 37 by reversing the plot structures.

Formulas and stereotyped patterns appear widely in the scene. A commission SPEECH (v. 2) employs vocabulary patterns common to the category. In the dialogue between Joseph and the brothers, SPEECHES from a legal context—such as ACCUSATION and SELF-DEFENSE—serve the development of the story. The OATHS in vv. 15 and 16 begin with a typical formula: "By the life of the pharaoh (*ḥê par'ōh*)." → 1 Sam 1:26; 17:55; 20:3; 25:26; 2 Sam 11:11; 14:19; 15:21; 2 Kgs 2:2, 4, 6; Amos 8:14. The clause following the formula can be introduced by *'im*, as in v. 15. In this case, the content of the clause is negated, even though no negative particle appears. The following clause can also be introduced by *kî*, as in v. 16. In this case, the content of the clause is strengthened. The OATH in v. 37 follows a different structure. It sets out the conditions that will apply (you shall slay my two sons) if the guarantee of the oath cannot be fulfilled (if I do not bring him back to you). The KNOWLEDGE formula in vv. 33-34 presupposes a designation of conditions necessary for establishing an assertion. The conditions can appear first and can be designated in a brief, obscure form: "In this. . . ." The obscure reference is then spelled out in detail following the formula. The formula itself builds on an inflected form of the verb "know" (*yd'*), with a specification of the point to be established: "I shall know that you are honest men." The test in v. 16a is influenced by the same pattern. (On the details of the formula, see Zimmerli, 90-91.) Finally, in v. 36 a DIRGE focuses Jacob's reaction to the fate of his sons (cf. 37:34-35).

Setting

The scene cannot be separated from the Joseph story as a whole. Thus, questions about setting are irrelevant as far as this particular element is concerned.

Intention

This element heightens the crisis within Jacob's family by reversing the structural lines and the focus of tension as set out in ch. 37. The brothers committed Joseph to an unknown fate. Now, with corresponding deception, Joseph inflicts a cruel fate on the brothers, a fate understood by the brothers as the inexorable result of their act against Joseph. The results of the scheme are a more severe division in the family and an increased sense of despair for the future: Simeon sits in prison; a foreboding fate awaits Benjamin; Jacob laments. The family falls short of any hope for reconciliation.

Bibliography

W. Zimmerli, *Erkenntnis Gottes nach dem Buche Ezechiel. Eine theologische Studie* (ATANT 27; Zürich: Zwingli, 1954).

V. DENOUEMENT, 43:1 – 45:28

Structure

A. Transition	43:1
B. Development of the denouement	43:2–45:24
1. The brothers and Jacob in Canaan	43:2-14
a. Jacob's commission speech	2
b. Response from Judah	3-5
1) Citation from Joseph	3
2) Conditions for accepting commission	4
3) Conditions for rejecting commission	5a

This scene is fully integrated into the structure of the Joseph story as the resolution of tension in the story's plot. In keeping with its integral position, it develops motifs drawn from other elements of the story. Thus, the crisis between the brothers comes into full play. Joseph's position of power in the Egyptian administration provides necessary context, as does the pressure of famine that brought Joseph to power. The scene begins as a continuation of the complication in ch. 42. The brothers cannot return to Egypt without Benjamin. Moreover, the basic structure of the scene is like that of the scene in ch. 42. A transition in v. 1 implies passage of time with a simple note, constructed in nominal sentence order: "The famine was severe in the land." The principal body of narration, though more complex, is also similar. A series of panels sets the brothers before Jacob in Canaan, then Joseph in Egypt. Then they confront a steward on the way back to Canaan, and once again Joseph in Egypt. Following the high point in the scene, a final panel sets the brothers before Jacob in Canaan, a concluding report on the developments within the structure of the family.

Following the transition, the first panel develops the crisis from ch. 42 in a way that is structurally similar to ch. 42. Jacob commissions his sons for a trip to Egypt in order to buy food. The circumstances provoking the commission are spelled out in v. 2a, amplifying the transition note. The grain brought from the previous trip has been exhausted. An implication of this note is that during the undefined period of time required for depleting the grain reserve Simeon remained in prison, unjustly confined (cf. the transition between chs. 40 and 41). Jacob's commission speech in v. 2b is like the one in 42:2. But contrary to ch. 42, here the spokesman for the brothers, Judah, objects to the commission.

Jacob responds to the objection by accusing the brothers of telling the Egyptian too much about the family. The brothers defend themselves with a manufactured alibi, like the one in 37:31-32. Thus, deception continues to be the basis for the relationship between father and sons (see Coats, *From Canaan*). Judah's speech in vv. 8-10 is an effort to break the stalemate. He asks Jacob to send Benjamin, then bases his request on the same life-and-death argument Jacob used in 42:2. For additional support he swears a self-curse as surety for Benjamin's safe return. The oath is not as obviously severe as Reuben's in ch. 42. Yet, its severity should not be underestimated: "I shall be guilty before you all the days." Jacob cannot refuse. His reply is a new commission speech, vv. 11-14, setting out plans for a return to Egypt that meet the necessary conditions. Benjamin shall accompany the brothers. V. 14 echoes the note of fate already apparent in ch. 42. Jacob blesses the sons for success in the trip, not so much in negotiating for food, but in securing a safe return of Benjamin and "the other brother." There is an element of hope, then, anchored in the name El Shaddai. But he also laments for his children, as if he sees an inexorable fate depriving him of his pride, indeed, the promise associated with El Shaddai. And with the lament the crisis of the story is again apparent.

The second panel, 43:15-34, is an apparent resolution of the tension in the story. The brothers now stand in Egypt, invited to a banquet. But the invitation is full of mystery. The anxiety of the mystery is highlighted by the brothers' confession to one another. The invitation, so the brothers believe, must be a trick of the inexorable fate that has moved them in the past. The mystery is increased by the brothers' exchange with the steward, vv. 19-23. Their speech begins with a formula of supplication, then recites the events of the previous scene. The motive is a declaration of intent to pay for what they have received and of their innocence in the matter of the mysterious money in the food sacks. But rather than accusation, the steward pronounces them innocent, acquitted of any charges. To make matters better, he also restores Simeon to them. Their fate is again attributed to God. But in this case (contrast 42:28), it is a good fate.

The final element in the panel describes the banquet with Joseph, an apparent confirmation of the good so unexpected. When Joseph arrives, the brothers bow in full obeisance to their lord (cf. 37:5-8). And after Joseph's inquiry about family welfare, they bow again. Joseph's inquiry about Benjamin brings no response from the brothers. Rather, he moves immediately to a blessing for the little brother. The weeping motif here serves the description of his reaction. It may well be that the weeping motif here parallels the narration in 42:24 and that both anticipate Joseph's reaction in the final reconciliation, although the weeping here seems to be provoked particularly by the sight of Benjamin. In any case, the banquet seems to confirm the good fortune developing in the panel. A type of reconciliation is apparent, even if the brothers cannot understand the events, even though Joseph remains incognito.

The reconciliation is only apparent, however. The third panel, 44:1-13, rebuilds the tension, and it is clear that Joseph does this as an explicit game. He first instructs his steward to construct evidence for a false accusation (cf. 39:13-14). The evidence in this case uses two items. Money is again hidden in the food sacks, but the focal point is a silver cup, concealed in Benjamin's bag. Then, after the brothers have been dismissed for the trip home, Joseph instructs his steward to pursue them and confront them with a new accusation: "Why have you exchanged evil for good?" The scene unfolds accordingly. And in response to a fate turned cruel again, the brothers fall all over themselves in an attempt to show their innocence. Their speech moves with the same unorganized flow that characterizes the self-defense in 42:10-11. The conclusion for this speech, however, lies in an oath, a desperate effort to secure their appeal. The man whose sack reveals the evidence will die, and all the others will be reduced to slavery ($\rightarrow$ 31:32). The desperate character of the oath demonstrates the brothers' confidence in their innocence. But the fate so characteristic of the scene cannot be denied.

The final panel in the major body of the scene, 44:14–45:24, brings the Joseph story to a genuine denouement. The panel opens with a shift in location, back to Joseph in the city. An audience with Joseph now labors under hostile conditions, so contrary to the previous audience. It is significant that the hostile audience is one that has been carefully constructed by Joseph. But the goal of his scheme is not clear. He has achieved his desire to see Benjamin, and his new scheme seems to be designed to detain Benjamin in Egypt while the other brothers return home. Judah responds to the sentence with one of the two most important speeches in the entire unit, 44:18-34. This speech does not develop in an uncontrolled, panic-stricken flow. Rather, it is carefully constructed. It begins with a polite supplication to Joseph, then builds a case by citing previous conversations with both Joseph and their father. The conclusion Judah draws is that to detain Benjamin would mean death for the father. And on the basis of that point, he makes his appeal: He, Judah, should be detained in the place of Benjamin, in order to allow Benjamin the freedom to return home.

The pressure of the confrontation brings the Joseph story to a turning point. The plot cannot develop any further without aborting the primary concern to resolve the alienation of the family. Joseph's following move, then, changes the audience from a hostile mood dominated by a legal exchange of accusation and defense to a more personal encounter. Vv. 1-3 entwine Joseph's self-revelation with the weeping motif. V. 3a, with its self-revelation formula and question about Joseph's father, contains the explicit reversal in the plot. Joseph held an advantage over the brothers because they did not recognize him. Now the advantage disappears; the brothers can understand what is happening. But, even though the plot has reached a turning point, the resolution is not yet complete—there is as yet no reconciliation. The brothers' response in v. 3b demonstrates that point. The crucial self-revelation speech, vv. 4-13, begins in v. 4a with one last delay in building tension. Joseph asks his brothers to come closer, and they obey. With that, Joseph's crucial movement unfolds. The speech asserts first the self-revelation formula, then a series of theological reflections on the events that brought Joseph to his position of power, and finally a set of instructions for bringing Jacob to Egypt. At last the family can be reconciled.

The genuine character of the reconciliation is confirmed by the narration at the end of the speech, vv. 14-15. Joseph kissed his brothers, wept again, and then the group talked together. The contrast between this scene and 37:4 is explicit. Moreover, the pharaoh's speech in vv. 16-20 gives the move an additional hearing, as if to add official sanction to the reconciliation. The panel ends in vv. 21-24 with a notation that the pharaoh's instructions were executed.

The final element in the scene, a new panel in vv. 25-28, contains a necessary conclusion. Following a transition in location, the brothers stand before Jacob in Canaan. Their speech is a report of the events in Egypt (cf. 42:30-34). But they are not concerned here with the entire scope of the trip. The report develops only Joseph's self-revelation, the point of climax for the entire plot. Vv. 26b-27 narrate Jacob's response, with no indication about a break in the brothers' deception pattern. The point is no longer at issue. To the contrary, the family can now be reconciled in fact. Accordingly, the father receives the news and the supporting evidence to establish the validity of the news. He responds in a speech that confirms the reconciliation: he will go to Egypt. In this case, reconciliation involves physical reunion of the family (contrast 33:15-17). Thus, the scope of the story, Jacob in Canaan, Israel in Egypt, approaches its limits.

The scene is a unit. It has duplication in speeches, but the duplications serve as a structural emphasis at crucial points, not as indications of parallel narration (so, the two self-revelation speeches). Moreover, the variation between names, particularly Jacob and Israel, does not suggest two layers of narration, but a scheme of unity in the scope of the plot (see Coats, *From Canaan*). For a discussion of sources in the Joseph story, → Genesis 37; 39–47.

Genre

The scene functions in the plot of the story as a peripeteia, a reversal of direction and a denouement of tension. Thus, the major motifs characteristic for the plot come to an end in development here. But no genre definition for the scene as a unit in itself is possible.

Stereotyped formulas appear in abundance. The following deserve notice: an ACCUSATION formula (43:6; 44:4-5, 15) as well as a SELF-DEFENSE SPEECH from legal contexts (43:7; 44:7-8), a BLESSING (43:14, 29), DIRGE (43:14), SUPPLICATION formula (43:20; 44:18), MESSENGER COMMISSION formula (44:4; 45:17, 18), MESSENGER formula (45:9), COMPLAINT (44:7), CONFESSION OF GUILT (44:16), SELF-REVELATION formula (45:3, 4).

Setting

The scene has no setting apart from the setting for the Joseph story as a whole.

Intention

This segment of the story brings the span of tension in the story's plot to its resolution. Thus, the principal elements of intention in the Joseph story itself can be seen most clearly here. (1) The story moves Jacob and his family from Canaan to Egypt and sets the stage for preservation of the family from the threat of starvation. The great survivors (45:7) constitute the substance for a bridge from patriarchs to exodus. (2) The story effects reconciliation in a broken family without basing the reconciliation on the merit of any one of its members or repentance-forgiveness schemes. (3) Political power used without wisdom and discretion can be destructive, a source for continuing alienation. But used with wisdom and discretion, it can provide blessing for all subjects.

VI. CONCLUSION, 46:1 – 47:27

Structure

A. Itinerary	46:1a
B. Theophany report	1b-4
C. Itinerary	5-7
D. Name list	8-27
E. Jacob and the brothers before Joseph	46:28–47:12
1. Reunion	46:28-34
a. Narration of the reconciliation	28-29
b. Jacob's farewell speech	30
c. Preparation for audience	31-34
2. Audience with the pharaoh	47:1-10
a. The brothers	1-6
1) Announcement to the pharaoh	1
2) Narration of the presentation	2
3) The pharaoh's inquiry about occupation	3a
4) Response	3b
5) Request	4
6) The pharaoh's proclamation to Joseph	5-6
b. The father	7-10
1) Narration of the presentation	7
2) The pharaoh's inquiry about age	8
3) Response	9
4) Jacob's blessing	10
3. Conclusion to the Joseph story	11-12
F. Administration report	13-26
G. Conclusion to the Joseph story	27

This scene develops the narration of the story beyond the denouement in the preceding section. It is here that Jacob moves with his families from Canaan to Egypt. Here appears the reunion between Jacob and Joseph, here Jacob's final settlement under Joseph's protective care. The element is thus an anticlimax, yet fully an integral part of the primary structure in the story.

The basic unity of the scene, indeed, the device for suggesting movement from Canaan to Egypt as the conclusion of the story, is provided by an itinerary scheme. V. 1a opens the narration with an itinerary formula, composed of a notice of departure from one site and arrival at another. In this case, no place-name qualifies the designation of departure. The pattern of the formula is nonetheless obvious. Vv. 5-7 continue the chain, forming a bracket around vv. 1b-4. Moreover, the bracketing structure continues in the jump from vv. 5-7 to vv. 28-30, around vv. 8-27. Vv. 28-30 break the stereotyped pattern of the itinerary somewhat. Yet, they provide clear contact with the chain in vv. 5-7 by establishing a more detailed designation of the destination. Vv. 6-7 mark the arrival simply in Egypt, while v. 28 defines the site as Goshen. Thus, the itinerary carries the weight of the conclusion by presenting Jacob's arrival in Goshen and reunion with Joseph. The speech in v. 30 also facilitates a sense of unity with the denouement by establishing a point of contact with the speech in 45:28. The reunion anticipated in the denouement is finally complete.

Narration of the reconciliation between Joseph and Jacob stands in close relationship, moreover, with a description of an audience with the pharaoh. Vv. 31-34 mark the preparation of the audience with instructions for proper behavior before the king. But the instructions contradict the report of the audience in the following chapter. The reason for the particular formulation here seems to be provision of context for the saying in v. 34 (for details, see Coats, *From Canaan*). The audience itself is divided into two sections. The first one, 47:1-6, presents the brothers before the pharaoh. The brothers define their purpose in coming to Egypt with a distinct appeal to their profession as shepherds, then pose a request for the pharaoh's permission to settle in Goshen. The audience is thus related to the goal of describing the final settlement in Egypt. The second section of the audience, vv. 7-10, presents the father. V. 7 narrates the presentation, with Jacob's blessing for the pharaoh an immediate consequence. The exchange of dialogue in vv. 8-9 centers on a point of curiosity, Jacob's age. But the age serves to intensify the blessing, for an older man at the end of his career stands in the most advantageous position to give blessing (cf. Genesis 48). Finally, the text narrates the blessing again as the crucial element of the unit, the consequence of Jacob's move to Egypt. But in neither case does a blessing speech appear.

Vv. 11-12 are a concluding statement for the Joseph story, Jacob's final settlement in Goshen under Joseph's provision and protection just as the pharaoh had commanded. V. 27 completes this conclusion, thus establishing an inclusion for part VI (vv. 13-26). V. 27a is constructed in exact parallel with the opening sentence of the Joseph story (see 37:1). V. 27b introduces a distinct theme: Jacob and his people not only settle on the land but increase in number and power (cf. Exod 1:7).

The bracketing accomplished by the itinerary chain and the inclusion established by dividing the conclusion into two parts embrace three items that appear to be secondary in the scene: the theophany report in 46:1b-4, the name list in 46:8-27, and the administration report in 47:13-26. (For details on these parts, see the following units.)

Source analysis and tradition history explain a part of the composite structure of the unit. 47:27b belongs to P (cf. Exod 1:7, with its terminology for Israel's increase). The remaining parts of the scene can be ascribed to the older sources. But even here the material shows levels of growth. The itinerary provides context for the theophany report, perhaps an expansion to include the Beer-sheba site. The audience between the brothers and the pharaoh has been expanded to include the saying about shepherds. And the description of Joseph's administration has been spliced into the scene. Presumably, the original conclusion would have noted at least Jacob's departure from Canaan and arrival in Goshen (the itinerary context), his reunion with Joseph, and his blessing for the pharaoh. This part, like the major body of the Joseph story, would derive from J. The redaction process bringing such diverse elements together would belong to the latest layer. The adjustment in the audience in order to provide context for the shepherds' saying may also be a part of that redactional stage, although the point must remain moot. The saying itself is probably older, an element of oral tradition.

Genre

The unit as a whole is dependent on the structure of the Joseph story, an anticlimax bringing the lines of narration to their final conclusion. Thus, no genre definition for the unit apart from its role in the larger story can be made.

Within the unit, several distinct genres or genre elements can be seen. 46:1a is an ITINERARY formula (cf. Exod 12:37). Vv. 5-7 are constructed on the pattern of an ITINERARY and, with v. 1a, form a framework around vv. 1b-4. The speech in 46:30 should be seen as a FAREWELL SPEECH (cf. Luke 2:29-32). A MESSENGER COMMISSION formula appears in 46:34.

Setting

The conclusion belongs primarily to the Joseph story, thus reflecting no independent setting. The expansions point to redactional activity on the Joseph story text at at least two levels. The theophany report reflects an Elohistic expansion (Rje), while the remaining elements point to a priestly expansion (Psup).

Intention

Within the larger scope of the Joseph story, this unit completes the narration by depicting Jacob's final settlement in Egypt with his family. The theophany report comments on the conclusion by making the ties between the Joseph story and the patriarchal traditions explicit and casting the focus of the Joseph tradition on a descent into Egypt. The name list complements that pattern, with the etiology simply an appendix.

JACOB'S THEOPHANY REPORT, 46:1b-4

Structure

I.	Statement of location	1b
II.	Call to attention	2a
III.	Response	2b
IV.	Self-revelation speech	3-4
	A. Self-revelation formula	
	B. Admonition not to fear	
	C. Reasons	

The theophany report is not from the same narrative mold as the Joseph story (Redford, 18-20). V. 1b ties the theophany to the traditional cultic center at Beer-sheba, with sacrifice offered there to the God of Isaac. There is no allusion to unusual natural phenomena. To the contrary, with only a commentary to define the theophany as a vision of the night, an opening dialogue establishes the scene. But the dialogue itself is typical: a call to attention by means of a twice-repeated call of Jacob's name, a brief response from Jacob, and then a self-revelation formula (cf. Exod 3:4-6). Moreover, the formula relates the God who speaks to the patriarchal tradition. The principal content of the theophany comes in God's admonition to Jacob not to fear, followed by a promise for divine assistance. In four distinct promises, God assures Jacob of divine presence for the descent from Canaan into Egypt and of the corresponding exodus from Egypt to Canaan, of fulfillment of the promise for great posterity and for a death in keeping with family unity. Thus, although style and tradition break out of the pattern in the Joseph story, the report corresponds directly with the Joseph story plot. Given its position in the context of the story's conclusion, it complements the story as a bridge from the patriarchs to the exodus. The report is perhaps originally from E, the Elohistic parallel to the Joseph story at large that derives essentially from J (so, Steck). But it relates intimately to the Joseph story context. It assumes that among the other sons Joseph maintains a primary position of authority, for Joseph will be the son to close Jacob's eyes in death. And it focuses on the crucial movement for Jacob from Canaan to Egypt. It would seem to be, perhaps from the beginning, a commentary on the conclusion of the Joseph story, introducing explicit patriarchal themes.

Genre
The unit develops along stereotyped lines. Formulas include the CALL TO ATTENTION with a double name (cf. Exod 3:4), the response (cf. Exod 3:4), and the SELF-REVELATION formula (cf. Exod 4:6). The speech in vv. 3-4 appears as an ORACLE OF SALVATION, including a promise patterned on the basis of an (→) assistance formula. As a whole, the unit is a theophany REPORT.

Setting
Beyond the setting in the Joseph story, the theophany report derives from the context of family cultic traditions, perhaps closely tied to the site in Beer-sheba.

Intention
In the Joseph story, the theophany report comments on the character of the tradition as a bridge between Canaan and Egypt, between patriarchs and exodus. If the report was originally independent of its Joseph story context, it would nevertheless have provided transition from the patriarchal traditions to the exodus traditions and established a justification for the patriarch's fundamental move.

Bibliography
O. H. Steck, *Die Paradieserzählung. Eine Auslegung von Genesis 2:4b–3:24* (BibS[N] 60; Neukirchen: Neukirchener Verlag, 1970) 120-24 n. 291.

NAME LIST FOR JACOB'S FAMILIES, 46:8-27

Structure

I. Introduction   8a

As a part of the conclusion to the Joseph story, the name list gives formal expression to the process that brought Jacob and his families from Canaan to Egypt. Thus, embraced by the framework provided by the itinerary, it develops a basic harmony with that context. It begins with a stereotyped introduction: "These are the names of . . ." (cf. Exod 1:2; Num 13:15). The continuation defines the content of the list: ". . . the sons of Israel who came to Egypt, Jacob and his sons." Structure in the list is controlled by stereotyped conclusions, dividing the list into four groups: sons of Leah, sons of Zilpah, sons of Rachel, sons of Bilhah. Moreover, the conclusions to each group regularly note the total number of the group. The allusion to a daughter in the Leah group is necessary in order to complete the number of the group and finally the number of the whole unit. But it also serves to pick up the story in Genesis 34 and suggests that the name list has not only the Joseph story in view, but a larger collection of patriarchal traditions (→ Genesis 12–50). As a part of the larger collection, however, the list establishes the character of the context as a bridge, a demonstration of the move from Canaan to Egypt. As a part of the larger collection, moreover, the list would belong to the final redaction of the text.

Genre

The name LIST is similar to a (→) genealogy (cf. Exod 6:14-16). But contrary to genealogy, the list does not focus on the family relationship, but rather on the organization characterized by the segments. It concludes each segment as well as the final summary with a number representing the total number of people encompassed by the list. Its generic quality has thus shifted to administration. It is now like the census lists of Numbers 1 and 26 (cf. also Exod 1:2-4), an organizational catalogue adapted for describing the people who descended into Egypt with Jacob.

Setting

The setting within the context is redactional. As an administrative genre, the list derives from the context of institutions responsible for organizing people into functional groups.

Intention

The list organizes the families of Jacob into their tribal groups in order to depict the shape of the entire body, ready for movement. As a part of the conclusion, it casts the body as a people who entered Egypt. As a demonstration of the move from Canaan to Egypt, it highlights the character of the context as a bridge between patriarchs and exodus.

TAX ETIOLOGY, 47:13-26

Structure

I. Exposition   13-14

Between the two parts of the conclusion to the Joseph story is a distinct unit about Joseph's role as administrator in the pharaoh's service. The narration begins by defining the context for the events to be described as the famine that brought Joseph to power in Egypt. Joseph appears as the grain steward, but no reference to Jacob or the brothers appears. The unit thus has more in common with the digression in chs. 39–41 (so, Gunkel, "Komposition"). Yet, it is not simply an extension of the scene from ch. 41. It does not present Joseph as a discreet and wise administrator. To the contrary, it builds an etiology for a perpetual tax system, an isolated element in the conclusion of the Joseph story.

To that end, the structure sets the context with an exposition, then lays out a series of business negotiations as the foundation for a tax proclamation. The negotiations series displays two distinct elements. In the first, the people request that Joseph sell them grain. Then Joseph sets the price for the transaction, and a narrative element notes the completion of the arrangement. In the second, the people again request a transaction. But the scene in this case has the people designate the price. And the narration shows that the contract was accepted. With the exception of the priesthood, all the people have become slaves to the king. All the land has reverted to the crown. This state of total slavery is made practicable by Joseph's speech in vv. 23-24, a proclamation of the tax law. The pharaoh will give the people land, as well as seed for their crops. In return, he expects a fifth of their income. The people agree, and the narration concludes in v. 26 with a formula confirming the legitimacy of the tax for successive generations.

The report thus builds its system without intrinsic contacts with the conclusion of the Joseph story; indeed, it interrupts the conclusion and hangs as an isolated appendix without altering the fundamental character of the story. In itself, it shows no signs of source duplication or growth. It appears to be from J, attached in the total construction of the Yahwist to the conclusion of the Joseph story.

Genre

The unit is a narrative justification for the tax proclamation. The concluding formula shows the validity of the proclamation for succeeding generations. It is to be defined, then, as ETIOLOGY.

Setting

The etiology is related superficially to the Joseph story, indeed, to the patriarchal traditions. As an isolated piece, it may derive from a distinct political context, adapted for inclusion in the story in order to preserve it (cf. Genesis 41).

Intention

The etiology develops its own intention without altering the shape of the conclusion to the Joseph story. As a distinct tradition, it establishes the basis of tax law by reference to the situation that provoked the tax proclamation.

THE JACOB DEATH REPORT, 47:28 – 50:14

Structure

I. Exposition	47:28
II. Narration of the deathbed scene	47:29-31
A. Transition: passage of time	29aαa
B. Oath dialogue	29aαb-31a
1. Israel's instructions for an oath	29aαb-30a
2. Joseph's agreement	30b
3. Israel's instructions for an oath	31aα
4. Narration of instructions executed	31aβ
C. Preparation for death	31b
III. Adoption for Manasseh-Ephraim	48:1-12a
IV. Continuation of deathbed scene	48:12b
V. Blessing for Ephraim-Manasseh	48:13-20
VI. Continuation of deathbed scene: Jacob's farewell speech	48:21-22
A. Announcement of death	
B. Promise for God's presence	
1. Assistance formula	
2. Promise for possession of land	
C. Designation of land for Joseph	
VII. Tribal sayings speech	49:1-28
VIII. Continuation of deathbed scene	49:29 – 50:14
A. Israel's farewell speech	49:29-32
1. Announcement of death	
2. Instructions for burial	
B. Death report	49:33
C. Dirge	50:1-3
D. Execution of burial instructions	50:4-14
1. Transition: passage of time	4aα
2. Joseph's request	4aβ-5
a. Supplication formula to the pharaoh's house	
b. Message commission formula	
c. Message	
1) Citation from Jacob's burial instructions	

The Jacob death report presupposes the Joseph story. Jacob now dwells in Egypt. Joseph exercises power as an administrative officer in the pharaoh's court, dependent nonetheless on the pharaoh for permission to leave the land. He attends Jacob's illness and supports him in death (cf. 46:4). Moreover, the report has been secondarily incorporated into the Joseph story itself by means of a repetition of the story's denouement (→ 50:15-21).

The narration is not in itself a story. It develops no point of tension but moves instead through a series of scenes with appropriate speeches in order to describe the last days of Jacob. Moreover, as a sequence of scenes, this report provides a structural framework for three distinct elements: a narration of Jacob's adoption for Ephraim and Manasseh in 48:1-12a, a narration of Jacob's blessing on the same two sons in 48:13-20, and a collection of tribal sayings in 49:1-28. These elements appear to be independent units, not originally created for a position in the Jacob death report.

The report is introduced by a brief exposition in 47:28. Pointing to the focal interest for the report, this verse exposes two items of information typical for the summarizing role of the unit as a whole (cf. 50:22). The first one, the number of years Jacob lived in Egypt, establishes an immediate tie with the Joseph story. But it also sets the tone for the report by suggesting a summary of Jacob's life. The same point applies for the second element, the total number of years in Jacob's life. In both cases, the summary indicates completion of a life span (cf. 5:4-5; 25:7-11).

The initial sequence in the report begins with a transition note about passage of time. But the note establishes the purpose of the entire unit: "The time drew near that Israel must die." The ensuing dialogue centers on an oath defining the circumstances for the burial. The initial speech is structured as a conditional request. The request employs a stereotyped supplication formula (cf. 50:4), and it carries a call for the addressee to accept an oath. The call specifies not only the content of the oath, instructions for the burial, but also an ancient ritual for establishing the oath (see von Rad, *Genesis,* 414). Joseph responds to the call with a simple statement of agreement. The speech is thus not an oath but only implies one. V. 31a repeats the process. The call for the oath is a brief speech, employing the verb "to swear" (*šbʻ*). But again, the call is not confirmed by an oath speech, but only by a narrative notation.

V. 31b concludes the oath dialogue. In some sense, this statement might be taken as a conclusion for the deathbed narration as a whole, an indication that Jacob was ready to die (so, Redford, 22). But no reference to his death appears. To the contrary, the narration breaks off and the unit on Jacob's adoption of

301

Ephraim and Manasseh begins. There is obviously some discontinuity in the movement. But the discontinuity does not call for a reconstruction of the scene, or even an evaluation of the scene as a combination of disharmonious layers of literary sources. To the contrary, it points to the role of the death report as a framework narrative. Thus, the narrative leaves an opening for the new element. There is appropriately no explicit notation in 47:31 that Jacob lay on the verge of death, no notation of his death. The note in v. 31 breaks off the scene and allows the new unit, still set in the context of the deathbed moments, to begin. Moreover, the new unit breaks off in 48:12a with a notation that summarizes the adoption procedure (cf. also 50:23). V. 12b repeats the moment described in 47:31b, with the same verb "bow himself" (ḥwh) as the unifying motif. And again there is no notation of immediate death. Rather, the framework provides context at the deathbed for the following unit, a blessing.

The blessing in 48:13-20 also comes to its own natural conclusion without concluding the death report. To the contrary, the speech in 48:21-22 moves beyond the blessing to a farewell statement, a continuation of the death report. The farewell begins with an announcement of Jacob's coming death, a crucial element for farewell speeches (cf. Gen 50:5, 24; Deut 4:22). The continuation carries a promise directed to Joseph. The first element of the promise is an assistance formula: "God will be with you." But contrary to the narrative form of the assistance formula in 39:2, 21, where the object is Joseph alone, here the object is plural. Moreover, the promise continues with an allusion to the land of the fathers, and again the object is plural. The promise could hardly intend only Joseph and his sons. To the contrary, all the sons constitute the point of reference. But the promise in v. 22 intends only Joseph (and his sons?) and builds on a singular pattern. The subject of the promise is again a land, but in this case the land is not a motif in a broad tradition, like the subject of v. 21. It is rather a particular piece of land. If the promise reflects a tradition of long-standing for the Joseph tribes, its character cannot be so easily reconstructed.

The collection of tribal sayings in 49:1-28 is introduced as a continuation of the deathbed scene. Thus, Jacob now summons all his sons. Again, the death-bed moment is appropriate for the blessing context of the sayings. V. 28 rounds off the sayings collection with a commentary defining the collection as a whole as the blessing of the father for his sons. It thus presupposes the position of the series of sayings in the deathbed scene, a continuation of the farewell address in 48:21-22. The death report continues in v. 29 with events described as a continuation of the sayings collection. The speech in 49:29-33, addressed to all the sons, is again a farewell address, similar in construction to 48:21-22 (48:21a par. 49:29a). Moreover, the principal content of the speech parallels 47:29-31 by detailing instructions for Jacob's burial, now a responsibility for all the sons. Immediately following the speech is, finally, an explicit note of Jacob's death (49:33).

The death report ends in 50:1-14 with a description of the dirge over Jacob, vv. 1-3, and a detailed report that the burial instructions were properly executed. It is interesting that the process of executing the instructions starts with a Joseph speech to the household of the pharaoh, rather than to the pharaoh himself. It begins with a supplication formula (cf. 47:29), then commissions the household to take a message to the pharaoh (note the messenger commission formula). The message founds a request for permission to leave Egypt on a citation of Jacob's

302

farewell speech with its burial instructions. The pharaoh grants permission and Joseph, with his retinue, leaves (cf. the exodus images in vv. 7-9). The dirge in vv. 10-11, marking the arrival in Canaan, provides the foundation for an etiology for the place-name, Abel-mizraim. V. 10 notes the dirge at the threshing floor of Atad, and v. 11, the Canaanites' reaction with an appropriate saying. The place-name is derived from the saying. Finally, vv. 12-13 note that the burial instructions were executed properly, and v. 14 Joseph's return with his people to Egypt. The death report has ended.

The framework narration shows no signs of structural duplication that might suggest plural sources. Duplication appears, but it facilitates the function of the report as a framework for independent units. The entire series belongs to a single conception, a redactional device for incorporating other traditions into a narrative context (see Coats, "Redactional Unity"). The death report may also have had a life of its own apart from its structural pattern as a framework narrative (→ Genesis 37–50).

Genre

The unit as a whole is cast as a death REPORT. The structural function of the unit qualifies the report as a framework narrative. The point of unity for the elements in the framework lies in a series of FAREWELL SPEECHES, particularly 47:29-31; 48:11, 21-22; 49:29-32. Moreover, the speeches in 48:3-7, 15-16, 20; 49:1-28 are also typed as FAREWELL SPEECHES in the final form of the narrative, drawing on the deathbed setting for their principal character.

Stereotyped formulas in this report include a SUPPLICATION formula (47:29; 50:4), patriarchal land promise (48:4, 21), ASSISTANCE formula (48:22), MESSENGER COMMISSION formula (50:4), and ETIOLOGICAL formula (50:11).

Setting

The death report now reflects a literary setting, a redactional device for bringing a number of independent traditions together into a single unit. The farewell speech, crucial to the narration, belongs primarily in the deathbed room, the context of a dying patriarch with his family, friends, or even strangers around. It is in this context that a patriarchal blessing has its natural setting. The blessing from a dying patriarch has peculiar efficacy. Taken together, the farewell speeches and blessings constitute the substance of the death report, a structure for preserving family traditions.

Intention

The report as a unit intends (1) to provide a narrative context for distinct and independent traditions, and (2) to depict the last events in Jacob's life, a part of family tradition. The farewell speech gives the last testimony of the dying patriarch to his family, the inheritance, a blessing, or even a curse (cf. 27:27-29, 39-40).

Bibliography
G. W. Coats, "Redactional Unity in Genesis 37–50," *JBL* 93 (1974) 15-21.

ADOPTION REPORT, 48:1-12

Structure

I. Exposition   1-2

The unit relates rather woodenly to the context established by the death report (→ 47:28–50:21). In the final form of the text, it is intended as an extension of the deathbed scene. But Jacob is not at the point of death; he is ill, but his death is postponed.

The structure of the unit illustrates the problem, as well as the basic tendency of the tradition. The substance of the scene lies in element II, structured as a dialogue and framed by an exposition and a brief, narrated conclusion. The exposition, vv. 1-2, establishes the contact between Joseph (with his sons) and Jacob. This point does not harmonize with the established relationship in 47:29-31. Moreover, the structure of the exposition, provided by two speeches reporting Jacob's illness to Joseph and Joseph's going to Jacob, establishes the context for an audience. The occasion is Jacob's illness. The illness may imply that he is dying, but the death is not imminent. The audience does not depend on an imminent death. The exposition thus suggests that the unit has been inserted into the death report, and that its insertion disrupts the context.

The series of speeches in the dialogue is interrupted only by an extensive narration of instructions executed in v. 10. The first speech in the series is complex and does not fit well with the remaining part of the unit. Jacob addresses Joseph first with a recitation of a past event, the theophany of El Shaddai at Luz (Bethel). The recitation includes a citation of a divine speech, the promise to Jacob for great progeny and possession of a land (vv. 3-4). On the basis of the citation, the speech moves to an adoption proclamation (vv. 5-6). On the basis of the promise for progeny, Jacob obtains new sons. Two parts of the proclamation define Jacob's relationship with Ephraim and Manasseh (v. 5) and Joseph's relationship with any other children born to him (v. 6). By direct proclamation before witnesses (Joseph), the speech formally establishes a father-son relationship, thus including Ephraim and Manasseh directly as a part of the promise in vv. 3-4. The speech ends in v. 7 with a renewed recitation, Rachel's death. The precise relationship between this element and the preceding parts of the speech is unclear. Perhaps it is intended only to maintain the deathbed mood for the adoption speech, otherwise not necessarily at home in such a scene.

A discontinuity within the dialogue can be seen, moreover, in the transition from the first speech to the remaining parts of the exchange. Jacob's question in

v. 8 is again addressed to Joseph. The content of the question does not imply that Jacob sees Joseph's sons for the first time at this point, however. To the contrary, the gloss in v. 10a makes clear that the question arises from Jacob's poor eyesight. But it does suggest that the sons have not been previously presented to Jacob in this scene. Moreover, the designation of Jacob's instructions in v. 9b as a call for blessing, as well as a speech in v. 11 that recalls the context of the scene in a death report (cf. 45:28), suggests that the focus may have shifted from the adoption. Yet, the focus is still on the two sons, now kissed and embraced by the patriarch (v. 10b). That movement would apparently confirm the adoption. Furthermore, the adoption pattern influences the conclusion, v. 12a, with its designation of the locale for the sons during the process as the "knees" of the patriarch (mē'im birkāyw), a symbol closely associated with adoption (cf. Gen 40:23, 'al birkê yôsēp ["on the knees of Joseph"]).

The discontinuity derives, perhaps, from a combination of literary sources. The speech in vv. 3-6 (7) is commonly attributed to P, the remaining parts of the report to an older source. If the report should properly break in such a fashion, it would be significant that both sources would maintain some form of an adoption tradition for Ephraim and Manasseh.

Genre
As a unit, these verses present a REPORT of a legal process for adoption. The adoption SPEECH in vv. 3-7 is most clearly cast in such a fashion. Characteristic for the speech is the proclamation of adoption in v. 5: "Now your two sons born to you in the land of Egypt before I came to you in Egypt are mine. Ephraim and Manasseh, like Reuben and Simeon, are mine." The remaining verses are less clearly cast in the role of adoption. They may, indeed, reflect accommodation to the death REPORT context. But the shape of the adoption proceeding is nevertheless present, if not in vv. 9b and 11, then in the narrative conclusion, v. 12a.

Setting
A report of a legal process for adoption does not belong necessarily to a deathbed scene (contrast 30:3). The setting in the tradition, then, is not necessarily the natural one and may cause some of the discontinuity with the context. The more natural setting for the process, as well as construction of a report to describe the process, would be the legal context of the family.

Intention
In the larger context, the report adds to the deathbed scene by depicting one of the acts in the last days of Jacob. The function of the report, formulated within the larger scope of Jacob tradition, would be to establish Ephraim and Manasseh as sons of Jacob, a reflection in the tradition to account for the split of Joseph in response to the loss of Levi.

BLESSING REPORT, 48:13-20

Structure

I. Exposition	13-14
II. Blessing dialogue	15-20a

A. Israel's blessing for Joseph's sons	15-16
B. Joseph's response	17-18
1. Narration of Joseph's displeasure	17
2. Joseph's correction speech	18
C. Blessing speech	19
D. Blessing (tribal saying) speech	20a
III. Conclusion	20b

This unit is more harmonious with the context provided by the death report than is the unit in 48:1-12. One may properly expect the process of blessing to unfold in the framework of a deathbed scene. Yet, the scene does not flow easily from the notation in v. 12b. Moreover, the physical circumstances surrounding the adoption report seem altered. Thus, while some proper context is offered by the death report, the unit seems nonetheless distinct, perhaps disruptive.

Structure in the report focuses on the blessing speeches of Jacob, with a response from Joseph, framed by an exposition and a brief conclusion. The exposition, vv. 13-14, sets the stage for the blessing conclusion. The exposition, vv. 13-14, sets the stage for the blessing by narrating a new presentation of Joseph's sons, with no clear indication of consequences from the presentation in vv. 1-2. The complicated description of the presentation in v. 14 anticipates the exchange between Joseph and Jacob in vv. 17-20, thus binding the elements of the narration closely together. The point of the unusual process in establishing the position for Jacob's hands is to provide the primary blessing (thus, the right-hand blessing) for Ephraim. Vv. 17-19 then narrate an exchange between Joseph and Jacob, developing Joseph's objection to this act of preference: Ephraim is the younger of the two sons. The father responds in v. 19 with a promise in line with the patriarchal promise: Both sons shall participate in the proclivity for great posterity characteristic of the family. The speech is thus parallel to the adoption speech in vv. 3-7. But in addition, Jacob's speech elevates Ephraim to the more prominent position (cf. 21:12-13). The conclusion in v. 20b marks the Ephraim elevation as the primary result of this section.

The speech in vv. 15-16 fits into the middle of the exchange between Jacob and Joseph. It is addressed to Joseph, thus structurally a part of the exchange. But it contains a patriarchal blessing for Ephraim and Manasseh, referring to the two sons in the third person. The initial part of the speech is the invocation for the blessing, with the blessing proclamation in v. 16a designating the two sons together, a single unit. Moreover, the continuation incorporates the two into the patriarchal promise. It thus occupies an additional parallel position to the adoption speech. But contrary to the exchange in vv. 17-19, in the blessing speech nothing of a preference for Ephraim can be seen. They do not stand over against each other. One must conclude that the speech represents a distinct stage of tradition incorporated into the description of the audience between the patriarch and Joseph.

The speech in v. 20a is more problematic. It is parallel to the tribal sayings collected in 49:1-28 (cf. vv. 3-4). Thus, the names of the two tribal fathers are cited in the direct address. And the groups are considered as a single unit, as in vv. 15-16. To be sure, the order of the names places Ephraim first, a point in harmony with the elevation of Ephraim noted in v. 20b. Yet, no other sign of Ephraim's elevation can be seen. Both tribes share the same saying. One must ask, then, whether this speech, like vv. 15-16, reflects an earlier stage in the history of the tradition, as yet unaffected by the elevation of the one tribe over the other. It is important to note, however, that the signs of discontinuity in the unit do not point to a combination of literary sources. The layers doubtlessly reflect the oral tradition history of the unit.

Genre

As a unit, these verses present a REPORT of a BLESSING, with three distinct blessing SPEECHES to carry the weight of the process. The final speech, v. 20a, is parallel to the speeches in the collection of tribal sayings, 49:1-28.

Setting

A report of a blessing fits naturally into the context of a deathbed scene, a part of the final acts of the patriarch. The setting in the tradition is thus harmonious with the natural setting in the family structure of the society. The particular interests of the two tribal groups, particularly the Ephraimite group, suggest that the family setting may be quite specific.

Intention

In the larger context of the Jacob death report, the blessing process adds detail to the presentation. The function of the report at its latest level is to establish Ephraim as the heir to the family over the brother. At earlier levels, the tradition functions simply to incorporate the two tribes into the tribal structure by providing patriarchal blessing. The saying in v. 20a functions in a similar way, yet, it designates a particular characteristic for these tribes among the other members of the group. It thus provides for tradition to supplement the collection in the following chapter.

Bibliography

E. C. Kingsbury, "He Sat Ephraim Before Manasseh," *HUCA* 38 (1967) 129-36.

COLLECTION OF TRIBAL SAYINGS, 49:1-28

Structure

I. Speech introduction: Jacob to his sons	1a
II. Speech: the tribal sayings	1b-27
A. Call to attention	1b-2
B. Address to Reuben	3-4
1. Designation of firstborn status	3
2. Judgment	4
a. Denial of firstborn status	
b. Reason	
C. Statement about Simeon and Levi	5-7
1. Definition of relationship	5a
2. Judgment	5b-6
a. Reason	5b
b. Denial of presence to them	6a
c. Reason	6b
3. Curse	7a

307

This unit is constructed as a speech, a natural element in the larger context of the Jacob death report. In keeping with the context, elements I and III define the unit as a speech at the moment of Jacob's death, the patriarchal blessing to the sons. The sayings in the speech, however, were originally independent of the deathbed context.

Structure in the collection of sayings, element II, is defined by the order of names in the Israelite confederation. But the order is problematic. The collection begins with the Leah tribes, a regular point in the sequence. The last two names in the group are not controlled by a stereotyped pattern, however (see 46:13-14 for the more common order, Issachar-Zebulun). The Bilhah and Zilpah tribes intervene between the Leah and Rachel groups (so 29:32–30:24). In this case, however, the Bilhah tribes have been split, with the Zilpah tribes inserted in the common order between them (contrast Num 13:4-16). Then the Rachel tribes appear in order at the end of the list. The constant elements in the order of the tribes are the Leah and Rachel groups, with the exception of a more fluid position for Issachar and Zebulun (see also 30:14-20). The inconstant elements are the Zilpah and Bilhah groups, as well as Issachar and Zebulun (see Coppens).

Within the framework of a twelve-tribe order, this collection of sayings poses one additional problem. It contains only eleven sayings or groups of sayings—the tribes of Simeon and Levi have been combined. This problem may reflect the stage in the history of the tribal list when Levi had been dropped. The normal procedure, in that case, would have been to replace Joseph with two distinct entries, Ephraim and Manasseh (so, 48:1-12a). But Joseph remains in place. Perhaps a saying for Ephraim lies behind v. 22 (see Zobel, 21-23). Perhaps the twelfth entry is to be found in 48:20, a saying significantly combining Ephraim and Manasseh. Or perhaps the collection reflects a stage in the history of the list that did not depend on the number twelve (see also Deut 33:6-25).

The speech itself begins with a call to attention, addressed in plural to all the sons. The first element in the call, v. 1b, is constructed in parallel to the first element in v. 2a, while the second element in v. 2a is paralleled in v. 2b. The harmony of the parallel suggests that the call is a unit, not to be split into two distinct parts (contrast the *RSV*).

The entries in the collection most frequently have only one saying for each tribal unit, or in the case of Simeon and Levi, one saying for two tribal units (so, 48:20). For Judah, Dan, and Joseph, multiple sayings appear. In addition, v. 18 is a gloss on the Dan sayings (see Zobel, 19). The sayings can be constructed as a simple assertion about the tribal father, with reference to the patriarch in the third person (vv. 9, 16, 17, 19, 20, 21, 22, 27). Moreover, the assertion may be a short statement, drawing on a wordplay: "Dan shall judge his people as one of the tribes of Israel." In v. 16, the assertion draws on a wordplay between the name of the tribe and the verb "judge" (*dān yādîn*). For other wordplays, see vv. 8, 13, 19. Or the assertion may, as v. 17, build on a metaphor: "Dan shall be a serpent in the way, a viper in the path. . . ." For other metaphors, see vv. 9, 14-15, 20, 21, 22, 27 (cf. 16:12).

The assertion may also be more complex. Some entries build on the pattern of an assertion but extend the saying to include new statements or a commentary on the lead statement (so, vv. 5-7, 10-12, 13, 14-15, 23-24a). The saying in vv. 5-7, e.g., opens with a definition of relationship between the two tribal units, followed by an assertion about the groups. But the continuation develops a first-person self-admonition to avoid the tribes (v. 6) and ends with a curse formula (v. 7a) and a final judgment on the tribes (v. 7b; cf. 27:29). The curse formula is, in effect, an indictment leading to the judgment, with the substance of the indictment expressed in the dependent (*kî*) clause. And both indictment and judgment stand together as integral parts of the saying (Zobel, 7-9). Vv. 10-12 follow a similar pattern, with v. 10 a lead assertion, vv. 11-12 then bound tightly to it (see Zobel, 12-15). Whether these verses constitute a secondary extension of v. 9 is not altogether clear (contrast Zobel).

V. 13 is somewhat different. In a saying composed of three members, the tribe is defined in terms of its territory. The structure of the saying, however, does not draw on three assertions, but on a single assertion in the first member, qualified by the following two parts. Finally, the entries in vv. 14-15 and 22-24 present a particular kind of extension. The opening assertion, vv. 14-22, employs a metaphor, and the continuation in vv. 15 and 23-24a is bound to the metaphor. But in content, the extension has relatively little to do with its point of contact (see Zobel, 22-23, particularly on vv. 23-24a).

Direct-address sayings are less common in the collection and constructed in more complex patterns (so, vv. 3-4, 8, 24b-26; cf. also 48:20; v. 9 also has second-person elements, yet these derive from redactional adjustments in relationship to v. 8; see Zobel, 14-15). The sayings in 48:20 and 49:24b-26 associate a second-person address with a third-person assertion about the tribe. In 48:20, the construction is clearer. The third-person assertion functions as a citation within the second-person address. The assertion may then be the kernel at the base of the saying. In 49:24b-26 the problems are more difficult. The distinction between this saying and the one in vv. 23-24 is not altogether clear. V. 25aα could be taken as a continuation of v. 24b (cf. the construction with *min* ["by means of"]). But the address now involves second-person elements, in contrast to vv. 23-24, with perhaps the exception of v. 26b. Could it not be that the distinctions in vv. 22-26 reflect growth in a single tribal saying (contrast Zobel)?

The remaining sayings, vv. 3-4 and 8, are not so complex. Yet, they also present problems in structure. The first one begins with a simple assertion, a definition of Reuben's rights as firstborn. The second element reverses that definition with a new figure of speech. The reversal can be understood as a curse with its justification, in effect, an indictment like vv. 5-7 (see Zobel, 6-7). But it has no formal curse statement and stands simply as an elaboration of the initial assertion. V. 8 is a collection of three assertions about Judah's fortunate position, addressed to Judah directly. The first and third define Judah's relationship with his brothers, with the second some justification for the relationship (see Zobel, 10-11).

Each assertion reflects a peculiar position in the history of the confederation. Unity of the sayings in a single collection derives from a period in the tradition's history when the formulation of the confederation was not bound by a fixed series. The six-tribe group related to Leah seems relatively firm, although Levi's position in the group is problematic. Joseph's position has not yet been displaced by Ephraim and Manasseh. Thus, the point in the tradition's history seems to be relatively early, with the list and thus the organization rather fluid. It is not possible, however, to attach all the sayings to the same stage in the history of the tradition. Moreover, it is clear that the collection cannot be attributed to any one of the early sources with any degree of confidence. It was, to the contrary, taken into one of the sources, probably J, through the device provided by the framework narrative.

Genre

In the final form of the text, the unit is a COLLECTION of tribal SAYINGS, constructed as a deathbed BLESSING (see Deuteronomy 33). The individual elements in the speech are tribal sayings, intimately related to, but not the same as, tribal blessing. But finer specification must be sought. The term "saying" is in itself broad, encompassing various genres (→ SAYING). The simplest saying is an (→) epigram (Lindblom, 79) or (→) aphorism (von Rad, *Genesis,* 421), perhaps a tribal (→) proverb constructed as a brief sentence employing a metaphor, a wordplay, or some other description of tribal character. Or the saying may develop oracular quality, either in terms of a simple definition of future tribal character, or in more complex forms. The statement in vv. 5-7 is a prophetic CURSE, with Jacob representing the prophetic messenger with a divine speech (so, Zobel, 9). The address in vv. 3-4 has much in common with a curse (see Zobel, 6). The contrary form can also be seen, a blessing for Joseph (vv. 25-26).

Setting

As a part of the deathbed scene, the collection shares a redactional setting with the narrative. As an earlier collection of sayings preserving reflections about characteristics of tribal groups, the collection belongs to the political life of the confederation, with the power structures apparent (so, Gunneweg). A more precise definition does not appear feasible (but see Gunneweg). The tribal proverbs may derive from folk wisdom (cf. Prov 28:15), the oracles from a prophetic tribal ritual (see Zobel).

Intention

The collection of tribal sayings orients from the blessing or cursing context of the deathbed scene to define the characteristics of each tribe or group of tribes. The saying is related to the blessing by virtue of the performative character in its pronouncement. But its primary intention lies in depicting the quality of the tribe (see Gunneweg).

Bibliography

J. Coppens, "La bénédiction de Jacob. Son cadre historique à la lumière des parallèles ougaritiques," in *Volume du congrès Strasbourg* (VTSup 4; Leiden: Brill, 1957) 97-115; A. H. J. Gunneweg, "Über den Sitz im Leben der sog. Stammessprüche," *ZAW* 76 (1964) 245-55; J. Lindblom, "The Political Background of the Shiloh Oracle," in *Congress Volume Copenhagen* (VTSup 1; Leiden: Brill, 1953) 78-87; H.-J. Zobel, *Stammesspruch und Geschichte. Die Angaben der Stammessprüche von Gen 49, Dtn 33 und Jdc 5 über die politischen und kultischen Zustände im damaligen 'Israel'* (BZAW 95; Berlin: Töpelmann, 1965).

RECAPITULATION OF JOSEPH STORY
DENOUEMENT, 50:15-21

Structure

I. Transition	15aα
II. The brothers' speech: an explanation for following action	15aβb
III. The brothers' messenger speech to Joseph	16-17a
A. Reason for request	16-17aα
1. Introduction to a citation from Jacob	16
2. Citation from Jacob	17aα
B. Request	17aβ
IV. Narration of Joseph's response	17b
V. Audience with Joseph	18-21a
A. The brothers' commitment as Joseph's slaves	18
B. Joseph's reconciliation speech	19-21a
1. Assurance of reconciliation	
a. Formula against fear	
b. Theological explanation	
2. Assurance of reconciliation	
a. Formula against fear	
b. Promise for provision	
VI. Conclusion	21b

This unit depends on the context provided by the death report in 47:28–50:14. But it also depends on the Joseph novella. To be sure, the Joseph novella ends in

47:27, with no strands of plot left open. Rather than a continuation of the story, with a new line of development for one or more of its principal motifs, this short section represents a recapitulation of the denouement, adapted for a position after the Jacob death report.

The unit opens with a brief transition from the deathbed scene, then sets the context with two relatively distinct speeches. These two speeches reproduce the crisis immediately preceding the denouement, 45:1-3. To discover that the potentate who controlled their fate was Joseph dismayed the brothers. Now to stand before Joseph without Jacob to protect them reactivates the brothers' anxiety. Thus, an apparent new breach in the family relationships occurs, a breach caused not simply by the death of the father, but explicitly by anticipation of Joseph's response to their earlier treachery.

The second speech is addressed to Joseph through a messenger, as the context suggests. And the messenger speech intensifies the tense relationships. The brothers do not go to Joseph personally with their plea. Moreover, they build their plea on a citation from Jacob that recalls patterns of deception from ch. 43 (see particularly v. 7). The first part of the speech, an introduction to a citation from Jacob (v. 16), drives the point home. Jacob had addressed a request to the brothers before he died, a speech Joseph did not hear. The citation itself begins with a messenger commission formula. The brothers stand under the now dead father's commission to relay a message to Joseph. And the message instructs Joseph to forgive the brothers for their treachery. Then, on the basis of the citation, the brothers pose their request for forgiveness. Thus, contrary to the scene in ch. 45 where the brothers take no initiative for asking forgiveness, here they pose their own request that Joseph forgive their treachery. Yet, the speech suggests more about the brothers' unchanged character than about their desire for forgiveness. The plan the brothers hatch is painfully transparent. No speech like the one cited as the basis for the appeal appears in this unit or in any other section of the death report of the Joseph story proper. The impact of this point is not that the speech has dropped out of the transmitted material. It is that as in 43:3-5, so here the brothers manufacture a defense. They still depend on deception as a way of life.

Element IV contains Joseph's response to the message, a recapitulation of the weeping motif from the Joseph story. Thus, v. 17b has parallels in 42:24; 43:30; 45:2, 14. In each case, the motif points toward the final resolution of the tension between Joseph and his brothers. Here the motif also sets the stage for the denouement. Element V then carries the weight of the scene, an audience between Joseph and his brothers (see chs. 43-45). The brothers open the audience by proclaiming themselves Joseph's servants (see 44:16). Joseph responds with a speech constructed on the pattern of an oracle of salvation (cf. 45:4-8). Moreover, Joseph's point following the formula against fear is a duplication of the theological interpretation in 45:5, 7, 8. Here the contrast between the brothers' intention and God's intention has been abstracted from the family context: "You meant evil. . . . But God meant it for good, to bring it about that many people should be kept alive." The tie with patriarchal tradition apparent in 45:4-8 has been broken. Joseph's role in Egypt now does not relate to preserving the family of Jacob, but to preserving many people without reference explicitly to familial ties. The speech continues with a new formula from the oracle of salvation pattern, followed in this case by a promise for provision (cf. 45:11; 47:12). The unit concludes with a notation that Joseph offset their anxiety. The reconciliation is again complete.

The unit shows no structural doublets, no problem in unity. It derives from a single source, a product of the same literary movement that brought the narration of Jacob's death into the overall collection of tradition about Jacob and his sons.

Genre
The unit cannot be classified as a distinct genre apart from its role as a recapitulation, a literary device in the overall redaction of Genesis 37–50. To be sure, it reflects a point of tension and its resolution. And while it is dependent on the death (→) report preceding it, it is a new movement in the narration. Yet, all major lines of development in the unit have parallels in the denouement of the Joseph story. Some differences can be seen, but the differences derive from the context following the death report and do not undercut a definition of the unit as recapitulation.

The speech in vv. 16-17a is cast as a MESSAGE. Yet, it has no (→) messenger commission formula, no messenger formula. Within the speech, a citation from Jacob to the brothers is also cast as a MESSAGE, in this case with a MESSENGER COMMISSION formula. The speeches in vv. 18-21a appear as an audience DIALOGUE, an exchange between a person of high rank with subjects under his power. An audience dialogue can be decorated with formulas demonstrating the differences in rank, such as self-abasement formulas or supplication formulas. These formulas do not appear here. But the brothers' commitment to Joseph as slaves follows the same line. Contrary to 45:4, Joseph's speech in vv. 19-21 is structured as an ORACLE OF SALVATION, including two formulas against fear and a promise for provision (corresponding with a typical promise for salvation).

Setting
This unit belongs to the literary redaction responsible for including the death report of 47:28–50:14 as a part of the overall unit on Jacob and his sons. It does not have any other setting than the setting in the literary redaction.

Intention
The unit as a whole functions as a redactional device for binding the death report of 47:28–50:14 into the Joseph story (so, Coats, "Redactional Unity").

Bibliography
G. W. Coats, "Redactional Unity in Genesis 37–50," *JBL* 93 (1974) 15-21.

THE JOSEPH DEATH REPORT, 50:22-26

Structure
I. Exposition	22
II. Patriarchal adoption of the children of Machir	23
III. Farewell speech to the brothers	24
A. Announcement of coming death	
B. Promise for exodus and possession of the land	

This unit concludes the series of narratives in Genesis 37–50, indeed, in Genesis 12–50. It presupposes not only the Joseph story, thus Joseph's position of power in Egypt, but the Jacob death report as well. In addition, it points forward to the wilderness theme (Exod 13:19) and the conquest (Josh 24:32). Thus, it relates to a large context of narrative material.

The elements of structure in the report seem to be loosely joined without clear lines of development from one point to another. The pattern of structure is nevertheless clear, developed on the basis of a parallel with the Jacob death report in 47:28–50:14. It begins with a summary of Joseph's life, an exposition for the report developed in parallel to 47:28. Both expositions open with a statement about the life of the subject in Egypt. However, the verb in the statement is different from the verb of 47:28 but the same as the verb in 47:27. This unit may thus reflect a stage in the redaction when the Joseph novella and the Jacob death report had already been combined. Moreover, this verse makes no reference to the number of years Joseph lived in Egypt. The parallel seems nonetheless present. In addition, both texts continue with a note about the total number of years in the subject's life. Thus, as in 47:28, so here the exposition sets the mood of the narration by summarizing the scope of Joseph's life.

The second element in the narration defines the relationship Joseph held with the children of Ephraim and Manasseh to the third generation. This description suggests a parallel with 48:3-12. Although no explicit adoption formula appears, the expression "born on Joseph's knees" points to the process (see 48:12). The farewell speech in v. 24 parallels the farewell speech in 48:21 with an announcement of Joseph's coming death and a promise to the survivors for possession of the land. In this case, as in 48:21, the land is identified in relationship to the fathers. But contrary to Jacob's speech, this speech ties the land to an explicit promise to the patriarchs. And the patriarchs are identified by the formula "Abraham, Isaac, and Jacob," presupposing unification of the patriarchal traditions (→ Genesis 12–50).

The speech in v. 25 is identified as an oath. It gives burial instructions (cf. 47:31) specifically with an allusion to the exodus. No detailed description of a burial place, parallel to 49:29-32, appears here. To the contrary, Joseph secures an oath only to have his bones taken out of Egypt at the exodus (cf. Exod 13:19, a citation of this speech, and Josh 24:32). But the parallel with Jacob's burial instruction speech cannot be mistaken. The unit ends in v. 26 with an explicit note of the death, a repetition summary by reference to total age, and a designation of execution for the burial instructions.

The report is not composed from segments of different sources. It presupposes a late stage in the development of the redaction, including the position of the adoption speech in 48:3-7.

Genre

The unit is a death REPORT for Joseph. It is, moreover, a part of a larger whole, with no independent existence (→ Genesis 12–50).

Setting

The unit derives from a literary setting in the redaction responsible for bringing a large section of narrative material together into a single whole (→ Genesis 12–50).

Intention

As a literary device, the report provides a point of contact in unifying structure in a large collection of material, Genesis 12–50. Indeed, it sets a key for structural unity with other framework elements such as Exod 13:19 and Josh 24:32. As a death report, the unit marks the end of the Joseph-Jacob series, indeed, the end of the patriarchal tradition, by narrating the end of the last principal in the series.

GLOSSARY

GENRES

ANECDOTE (Anekdote). A particular kind of report that records an event as an experience in the life of a person. (Gen 25:29-34; 35:21-22a; 36:6-8)

ANNALS (Annalen). A report from the archives of the royal court. (Gen 14:1-24)

ANNUNCIATION OF BIRTH (Geburtsankündigung). A speech, commonly delivered by Yahweh or a representative of Yahweh, announcing the imminent birth of a child. (Gen 18:1-15)

APHORISM (Lehrspruch). A terse saying, embodying a general truth or a characteristic typical for the addressee.

APOPHTHEGM (Merkspruch, Logion). A short and pointed saying, commonly supported by a narrative framework. The form-critical assumption is that for the intention of the apophthegm, the saying is primary. (Gen 9:18-29)

BIOGRAPHY (Biographie). A kind of history writing that documents events of a particular life throughout its duration. The structure is controlled by the record of events in the chronology of life.

BLESSING (Segen, Segnung). A speech, structured in either a subjunctive (imperative, cohortative, jussive) or indicative mood, designed to enhance the object of the blessing with the creative power of the performative word.

CHRONICLE (Chronik). A narrative account of outstanding achievements by some particular historical figure. The events and deeds will be in some manner unique and suggest reason for remembering the principal figure. Related genre: (→) Annals.

COLLECTION (Sammlung). A general term describing any combination of genres. Thus, a collection of sayings would be a combination of individual tribal sayings organized according to the traditional list of the twelve tribes.

CURSE (Fluch). A speech, structured in a subjunctive (imperative, cohortative, jussive) or indicative mood, designed to diminish the object of the curse with the creative power of the performative word.

DIALOGUE (Dialog, Zwiegespräch). A combination of speeches, each in response to the other, with the pattern of response significant for special types of dialogue. The term is thus more appropriate for referring to structure than genre.

DIRGE (Leichenlied, Leichenklage, Leichenklagelied, Trauerlied, Grabgesang). A speech spoken at the death of an associate, or by a professional or gifted individual. It may be marked by a particular rhythm or meter. The typical meter is three plus two beats in the line (*qînâ*).

317

EPIGRAM (Inschrift). A witty, ingenious, or pointed saying, tersely expressed. A tribal epigram would characterize the subject "with regard to distinguishing features, customs, or dwelling places, often with a humorous or satiric sting" (J. Lindblom, "The Political Background of the Shiloh Oracle," in *Congress Volume Copenhagen* [VTSup 1; Leiden: Brill, 1953] 79).

ETIOLOGY (Ätiologie). A narrative designed in its basic structure to support some kind of explanation for a situation or name that exists at the time of the storyteller. It builds a connection between a saying in the body of the genre and a conclusion that provides the explanation. Sometimes it is a simple wordplay. (Gen 32:2-3)

EXAMPLE STORY (Beispielerzählung). Provides a concrete example to illustrate a point. (Gen 24:1-67)

FABLE (Fabel). Depicts a world of fantasy with the principal figures drawn from both human and subhuman creatures. Describes a static situation. Typically, a presumptuous character has an overblown ego pricked by a pointed moral.

GENEALOGY (Stammbaum, Genealogie). Builds on a system of enumeration rather than narration. It is more nearly akin to (→) list, but can incorporate (→) story in its scope. It derives ultimately from tribal circles as a means for the history and validation of tribal units.
Linear Genealogy (Gen 4:1-26; 5:1–9:29; 11:10–25:11; 22:20-24; 25:1-6)
Segmented Genealogy (Gen 10:1-32; 25:12-16; 36:9-14)

HIEROS LOGOS (Heiligtumslegende). Sacred words used for showing the origin of a holy place; cultic legend intended as an account of the foundation of a sanctuary by a depiction of the event of the construction that marked the place as holy. (Gen 28:10-22; 33:18-20; 35:1-7; 35:9-15)

HISTORY (Geschichtsschreibung). Designed to record events of the past as they actually occurred. The structure is controlled by chronological stages or cause-effect sequences of events as the author(s) understood them.

HYMN (Loblied, Hymnus). A song of praise highlighting particular deeds or particular characteristics of the person praised, typically the Lord.

ITINERARY (Wegverzeichnis, Itinerar). A list of itinerary formulas, each marking the place of departure and the place of arrival for the subject of the list. The genre shows movement of the subject physically, but it also can depict movement for various pieces of literature such as battle reports, tales, legends. Related genres: (→) Annals, (→) Chronicle.

LEGEND (Legende). Static narration with recurring emphasis on some particular characteristic of the narrative's hero, usually a virtue of high value. The goal is edification of the audience. (Gen 22:1-19; 39–41)

LIST (Liste). A serial document, organizing the items in the serial in a representative, functional order.
King list (Gen 36:31-39)
Name List (Gen 35:22b-26; 36:15-19; 36:40-43; 46:8-27)

MESSAGE (Botschaft). A communication, typically a (→) speech, sent from one subject to another by a third party, designed to deliver information or instruction for some particular goal.

MYTH (Mythos, Mythe). A narrative form set in a fantasy world designed to account for the real world by reference to activities of the gods in the divine world. (Gen 6:1-4)

NOVELLA (Novelle). Develops a point of tension to a final resolution. The perspective is this world. The structural character is complex; it may employ subplots. It is not set within the process of oral tradition. (Genesis 13–14; 18–19; 16:1–21:21; 24:1-67; 26:34–33:20; 29:1–32:1; 32:4–33:17; 37:1–47:27; 38:1-30)

OATH (Eid, Schwur). A speech that binds the speaker to a particular act or position for future acts.

ORACLE (Orakel). A speech of God, delivered by a prophet or some other duly commissioned individual.

ORACLE OF SALVATION (Heilsorakel, Heilsspruch, Heilsankündigung). (Gen 15:1-21)

PROVERB (Sprichwort, Weisheitswort). A saying based on observation or other kinds of experience.

Related genres: (→) Saying, (→) Epigram, (→) Aphorism.

REGISTER (Register). A name list containing the membership of a particular entity.

REPORT (Bericht). Shares with (→) history the intention to record without developing the points of tension characteristic for a plot. It is brief. (Gen 1:1–2:4a; 19:30-38; 35:21-22a; 36:6-8)

There are several types of reports:

(1) Adoption (Gen 48:1-12)

(2) Battle (Gen 14:1-24)

(3) Birth (Gen 25:19-26; 36:1-5)

(4) Blessing (Gen 48:13-20)

(5) Death (Gen 23:1-20; 25:7-11; 25:17-18; 35:8; 35:16-20; 35:27-29)

(6) Dream (Gen 37:5-11)

(7) Theophany (Gen 46:1b-4)

(8) Marriage (Gen 36:2-3)

SAGA (Sage). A long, prose, traditional narrative having an episodic structure developed around stereotyped themes or objects. It may include narratives that represent distinct genres in themselves. The episodes narrate deeds or virtues from the past insofar as they contribute to the composition of the present narrator's world.

Types of sagas are:

(1) Primeval Saga. Narrative account of the beginning of time, the time that produced the world as it is from an original ideal world. Episodic series. (Yahwist's version, Genesis 1–11)

(2) Family Saga. Narrative account of the events that compose the past of a family unit, exemplified primarily by the affairs of the patriarchal head of the family. Episodic series. (Yahwist's version of the Abraham Saga, Genesis 12–26)

(3) Heroic Saga. Narrative account of the events that compose the past of a people's leader who, by virtue of his identification with his people, made it possible for them to endure. Episodic units. (Yahwist's version of the Moses Saga).

319

SAYING (Spruch). A general term describing a brief speech of intrinsic value. Related genres: (→) Wisdom Saying, (→) Proverb.

SONG (Gesang, Lied). A poetic composition performed by an individual or group. Boasting. (Gen 4:23-24)

SPEECH (Rede). A general term describing any oral communication enacted by one of the principals of a pericope. More detailed definition of speech is desirable. For example, a speech may be an oath, an oracle, an accusation.

TALE (Sage, volkstümliche Geschichte oder Erzählung). A short narrative characterized by a minimum number of characters, single scene, and plot. It employs exposition, development of tension, and resolution. Complexity of plot is limited. (Gen 2:4b–3:24; 4:1-16; 11:1-9; 16:1-16; 18:1-15; 21:1-21; 12:9–13:1; 19:1-29; 20:1-18; 21:22-34; 26:1-17; 26:34–28:9; 34:1-31)

TORAH (Unterweisung). A unique combination of story and commandment that makes a fundamental statement about what God expects by saying as forcefully as possible what the people of God is. (Pentateuch)

FORMULAS

ACCUSATION (Anklageformel). Typically begins with the interrogative particle *lāmmâ*, "Why have you done this thing?", or *mah-zō't 'āśît*, "What have you done?" The formula is constructed in the 2nd person as a direct challenge to some previous act. (Gen 3:13; 4:6, 10; 12:18-19a; 16:5a; 20:9; 26:9a, 10; 31:26-28a; 31:30; 31:36b-37aα; 29:25b; 42:1b; 43:6; 44:4-5, 15)

AGE (Alters-). Establishes the statistic in relationship to a particular event of seminal importance for the subject's life. (Gen 7:6)

ASSISTANCE (Beistands-). "I am with you." (Gen 26:3aβb; 26:24; 28:15; 31:3; 39:2-3, 21; 48:22)

AUTHORIZATION (Bevollmächtigungs-). (Gen 41:44)

BEGINNING DIALOGUE (Dialogeröffnungs-). (Gen 27:1, 18)

BLESSING (Segens-). Introduced with the word "to bless" (*wayĕbārek*) and constructed with imperatives. (Gen 1:28; 8:17b; 9:1-2; 9:26-27; 10:8a; 12:2-3; 27:29; 28:3-4; 28:24b; 32:30b (*RSV* 29b); 43:14, 29; 48:13-20; 48:19)

CALL TO ATTENTION (Lehreröffnungs-, Aufforderung zum Hören-). (Gen 46:2a)

COMMISSION SPEECH (Sendungsrede-). (Gen 37:13-14a; 42:2)

COMPLAINT (Klagende Bitt-). (Gen 44:7)

CONCLUDING (FOR GENEALOGIES) (Schluss-). (Gen 25:4b; 25:16; 35:26b; 36:5b; 36:17b)

CONCLUSION (Gen 2:1; 2:4a; 1:5b; 1:8b; 1:13; 1:19; 1:23; 1:31b)

CONFESSION OF GUILT (Schuldbekenntnis-, Schuldgeständnis-). (Gen 44:16)

CONVERSATION (Gesprächs-). With the vocative as a call to attention and the response constructed with the particle *hinnēh* plus suffix. (Gen 22:1, 7, 11)

COVENANT (Bundes-). "I shall be your god; you shall be my people." (Gen 9:9-11; 9:12-16; 17:10a)

320

CURSE (Fluch-). Employs the passive participle *'ārûr* ("cursed") with a definition of the one to be cursed and the content of the curse. (Gen 3:14; 3:17-19; 4:11-12; 9:25; 27:27b-29; 27:39-40; 49:7)

DATING (Datierungs-). Attests an event by fixing the year, the month, the day the event occurred. (Gen 7:11; 8:4, 5, 13, 14)

DIRGE (Leichenklage-, Leichenklagelied-, Leichenlied-, Trauerlied-, Grabgesang-). (Gen 37:34-35; 42:36; 43:14; 50:1-3)

ETIOLOGICAL (ätiologische-). (Gen 2:24; 4:25; 16:13-14; 19:22; 19:37; 19:38; 21:31; 26:20b; 26:21b; 26:22aβb; 26:33; 28:16-17; 31:48-49; 32:3b; 32:31; 32:32-33; 38:29b; 38:30; 50:11)

EXECUTION (Vollzugs-). "And it was so." (Gen 1:3b; 1:7b; 1:9b; 1:11b; 1:15b; 1:24b; 1:31a; 7:18-19; 7:5, 9)

FAREWELL SPEECH (Abschiedsrede-). (Gen 46:30; 47:29-31; 48:11, 21-22; 49:29-22)

IDENTIFYING EVIDENCE (Beweissmittel-). (Gen 38:25b)

INTRODUCTORY (Einleitungs-). (Gen 25:13a; 35:22b; 36:9; 36:11a; 36:13a; 36:14a; 36:15bα; 36:17aα; 36:20a; 36:22aα; 36:23aα; 36:24aα; 36:25aα; 36:26a; 36:27a; 36:28a, 29a; 36:31; 36:40)

ITINERARY (Itinerar-). (Gen 12:8-9; 13:1; 13:18; 13:3; 20:1; 26:17; 26:22aα; 26:23; 28:10; 33:18; 35:16a; 35:21; 46:1a; 46:5-7)

JUDGMENT (Urteils-). From God to the addressee; typically employs some statement of indictment as the foundation for a sentence as divine judgment. (Gen 2:17; 3:14-15; 6:13; 7:1-4; 7:11-12; 7:17-21; 6:4; 11:8; 20:3)

KINSHIP (Verwandtschafts-). (Gen 2:23; 29:14)

KNOWLEDGE (Kenntnis-). (Gen 42:33a; 42:34ab)

MESSENGER (Boten-). Part of the speech commissioned by the sender for delivery to the recipient. It functions to identify the sender for the recipient, if not also to claim the authority of the sender for the message. (Gen 32:5bβ-6 [*RSV* 4bβ-5]; 45:9; 24:30)

MESSENGER COMMISSION (Botensendungs-, Botenbeauftragungs-). Addresses the messengers directly with the commission to act for the sender as bearers of a message. (Gen 32:4-5bα [*RSV* 3-4bα]; 44:4; 45:17, 18; 46:34; 50:4)

NAME LIST (Namenslisten-). (Gen 36:20b-21a; 36:22aβ; 36:23aβb; 36:24aβ; 36:25aβb; 36:26b; 36:27b; 36:28b; 36:29b-30a)

NAMING (Namensgebungs-). "God named the day." Can commonly be combined with an inflected form of the verb "name" and reveals a wordplay with a preceding or following element. (Gen 1:19aβb-20a; 2:11-14; 2:23b; 3:20; 4:25; 4:26; 5:29a)

NARRATIVE (Erzählungs-). "After these things. . . ." (Gen 15:1; 22:1aα)

NARRATIVE INTRODUCTION (Erzählungseinleitungs-). "It happened at that time. . . ." (Gen 38:1)

OATH (Eides-, Schwur-). (Gen 24:41; 26:31a; 42:15, 16; 42:37; 44:10; 47:29-32)

ORACLE OF SALVATION (Heilsorakel-, Heilsspruchs-, Heilsankündigungs-). (Gen 46:3-4; 21:17; 28:13aβb-14; 31:24b; 31:11-13)

REASSURANCE (Bestätigungs-). (Gen 15:1b)

SELF-ABASEMENT (Selbsterniedrigungs-, Selbstdemütigungs-). (Gen 18:27)

SELF-DEFENSE. (Selbstverteidigungs-). (Gen 42:10, 11, 13; 43:7; 44:7-9)

SELF-REVELATION (IDENTIFICATION) (Selbstoffenbarungs-, Selbstenthüllungs-). Constructed with the first-person pronoun "I" (*'ānî*) plus a proper noun. (Gen 15:1b; 15:7; 17:1bα; 24:24; 26:24; 27:19; 28:13aβ; 31:13a; 35:11-12; 45:39; 45:3, 4; 46:3-4)

SPEECH (Rede-). Introduces speeches by designating who the speaker is and, commonly, to whom he speaks. (Gen 3:2; 4:6, 8, 9, 10, 13, 15; 4:23aα; 13:8, 14; 15:2, 3, 5a, 5b, 7; 15:8, 9, 13aα, 18a; 16:9, 10, 11; 17:15, 16; 18:10; 20:10; 22:15; 25:36a; 31:4-5aα; 38:28aba, 29aa; 34:13-14aα; 34:20)

STATEMENT OF LOCATION (Ortsangabe-). (Gen 37:1; 4:16; 13:18; 19:30; 20:1; 21:20; 22:19; 26:6, 17; 36:8; 50:22)

SUMMARY (Zusammenfassungs-). (Gen 25:7a; 25:17a)

SUPPLICATION (Bittgebets-). Casts a petition in the negative jussive with *'al* or *hinnēh nā'* ("Behold now"). (Gen 18:30a; 18:32a; 18:31a; 43:19; 43:20; 44:18; 47:29; 50:4)

TESTIMONY (Zeugnis-). (Gen 47:26)

TOLEDOTH (Generationenverzeichnis-). "These are the generations of. . . ." A demonstrative pronoun, *'ēlleh,* introduces the technical term *tôlĕdôt,* and the context of the generation is named. Functions to head a story or larger unit of stories about the subject of the formula. (Gen 2:4a; 5:1; 6:9; 10:1; 11:10; 11:27; 25:12; 25:19; 36:1, 9; 37:2)

TRANSITION (Überleitungs-). "At that time" (*wayĕhî bā'ēt hahiw'*). (Gen 21:22aα; 25:27aα; 39:7aα; 40:1aα; 22:1; 41:1; 4:3; 8:6)

VALUATION (Bewertungs-). (Gen 1:10b; 1:12b; 1:18b; 1:21b; 1:25b; 1:31b; 2:20b; 2:23a; 6:6)

VENGEANCE (Rache-). (Gen 4:24)

VOW (Gelübde-). (Gen 28:20-22)

WORD (Wortereignis-). "The word of the Lord came to. . . ." (Gen 15:1a; 15:4)